Insight and Innovation in International Development

Edited by International Development Research Centre
Ottawa, Ontario, Canada

For further volumes:
http://www.springer.com/series/8850

Elias T. Ayuk • Samuel T. Kaboré
Editors

Wealth Through Integration

Regional Integration and Poverty-Reduction
Strategies in West Africa

Springer

International Development Research Centre
Ottawa • Caire • Dakar • Montevideo • Nairobi • New Delhi • Singapore

Editors

Elias T. Ayuk
United Nations University
Institute for Natural
    Resources in Africa
Accra, Ghana

Samuel T. Kaboré
University of Ouagadougou
Boulevard Charles de Gaulle
Ouagadougou, Burkina Faso

Originally published in French as Ayuk, Elias T. and Kaboré, Samuel T. (Réd.), *S'intégrer pour s'enrichir*, Springer, 2012, ISBN 978-1-4614-1233-5.

A copublication with the
International Development Research Centre
PO Box 8500
Ottawa, ON, Canada K1G 3H9
info@idrc.ca/www.idrc.ca
ISBN 978-1-55250-544-1 (e-book)

ISBN 978-1-4614-4414-5   ISBN 978-1-4614-4415-2 (eBook)
DOI 10.1007/978-1-4614-4415-2
Springer New York Heidelberg Dordrecht London

Library of Congress Control Number: 2012944175

Printed on acid-free paper

Springer is part of Springer Science+Business Media (www.springer.com)

Contents

1   **Introduction: Why Integrate?**   1
     Elias T. Ayuk and Samuel T. Kaboré

Part I   Economic Convergence and Fighting Poverty

2   **Fifteen Years of WAEMU: Results and Strategies
     for the Future**   19
     Diery Seck

3   **Growth and Convergence in Africa: A Dynamic
     Panel Approach**   43
     Pierre Joubert Nguetse Tegoum, Pascal Nakelse, and Roland Ngwesse

4   **Has There Been Real and Structural Convergence
     in WAEMU Countries?**   69
     Nacisse Palissy Chassem

5   **The Impact of the Convergence, Stability and Growth
     Pact in the WAEMU**   91
     Adama Combey and Komla Mally

6   **Real Convergence in the WAEMU Area: A Bayesian Analysis** 111
     Claude Wetta and Antoine Yerbanga

7   **The Effects of Credit Constraints on Economic Convergence:
     The Case of the WAEMU Countries** 131
     Abdoulaye Diagne and Abdou-Aziz Niang

8   **Free Movement of Goods in WAEMU and the European
     Union: Community Law a Comparative Study from
     the Perspective of Trade** 147
     Ousmane Bougouma

Part II   Regional Financing Instruments and Fighting Poverty

 **9   The Role of Cash Transfers from Migrants in Promoting
      the Financing of Economic Development
      in WAEMU Countries** 171
      Ameth Saloum Ndiaye

**10   Efficiency of Credit That Targets the Poor: Measures
      and Application of Agricultural Credit in Burkina Faso** 189
      Samuel Tambi Kaboré

**11   Performance and Effectiveness of the Decentralised
      Financial System and Poverty Reduction in Niger** 211
      Insa Abary Noufou

**12   Financing Agriculture and the Food Crisis in Africa:
      What Role Can Microfinance Play?** 227
      Sandra Kendo

**13   Common External Tariff (CET) and Targeting
      the Poor in Mali** 247
      Massa Coulibaly and Balla Keita

14   How Does Communication Enrich Integration Policies 267
      Ahmed Barry, Augustin Niango, and Kathryn Touré

**15   Conclusions and Prospects: Creating Wealth
      through Integration** 287
      Elias T. Ayuk and Samuel T. Kaboré

Index 295

Acknowledgements

The chapters found in this book result from a regional conference that was jointly funded by the Canadian International Development Agency (CIDA), the International Development Research Centre (IDRC) and the West Africa Economic and Monetary Union (WAEMU). The University of Ouagadougou's Institut Supérieur des Sciences de la Population (ISSP), a WAEMU centre of excellence, organised the conference in collaboration with the WAEMU Commission and the IDRC. A scientific committee led the competitive selection process for papers, while an organising committee handled organisational tasks. The members of these two committees are listed below. The editors would like to express their sincere gratitude to all these people and institutions for their vital contributions.

About the Authors

Elias T. Ayuk is director of the United Nations University' Institute for Natural Resources in Africa (UNU-INRA) based in Accra, Ghana. At the time this work was carried out, he was senior programme specialist at the regional office of the International Development Research Centre (IDRC) in Dakar, Senegal.

Newton Ahmed Barry is a specialised investigative journalist. After a decade hosting the evening news on national television in Burkina, in 2001, he co-founded the newspaper *L'Evénement*, one of Burkina Faso's widely read newspapers.

Ousmane Bougouma is a doctoral candidate at the University of Rouen and UFR/SJP (Research and Training Centre in Law and Political Sciences) at the University of Ouagadougou. He is also a part-time lecturer at the University of Ouagadougou (responsible for tutorials) and an auditor with the CFA-Afrique agency (a legal and fiscal consulting agency).

Nacisse P. T. Chassem is a statistician and an economist. He teaches econometrics at the Institute for Statistics and Applied Economics (ISSEA), located in Yaoundé, Cameroon. He is also an advisor at the Cameroon Ministry of Economy, Planning and Regional Development.

Adama Combey is an economist at the Centre for study, research and training in Economics and Management of the University of Lomé, Togo.

Massa Coulibaly is professor of econometrics and research methodology at the University of Bamako. He is also a researcher at the Groupe de Recherche en Economie Appliquée et Théorique (GREAT), of which he is executive director.

Abdoulaye Diagne is a tenured professor at the Faculty of Economics and Management at the Cheikh Anta Diop University (UCAD) and director of the Consortium pour la Recherche Économique et Sociale (CRES) in Dakar. He runs the Africa department of the Poverty and Economic Policy (PEP) research network.

Samuel T. Kaboré is assistant professor at the UFR/SEG (Research and Training Centre in Economics and Management) at the University of Ouagadougou II, Burkina Faso. He was also an associate researcher at the University of Ouagadougou's Institut Supérieur des Sciences de la Population (ISSP).

Balla Keita is a statistician. He joined the National Institute of Statistics, Mali (INSTAT) in 2000.

Sandra Kendo is a doctoral candidate at the University of Lorraine/and University of Yaoundé II.

Komla Mally is an economist at the Centre for study, research and training in Economics and Management of the University of Lomé, Togo.

Pascal Nakelse is statistican/economist at the National Institute of Statistics and Demography in Burkina Faso.

Abdou-Aziz Niang is a doctoral candidate in economics at the University of Bourgogne (Dijon, France).

Ameth Saloum Ndiaye is an economist and researcher at the Faculty of Economics and Management (FASEG) at the Cheikh Anta Diop University in Dakar (UCAD). He has worked as an economist at the Centre d'Études de Politiques pour le Développement (CEPOD), at the Senegal Ministry of Economics and Finance.

Pierre Joubert Nguetse Tegoum is a statistician/economist, and is an assistant advisor at the Cameroon Ministry of Economy, Planning and Regional Development. He is also a researcher and consultant.

Roland Ngwesse is a statistician/economist with the Cameroon Ministry of Economy, Planning and Regional Development.

Augustin Niango works at the West Africa Economic and Monetary Union (WAEMU) Commission, and is responsible for technical coordination of the Higher Education, Research, Health and Culture Department.

Insa Abary Noufou is a macroeconomist and doctoral candidate at the Cheikh Anta Diop University in Dakar. He is currently a key advisor to the Prime Minister of Niger and head of the Department of Economic and Financial Affairs for the Prime Minister.

Diery Seck is an economist and director of the CREPOL (Centre for Research in Political Economy) in Dakar, Senegal.

Kathryn Touré has worked for 20 years promoting African expertise and knowledge sharing to encourage useful discussions related to societal development. Since 2008, she has been based in Dakar as Regional Director of the Canadian International Development Research Centre (IDRC).

Antoine Yerbanga is a doctoral candidate at the UFR/SEG (Research and Training Centre in Economics and Management) of the University of Ouagadougou II. He is a junior researcher in the Profiling team of the Advanced Poverty Analysis Unit.

Claude Wetta is assistant professor at the UFR/SEG (Research and Training Centre in Economics and Management) of the University of Ouagadougou II, as well as a researcher and Profiling team leader of the Advanced Poverty Analysis Unit (UAAP). He was the department head and coordinator of the UAAP.

The work presented in this book draws from papers presented at the conference, whose scientific committee and organizational committee members are listed hereafter.

Scientific committee
Elias T. Ayuk (IDRC)
Asséta Diallo (IFDC)
Eloges Houessou (WAEMU)
Samuel T. Kaboré (ISSP/PARSEP)
Dieudonné Ouedraogo (ISSP/PARSEP)
Bréhima Tounkara (WAEMU)

Organizational committee
Elias T. Ayuk (IDRC)
Badjibassa Babaka (WAEMU)
Mariam Compaore (ISSP/PARSEP)
Edith Coulibaly (ISSP)
Salifou Darankoum (ISSP)
Jérôme Gerard (IDRC)
Samuel T. Kaboré (ISSP/PARSEP)
Odile Kinde Ouoba (WAEMU)
Rasmané Zabre (ISSP)
Hamidou Kone (ISSP/PARSEP)
Mamadou Ndao (MediaDev Africa)
Augustin Niango (WAEMU)
Drissa Ouattara (WAEMU)
Dieudonné Ouedraogo (ISSP/PARSEP)
Sié Offi Some (ISSP)
Kathryn Touré (IDRC)
Perpétue Yameogo (ISSP)

List of Tables

Table 2.1	WAEMU country intra-community exports, in millions of CFA francs	26
Table 2.2	FOB export growth rate correlation matrix for WAEMU countries from 1990 to 2008	27
Table 2.3	Achievement of convergence criteria in WAEMA countries	29
Table 2.4	Assessment of WAEMU's institutional and operational set-up	31
Table 2.5	WAEMU country human development index (UNDP) ranking, 1990–2007	32
Table 2.6	Gross domestic product per capita in WAEMU countries in current dollars, 1990–2007 (PPP, in $US)	32
Table 2.7	WAEMU country inflation rates for five prior years	33
Table 2.8	Money supply ratio relative to GDP in WAEMU countries	34
Table 2.9	Ratio of private sector credit to GDP in WAEMU countries	35
Table 3.1	Estimation results for Africa	60
Table 3.2	β-Convergence test results in RECs	60
Table 3.3	Characterisation of convergence	61
Table 3.4	Explanation of conditional convergence	62
Table 4.1	Results of β-convergence equation estimations	85
Table 5.1	Fixed effects and GMM system results	104
Table 6.1	Parameters of the absolute convergence model using the Bayesian method	120
Table 6.2	Speeds of absolute convergence	120
Table 6.3	Parameters and speeds of conditional convergence	121

Table 7.1   Descriptive statistics (panel (1984–2004)) 143
Table 7.2   WAEMU country convergence speeds
               (country 1: United States) 143
Table 7.3   Estimation results (country 1: United States) 143
Table 7.4   Estimation results (country 1: France) 144
Table 7.5   WAEMU country convergence speeds
               (country 1: France) 144
Table 7.6   Estimation results (country 1: Nigeria) 144

Table 9.1   Descriptive statistics of cash transfers
               in the WAEMU, 1974–2006 (millions of US$) 174
Table 9.2   Cash transfer impact indicators in the WAEMU,
               1974–2006 175
Table 9.3   The impact of cash transfers on economic growth
               in the WAEMU 180
Table 9.4   Impact of cash transfers on domestic investment
               in the WAEMU 181
Table 9.5   Financial system, cash transfers and domestic
               investment in the WAEMU 182
Table 9.A.1   Cash transfers in the WAEMU, 1974–2006 (*million* US$
               and % of GDP) 185
Table 9.A.2   Cost of cash transfer for a sum of 300 euros
               sent from France 185
Table 9.A.3   Definition of sources of variables 186

Table 10.1   Agricultural credit efficiency indices 200
Table 10.A.1   Percentage (%) of poor and non-poor households
               based on a few targeting indicators 206
Table 10.A.2   Efficiency indices for credit targeted based on
               major activities of poor households 207
Table 10.A.3   Efficiency indices for credit targeted based
               on sustainable assets and goods held
               by poor households 208

Table 11.1   Performance and financial viability indicators 217
Table 11.2   Proportion of poor people using DFS services
               by region (in %) 219
Table 11.3   Results of the logistic regression between poverty
               and DFS variables 221

Table 12.1   Descriptive statistics of variables 242
Table 12.2   Estimation of the impact on productivity 242
Table 12.3   Marginal effects on productivity 243
Table 12.4   Estimations of impact on poverty 243
Table 12.5   Marginal effects on poverty 244

Table 13.1   Tariff structure of imports and taxes and duties in Mali
              in 2006 (millions of CFA francs) 250
Table 13.2   Geographic structure of imports in Mali in 2006 (in %) 251
Table 13.3   Geographic structure of customs income in Mali
              in 2006 (in %) 251
Table 13.4   Geographic structure of customs burden in Mali
              in 2006 (%) 252
Table 13.5   Tariff structure of household import expenditure
              (millions of CFA francs) 252
Table 13.6   Potential taxation on non-traded products in Mali
              in 2006 (%) 253
Table 13.7   Distribution of poverty and poor people in Mali
              in 2006 (%) 256
Table 13.8   Distribution of consumers and buyers
              per product category 257
Table 13.9   Distribution of consumption and percentage
              of consumption (millions of CFA francs and %) 258
Table 13.10   Standard percentage (%) of poor people's
              consumption 258
Table 13.11   Distribution of consumption and percentage
              of consumption by milieu (millions of CFA
              francs and %) 259
Table 13.12   Standard percentage (%) of consumption
              by the poor by milieu 259
Table 13.13   Distribution of purchases and percentage
              of purchases (millions of CFA francs and %) 260
Table 13.14   Standardised percentage of purchases by the poor 261
Table 13.15   Standard percentage of import duty for the port
              (millions of CFA francs and %) 262
Table 13.16   Standard part of actual port duties paid
              by the poor (millions of CFA francs and %) 263
Table 13.17   Standard percentage of exemptions for the poor
              (millions of CFA francs and %) 263
Table 13.18   Standard part of urban poor people's
              exemptions ($P_0 = 20.9\%$) 264

List of Figures

Fig. 3.1　Evolution of standard deviation of per capita gross
domestic product 54

Fig. 3.2　ECOWAS: evolution of standard deviation of per capita
gross domestic product 55

Fig. 3.3　WAEMU: evolution of standard deviation of per capita
domestic product 55

Fig. 3.4　CEMAC: evolution of standard deviation of per capita
gross domestic product 57

Fig. 3.5　SADC: evolution of standard deviation of per
capita gross domestic product 58

Fig. 3.6　COMESA: evolution of standard deviation of per capita
gross domestic product 58

Fig. 3.7　Per capita income convergence, 1985–2005 59

Fig. 4.1　First derivative of real per capital gross capital formation
distribution trend (WAEMU) – *dotted lines* are 95%
confidence interval points of the continuous curve 77

Fig. 4.2　Evolution of the first derivative of the total factor
production distribution trend (WAEMU) – *dotted lines* show
the 95% confidence intervals of the continuous line 78

Fig. 4.3　First-derivative plot of per capita GDP distribution
trend (WAEMU) – the *dotted lines* show the 95%
confidence interval of the continuous line 79

Fig. 4.4　First-derivative plot of per capita GDP distribution trend
(WAEMU with the exception of Côte d'Ivoire) – the *dotted lines*
show the 95% confidence interval of the continuous line 80

Fig. 4.5　Evolution of real per capita GDP
in WAEMU countries 84

Fig. 4.6　Evolution of real per capita GCF
in WAEMU countries 84

Fig. 4.7　Evolution of TFP in WAEMU countries 84

Fig. 4.8   Changes in first-derivatives of per capita GDP deviations
             with respect to the WAEMU average 85
Fig. 4.9   Changes in first-derivatives of per capita gross capital formation
             (GCF) deviations with respect to the WAEMU average 86
Fig. 4.10   Changes in first-derivatives of total factor productivity (TFP)
             deviations with respect to the WAEMU average 87

Fig. 5.1   Real GDP growth rate and average number of criteria
             respected (1997–2008) 100
Fig. 5.2   Evolution of distribution of the log of real per capita
             GDP for 1997–2008 101
Fig. 5.3   Evolution of the log of real per capita GDP
             for WAEMU countries from 1997 to 2008 102
Fig. 5.4   Distribution of the log of per capita GDP
             for the period 1997–1999 103
Fig. 5.5   Distribution of the log of per capita GDP
             for the period 2005–2007 103

Fig. 6.1   Evolution of the variance ratio 124

Fig. 9.1   Cash transfers in the franc zone (FZ), 1974–2005
             (million US$ and % of GDP) (a) Total cash transfers in FZ,
             1974–2005 (millions of US$) (b) Total cash transfers in FZ
             in % of GDP, 1974–2005 173
Fig. 9.2   Cash transfers, aid and foreign direct investment
             in the WAEMU, 1974–2006 (million US$) 174

Fig. 10.1   Analysis of targeting policies 192

Fig. 11.1   Trend of impact indicators for MFI in Niger (in millions
             of CFA francs) 215
Fig. 11.2   Households with access to microfinance services 218
Fig. 11.3   Number of MFI service beneficiaries by gender 220
Fig. 11.4   Proximity of MFI in Niger 222

Fig. 14.1   Stereotypologies of decision makers and researchers 270
Fig. 14.2   Representation of the three-way dialogue between
             researchers, decision makers and citizens 272
Fig. 14.3   Representation of a dialogue stripped of all ideas
             of superiority, in which communicators occupy a space
             at the crossroad 273

Acronyms and Abbreviations

ACBF	African Capacity Building Foundation
AfDB	African Development Bank
AFD	French Development Agency
AFRACA	African Rural and Agricultural Credit Association
AIDS	Acquired Immune Deficiency Syndrome
BCEAO	Central Bank of West African States
BRS	Banque Régionale de Solidarité
BRVM	Bourse Régionale des Valeurs Mobilières (regional stock market)
CASHPOR	Credit and Saving for the Hard-Core Poor
CEMAC	Central African Economic and Monetary Community
CERDI	International Development Research Studies Centre
CERISE	Comité d'Echanges de Réflexion et d'Information sur les Systèmes d'Epargne
CET	Common external tariff
CFA	African Financial Community
CGAP	Consultative Group to Assist the Poorest
CIDA	Canadian International Development Agency
CIRAD	Centre de Coopération Internationale en Recherche pour le Développement
CJEC	Court of Justice of the European Community
CNCA	Caisse Nationale de Crédit Agricole
CNRS	National Centre for Scientific Research
CODESRIA	Council for the Development of Social Science Research in Africa
COMESA	Common Market for Eastern and Southern Africa
CREPOL	Centre for Research in Political Economy
CRES	Consortium pour la Recherche Économique et Sociale
CSGP	Convergence, Stability and Growth Pact
DCF	Development and cohesion fund
DFS	Decentralised financial system

EAC	East African Community
EBCVM	Burkina Faso survey on household living conditions
ECA	Economic Commission for Africa
ECCES	Economic Community of Central African States
ECOWAS	Economic Community of West African States
EPA	Economic Partnership Agreement
EPD	Economic Policy Department
EU	European Union
FAARF	Support fund for women's gainful activities
FAO	Food and Agriculture Organisation of the United Nations
FASEG	School of Economics and Management
FDI	Foreign direct investments
FENU	United Nationas Capital Development Fund
FZ	Franc Zone
GCF	Gross capital formation
GDP	Gross domestic product
GMM	Generalised method of moments
GREAT	Groupe de Recherche en Economie Appliquée et Théorique
GTZ	German Development Cooperation
HDI	Human development index
HICP	Harmonised index of consumer prices
HIES	National household income expenditure survey
HIV	Human immunodeficiency virus
ICOR	Incremental Capital Output Ratio
IDRC	International Development Research Centre
IFPRI	International Food Policy Research Institute
IGA	Income-generating activity
ILCR	Incremental Labor to Capital Ratio
IMF	International Monetary Fund
INADES	African Institute for Economic and Social Development
INSD	National Institute of Statistics and Demography
INSTAT	Malian National Statistics Institute
ISSP	Institut Supérieur des Sciences de la Population
MDG	Millenium Development Goals
MEF	Ministry of Economy and Finance
MFB	Ministry of Finance and Budget
MFI	Micro-finance institutions
NMU	National micro-finance unit
ODA	Official development assistance
OECD	Organisation for Economic Cooperation and Development

OLs	Ordinary least square
ONG	Non-governmental organisation
OPA	Observatory of abnormal practices
PARSEP	Projet Régional d'appui aux cadres nationaux de suivi évaluation des stratégies de réduction de la pauvrété
PAT	Poverty Assessment Tool
PPP	Purchasing power parity
PPTE	Heavily indebted poor countries
PTCI	Inter-university postgraduate degree programme
PWR	Participatory Wealth Ranking
QUIBB	Core Welfare Indicator Questionnaire
R&D	Research and development
RADF	Regional Agricultural Development Fund
REC	Regional economic community
RIAF	Regional Integration Aid Fund
RME	Rural micro-enterprises
SACU	Southern African Customs Union
SADC	Southern African Development Community
SEF	Small Enterprise Foundation
SHD	Sustainable human development
SKS	Swayam Krishi Sangam
SME/SMI	Small and medium enterprise/small and medium industry
SNV	Netherlands Development Cooperation
SOFITEX	Société des Fibres Textiles
SYSCOA	West African accounting system
TFP	Technical and financial partner
TFP	Total factor productivity
UMAC	Central African Monetary Union
UNDP	United Nations Development Programme
UNESCO	United Nations Educational, Scientific and Cultural Organisation
UNFPA	United Nations Population Fund
UNICEF	United Nations Children's Fund
USA	United States of America
USAID	United States Agency for International Development
VAT	Value-added tax
VIP	Visual Indicators of Poverty
WADB	West African Development Bank
WAEMU	West African Economic and Monetary Union
WAMU	West African Monetary Union
WB	World Bank

WBI	World Bank Institute
WEEC	Women Economic Empowerment Consortium
WFP	World Food Programme
WHO	World Health Organisation

Preface

In December 2008, when I met with the president of the International Development Research Centre (IDRC), I was far from imagining that the work we wanted to do together would become a reality so quickly. As early as the beginning of 2009, we were given a unique opportunity to share our respective experiences through the celebration, throughout 2009, of 15 years of the West African Economic and Monetary Union (WAEMU). For the IDRC, this was a good opportunity to make the large network of researchers it has been supporting for years available to support a regional ambition. For the WAEMU, celebrating this anniversary was the occasion to step back and take a critical look at the past 15 years of regional integration efforts.

Once the decision was made, it was time to make this shared determination a reality. What was said was done, and with contributions from our respective specialists, preparation for the conference *Regional Integration and Poverty-reduction Strategies in WAEMU Member Countries* conference kicked off.

After several preparatory meetings and a call for proposals, the conference was held on December 8 to 10, 2009 in Ouagadougou, Burkina Faso, attracting over a hundred researchers, journalists, representatives of civil society, national leaders and WAEMU experts. During this conference, the development, implementation and monitoring of regional poverty-reduction policies were compared and discussed by researchers, journalists and various members of civil society.

These three intense days of discussion enabled WAEMU to take a look in the mirror, focussing on a number of equally important questions:

Has WAEMU made the best choices and adopted good methods?

Has WAEMU been sufficiently attentive to the populations and responded to their expectations?

Has stakeholder commitment to the integration process been equal to the challenges?

How can we envision the future of the Union so that its populations are more at the heart of regional policies?

How can information about the WAEMU be shared with the Union's citizens?

Participants in the conference attempted to find hard-hitting answers to these questions. Researchers, the media and members of civil society spoke candidly. The Union's choices were examined in minute detail. Some elements of these analyses deserve to be recalled: the convergence of WAEMU Member States remains a great challenge, poverty in the zone persists despite the institutional and regulatory advances that have been made, and weak intra-community exchanges remain a concern despite internal tariff removal.

In addition, the Union's strategic choices were critically reviewed and the issue of the various parties' participation in developing and evaluating community policies was the object of long discussions and analyses. Many of these are presented in this book.

Regarding this last point, it is interesting to highlight that this book takes into account relevant recommendations made by researchers while learning from this experience that is still rare in West Africa, and demonstrates to what extent discussions among researchers, decision-makers and journalists are essential in enabling as many people as possible to make quality contributions to the process of regional integration.

This book is filling a need and also demonstrates the need and urgency of setting up regular exchange platforms among decision-makers, researchers and the media so that regional integration not be a matter for a select few but a participative process that involves as many people as possible.

It is also an excellent—and even indispensable—reference for researchers and the general public, as well as for the leaders of WAEMU and other African integration institutions.

This is why the WAEMU Commission, which made every effort to make the joint work possible, is happy to have contributed to producing this reference book on regional integration in West Africa. This is a good opportunity to congratulate the Canadian IDRC and the CIDA, the researchers, the Member State decision-makers and the journalists for this major intellectual contribution. Let them all be thanked here for their involvement, which will, I am sure, contribute to a regional integration that is advancing slowly but surely.

President of the WAEMU Commission   Soumaïla Cissé

Chapter 1
Introduction: Why Integrate?

Elias T. Ayuk and Samuel T. Kaboré

Abstract This book explores two issues that are topical in developing countries: regional integration and poverty-reduction strategies. Economic grouping provides opportunities for improving the living conditions of populations. They are accompanied by allocation and accumulation effects, which are two major beneficial pillars of regional integration. The 15 chapters in this book do not only examine what is required for the convergence of African economies, which constitutes an absolute prerequisite for improving the welfare of populations, but they also look at some instruments that could play a central role in poverty-reduction strategies.

I Introduction

Trade between nations has positive economic effects but can also be impeded by structural imbalances and gaps in the endowment of resources that exist between nations. Despite the large increase in global trade, the lack of a corresponding increase in world economic growth attests to the fact that current trade practices fail to lead to development. Globalisation has made it such that the different countries around the world can benefit from resources that are not available within their national borders. For developing countries, the liberalisation of trade has not yielded the expected return. In response, a new paradigm emerged, suggesting that to lead to economic growth public investment should accompany trade liberalisation. Some researchers have identified problems with this school of thought. They have

E.T. Ayuk (✉)
United Nations University, Institute for Natural Resources in Africa (UNU-INRA),
Accra, Ghana
e-mail: ayuk@inra.unu.edu

S.T. Kaboré
Research and Training Centre in Economics and Management, University of Ouagadougou II,
Ouagadougou, Burkina Faso

E.T. Ayuk and S.T. Kaboré (eds.), *Wealth Through Integration*, Insight and Innovation
in International Development 4, DOI 10.1007/978-1-4614-4415-2_1,
© International Development Research Centre 2013

argued that due to the very nature of the liberalisation of trade, which requires the removal of customs duties and taxes, governments in developing countries no longer benefit from the revenue that could have been generated by the tariffs and therefore are not able to supply the resources needed to make public investments. In recent years, solid arguments have been put forward to encourage developing countries to emphasise regional integration first before seeking to access the worldwide market.

The crisis the eurozone is experiencing is, in part, due to the fact that certain macroeconomic basics related to common trade zones were not respected. When new countries joined the Union, some of them did not meet the required convergence criteria. The monetary policy was too strict for some countries and too free for others. This book looks into the issues linked to regional integration in West Africa (the WAEMU zone) and should be of interest to researchers worldwide who work on this topic.

One of the key innovations found in this book is that it presents empirical data related to the efforts made by the West African Economic and Monetary Union (WAEMU) countries to converge their economies—an element that is very important for regional integration. This book also examines certain instruments that are necessary for regional integration and the way the latter have influenced poverty reduction in the Union's countries.

WAEMU was founded in 1994 to promote the economic and monetary integration of eight West African countries that shared a single currency, the CFA franc. From December 8–10, 2009, to celebrate 15 years of WAEMU's existence, it organised a regional conference with the International Development Research Centre (IDRC) and the Canadian International Development Agency (CIDA) on the topic of "regional integration and poverty-reduction strategies". The IDRC and the CIDA supported research in four West African countries focussed on poverty-reduction strategies. The various chapters in this book were written by researchers and were selected by a scientific committee following a competitive call for papers. The papers were presented at the conference and were discussed within the region's scientific community.

II   The Concept of Regional Integration

Regional integration can take very different forms depending on its stage and scope, which refers to the number of countries involved (Balassa 1961). The five forms or stages of regional integration include free-trade zones, customs union, common market, economic and monetary union and complete political union. Member countries in free-trade zones remove trade barriers among themselves but maintain their own national barriers against third countries. In customs unions, member countries remove the obstacles among themselves while also adopting and applying common customs duties to third countries. The situation in common markets is the same as in customs unions, except that in addition, the member countries allow full production factor mobility within the union. The characteristics of common markets apply to economic and monetary unions, including a full harmonisation of monetary, budgetary, industrial and social policies. These unions also implement a common external relations policy. Complete political union consists of integrating a region's political and economic affairs.

Among the advantages and benefits associated with regional integration, one can mention benefiting from economies of scale, improving competitiveness and attracting investment. The literature contains contradictions regarding the manner in which the openness of trade, which is often linked to regional integration, could affect economic growth and therefore play a role in reducing poverty (Mealy 2005; Rodrik and Rodriguez 2001; Winters et al. 2004). One of the negative consequences of regional integration that has been advanced is the closing of local industries, which leads to unemployment (Balassa 1961).

Regional integration has followed a variety of models around the world, which have led to successful experiences as well as bringing to light key problems linked to the process. In Europe, political determination and a robust institutional set-up led to huge markets and the free circulation of goods and services. The recent crisis in the eurozone brings to the forefront crucial issues that can arise when the economies are of different sizes and/or when certain countries have larger debt than others. In Latin America, Mercosur experienced an increase in intra-regional trade and investment flow, set up a common external tariff structure, formed a negotiation bloc and promoted the consolidation of the democratic process and the harmonisation of macroeconomic policies (Paiva and Gazel 2003). Some of the gains stemming from the common market and the coordination of economic policies experienced setbacks due to financial troubles in the region. The North American Free Trade Agreement (NAFTA), which places less emphasis on formal institutional cooperation, raised questions about the momentum of synergy in institutional cooperation and economic interdependence. Mexico benefited from these measures by adopting a stronger policy framework. There was an increased flow of cross-border trade that contributed to greater synchronisation of Mexico's economic cycles with those of the United States and Canada. Asia's experience seems to have been based on "the market" with less emphasis on strengthening institutions. Emphasis was placed on intra-industry rather than inter-industry trade and cross-border trade flows.

African regional groupings have not experienced much success. This is due to traditionally weak intra-regional trade on the continent, to serious macroeconomic imbalances, to the burden of foreign debt, the over-evaluation of the currencies, the lack of funding for trade and a tight fiscal base, with customs duties representing a substantial source of revenue. The import substitution protection strategies adopted by the majority of countries since independence have led to a multitude of regulations restricting trade, such as licences, currency allocation, special taxes on acquisition, trade and deposits. As a result, the economic context has not been favourable to the development of regional commitments. One can note, nonetheless, that some progress has been made, such as the free circulation of goods and people and the implementation of a common external tariff.

In sub-Saharan Africa, there are around 14 regional trade zones. The four largest, each at a different stage in their move towards integration, are the West African Economic and Monetary Union (WAEMU), the Southern African Customs Union (SACU), the Central African Economic and Monetary Union (CEMAC) and the East African Community (EAC). These four groups count over 24 countries. There are also four other regional groups that cover a total of 53 countries that are at various stages of progression towards a free-trade zone. These are the Economic Community of West African States (ECOWAS), the Economic Community of Central African States (ECCAS), the Common Market for Eastern and Southern Africa (COMESA) and the Southern African Development Community (SADC). These groupings are facing a number of challenges that include implementing the signed agreements, the multiplicity of affiliations, the need for mechanisms to compensate for loss of tax revenue, implementing clear procedures to face non-tariff-based barriers, and the lack of means to support regional integration (Mfunwa and Mzwanele 2008).

III   Theoretical Considerations

In this section, we will examine the theoretical foundation for regional integration and its connection to poverty reduction. Several authors have made theoretical contributions to the various dimensions of regional integration and to their effects. This section briefly summarises these contributions and lists the main advantages expected from the integration process.

The theoretical basis for trade among nations dates from the economist Ricardo's theory of comparative advantage. According to Ricardo, a country will export the goods with which it has a comparative advantage. A difference in technology is, therefore, the basis for the trade. The direction of the trade depends on a relative comparison of isolated prices (without trade). It goes without saying that consumers in the importing country benefit, as they pay a lower price than they would have paid if the product were to have been produced in their own country. According to the Ricardo model, if two countries have identical technology, there is no comparative advantage and therefore no need for trade.

The Ricardo-Viner model suggests that even if two countries have identical production technologies, the fact of having a larger endowment of factors could create a comparative advantage. In this model, there is one factor that is mobile and factors that are specific to each sector. The distributive effects of trade and tariffs are specific to each sector.

Viner (1950) demonstrated, in the context of customs unions, that regional integration could lead to "the expansion of trade" and to the "diversion of trade". Expanding trade results from new commercial opportunities created by movement of the demand from the high-cost country towards the low-cost country. Cernat (2001) demonstrates expansion of trade for three African commercial blocs, the COMESA, the ECOWAS and the SADC. A study by Gbetnkom (2008) shows the positive overall impact of economic integration on the creation of trade flows in the CEMAC zone. In certain cases, partner country production can be replaced by low-cost importations coming from outside the partnership zone. This situation denotes diversion of trade that does not benefit consumers.

Heckscher-Ohlin-Samuelson present a long-term model that tries to explain the composition of trade between countries and how trade is involved in revenue distribution within the countries. The model explains what determines the comparative advantage and demonstrates that the difference in production factor endowment is a basis for commercial trade between countries. A country will export the goods produced intensively with abundant factors and will import the goods produced intensively with less abundant factors.

Balassa (1961) worked on the theoretical foundation for economic integration. For this author, trade barriers between markets lessen with an increase in economic integration. The author puts forth that common markets between countries, with the free circulation of production factors, naturally generate demand for more integration.

Krugman (1993a) states that the liberalisation of trade enables countries to specialise by taking into account their comparative advantage and possibly also a divergence in trade cycles in the union's countries. Krugman (1991) also demonstrates that trading blocs often have a positive effect on people's welfare.

In a 1998 study, Frankel and Rose stipulate that commercial links and monetary integration reduce the asymmetry of clashes between countries. In this way, strong economic integration is accompanied by a strong correlation in economic cycles.

Baldwin (1997) identified two theoretical advantages that justify the formation of trading blocs: the allocation effect and the accumulation effect. The allocation effect refers to more efficient allocation of resources resulting from the elimination of trade obstacles in the context of regional integration. Indeed, according to economic theory, in a competitive economy, demand for a product channels productive resources towards the production of the product. This demand is therefore an important signal between consumers and producers. However, tariff and non-tariff barriers between countries confuse the signal. Regional integration that is accompanied by the elimination of obstacles to the circulation of persons and goods therefore generates the efficient allocation of resources.

Baldwin (1997) also notes a corollary with the allocation effect—the "scale and variety effects". At the time of import-replacement policies, protecting inefficient industries was a regular practice in developing countries. It led them to maintain in place enterprises that, in several cases, were operating at an inefficient scale. Regional integration, with markets that open within the grouping that accompanies it, reduces this protection and can help, through the reallocation of resources, to rationalise entire industries. It goes without saying that the creation of vast markets could enable small enterprises to reach their optimal size. That could engender a decrease in average costs and also in consumer prices.

The variety effect is simply the choice of a variety of products from which consumers benefit thanks to the large market that stems from regional integration. The broader choice and the competition that follows could lower consumer prices. For enterprises, the possibility and the possible availability of a larger choice of production factors could help enterprises to use the most appropriate input, which could have a significant and positive effect on their productivity.

The second major effect of regional integration is the accumulation effect. This can be observed in investment and trade circuits. The development of regional markets attracts more suppliers and enables enterprises to specialise. The result of this process is a decrease in average production costs inside the grouping and an increase in production factor yield, resulting in an accumulation of material and non-material factors. Economists agree on the fact that globalisation and regional integration increase the mobility of human and financial resources and have technological consequences that lead to improved productivity and lower production costs, which in turn attract other investments and promote an accumulation of factors (CNUCED 2009). Considering the combined effects of regional integration on efficiency and accumulation, there is no doubt that it can contribute to economic growth and poverty reduction.

In developing countries, there are other reasons that strongly support greater interest in regional markets over worldwide markets. First, regional neighbours tend to be at the same stage of development, thus avoiding the David versus Goliath syndrome. Secondly, the value created in production and trade remains in the region and is not exported outside the region. And finally, this type of trade enables countries to save their foreign currency reserves (Palley 2002, 2003).

WAEMU's approach to economic integration consists of implementing a variety of policies, programmes and incentives to ensure convergence of its economies. Economic convergence is perceived to be the progressive lessening of gaps between the countries with regard to a certain number of economic variables. There are three types of convergence. Nominal convergence is relative to macro-economic stability variables such as inflation, debt and budget deficit. WAEMU monitors this through convergence criteria. Real convergence impacts standard of living, which is generally measured by real per capita GDP. Finally, structural convergence concerns the structural characteristics of the economies and is perceived through the structure of demand (consumption rates, demographic growth rates) or the structure of supply (investment, factor productivity, production technology). Testing convergence consists in measuring the degree of similitude levelling up among countries, both in terms of the management and structure of the economies (structural or beta-convergence) and in terms of performance and standard of living (real or sigma-convergence). The presence of structural convergence means there is a progressive decrease in gaps and an economic similarity in terms of the structure of demand or supply (the countries that are behind change and advance rapidly to reduce the gaps and catch up with the more advanced or leading countries). The presence of real convergence means that the standard of living, in terms of income and people's welfare, is gradually levelling up.

Regional Integration and Poverty

Poverty refers to unacceptable deprivation in one or several dimensions of welfare (Ravallion 1996). There are several forms of poverty depending on the dimension that is lacking, such as monetary poverty when income or consumption is insufficient or below an acceptable threshold. Reducing poverty consists of eliminating or reducing the deprivation of those who suffer from it, which implies reducing welfare differences. Through real convergence, regional integration is an instrument for reducing poverty. Indeed, real convergence implies progressively reducing the gaps between countries in standard of living, which is generally measured by real GDP per capita. Real convergence means that the standard of living in poor countries and that of the inhabitants gets closer to that found in richer countries, which implies a reduction in poverty. Social and growth policies that are implemented nationally or regionally also contribute to reducing poverty. Public policies aimed to produce growth and/or to fairly distribute the fruit of this growth contribute to reducing poverty (Ravallion and Huppi 1991; Datt and Ravallion 1992; Bigsten and Levin 2000; Ravallion and Datt 2002; Buccanfuso and Kaboré 2004).

At the regional level, the 33rd Ordinary Session of ECOWAS Conference of Heads of State, held on January 18 in Ouagadougou, endorsed a West Africa poverty-reduction regional strategy document (DSRRP-AO). In the countries, poverty-reduction strategies have been implemented since the beginning of the 2000s. These strategies have combined with the economic effects of integration to produce gains in welfare and poverty reduction.

Good knowledge of real trends towards integration is essential and enables authorities to take adequate measures. Chapters 3, 4, 5 and 6 use more or less complex methods to test convergence in order to provide as much scientific certitude as possible to confirm or disprove the gap-reduction trend among WAEMU countries.

If countries that are part of an economic grouping manage to converge their economies, then wealth accumulates with effects on prices that are beneficial to consumers, leading to increased welfare and reduced poverty. WAEMU countries that have undertaken poverty-reduction strategies need their economies to converge.

IV Chapter Overview

Part I: Economic Convergence and Fighting Poverty

In Chap. 2, Diery Seck uses a critical review of the literature to give a summary of WAEMU's first 15 years, draws key conclusions and uncovers prospects for the future that should govern WAEMU's actions in the years to come. The author summarises WAEMU from three main perspectives: an economic and social overview, a monetary and financial overview and convergence among the Union's national economies.

The economic and social review brings to light two major facts: (1) the average ranking of WAEMU zone countries in terms of human development index (HDI) regressed continually from 1990 to 2007, making the Union one of the most disadvantaged community areas in the world, and (2) there is significant and growing income disparity (GDP per capita) among its members, with an income gap between the lowest-income countries (Guinea-Bissau, Niger, and Togo) and the three highest-income countries (Côte d'Ivoire, Senegal and Benin) that increased by 56% between 1990 and 2007 in favour of the richest, growing from US$594 to US$926.

In terms of the financial overview, there are four key points to note. The first is that the Union has maintained its tradition of low inflation that dates from before the devaluation of the CFA franc—cf. the 1990 rates—and has been able to create uniformity in this area. It has also respected its primary convergence criteria related to inflation, which prescribed that the rate not exceed 3% annually, with exception made for Guinea-Bissau, which was coping with a civil war and the first period of CFA franc devaluation. The second key point is the notable progress recorded in the money supply (M2) ratio over the GDP since the creation of WAEMU, except for Niger whose situation calls for specific attention with regard to its low level of monetisation. The third concerns progress in financing the economy, thanks to an improvement in the ratio of private sector funding relative to GDP in the member countries, with the exception of the Côte d'Ivoire due to a socio-economic crisis, and Niger and Guinea-Bissau, which have low credit access levels. Finally, the fourth key point is the integrating nature of the regional stock market (BRVM) and its capacity to mobilise community and external savings, which is one of WAEMU's major accomplishments in the financial arena, even if the concentration that benefits Senegal and the Côte d'Ivoire remains too pronounced, accentuating the imbalance that has already been observed on the private sector credit market.

One of WAEMU's main measures of success resides in the convergence of its member states economies towards sustained growth, marked by the weaker members catching up with the more advanced members. The track record of convergence, based on the Union's performance in two types of measures—absolute or β-convergence and σ-convergence—which shows through the decrease over time of the dispersion coefficient of respective values of a variable between the countries that they are increasingly becoming similar. The majority of this work concludes that there is an absence of σ-convergence, which for the WAEMU indicates that the richest countries remain so over time and the poorest remain the poorest, a result that corresponds to the growing disparity mentioned above. Sigma-convergence tests were also performed on other economic indicators such as investment relative to GDP, gross savings relative to GDP and lender interest rates relative to borrower rates and show contradicting results that confirm or reject the existence of convergence among WAEMU countries. The rare absolute (β-convergence) tests on WAEMU-country economies gave the same controversial results on the existence or non-existence of absolute convergence.

Chapter 2 concludes that the track record is not very satisfactory both in terms of reducing disparity among the WAEMU member country economies and in terms of the speed at which trailing countries are catching up with the leading countries. The author indicates that future strategic actions could be organised in four major directions: (1) boosting the Commission's regional policy competence, (2) setting in motion a more vigorous policy regarding the Union's weaker countries, (3) creating a Social Pact and (4) increasing the mobility of goods, people and capital.

In Chapter 3, Pierre Nguetse Tegoum, Pascal Nakelse and Roland Ngwesse find the absence of income convergence in all African countries. This non-convergence is mainly due to the great heterogeneity that exists among these countries. However, the examination of Regional Economic Communities (REC) sometimes reveals a process of beta-convergence. Indeed, out of the five groupings that were considered, four constitute convergence clubs. These are the ECOWAS, CEMAC, WAEMU and SADC zones. An analysis of the fixed effects was carried out on these RECs. It revealed that the ratio of investment on GDP is significantly linked to unobservable structural disparities. Demographic growth influences income level convergence in the ECOWAS, while trade supports income convergence in the WAEMU space and proved to be insignificant in the other RECs. This situation could be inherent to weak intra-regional trade in the various RECs (less than 13%). The study recommends policy measures that aim to promote intra-regional trade, to harmonise investment policies in the various RECs and to make the African Union more effective in order to facilitate African integration and, in doing so, standard of living convergence.

In Chapter 4, Nacisse Palissy Chassem examines real and structural convergence in WAEMU countries from 1970 to 2005. This evaluation is carried out using δ-convergence indices smoothed out with regression pline and using β-convergence regressions. Real convergence is measured using the real per capital gross domestic product, while structural convergence is evaluated with the real gross capital formation per capita and total factor productivity. The results reveal the existence of real convergence and structural convergence for the 1975–1991 period, but real and structural divergence for the 1970–1974 and 1992–2005 periods.

In Chapter 5, Combey and Mally analyse the effect of the convergence, stability and growth pact (PCSC) on the dynamics of real convergence within WAEMU. After examining the concept of sigma-convergence and distribution convergence, the authors use the beta-convergence approach with panel data to take into account state of technology differences among the countries. After correcting the endogeneity bias using the generalised method of moments (GMM), the results suggest that one cannot reject the hypothesis of conditional convergence and that the pact tripled the speed of reconciliation of real per capita GDP in WAEMA member countries from 1997 to 2008. As a result, adopting the PCSC improved overall standard of living in the Union's member countries. The study does, however, have some limitations, notably the reduced temporal dimension and the fact that it does not take into account the non-monetary aspects of poverty.

In Chapter 6, Wetta and Yerbanga use the Bayesian estimation method to determine the speed of convergence (absolute and conditional) in each country.

The results of the study show that there is weak absolute convergence within the Union and that educative policies, just like openness policies, could accelerate growth and convergence in the countries. The study also notes the presence of sigma-convergence for the periods 1980–1994 and 2000–2008, but an absence of this convergence for the period 1994–2000. The authors consider the first period to be a "before-integration period" and the second to be an "after-integration" period. The absence of sigma-convergence during the 1994–2000 period, far from bringing into question the positive impact of integration on sigma-convergence, could correspond to a certain latency or to the time it took the countries and the economies to adapt and to react to the new rules set up by the treaty. The heterogeneity of data sources, data series gaps for certain countries such as Guinea-Bissau and the lack of relevant variables to measure the quality of institutions such as democracy, good governance, property rights protection, and so on all represent difficulties that are brought to light in this chapter as representing serious limitations to the analysis of convergence within the WAEMU.

Chapter 7 by Diagne and Niang focuses on the effects of the weak financial system on WAEMU-country convergence towards the worldwide growth limit. According to the authors, there is a critical level of private credit that equals 13.77% of the GDP, and WAEMU countries that record a level of private credit that is less than this threshold diverge from the American development limit. They consider the United States to be the leading country, with a rate of economic growth that represents the limit of growth. In this case, Burkina Faso, Guinea-Bissau and Niger diverge due to their low levels of private credit, equalling 11.49, 12.29 and 9.74%, respectively. Furthermore, taking into account the economic history between France and WAEMU countries, the authors also consider the case in which France is the leading country. The result lowers the critical private credit threshold from 13.77 to 11.37% of GDP. Considering France as the leader leaves only Niger diverging. The chapter concludes that credit constraints impede the countries from fully benefiting from technology transfers and push them to distance themselves from the growth limit by considerably reducing their convergence speed. Financial policy measures should aim at quickly improving credit access for all member countries and particularly for Niger, Burkina Faso and Guinea-Bissau, which have the lowest credit levels in the Union.

In Chapter 8, Ousmane Bougouma undertakes a comparative analysis of WAEMU and European Union texts from a trade-related angle. The author places a priority on examining WAEMU's legal framework for the free circulation of merchandise. The free circulation of merchandise in one of the four community freedoms recognized by the EC and WAEMU treaties that the four "pillars" of the common market. The alter ego of the European Union EC treaty articles 23–31 can be found in articles 4 and 77–81 of the WAEMU treaty. These two texts have the same ambition, that of liberalising trade among member states by establishing a principle of free circulation of all products that are appreciable in terms of money and susceptible as such to be the object of commercial transactions. The free circulation of merchandise is, in effect, an essential community freedom. Community freedoms have a daily influence on the lives of community citizens, and without these free circulation regimes, no community progress would be possible. They are of interest both member states and enterprises, which are economic players. WAEMU is a dynamic but young integration organisation and its rules have not yet been tested by practice or by jurisprudence, which explains the call on the successful EU experience to throw light on the analyses. However, European material law should not be perceived as ready-made for WAEMU.

Bougouma insists on the necessity of avoiding the establishment of a symmetric lineage between WAEMU and EU law. Adaptations of the WAEMU free circulation of merchandise system are necessary to take into account the specific characteristics of the community area. Completing its common market requires, however, a certain number of actions. It is first necessary to improve its regulatory framework with secondary legislation and by making it more restrictive. WAEMU must also work to reduce the time-span that exists between taking resolutions and their implementation. In effect, the States do not hesitate to marginalise the right to free circulation of merchandise, particularly because it leads to a loss of budgetary income. The lack of a legal and judicial element within the Union is a primary cause. The Commission must ensure that community law deploys all its effects (primacy, direct and immediate application) throughout the WAEMU space. This will also enable community jurisdiction to play its role in building the community space because in the EU, when politicians hesitate, the Court of Justice of the European Communities (CJEC) decides and the European Community machine advances. It is then necessary to act upon member states by establishing a schedule for eliminating the obstacles for free circulation of merchandise after a complete diagnosis of the tariff- and non-tariff-related obstacles that continue to persist in the community space. Finally, it is necessary to interact with the economic operators by involving them more in the normative process. Indeed, economic players have lacked preparation for the liberalisation of trade. Strengthening the common market in general and free circulation of merchandise in particular are the prerequisite for economic development within the WAEMU space. The author's comments and observations are in line with the ideas put forth by Lamy (2010).

Part II: Regional Financial Instruments and Fighting Poverty

Ameth Saloum Ndiaye (Chapter 9) analyses the role migrant fund transfers play in promoting economic development in WAEMU. He approaches the issue of migrant fund remittances as a new source of development funding. The author focuses on WAEMU countries from 1974 to 2006 and shows that money transfers promote economic growth and that these resources contribute to increasing domestic investment. This result reveals that productive investment constitutes an important channel through which fund transfers influence growth. For the entire period from 1974 to 2006, WAEMU countries recorded a total money transfer volume of around US$18.2 billion, representing an average of US$79.8 million a year. Econometric analysis also reveals that money remittances act de facto like a substitute for financial services to promote productive investment and, as a result, growth in this zone. This result thus demonstrates that the influence of fund remittances on investment occurs in a shallow financial system marked by the presence of liquidity limitations with, notably, low levels of deposits and limited access to credit. The main implication is that it is essential to channel money remittances more towards productive investments, on one hand by pushing migrants into the banking system, enabling the financial system to offer savings products and entrepreneurial credit, and on the other hand by putting into place both financial and non-financial support structures. From this point of view, the study recommends the creation of a regional diaspora investment support fund that could be responsible for identifying migrant-led projects and for providing financial and technical support in order to improve their capacity to undertake and manage productive activities.

In Chapter 10, Samuel Kaboré analyses the efficiency of targeted credit on the poor by using a variety of indicators applied to Burkina Faso agricultural loans. The study proposes a targeted credit efficiency index for the poor that is calculated based on the efficacy of targeted indicators. This efficiency index measures the percentage of the total amount that arrives to the poor. The empirical results indicate that targeting farming enables agricultural loans to potentially reach at least 89% of monetarily poor households, with an efficiency index of less than 42%. This eligibility of the poor fell to 13.2% of poor households in 1998 and 22% in 2003 when one targets the actual seekers of agricultural loans. In reality, agricultural loans reach fewer than 11% of monetarily poor households, with an effective efficiency of at most 42%. This major gap between the potential and real eligibility of the poor suggests an eviction of the poor due to a variety of implicit indicators whose in-depth analysis would enable loans to be better adapted. Targeting through the use of other indicators, such as major grains like sorghum, small ruminant breeding or the possession of arable land, is effective on the eligibility of poor households, but ineffective in eliminating the non-poor, which translates into an efficiency index of at most 42%, even if the financial administration is very efficient in transferring the funds to the poor. In order to reach a larger number of the poor, agricultural loans need to be adapted to the conditions faced by the poorest households, whereas agrarian reforms that could give a legal hold on the land would offer the poor greater access to credit.

In Chapter 11, Insa Abary Noufou examines the performance and effectiveness of Niger's decentralised financial system. The conditions required by the classical banking system and financial institutions place serious limitations on the access households have and notably the access the poor have to credit. The decentralised financial system (DFS) is supposed to facilitate participation by the poor in economic activities through a savings and loan system that tries to be financially viable and profitable. In Niger, this DFS continues to develop and to structure itself into a tool supplying financial services to the most disadvantaged population. As a result, after many years of experimenting with micro-savings and loan projects, it is important to assess the performance of the microfinance sector and its contribution to Niger's economic and social development. The study shows that despite relatively high interest rates and usury, the microfinance system is developing at full speed in Niger, with an increase in the number of microfinance institutions, the volume of loans granted and jobs created, along with an increasing number of beneficiaries, primarily women.

Despite the obstacles to long-term viability, micro-credit remains a financial possibility that is of vital importance to the poor and therefore essential for poverty reduction in Niger. To make the DFS more effective, the study recommends targeting the poor and identifying their financial needs, but also considering DFS customers not as people looking for charity but as stakeholders seeking to do business when they have access to basic tools (capital and training) that are adapted to their needs.

Chapter 12 by Sandra Kendo examines the relations that exist between financing farming activities and the food crisis. In a context of a growing food crisis where more than a billion people are suffering from hunger, the study of how to optimise the agricultural sector by boosting funding in view of serving the largest possible number of poor people proves its importance. The author set the goal of analysing how microfinance can enhance the funding of farming in view of improving living conditions for poor populations. This financing can be improved and ensured efficiently if microfinance services are innovated and adapted to this purpose. The capacity of farming households has a twofold influence on the poverty-reduction process through, on one hand, farming productivity and, on the other, income distribution. The study assesses successively the impact of available credit on agricultural productivity and then that of agricultural productivity on poverty. It shows that the financial sector, having achieved its current level of development, is not contributing to improving productivity, but it is a key factor that has a positive impact on poverty reduction. In addition, there is a negative relationship to the non-linear trend between farming productivity and poverty. Yet, in view of improving the financial sector's actions among farmers, a framework could be developed to promote financial intermediation based on microfinance. In this way, it is necessary to value and popularise among farmers the activities of those involved in microfinance. The development of adequate and adapted financing through microfinancing in the agricultural sector should be a priority for West African countries. Such financing has a positive influence both on improving productivity processes and on poverty reduction.

In Chapter 13, Coulibaly and Keita assess the impact of the common external tariff (CET) on households, particularly those with a modest standard of living in Mali. In concrete terms, they use consumer budget survey data to determine if application of the CET is such that households with modest levels of consumption or purchase of tradable goods can bear tax pressure that is proportionally lower than those with higher income. To do so, the study makes use of indicators that target the poor, notably those used in assessing poverty-reduction programmes. The results indicate that CET on category 0 social goods benefits proportionally more those who are not poor than those who are poor. The same applies to poor buyers of products of primary necessity found in CET category 1. Chapter 13 concludes by highlighting the necessity of more in-depth and broader evaluation of the CET and integration of the "poverty" dimension into the development and implementation of the Union's commercial policy.

During this conference, communications specialists participated and were able to appreciate how researchers were communicating the results of their work. In Chapter 14, Barry, Niango and Touré review the importance of better communication in order to better inform decision-makers. This critical perspective makes it possible to bring technical concepts to an easy level of understanding for non-economists.

In the final chapter (Chapter 15), Elias T. Ayuk and Samuel T. Kaboré summarise the conclusions and prospects for regional integration in West Africa. The prospects that are presented respond to the question of how better to ensure integration that creates wealth and reduces poverty. In a word, WAEMU member countries have a lot of integration and poverty-reduction potential as long as appropriate economic policy measures are used to overcome certain limitations that have been highlighted.

References

Balassa, Bela (1961), *The Theory of Economic Integration*, Richard D. Irwin, INC, Homewood, Illinois.

Baldwin, R.E. (1997), 'Review of the theoretical developments on regional integration' in Oyejide A., Elbadawi I. and Collier P. (eds.) *Regional Integration and Trade Liberalization in Sub-Saharan Africa*. Volume 1: Framework, Issues and Methodological Perspectives. Londres: Macmillan Press Ltd: 24–88.

Bigsten, A. and Levin J., (2000), 'Growth, Income Distribution and Poverty: A review', *Working Paper in Economics* No. 32. JEL-Classification 01, 02. Göteborg University.

Buccanfuso, D. and T.S. Kaboré, (2004). 'Croissance, Inégalité et Pauvreté dans les années 90 au Burkina Faso et au Sénégal, *Revue d'Économie du Développement*, Vol 2: 9–36, June 2004.

Cernat, L. (2001), 'Assessing regional trade arrangements: Are South-South RTAs more trade diverting?' Dans *Policy Issues in International Trade and Commodities Study Series, no 16*, CNUCED, New York and Genève.

CNUCED (2009), *Le Développement Economique en Afrique Rapport 2009: Renforcer l'Intégration Economique Régionale pour le Développement de l'Afrique*. Nations Unies, New York and Geneva, 126 pages.

Datt, G. and M. Ravallion, (1992), 'Growth and Redistribution Components of Changes in Poverty Measures: A decomposition with applications to Brazil and India in 1980s'. *Journal of Development Economics*, 38 (1992): 275–295.

Frankel, J. and A.K. Rose (1998), 'Endogeneity of the optimum Currency Criteria', *Economic Journal*, 108:1009–1025.

Gbetnkom, D. (2008), 'Is South-South regionalism always a diversion? Empirical evidence from CEMAC', *International Trade Journal*, 22 (1): 85–112.

Krugman, Paul R. (1991), Geography and Trade, Cambridge, MA: MIT Press

Krugman, Paul R. (1993a), "The Narrow and Broad Arguments for Free Trade", *American Economic Review*, 83: 362–366.

Lamy, Pascal (2010), 'Intégration régionales en Afrique: ambitions et vicissitudes'. Notre Europe *Policy paper no. 43*.

Mealy, M.P. (2005), "Linkages between Trade, Development and Poverty Reduction: Stakeholders' Views from Asia on Pro-poor Trade Policies", Report Prepared for CUTS-Centre for International Trade, Economics & Environment (CITEE).

Mfunwa, Mzwanele, G. (2008), 'Achieving a free trade area and customs union: Emerging challenges and opportunities for Southern Africa', Featured article at the Fourteenth Meeting of the Intergovernmental Committee of Experts for Southern Africa (ICE), UNECA

Paiva, Paulo and Ricardo Gazel (2003), 'Mercosur: past, present and future', *Nova Economica, Belo Horizonte*, 13 (2): 115–135.

Palley, T.I. (2002), 'A New Development Paradigm: Domestic Demand-Led Growth, *Foreign Policy in Focus*, September 2002, at: www.fpif.org.

Palley, T.I. (2003), 'Export-Led Growth: Is There Any Evidence of Crowding-out?' in Arestis et al. (eds.), Globalization, Regionalism and Economic Activity. Cheltenham, UK. Edward Elgar, 2003.

Ravallion M., (1996), 'Comparaisons de la Pauvreté, Concepts et Méthodes', *LSMS Document de travail N° 122*. Banque Mondiale, Washington, D.C.

Ravallion M. and G. Datt, (2002), 'Why has Economic Growth been more Pro-poor in some states of India than others ?' *Journal of Development Economics*, 6 (2002):381–400.

Ravallion M. and Huppi, M. (1991), 'Measuring Changes in Poverty: A Methodological Case Study of Indonesia during an Adjustment Period', *The World Bank Economic Review*. Vol. 5, No. 1: 57–82.

Rodrik, D. and F. Rodriguez (2001), 'Trade Policy and Economic Growth: A Skeptic's Guide to The Gross-National Evidence', B. Bernanke and K.S.Rogoff (eds), *Macroeconomics Annual*; 2000, Cambridge, MA: MIT Press for NBER

Viner, J. (1950), The *Customs Union Issue*, Carnegie Endowment for International Peace, New York.

Winters, L.A, N. McCulloch, and A. McKay (2004), 'Trade Liberalization and Poverty: The Evidence so Far', *Journal of Economic Literature*, XLII (March): 72–115.

Part I
Economic Convergence
and Fighting Poverty

Chapter 2
Fifteen Years of WAEMU: Results and Strategies for the Future

Diery Seck

Abstract After 15 years of existence, WAEMU has recorded some undeniable successes, particularly in its currency management, its exchange policy and in the organisation of its stock market. It has also managed to preserve the solidity and reliability of its institutions and its members' adhesion to the community project. However, although there continues to be respect for its neutrality, independence and authority, it is facing difficulties improving in other areas that are, certainly, new to its scope of responsibilities. WAEMU is one of the most disadvantaged community areas in the world in terms of human development, and according to UNDP human development index (HDI) its ranking continues to regress. Furthermore, the growing economic divergence between the richest and the poorest countries highlights the failure of national policies in individual countries and the Union's inability to help these countries in a significant manner within the current framework, which is an element that could threaten cohesion.

The significant improvements that one can expect of the Union are not in the monetary arena, where it has managed to preserve and strengthen the gains from the West African Monetary Union (WAMU) that preceded it, but rather they are in those areas that continue to fall under national competence. There are four kinds of priority strategic actions that emerged from the analysis of WAEMA's institutional and programming results. First, WAEMU's economic and social—and therefore budgetary—policy competence should be broadened beyond monetary issues, and the states should envision conceding part of their sovereignty, which would strengthen the Union's ability to exploit its full potential. Increasing the Commission's revenues would make it easier to implement community projects that have been suspended or abandoned due to a lack of funding.

Secondly, the Union should focus on strengthening the weakest countries, both to improve the social situation of residents of those countries and to facilitate the

D. Seck (✉)
CREPOL (Centre for Research in Political Economy), Dakar, Senegal
e-mail: d.seck@crepol.org

E.T. Ayuk and S.T. Kaboré (eds.), *Wealth Through Integration*, Insight and Innovation in International Development 4, DOI 10.1007/978-1-4614-4415-2_2,
© International Development Research Centre 2013

equalisation process, which is key to all community projects. Thirdly, the Union should enact a social pact whose main goal would be to improve the standard of living of all its residents. Implementing the social pact would occur at the community level, under the Commission's overall authority and adequate financing. The fourth strategic priority would consist of increasing mobility within the Union to remove non-tariff barriers and untimely roadblocks, of encouraging the development of cross-national value chains within the Union and of reinforcing the creation of infrastructures that promote mobility.

I Introduction

WAEMU was founded in January 1994 to replace the WAMU and to serve as a framework for the formulation and implementation of development policies in the West African franc zone following the devaluation of the CFA franc. The economic and social conditions that led to its foundations can be succinctly summarised as follows. Although the WAMU zone experienced average GDP growth that was higher than that of sub-Saharan African countries from 1970 to 1985, its situation gradually deteriorated between 1985 and 1993 due to deteriorating terms of trade, which decreased by 40% during this period. The drop in the US dollar relative to the French franc, to which the CFA franc had been pegged through fixed parity, significantly reduced competitiveness of the zone's exports. In addition, coffee and cacao prices continued to fall, deepening trade balance deficits in member countries and affecting their foreign exchange reserves.

The public sector wage bill proved to be particularly high in the face of the rising budget deficit and had negative repercussions on performance in the private sector, which was facing high taxes, considerable arrears of the state and the expensive alignment of its pay scales with that of the public administration's higher scales. It followed that, despite moderate inflation rates, the monetary situation worsened quickly, due to capital drain and the monetisation of the states' budget deficits, which worked around the statutory pre-financing ceilings of the West African States Central Bank (BCEAO) by having recourse to loans from commercial banks that refinanced the monetary authority. Consequently, budget discipline slackened to relieve social tensions, aggravating the crowding out of private enterprises from the credit market and thus impacting investment and production. A vicious circle had taken hold and called for radical measures.

Considering the states' weak capacity to mobilise more budget proceeds, the erosion of the zone's real effective exchange rates, the inefficiency of Bretton Woods Institutions' aid programmes and the immobility of salaries in the formal labour market, it became necessary to change the parity of the CFA franc as an inevitable measure that needed to be accompanied by daring reforms to prevent the major internal and external imbalances of the previous decade.

WAEMU was created as an appropriate framework for the development and execution of reforms and initiatives related to restoring macroeconomic equilibrium among the zone's countries, building the credibility of the currency, revitalising the economy through private investment, intensifying intra-zone trade and returning to budgetary discipline. The new line of measures targeted the zone's greater integration, with an ultimate goal of improving the standard of living of its residents. For the theory of Optimum Currency Areas, see Mundell (1961) and Kenen (1969). Many of these measures were implemented both at the community and national levels, with varying results. The purpose of this study is to review those results and draw up the most relevant conclusions from them in order to develop prospects that should govern WAEMU's future actions.

Requirements for WAEMU's Success

Necessary Monetary and Economic Arrangements

In view of the texts that govern WAEMU, notably the primary criteria for convergence, the project's monetary nature seems to dominate, reinforced by its economic aspects. Also, it is appropriate to study the factors that contribute to the success of monetary unions in light of past experiences. One can draw up four key lessons.[1] First, the success of the monetary union depends above all on the determination of its members to individually and irrevocably renounce monetary sovereignty and any use of monetary or exchange policy instruments in order to create a common regional institution that has the exclusive power to develop and apply monetary and exchange policy. In addition, the union must have a single currency and, if it has another one, the latter must have a fixed, unchanging nominal exchange rate with respect to the primary currency and free and unlimited convertibility so that the two currencies are perfect substitutes for each other.

Secondly, the monetary authority must be able to prevent, without pressure from the member states or the possibility of them working around the measures, any monetisation of their budget deficits, which is made easier if it has oversight on the level of budgetary expansion and therefore a certain capacity to discuss with its members. Indeed, it is essential that in its policy to defend the currency, it can juggle the inflationist trends that could result in excessive recourse to monetary creation through direct loans from the monetary authority or indirect ones from commercial banks. Thirdly, the success of a monetary union could depend on its organisation around a strong and stable economy or simply around the latter's currency, be it an officially fixed parity or a parity to which the members adhere freely but respect scrupulously.[2] This arrangement gives members of the union the benefit of externally-imposed discipline considering that monetary stability must be based on fiscal

---

[1] See Masson and Patillo (2001a, b).

[2] WAEMU, the Central African Economic and Monetary Union (CEMAC) and the Euro zone chose official fixed parity. WAEMU and CEMAC have the CFA franc that was pegged to the French franc and now to the euro, while the euro was organised around the Bundesbank and the German mark.

discipline not unlike that of an advanced economy. One of its main characteristics is strong fiscal discipline, which facilitates control of inflation. Finally, a monetary union cannot succeed without producing or being facilitated by the broader trade and institutional integration of its members. To achieve common goals other than monetary ones, the union may need to initiate additional reforms in harmony with monetary policy instruments and that have their own ambitions and implementation programme.

The success of an economic and monetary union hinges on an adequate institutional framework whose operational rules strengthen the effectiveness of its action. However, it also depends on controlling mechanisms through which the positive impact of integration efforts should be channelled. Six benchmarks enable the measurement of potential gains that could result from the union.

Increased Intra-zone Trade

Intensifying trade within the integrated zone benefits its economic agents and can stimulate private investment, create economies of scale and sometimes open up regions that are located on the main internal trade routes. The gains resulting from increased intra-zone trade depend on how complementary national production are, on how smoothly goods and people circulate throughout the union's territory and on the existence of fast and reliable means of payment along with a harmonised legal framework.

Weak Correlation of the Effects of Crises on Member Economies

Union members are better protected if the structure of their respective economies is safeguarded when other members suffer the impact of various crises, be they external such as changing world prices for certain products or variations in interest rates, nominal exchange rates or the level of worldwide economic activity, or internal; the overall impact is lessened.

Labour Mobility Within the Union

It becomes easier for union members to converge private investment profitability rates, unemployment rates and economic growth when labour circulates freely in the territory. The absence of barriers at the union's internal borders, freedom of residence and to acquire movable and immovable property, fiscal equality and the recognition of degrees and vocational certificates are factors that favourably impact labour mobility.

Union Competence in Budgetary Matters and Member Solidarity

A union can make great contributions to its members if it has the budgetary competence to help them accelerate economic convergence and face crises. This supposes full agreement on the methods used to calculate aid and the absence of hazardous moral behaviour by its members or one of its members, the fulfilment of whose needs could eventually drain the solidarity fund. Finally, it also requires constant solidarity among the members, even when they face crises simultaneously. Granting budgetary competence to the union constitutes a transfer of budgetary sovereignty that, even if limited or circumscribed to specifically defined cases, is symbolically important in the expression of the members' commitment to have a shared future.

Unilateral Irreversibility of Community Arrangements

A union member's possibility of influencing how the common monetary policy is led or the monetary authority's ability of unilaterally adjusting the budgetary expansion of its members would considerably reduce the efficiency of the community arrangement and would threaten its long-term viability. In both a perceived and real manner, the union members and the private sector must be convinced that the monetary authority has its hands bound and that the community arrangement cannot be subject to any exceptions, so that the central bank's monetary policy cannot be dependent on the states' budgetary policy, notably by way of the non-statutory monetisation of the latter's deficits.

Member Adhesion to Nominal Convergence Criteria

The consecrated use of strictly observed convergence criteria by the union's members constitutes a major requirement for the existence of a single institution in charge of monetary and exchange policy and for the rise of a viable common currency in the community territory. The underlying challenge is to lead economies that are different in their structure, size, performance, assets, challenges and history to observe these criteria and to stick to them over time and despite shocks that will certainly affect them differently. The task is all the more difficult if community aid mechanisms lack when a major crisis affects some of the members.

WAEMU's Institutional Framework and its Functioning

WAEMU's Institutional Framework

Benin, Burkina Faso, Côte d'Ivoire, Mali, Niger, Senegal and Togo signed a treaty on January 10, 1994, which took force on August 1, 1994, creating the WAEMU to complete the WAMU that preceded it. WAEMU's objectives were formulated as follows[3]: (a) strengthen the competitiveness of economic and financial activities in

---

[3] Guinea-Bissau became a member of the Union on May 2, 1997.

the member states in the framework of an open and competitive market and a rationalised and harmonised legal environment; (b) ensure the convergence of member state economic performance and policies by instituting a multilateral monitoring procedure; (c) create a common market among member states based on the free circulation of people, goods, services and capital and the right of establishment for people working independently or earning a wage, as well as a common external tariff and a common trade policy; (d) establish coordination of national sectorial policies by implementing common actions and eventually common policies, notably in the following areas: human resources, territorial planning, transport and telecommunications, environment, agriculture, energy, industry and mines; and (e) harmonise, as necessary for the good function of the market, member state legislations and, specifically, taxation.

To operate, the Union established the following bodies: the Conference of Heads of State and Government, the Council of Ministers, the Commission, the Court of Justice and the Court of Audit.

In addition, the Central Bank of West African States (BCEAO) and the West African Development Bank (WADB) are specialised WAEMU institutions, the former filling the role of central bank and the latter that of a subregional development bank. The Inter-parliamentary Committee and the Regional Consular Chamber complete the WAEMU institutional set-up. All of the Union's bodies have been in operation since 1998.

Convergence Criteria

In 1999, WAEMU members adopted the Convergence, Stability, Growth and Solidarity Pact, that was amended in 2003 and 2009. In virtue of the pact's current version, the Union established convergence criteria that have to be observed by all its members.

Primary criteria are a ratio of the basic fiscal balance to nominal GDP greater than or equal to 0%, an average annual inflation rate of 3% per year at most, a ratio of outstanding domestic and foreign debt to nominal GDP that does not exceed 70% and non-accumulation of domestic and external payment arrears in the current financial period.

Secondary criteria are a ratio of the wage bill to tax revenue that does not exceed 35%, a ratio of domestically financed public investment to tax revenue of at least 20%, a ratio of current exterior balance outside grants to nominal GDP of at least −5% and a tax-to-GDP ratio of at least 17%.

Additional Union Measures

The BCEAO and the WADB operate within the WAEMU as independent, specialised institutions, respectively, as the monetary authority and the investment bank. With the Union's goal of meeting its objectives, it has undertaken actions and adopted measures that can be described succinctly as follows. In terms of harmonising national legislation, it implemented the West African Accounting System (SYSCOA), the state budget classification and the State Accounting Plan. It has also harmonised legislation in terms of value-added tax (VAT) and created the Regional Stock Market (BRVM). The institution of the National Economic Policy Committees and the adoption of a harmonised consumer price index (HICP) are its key actions in terms of multilateral monitoring of macroeconomic policies.

As part of its efforts aimed at creating a common market, the Union proceeded with removing non-tariff barriers and set up free movement, completely free of duties and taxes, of local and craft-industry products. In addition, it progressively reduced customs duties on industrial products of unapproved origin and fully undid tariffs on 100% of industrial products from approved origins. It also adopted community competition legislation. The CET was set up and accompanied by a maximum customs duty of 20% to which is added a statistical fee of 1% and a community solidarity duty of 1%. Sectorial policies were adopted in the following areas: energy, industry, mines, agriculture, environment, maritime, telecommunications, road transport, air transport, teaching and scientific research, health, women and employment. To fund development, WAEMU set up the Regional Integration Aid Fund (RIAF) and the aid intervention programme for member countries.

Analysis of the WAEMU Institutional Set-Up

At its foundation, WAEMU benefited amply from the experience of WAMU, which preceded it, notably in that which concerns the role and powers of the central bank, cooperation among member states, subregional monetary policy and bank supervision. These gains were updated with the start of WAEMU without any significant reconsideration and were completed with new economic arrangements that strengthened the Union. In light of its 15 years of experience, the Union can be considered a success in three of its four institutional arenas. In effect, it has managed to ensure the commitment of its members to delegate their monetary sovereignty fully and completely to a central bank, the BCEAO, whose powers, although supervised by the political authority of the states, are exercised independently and without specific pressure from the latter, thus enhancing its credibility and as a result that of its currency. The BCEAO exclusively enacts monetary and exchange policies, and the CFA is the only legal currency in the Union's territory, with no competition from any other currency.

The monetary authority has, among other things, been granted the capacity to prevent inflationist pressure that could result from uncontrolled and monetised budgetary expansion by the states through monetary reconciliation. The growing tendency of member states to finance their budget deficit on the BRVM financial market via compulsory loans constitutes a market mechanism that amplifies the BCEAO's institutional credibility. Finally, pegging the CFA franc to the euro and

Table 2.1 WAEMU country intra-community exports, in millions of CFA francs

	1996	1997	1998	1999	2000	2001	2002	2003	2004	2005	2006
Benin	4.1	3.8	4.6	5.6	7.5	7.3	6.0	8.7	25.3	21.1	27.6
Burkina Faso	13.7	16.7	22.4	39.7	21.2	23.9	20.5	112.2	128.7	99.0	5.2
Côte d'Ivoire	249.7	311.6	344.8	391.3	422.6	406.3	390.1	320.8	349.9	417.0	455.5
Mali	49.4	37.6	45.2	26.8	38.8	15.6	37.9	18.6	42.4	52.4	39.3
Niger	9.1	7.1	8.9	8.0	8.0	3.8	7.4	3.5	15.5	8.3	6.4
Senegal	53.2	60.0	64.9	70.7	61.3	81.5	121.4	132.6	162.4	179.5	198.1
Togo	3.8	4.0	5.7	10.6	12.7	42.6	57.4	105.7	90.9	78.4	96.7

Source: WAEMU Commission

having the French Treasury guarantee of its convertibility strengthens the solidity of the Union because it encourages economic agents to compromise on their currency and to hold it without fear of it losing value.

However, the success of the Union has been less resounding on an economic level than on a monetary level due to this dimension being a more recent part of the community arrangement and to the national preponderance in budget policy, the tool of choice for economic policy. Although a large number of legal instruments and harmonisation tools have been issued in view of facilitating business practices and developing uniform standards, the Union's lack of budgetary competence has made WAEMU's economic policy the weak link compared with the scope of its monetary dimension. This institutional situation is not without consequences on the long-term prospects of the community project and therefore upon its final success.

Currently, the analysis will focus on the adequacy of the channels through which potential community gains can take form. The issues are those of increasing intra-zone trade, of reducing the correlation between the effects of crises on member economies, of labour mobility, of the scope of the Union's fiscal income based on member solidarity, of the irreversible unilateral community arrangements and of the member's adherence to conversion criteria.

Table 2.1 shows that intra-zone exports from the Union's large countries—Côte d'Ivoire, Senegal and Benin—increased greatly from 1996 to 2006. On the other hand, the landlocked countries of Burkino Faso, Mali and Niger experienced intra-community exports whose growth was more modest and more volatile. On the whole, WAEMU increased its cross-border trade, boosting the role of coastal states as suppliers to members without access to the sea and therefore integrating the whole of the Union more into a globalised world. Assessment of WAEMU's intra-regional trade performance has been conducted by Agbodji (2007), Bayoumi and Ostry (1995), Coulibaly (2007), Faroutan and Pritchett (1993) and Goretti and Weisfeld (2008).

Integration instruments, such as Organization for the Harmonization of Business Law in Africa (OHBLA), SYSCOA, the CET, the common road transport programme and the common air transport programme, play an important role in the expansion of intra-zone trade. However, the Union continues to suffer a negative impact from untimely roadblocks that delay delivery of merchandise, creating an additional economic cost.

It is generally admitted that the healthy economic growth of a developing country is based on export. As a result, any crisis that compromises exports could

Table 2.2 FOB export growth rate correlation matrix for WAEMU countries from 1990 to 2008

	Burkina Faso	Togo	Senegal	Niger	Mali	Côte d'Ivoire	Benin
Burkina Faso	1						
Togo	0.270	1					
Senegal	0.457	0.238	1				
Niger	0.327	−0.109	0.485	1			
Mali	0.209	−0.608	−0.023	−0.015	1		
Côte d'Ivoire	0.548	0.310	0.599	0.447	0.154	1	
Benin	−0.297	−0.001	−0.149	0.046	−0.006	0.035	1

Source: International Financial Statistics, IMF; author's calculations

impede economic growth. One of the reasons an economic union is desirable is that it provides an implicit assurance that results from there being a weak correlation between the impacts of crises and member exports. Table 2.2 shows the correlation among export growth rates in WAEMU member states, revealing a contrasting image. The two strongest economies—Côte d'Ivoire and Senegal—are the most correlated, at 0.599. The weakest economies have weak or negative correlation coefficients, which seems to indicate that they are less sensitive to external crises and that there is a better propensity to reassure each other.

On the whole, the correlation matrix highlights the significant gain that could result from the Union by mutualising the risks linked to the impact of crises on member economies. One must, however, note that WAEMU does not yet have a fund to guarantee its members' exports or any instrument that could compensate for a significant decrease in export proceeds. In addition, the community solidarity duty, which is 1% of non-community imports, could amplify the economic downside of a member state if the latter increases non-community imports to fill a passing production deficit.

WAEMU benefits from two factors that should make it easier to adjust to crises. The relatively large size of its informal sector in the labour market and its high capacity to adjust rapidly to crises constitutes a clear advantage that also impacts the formal sector. The second factor is linked to the Union's continued effort to facilitate the free movement of people by boosting development of the road infrastructure, removing visa requirements for Union residents and giving them the right to settle, work and acquire movable and non-movable property in every country in the community. WAEMU stands out due to its strong migratory flows as illustrated in the Burkina community found in Côte d'Ivoire, a third of whose population is considered to be of foreign origin.

Solidarity constitutes one of the economic and monetary union's key strong points and is based on the latter's capacity to help its members face temporary difficulties or to nudge the weaker members closer to the others, thus preserving cohesion and facilitating convergence. Upon analysis, WAEMU does not seem to have adequate resources to fulfil this role, despite the existence of the Regional Integration Aid Fund (RIAF) and the intervention programme. A lack of financial resources necessary to boost solidarity could weaken political determination to further the integration process and therefore limit the Union's development. From this point of view, taking into account how insufficient and relatively uncertain public development aid is, the 1% community solidarity duty on non-community imports could benefit from being increased in order to give the Union more sovereignty and presence in the future of its members. In comparison, the European Union (EU) has four types of budget resources: customs duties on extra-community imports, customs duties on certain food products imported from outside the Union, a percentage of the value-added tax collected by its members and a direct contribution from member states representing a certain percentage of their gross national product. The EU's financial resources represent around 1.24% of the Union's gross national product. WAEMU's most important economic programs are described in WAEMU (2006). They can be compared to those of the European Union: see Leonard (2005).

Since it was created, the WAEMU has been characterised by the strict adhesion to its governance principles and to an absence of unilateral modification in the rules that underlie how it conducts its monetary and exchange policy, whether it comes from the monetary authority or the member states. This stability in governance relations boosts the central bank's credibility and prevents uncontrolled budget expansion that would bet on a member state's deficit monetisation. On the other hand, it imposes that the latter confine itself to the strict management of the currency and therefore exclude the pursuit of other objectives that could conflict with defending the value of the CFA franc. In other words, the Union may need to develop and implement non-monetary policy instruments to pursue its economic goals.

It is commonly admitted that the keystone of a monetary union resides in the capacity of its members to work together to define convergence criteria and to respect them as much as possible. The eight criteria chosen by the WEMU are compatible with the Union's development and apply to all its members, although the deadline for conforming to them has been pushed to 2013. Table 2.3 details the member state's experience in this area.

Three key lessons can be drawn from the experience between 2004 and 2006, corresponding to 10 years after the foundation of the WAEMU. The first is that no criterion was respected by all the states in a given year and that no state respected any of the criteria every year. It is therefore appropriate to question the realism of levels demanded for each of the chosen criteria or of the Union's capacity to impose on its members conformity to commitments that have been made voluntarily. An alternative approach could consist of exploring a transfer of competences in certain areas—notably budgetary areas—that could facilitate the respect of certain criteria. The second lesson is that on average, the member states conformed to 3.88 criteria in 2004, 2.88 in 2005 and 3.25 in 2006, which represent less than half of the eight criteria and does not demonstrate any trend towards improvement over time. None of the criteria experienced an improvement in respect over time. One can therefore conclude that the WAEMU does not yet control how the respect of convergence criteria is evolving.

The third lesson resides in the differentiation between the most respected and the least respected criteria. Controlling inflation, a primary criterion, was the most observed but has the characteristic of being the most influenced by the monetary

Table 2.3 Achievement of convergence criteria in WAEMA countries

Convergence criteria (based on additional convergence indicators)	Achievement of criteria in 2006[a] by state and review of performance in 2004 and 2005 in WAEMU								Number of countries having respected the criteria		
	Benin	Burkina Faso	Côte d'Ivoire	Guinea-Bissau	Mali	Niger	Senegal	Togo	2006	2005	2004
1 Basic fiscal balance[b] to nominal GDP (norm ≥ 0)	0.8	−1.4	−1.9	−2.2	2.9	−0.5	−1.1	−0.1	2	4	4
2 Underlying inflation rate (norm ≤ 3%)	3.9	2.5	2.5	2.2	3.6	0.7	1.6	1.8	6	1	8
3 Total outstanding debt to nominal GDP (norm ≤ 70%)	14.8	17.1	80.5	323.8	23.9	25.6	40.5	95.9	5	5	4
4 Non-accumulation of payment arrears (in billions)	0	0	426.2	nd	0	nd	0	nd	4	4	5
4.1 Domestic payment arrears	0	0	23.7	nd	0	nd	0	nd	7	5	5
4.2 Foreign payment arrears	0	0	402.5	21.8	0	0	0	26.8	5	5	4
5 Wage bill to tax revenue[b] (norm ≤ 35%)	35.2	36.3	43.1	86.2	24.9	31	30.3	34.6	4	3	4
6 Domestically financed public investment to tax revenue[b] (norm ≥ 20%)	17.6	30.6	11.8	2.1	17.4	21.2	27.8	5.5	3	4	4
7 Current exterior balance outside grants to nominal GDP (norm ≥ −5%)	−7	−11.3	1.8	−12.2	−8.4	−9.9	−10.4	−20.1	1	1	1
8 Tax revenues (norm ≥ 17%)	15.3	12	15.1	10.9	14.7	11.4	19.1	14.2	1	1	1
Number of criteria respected by countries 2006	3	4	2	1	4	4	6	2			
2005	3	3	1	0	5	3	7	1			
2004	4	6	2	1	6	2	7	3			

Source: WAEMU Commission, April 2007

[a] Shaded areas show respected criteria

[b] Corrected for budget grants and HIPC resources

authority via controlling monetary expansion. The most violated criteria concern the public budget—basic budget balance and fiscal pressure rate—along with the current exterior account. These three variables are under national policy control and seem to indicate the areas that need more efforts to consolidate the Union.

To conclude this section, Table 2.4 summarises the efforts accepted by the WAEMU and proposes a measure of how adequate they are with regard to the member states' integration project. The measures that are under the monetary authority were observed and were executed relatively well. These are transferring monetary sovereignty from the member states, the development and implementation of monetary and exchange policy, pegging the CFA franc to a strong currency and guaranteeing convertibility, and the unilateral irreversibility of community monetary arrangements. Some, although insufficient, progress has been made in diversifying national economies, notably concerning exports and labour mobility. Greater attention must be paid to four major areas which are (1) strengthening WAEMU's capacity to lead regional economic policies that work together with national economic policies, (2) expanding intra-community trade, (3) increasing the Union's financial resources and budgetary competence and (4) strengthening the Union's capacity to get the countries to respect convergence criteria and to find alternative solutions that can promote the respect of those criteria.

II Review of WAEMU Results

This review of WAEMU's results after 15 years of existence covers three areas: a social and economic review, a monetary and financial review and a review of convergence between the Union's national economies.

Social and Economic Review

Table 2.5 gives an overview of human development in the Union's member states as measured by the UNDP's HDI. It raises three issues. First, the average ranking of WAEMU zone countries regressed continually from 1990 to 2007. In other words, the level of human development prior to the creation of WAEMU was greater than that it experienced after 15 years of existence. Secondly, between 1990 and 2007, with the exception of Benin which dropped 12 spots in the ranking, each state taken individually dropped by 20 spots or more, with the Côte d'Ivoire dropping by 40. Finally, the weak ranking of the countries and their continual decrease make the WAEMU one of the most disadvantaged community areas in the world and run the risk of keeping it there in the foreseeable future if determined action is not taken to remedy this situation. The social record of WAEMU is examined by Bleaney and Nishiyama (2004), Fielding (2004) and Konseiga (2005).

Table 2.4 Assessment of WAEMU's institutional and operational set-up

Criteria of success	Implementation	Degree of accomplished efforts
Institutional criteria		
Sovereignty and single regional currency	– Single, independent central bank – Total abandon of national monetary sovereignty – Single, convertible currency throughout the zone	+ + +
Controlling budgetary expansion and inflation	– BCEAO controls budgetary expansion, prevents deficit monetisation by members – BCEAO dialogues with states about their budgets – State budget deficits financed by compulsory loans	+ + +
Pegging to a strong and stable economy or currency	– Institutional pegging to euro – Unlimited convertibility of CFA franc guaranteed by French Treasury	+ + +
Additional measures for economic integration	– Standards and regulations enacted – Absence of internal execution capacity – Insufficient Commission budget for programme implementation – Limited Commission influence on states' economic policy	+
Operational criteria		
Increasing intra-zone trade	– Increased overall intra-zone trade – Noticeable improvement in coastal country exports – Weak increase and large variability in landlocked country exports	+
Weak correlation of the effects of crises on members' economies	– Moderate correlation between exports of two largest economies – Small country exports hardly or not at all correlated	+ +
Union budgetary competence	– Union funding insufficient for regional economic policy – Weak absorption capacity of the states (RIAF)	+
Manpower mobility	– National legislations favourable to mobility and settling for residents of the Union – Regional transport infrastructure is insufficient	+ +
Unilateral irreversibility of community arrangements	– Good set-up with very good credibility	+ + +
Member adherence to convergence criteria	– Adherence insufficient over time, for each criteria and for each country	+

Table 2.5 WAEMU country human development index (UNDP) ranking, 1990–2007

	1990	1995	2000	2005	2007
Benin	149	145	158	163	161
Burkina Faso	157	172	169	176	177
Côte d'Ivoire	123	148	156	166	163
Guinea-Bissau	152	164	167	175	173
Mali	155	171	164	173	178
Niger	156	173	172	174	182
Senegal	137	158	154	156	166
Togo	132	144	141	152	159
Average country rank	145.1	159.4	160.1	166.9	169.9
Total number of ranked countries	160	174	173	177	182
Average standardised rank (Cf. Note)	90.7	91.6	92.6	94.3	93.3

Source: United National Development Programme Report, 1992, 1998, 2002, 2007/2008, 2009
Note: The average standardised rank is the average rank relative to the total number of ranked countries multiplied by 100

Table 2.6 Gross domestic product per capita in WAEMU countries in current dollars, 1990–2007 (PPP, in $US)

	1990	1995	2000	2005	2007
Benin	1,043	1,800	990	1,141	1,312
Burkina Faso	618	784	976	1,213	1,124
Côte d'Ivoire	1,324	1,731	1,630	1,648	1,690
Guinea-Bissau	841	811	755	827	477
Mali	572	565	797	1,033	1,083
Niger	645	765	746	781	627
Senegal	1,248	1,815	1,510	1,792	1,666
Togo	734	1,167	1,442	1,506	788

Source: UNDP Human Development Reports, 1993, 1998, 2002, 2007/2008, 2009

The evolution of the per capita GDP in Union countries is presented in Table 2.6. It shows that the countries that were the richest in 1990—Côte d'Ivoire, Senegal and Benin—remained so and experienced respective growth in income. On the contrary, the economically weak countries such as Guinea-Bissau, Niger and Togo stagnated or fell behind. One should also note that the latter experienced high levels of income variability, which aggravated matters for them in their efforts at development and internal redistribution. The WAEMU has a major challenge in this area, which lies in the significant and growing income disparity among its members. For example, in 1990, the average income of the three richest countries was US$1,205, while the average income of its three poorest members was US$611, which represents a gap of US$594. In 2007, the average income of the former increased to US$1,556, while the latter was only US$630, creating a difference of US$926. As a result, the gap between the two groups increased by 56%. On the whole, these results highlight the urgent and necessary need for WAEMU to focus on its weakest members in order to bring them up to the level of the others, to help them meet their social challenges head on, as left without solutions the current situation could lead

Table 2.7 WAEMU
country inflation rates
for five prior years

	1990	1995	2000	2005	2007
Benin	n.d.	17.8	3.7	2.8	2.6
Burkina Faso	−0.4	6.7	2.4	3.0	2.0
Côte d'Ivoire	4.8	9.7	2.9	3.2	26
Guinea-Bissau	58.0	47.2	22.9	1.5	1.5
Mali	0.3	6.4	1.7	2.4	1.0
Niger	−3.0	6.6	2.7	2.6	1.3
Senegal	0.2	7.5	1.4	1.5	2.0
Togo	0.8	11.3	3.1	2.6	1.9
WAEMU	n.d.	11.0	2.4	2.8	2.3

Source: International financial statistics, IMF

to sociopolitical unrest. One should also note the major income gains recorded by Burkina Faso and Mali, two landlocked countries that made regular progress without too much variability. Several studies describe the macroeconomic characteristics of WAEMU and its challenges. They include Doré and Masson (2002), Fielding et al. (2005), Hinkle and Montiel (1999), Linjouom (2004), Masson and Patillo (2005), Nashabishi and Bazzouni (1994), Rogoff and Reihart (2003), Rosenberg (1995), Rother (1998), Roudet et al. (2007), and Yehoue (2006).

Monetary and Financial Review

A review of WAEMU's monetary results is carried out from the angle of inflation and financing the economy. A history of inflation rates in the Union's member countries is presented in Table 2.7. It shows that outside the inflationist period that followed the CFA franc's parity change in January 1994, inflation has been well controlled in all the countries, with the exception of Guinea-Bissau, which was experiencing a civil war and was taking its first steps in the Union. So, the Union maintained its tradition of having a low inflation rate that dated to before the devaluation of the CFA franc—cf. the 1990 rates—and was able to create uniformity in this area by respecting its first-order convergence criteria regarding inflation, which prescribes that the rate not exceed 3% annually. One should underline the preponderant role the monetary authority played in these achievements and perhaps be inspired by it for the development and implementation of non-monetary policies, considering the rather modest results of national development policies.

Financing the economy plays a key role in development zone such as WAEMU and contributes to its financial liberalisation. The monetary supply to GDP ratio gives a reliable indication and is presented in Table 2.8. Notable progress has been recorded in this area since WAEMU was founded, except in Niger, whose situation calls for special attention due to its low level of monetisation and the huge gap that separates it from the other members of the Union. One should note that countries such as Guinea-Bissau and Togo, whose per capita GDP is relatively low as shown in Table 2.6, benefited from a relative monetary supply level that could contribute to them catching up with the other members, without any particularly inflationist

Table 2.8 Money supply
ratio relative to GDP
in WAEMU countries

	1990	1995	2000	2005	2007
Benin	25.1	22.9	28.6	25.8	30.7
Burkina Faso	18.1	21.4	20.9	18.8	22.5
Côte d'Ivoire	28.8	28.7	21.8	22.7	28.2
Guinea-Bissau	8.0	9.4	42.7	31.5	36.5
Mali	20.1	18.7	21.4	26.3	28.4
Niger	19.8	14.1	8.8	6.5	9.1
Senegal	22.6	20.6	23.7	32.3	35.0
Togo	36.1	26.0	26.0	27.5	35.9

Source: International financial statistics, IMF

pressure, if the hypothesis that the currency plays a positive role in economic development proves to be true in the WAEMU space.

Our analysis will now look at the Union's financial results. The banking system faced tightening credit following the devaluation of the CFA franc and progressively was able to return to rates comparable to those that occurred in 1990, an evolution that was facilitated by the states' increasing use of compulsory loans to finance their budget deficits, thus reducing the displacement of the private sector from the credit market. This change is connected to economic growth in the Union's members that it accompanies. Outside of the Côte d'Ivoire, which experienced a situation of near-division on the sociopolitical level that tended to reduce banking activities in certain regions, greater attention should go to Guinea-Bissau and Niger, whose private sector suffered for a long time from a level of access to credit that was too low to be compatible with sustainable economic growth. For the Union, in general, and for these two countries in particular, more in-depth analysis of the causal connections between credit expansion in the economy and economic growth—respecting WAEMU's nominal convergence criteria—should be carried out to, perhaps, support development efforts.

The regional stock market (BRVM) has actively participated in funding the sub-region since it was founded in September 1998. According to the World Bank, the market capitalisation of listed companies represented 11.4% of its host country Côte d'Ivoire's GDP in 2000, 14.2% in 2005 and 42.2% in 2007. The integrating nature of BRVM and its capacity to mobilise community and foreign savings constitutes one of WAEMU's greatest financial achievements, even if too high a concentration benefits Senegal and the Côte d'Ivoire, thus accentuating the imbalance already observed on the private sector credit market.

Real Community Convergence

The records of nominal convergence and real convergence in the WAEMU have been evaluated by Bamba (2004), Bamba and Diomande (1998), Berthelemy and Vadourkakis (1996), Ndiaye (2007), Sy (2006) and Wane (2004). One of the key measures of WAEMU's success lies in the economic convergence of its member states towards sustained growth, marked by the weaker countries catching up with

Table 2.9 Ratio of private sector credit to GDP in WAEMU countries

	1990	1995	2000	2005	2007
Benin	19.1	7.4	11.6	15.3	18.4
Burkina Faso	16.8	6.1	11.7	16.0	16.0
Côte d'Ivoire	36.5	20.4	15.2	13.4	15.2
Guinea-Bissau	2.6	4.9	7.9	2.0	5.6
Mali	12.5	9.7	15.1	16.1	17.4
Niger	12.3	4.4	5.2	6.5	9.1
Senegal	26.4	14.7	18.7	21.6	21.9
Togo	22.6	17.1	15.6	17.1	20.4

Source: International financial statistics, IMF

the more advanced countries. Two types of convergence measures will be used to evaluate Union performance: absolute convergence—or β-convergence—and σ-convergence that shows—via a decrease over time of the value dispersion coefficient among the countries relative to a variable—growing similarity. Wane (2004), Van Den Boogaerde and Tsangarides (2005), Masson and Patillo (2005), and Ndiaye (2007) tested σ-convergence on per capita GDP in WAEMU countries. The majority of these studies conclude in a lack of σ-convergence, which in the case of WAEMU countries means that the richest countries remain so over time and the poorest remain the poorest, a result that concords with Table 2.6.

σ-Convergence tests have also been carried out on other economic indicators in WAEMU countries. Ndiaye (2007) demonstrated an absence of convergence for investment relative to GDP, while Van Den Boogaerde and Tsangarides (2005) found weak convergence. Van Den Boogaerde and Tsangarides (2005) results concerning savings rate measured by the ratio of gross savings relative to GDP indicate σ-divergence. Sy (2006) found growing divergence in the member states' banking sectors by measuring over time the change in dispersion between lender and borrower interest rate gaps (Table 2.9).

The rare tests of absolute convergence that have been done on WAEMU country economies have given the following results. For Wane (2004), convergence—measured by the negative sign of the β coefficient of per capita GDP on the lagged dependent variable of the latter—is slow, reaching 6% a year. On the contrary, Masson and Patillo (2005) use the Markov chains and find a process of GDP per capita divergence in the zone's countries. Finally, Sy (2006) suggests that there is no β-convergence in the case of the gaps between lender and borrower rates in WAEMU countries, which indicates an absence of integration in the Union's banking sector. Assessment of WAEMU's overall performance has been conducted by Clément et al. (1996), Goreux (1995), Hernandez-Cata et al. (1998), and Van Den Boogaerde and Tsangarides (2005).

In conclusion, the review relative to convergence of the real economic sectors in member states reveals results that are not particularly satisfactory from the viewpoint of both disparity reduction and speed at which the lagging countries are catching up with the leaders. The greatest challenges lie in the budgetary and economic policy arena rather than in the area of monetary policy, as the monetary authority has demonstrated strong control over inflation. One should then raise the question of the level of resources made available to the Commission in order to help the weaker countries better integrate the Union and facilitate its progress.

III   Recommended Strategies for the Future

What strategic priorities can be drawn up from this short analysis of WAEMU's institutional set-up and its operational results and performance in order to renew the Union's dynamism? The results that have been presented and that could drive specific actions can be organised along four main lines: (1) strengthening the Commission's regional policy competences, (2) implementing a more active policy to strengthen the Union's weaker countries, (3) the creation of a social pact and (4) increasing the mobility of goods, people and capital. First, it is essential to recall that the Union's main strength lies in its long experience and the quality of its monetary arrangement, which serves as a basis and could be the model it should follow to build the institutions that will ensure its future successes.

Strengthening Union's Policy Competences

The success of the BCEAO and of the BRVM and the difficulties the states are facing in their respective internal policies offer an interesting contrast and raise the issue of the need to confer more competences to the Commission in order for it to increase the quality of its policies, benefiting from economies of scale and taking inspiration from the experiences of its specialised institutions. Furthermore, delegating monetary sovereignty should be accompanied by a comparable, be it unequal, delegation of budgetary policy competences in order to provide the Union with greater benefits. Such a change will noticeably benefit the weaker countries, whose financial and human capacities cannot, for the time being at least, initiate policies that could result in development.

At its current stage, the Commission has focussed on establishing standards and regulations that could create a favourable development environment in the Union. Yet, due to a lack of resources, it has not yet undertaken the vast regional economic development programme the zone needs. However, this work is an important part of its mission. It is symptomatic that a large number of projects found in WAEMU's 2006–2010 strategic development document have not been undertaken due to a lack of funding. WAEMU could envision the possibility of having a number of national competences transferred to it and of receiving higher fiscal proceeds in compensation through a higher community duty or through funding that comes from the profits made by its specialised institutions.

Policies to Strengthen the Weaker Countries

Economic divergence and the inability of the weaker countries to catch up in the Union is one of the results that stand out the most in this study. Both from the point of view of their level of human development and their economic performance, Niger and Guinea-Bissau first, and Burkina Faso and Mali to a lesser extent, deserve special attention to help them rise to the level of the other member states.

There are three potential areas of intervention. First, an increased technical skills-transfer and direct support programme for national administrations could be developed to improve the process of developing and implementing national policies. The difficulties that states are facing to conform to nominal convergence criteria or to catch up to the level implied by real convergence can be, for the most part, attributed to deficiencies in national budgetary and trade policies.

The second possible area of intervention is increased funding of the economy and of the private sector in the weakest countries. The monetisation rate (M2/GDP) of their economies and the level of bank financing of the private sector cannot reasonably be considered compatible with sustainable economic development. One must also admit that the weak countries' low capacity for financial absorption and the private sector's low level are non-negligible limitations to the expansion of financial development in their economies. Thus, it is appropriate to explore the very means of reaching this objective that is so essential to the long-term success of the Union.

Fighting the large variability of economic indicators in the weakest countries is the third area of possible intervention. Several measures could be combined to contribute to reaching this goal. Among the more important ones is the diversification of exports by creating new sectors of comparative advantage, controlling water and the modernisation of cultural techniques, enhancing the level of agricultural supervision and implementing insurance programmes linked to export levels or to nominal GDP.

Creating a Social Pact

The WAEMU zone is one of the most disadvantaged in the world because its level of social development is one of the most modest. The majority of the region's social challenges are shared by all the member states and therefore justify synergistic collective action, as the weakest countries are facing many difficulties accomplishing alone the social progress required for their development. Following the example of the Convergence, Stability, Growth and Solidarity Pact, WAEMU members could join forces through a social pact whose goal would be to develop joint social policy that includes transfer of state competences to the Commission in the same spirit as for the New Partnership for Africa's Development (NEPAD). Such an undertaking could model itself after the operations and governance of WAEMU's specialised institutions such as the BCEAO, the WABD and the BRVM. Operational and financial independence and having a regional mission would make the social pact effective in a way that would be hard for a single country to attain.

As an example, social pact programmes could include healthcare (endemic diseases, vaccination and prevention campaigns, university hospitals), social habitat, water and higher education. The WAEMU could also run programmes in emergency zones such as where there are conflicts, epidemics or natural disasters, supported by the traditional international humanitarian involvement.

Increasing Mobility

Mobility of capital, goods and people is one of the building blocks of regional integration. Policies that aim to encourage the private sector to make cross-border investments should be actively pursued in order to promote the transfer of technology and know-how and also to promote banking credit of the economy, particularly in countries where this is low. The WAEMU could also benefit from persevering in efforts undertaken to remove non-tariff barriers and roadblocks in order to make intra-community economic trade smoother. Increased mobility of merchandise could promote the transformation of agricultural products in the WAEMU space thanks to their rapid and economical transfer from rural zones to industrial zones, thus creating more regional complementarity within the Union. Building new infrastructure should be one of the priorities in the effort to build mobility within the Union.

IV Conclusion

After 15 years of existence, WAEMU has recorded some undeniable successes, particularly in the management of its currency, its exchange policy and the organisation of its stock market. It has also managed to safeguard solid and reliable institutions as well as the adhesion of its members to the community project. Its neutrality, its independence and its authority continue to be respected, despite events such as the Côte d'Ivoire crisis and the disorder in Guinea-Bissau, which rocked the region. Yet, it should be noted that the Union has reached its limits, at least in its current configuration, with regard to pursuing some of its objectives. Just as its successes are confirmed over time, it continues to have trouble improving in certain areas, which are no doubt new areas of competence.

In effect, after 15 years of efforts, from a human development perspective, the WAEMU is still one of the most disadvantage community areas in the world and its average UNDP HDI ranking has continued to regress, being now lower than it was prior to the founding of the Union. As a result, it is urgent to improve the standard of living of its citizens. Furthermore, the growing economic divergence between the richest and the poorest countries in the Union highlights the failure of national policies undertaken individually and the Union's incapacity to help them in a significant manner as part of its current framework. Such a situation is not without risk for the Union's cohesion and could dampen the political determination of its members at the precise moment when it needs to be stronger to support a more ambitious community project.

The significant improvements that one can expect from the Union are not in the monetary area, where it has managed to safeguard and to strengthen the gains of the WAMU that preceded it, but rather in those areas that are still under national responsibility. In this, the model of the Union's specialised institutions to which it owes its most major successes deserves to be spread to other sectors. It would be a question of transferring certain competences that until now were national and that the states, particularly the weakest of them, are having trouble meeting to the Commission in exchange for greater budgetary resources. Several forms of additional funding for the Commission could be envisioned, including a community duty, the transfer to the Commission of part of the benefits of specialised institutions or recourse to the stock market combined with external contributions in the form of guarantees or co-reimbursement.

There are four kinds of priority strategic actions that have emerged from the analysis of WAEMA's institutional and programming results. First, WAEMU's economic and social—and therefore budgetary—policy competence should be broadened beyond monetary issues, and the states should envision conceding part of their sovereignty, which would reinforce the Union's ability to make the most of its full potential. Increasing the Commission's proceeds would make it easier to implement community projects that have been suspended or abandoned due to a lack of funding. Such a decision would bring many benefits to the weakest countries because it would back up their limited national capacities significantly and mutualise part of the budgetary resources transferred from stronger members.

Secondly, the Union should focus on strengthening the weakest countries, both to improve the social situation of residents of those countries and to facilitate the levelling-up process, which is key to all community projects. With this in mind, the Commission could initiate a technical competence transfer and support programme for national administrations in order to improve the process for developing national policies. It could also promote greater financing of the economies of these states, notably by stimulating credit to the private sector and by encouraging controlled monetary expansion that would reduce the degree of financial restrictions, as measured by an M2/GDP ratio that is too weak to be compatible with sustainable economic development. Finally, appropriate and lasting measures should be developed to fight the great variability of the key economic indicators in these countries.

Thirdly, the Union should enact a social pact whose main goal would be to improve the standard of living of all its residents. Implementing the social pact would occur at the community level, with the Commission's overall responsibility and adequate financing. The synergies and levelling among all the countries that would result would certainly strengthen the adhesion of all its members. The structure of the Union's specialised institutions could inspire the operationalisation of the social pact. The fourth strategic priority would consist of increasing mobility within the Union by removing non-tariff barriers and untimely roadblocks, encouraging the development of cross-national value chains within the Union, and of reinforcing the creation of infrastructures that promote mobility.

It is possible to pursue all these strategic priorities at once because currently, the political commitment of the states is intact. In addition, exterior factors such as globalisation and its challenges, which require a collective response and greater attachment to economic unions as recently illustrated in Europe in reaction to the economic crisis that shook the world, call for strengthening the Union and for stronger adhesion to the community project. It is therefore time for strong action, and the conditions are promising.

References

Agbodji, A. E. (2007), 'Intégration et Echanges Intra Sous-régionaux : Le Cas de l' UEMOA', *Revue africaine de l'intégration*, Vol. 1 No. 1, January 2007: 161–188.

Bamba, L. N. (2004), 'Analyse du Processus de Convergence dans la Zone UEMOA', Research Paper No. 2004/18, February, World Institute for Development Economics Research (WIDER), United Nations University, Helsinki.

Bamba, L.N. and K. Diomande (1998), 'Convergence Nominale vs Convergence Réelle et/ou Conver gence des Politiques Economiques vs Convergence des Structures Economiques dans les Pays de l'UEMOA', Symposium International sur 'L'Avenir de la Zone Franc avec l'Avènement de l'Euro', CODESRIA, Dakar, 4–6 November.

Bayoumi, T. and J. D. Ostry (1995), 'Macroeconomic Shocks and Trade Flows Within Sub-Saharan Africa: Implications for Optimum Currency Arrangements', IMF Working Paper No. 95/142, Washington D.C. International Monetary Fund.

Berthelemy J. C. and A. Vadourkakis (1996), 'Economic Growth, Convergence Clubs and the Role of Financial Development', *Oxford Economic Papers*, Vol. 48 No. 2: 300–328.

Bleaney, M. and A. Nishiyama (2004), 'Economic Growth, Income Distribution and Poverty: Time-series and Cross-country Evidence from the CFA-zone Countries of Sub-Saharan Africa', Research Paper No. 2004/03, January, World Institute for Development Economics Research (WIDER), United Nations University, Helsinki.

Clément, J., J. Mueller, S. Cossé, and J. LeDem (1996), 'Aftermath of CFA Franc Devaluation', Occasional Paper Paper No. 138, Washington D.C., International Monetary Fund.

Coulibaly, S. (2007), 'Evaluating the Trade Effect of Developing Regional Trade Agreements: A Semi-Parametric Approach', World Bank, *Policy Research Working Paper* No. WPS 4220.

Doré, O. and P.R. Masson (2002), 'Experience with Budgetary Convergence in the WAEMU', *IMF Working Paper* No. 02/108, Washington D.C. International Monetary Fund.

Faroutan, F. and L. Pritchett (1993), 'Intra-Sub-Saharan African Trade: Is There Too Little?' *Journal of African Economies*, Vol. 2:74–105.

Fielding, D. (2005), *Macroeconomic Policy in the Franc Zone*, Editor, Palgrave Macmillan, Houndmills Basingstoke, U.K.

Fielding, D. (2004), 'How Does Monetary Policy Affect the Poor? Evidence from the West African Economic and Monetary Union', *Research Paper No. 2004/02*, January, World Institute for Development Economics Research (WIDER), United Nations University, Helsinki

Fielding, D., K. Lee, and K. Shield (2004), 'The Characteristics of Macroeconomic Shocks in the CFA Franc Zone', *Research Paper No. 2004/21*, March, World Institute for Development Economics Research (WIDER), United Nations University, Helsinki.

Goretti, M. and H. Weisfeld (2008), 'Trade in the WAEMU: Development and Reform Opportunities', *IMF Working Paper* No. 08/68, Washington D.C., International Monetary Fund.

Goreux, L. M. (1995), ' La Dévaluation du Franc CFA: Un Premier Bilan en Décembre 1995', Rapport de consultation, 28 décembre 1995, Banque Mondiale, 152 pages.

Hernadez-Cata, E., C.A. Francois, P. Masson, P. Bouvier, P Peroz, D. Desruelle, and A. Vamvakidis (1998), 'The West African Economic and Monetary Union, Recent Developments and Policy Issues', Occasional Paper, Paper No. 170, Washington D.C., International Monetary Fund

Hinkle, L., and P. J. Montiel, (1999), 'Exchange Rate Misalignment: Concepts and Measurement for Developing Countries', Washington D. C., World Bank.

Kenen, P. B. (1969), 'The Theory of Optimum Currency Areas: An Eclectic View' in Monetary Problems of the International Economy, edited by Mundell, R., and A. Swoboda, University of Chicago Press, Chicago.

Konseiga, A. (2005), 'Regionalism in West Africa: Do Polar Countries Reap the Benefits? A Role for Migration', Institute for the Study of Labor (IZA), *IZA Discussion Paper No. 1516*, Bonn, Germany.

Leonard, D. (2005), *Guide to the European Union*, Profile Books, London.

Linjouom, M. (2004), 'The Costs and Benefits Analysis of CFA Membership: The Choice of an Exchange Rate Regime for the CFA Countries Zon',*Research Paper No. 2004/14*, February, World Institute for Development Economics Research (WIDER), United Nations University, Helsinki.

Masson, P., and C. Patillo (2001a), 'Monetary Union in West Africa: An Agency of Restraint for Fiscal Policy?', *IMF Working Paper* No. 01/34, Washington D.C., International Monetary Fund.

Masson, P., and C. Patillo (2001b), 'Monetary Union in West Africa (ECOWAS): Is It Desirable and How Could It Be Achieved?', *IMF Occasional Paper* No. 204, Washington D.C., International Monetary Fund.

Masson, P. and C. Patillo (2005), *The Monetary Geography of Africa*, Washington D.C., Brookings Institution.

Mundell, R. (1961), 'A Theory of Optimum Currency Areas', *American Economic Review*, Vol. 51, (November): 657–665.

Nashashibi, K. and S. Bazzoni (1994), 'Exchange Rate Strategies and Fiscal Performance in Sub-Saharan Africa', *IMF Staff Papers*, International Monetary Fund, Vol. 41, pp. 76–122.

Ndiaye, M. B. O. (2007), 'Respect des critères de convergence vs harmonisation des critères de convergence : étude comparative des performances des indicateurs de convergence économique dans la zone Franc en Afrique (UEMOA et CEMAC)', *Revue africaine de l'intégration*, Vol. 1 No. 2, July 2007 : 31–69.

Rogoff, K. and C. Reinhart (2003), 'FDI to Africa: The Role of Price Stability and Currency Instability', *IMF Working Paper* No. 03/10, Washington D.C. International Monetary Fund.

Rosenberg, C. (1995), 'Fiscal Policy Coordination in the WAEMU after the Devaluation', *IMF Working Paper* No. 95/25, Washington D.C. International Monetary Fund.

Rother, P. C.(1998), 'Money Demand and Regional Monetary Policy in the West African Economic and Monetary Union', *IMF Working Paper* No. 98/57, Washington D.C. International Monetary Fund.

Roudet, S., M. Saxegaard, and C. G. Tsangarides (2007), 'Estimation of Equilibrium Exchange Rates in the WAEMU: A Robustness Analysis', *IMF Working Paper* No. 07/194, Washington D.C. International Monetary Fund.

Sy, Amadou (2006), 'Financial Integration in the West African Economic and Monetary Union', *IMF Working Paper* No. 06/214, Washington D.C. International Monetary Fund.

Van Den Boogaerde, P. and C. G. Tsangarides (2005), 'Ten Years after the CFA Franc Devaluation: Progress Toward Regional Integration in the WAEMU', *IMF Working Paper* No. 05/145, Washington D.C. International Monetary Fund.

WAEMU (2006), *Le Programme économique et régional 2006 – 2010*, July.

Wane, A. A. (2004), 'Growth and Convergence in WAEMU Countries', *IMF Working Paper* No. 04/198, Washington D.C. International Monetary Fund.

Yehoue, E. (2006), 'On the Pattern of Currency Blocs in Africa', *Journal of African Development*, Spring 2006, Vol. 1, No. 1: 39–86.

Chapter 3
Growth and Convergence in Africa: A Dynamic Panel Approach

Pierre Joubert Nguetse Tegoum, Pascal Nakelse, and Roland Ngwesse

Abstract This study focuses on standard of living convergence within African countries. It evaluates the convergence process of per capita income using the concepts of σ-convergence and β-convergence. The analysis covers 46 countries from a variety of different regional economic communities (RECs); the period studied spans 1985–2005, using data from the World Bank's World Development Indicators (2007) database.

The methodology adopted to test the convergence hypothesis was inspired from that used by Evans and Karras (J Monet Econ 37:249–265, 1996). The originality of the latter is that it combines both panel data and determination of stochastic series dynamics for per capita income in each country. Two estimation techniques were applied: the generalised method of moments (GMM) and the least squares dummy variable corrector (LSDVC) model, which is more effective on smaller samples.

The results indicate an absence of income convergence for all African countries. This non-convergence is primarily due to the great heterogeneity that exists among the countries. However, analysis of the RECs shows some β-convergence. Indeed, out of the five groupings studied, four constituted convergence clubs: ECOWAS, CEMAC, WAEMU and SADC.

In these RECs, a fixed-effects analysis was carried out, showing that the investment-to-GDP ratio is significantly linked to unobservable structural disparities. For example, demographic growth influences convergence in income level in the ECOWAS, while trade supported income convergence in the WAEMU area and proved to be insignificant in other RECs. This situation could be inherent to the low levels of intra-regional trade in the various RECs (under 13%).

P.J.N. Tegoum (✉) • R. Ngwesse
Ministry of Economy, Planning and Regional Development, Cameroon
e-mail: ngueste_pierre@yahoo.fr

P. Nakelse
National Institute of Statistics and Demography, Burkina Faso

E.T. Ayuk and S.T. Kaboré (eds.), *Wealth Through Integration*, Insight and Innovation in International Development 4, DOI 10.1007/978-1-4614-4415-2_3,
© International Development Research Centre 2013

The study recommends policy measures aimed at promoting intra-regional trade, the harmonisation of investment policies in the various RECs, along with policies that aim at making the African Union more effective in order to facilitate African integration and, in this way, standard of living convergence.

I Introduction

In recent decades, per capita GDP growth in developing countries has remained very low in general and inferior to that found in industrialised countries as a whole, according to the World Bank estimates presented in Global Economic Prospects 2005. The average growth rate observed during the 1990s did not exceed 1.5% per year. This growth was unevenly distributed (World Bank 2005): per capital GDP in sub-Saharan African countries, for example, continued to decrease along the same lines as the previous trends (growth of per capita GDP: −1.2% in the 1980s and −0.2% in the 1990s). However, GDP growth picked up in the 2000s, although the gap with rich countries deepened.[1] This observation brings into question the possibility of poor countries catching up the rich countries.

In a study assessing the integration process in Africa, the Economic Commission for Africa (Hakim et al. 2007) identified the different objectives that led African countries to group together in regional economic communities (RECs). The study shows that the goal of economic growth is central for each country. Thus, the idea of generating a process of income growth is not only shared by all the countries, but the weight given to it tends to be significant. It is therefore not surprising that both theoretical and empirical studies present regional integration as a possible catalyser for income convergence (Beyaert 2007; Hakim et al. 2007). The idea of catching up as it was foreseen by the Solow model (1956) supposes that cooperation among the countries in a framework of regional integration will enable the poor countries to reach a level of income that the rich countries with which they are cooperating have already reached. Europe is a good illustration that goes in this direction. In effect, with the establishment of the European Union (EU), initially poor countries such as Spain and Poland reached the level of developed countries.

However, despite the progress in integration[2] observed in Africa, the process of income convergence within African countries remains weak, as demonstrated by Hakim et al. (2007), for example. Armed with this conclusion, it seemed necessary to evaluate convergence within the RECs based on new panel data test techniques. In other words, is it possible for there to be income convergence in the various regional groupings? And, where appropriate, what factors actively contribute to this convergence?

---

[1] According to the World Bank (Banque mondiale 2000), the average income in the 20 richest countries is 37 times higher than the average income in the 20 poorest countries.

[2] Country groupings into RECs, effective set-up of the African Union in 2002, etc.

In the literature, the concept of income convergence hinges on two key elements. β-Convergence, which assesses the process of income adjustment over time towards a path of growth, is subdivided into three categories; these are absolute convergence, conditional convergence and club convergence. Among these is also σ-convergence, which enables the measurement of income distribution based on an indicator such as variance or the variation coefficient. So the key objective of this work is to study income-level convergence in African countries. It sets out, specifically, to test the hypothesis of income convergence in African countries, to characterise β-convergence and, if possible, to look for factors that determine convergence.

The rest of the study is structured as follows: Section II presents the general analytical framework of the convergence problems and their measurement techniques. Section III covers the econometric specifications of the models to be implemented. Section IV illustrates the process of convergence and presents the results of estimations, leading to Section V that raises political implications and makes recommendation. Section VI concludes the paper and identifies gaps for future work.

II Growth and Convergence: A Review of the Theoretical and Empirical Literature

In this section, we present the theoretical basis of convergence and highlight the empirical evidence for income convergence. We first review the theoretical framework from which the notion of convergence derives.

The Theoretical Basis of Income Growth

This section presents the general framework from which derive the tools used to analyse issues of convergence between economies. The concept of convergence was used at first to describe the process by which the poorest economies catch up with those that have higher per capita income. It had been acknowledged that the recorded growth rate in developing countries should, over a long period, be higher than that of more economically advanced countries, which would enable a reduction in the gaps between development levels in these two groups of countries.

The explanation resides in the fact that in the first neoclassical growth models, notably that of Solow (1956), marginal productivity is supposed to decrease for each production factor. In this way, the less advanced economies should catch up with the more developed countries because the factors' marginal yields are higher in the countries that are behind, where there are greater margins of progression.

In effect, the pace of productivity gains slows as the economies near a situation of long-run equilibrium.

Below, we present the theoretical basis of the Solow model (1956) in order to grasp the connection to the concept of convergence.

Framework: The Neoclassical Solow Model

The Solow model (1956) offers a simple framework to understand growth through the process of capital accumulation. The basis of this model remains solid and serves in a number of studies of growth.[3]

The model describes a closed competitive economy with a single good, labelled Y, produced by a Neoclassical technology F (therefore with constant scale yields). Technical progress, labelled A, is neutral as described by Harrod, which means it improves work performance.

This leads to a production function as follows:

$$Y = F(K, AL) = K(AL)^{\alpha} \quad \text{avec } 0 < \alpha < 1 \tag{3.1}$$

Let n be the growth rate of the labour force L, s the rate of savings and g the growth rate of technical progress A, all supposed to be exogenous.

Capital accumulates through a foregoing consumption, with its evolution represented as follows:

$$\dot{K}_t = I_t - \delta K_t = sF(K, AL) - \delta K \tag{3.2}$$

with I, investment, and δ, depreciation of physical capital.

Below, we reason in terms of variables by effective work unit, symbolised by $K_t = K_t / AL_t$. In this way, the model's basic dynamic equation is:

$$\dot{k}_t = sf(k_t) - (n + g + \delta)k_t \tag{3.3}$$

which can be written as follows:

$$\gamma_k = \frac{\dot{k}}{k} = \frac{sf(k)}{k} - (n + g + \delta)$$

Under the hypothesis of decreasing marginal productivities of labour and capital, the economy converges towards its long-term state, that is, its path to growth equilibrium (SCE), upon which variables grow at the regular and exogenous rate g. This long-term state is independent of initial conditions and is given by:

---

[3] Including work in favour of alternative theories (theory of endogenous growth).

$$y* = \left(\frac{s}{g+n+\delta}\right)^{\frac{\alpha}{1-\alpha}} \tag{3.4}$$

One observes that an economy's wealth increased with greater savings and lower demographic growth. The long-term state also depends on economic policies that displace the production border or modify structural parameters (n and s) in a definitive manner.

The transformation of Eq. (3.4) gives a growth equation:

$$\ln y_t - \ln y_0 = \left(1 - e^{-\beta t}\right)\left[\ln y_0 - \frac{\alpha}{1-\alpha}(\ln s - \ln(n+g+\alpha))\right] \tag{3.5}$$

in which $\beta = (1-\alpha)(n+g+\alpha)$ is the coefficient that characterises the speed of convergence.

It translates the short-term dynamics, that is, that of transition towards the long-term state. From this coefficient, one can also calculate the half-life T, that is, the time needed to make half the adjustment, by the equation:

$$\exp(-\beta T) = \frac{1}{2}.$$

The tools traditionally used in the empirical analysis of economic growth are based on the above-described theoretical framework, as are the various concepts developed to explain the convergence phenomenon that it shows.

Convergence: Concept and Measurement

The concept of convergence is used in economic analysis to characterise the process of economies becoming more similar with regard to certain macroeconomic variables. Nonetheless, although convergence is an intuitively simple concept, it can be difficult to define precisely, and various methods can be used to carry out its empirical analysis. Indeed, overall it is possible to identify two ways to define the convergence of two series: on one hand, based on the average evolution of their difference and, on the other, based on the evolution of their distribution. Occasional average series variances are generally neglected when the analysis is done considering the average differences. On the contrary, the distribution of an entire series takes into account series fluctuations, which refers to their volatility.

Operationally speaking, two types of tests are generally used to study the convergence of economies: β-convergence and δ-convergence.

β-Convergence

β-Convergence refers to the economies' adjustment over time towards a path of growth or towards a reference value. The concept of β-convergence was developed in the framework of a neoclassical growth model. In this model, the idea that poor countries will catch up with rich countries if they reach a higher growth rate leads to the use of β-convergence testing. The latter consists of reversing the country i's annual per capita GDP growth rate (y_{it}) over its initial level (y_{i0}) while controlling the differences in terms of the stationary state, that is, the differences in preferences, savings rate, population increases, technologies, etc. All these variables are contained in vector x of the below equation, which can be estimated using panel data:

$$\frac{\Delta y_{it}}{y_{i,t-1}} = \alpha + \beta^* \ln(y_{i0}) + \gamma x_{it} + \varepsilon_{it} \tag{3.6}$$

The estimation of the above equation could lead to a β-convergence if the β coefficient is statistically negative. This β-convergence is called conditional if the γ parameter is different than zero (i.e. the x_{it} differs from one country to the next[4]). On the other hand, β-convergence is called absolute when $\gamma = 0$. The idea of β-convergence can also be based on the presence of a mechanism by which economic variables adjust over time towards a reference value (y^*) considered to be the attractor:

$$\Delta y_t = \beta^* (y_{t-1} - y^*)$$

In this case, there is convergence if there is a corrective mechanism for the variations relative to the reference value, that is, if the β coefficient is negative and statistically significant.

Club Convergence

Due to the existence of the multiple equilibriums that are revealed by the Solow model, we have seen a polarisation of the world economy into country groups. This has led to the introduction of the notion of convergence clubs. From this perspective, countries that share the same structural characteristics can converge in the long term only if their initial conditions are similar (Galor 1996).

σ-Convergence

It enables one to measure the degree of reconciliation over time between several economies in view of one or several indicators or criteria. Its analysis is based on the evolution of the considered series. There will be convergence of the entire sample when distribution diminishes over time. The per capita income distribution indicator could be the variance or the standard deviation of the series.

In this way, one can judge the process of convergence among economies, relative to a considered variable, from the graphic analysis of the evolution of variance (or of

---

[4] See Islam (1995) and Caselli et al. (1996).

standard deviation). The tendency for the distribution indication to reduce along with the evolution of the considered variable's average towards a set standard in the reference country could indicate the presence of a "good" process of convergence. It could be possible to talk about "perverse" convergence when, for example, in the case of σ-convergence, the lowering of the standard deviation is the result of a lower per capita GDP for the countries initially richer moving in the direction of the poorer countries.

Empirical Studies of Income Convergence

The idea that economic growth is accompanied by convergence in the countries' standard of living has led to a number of empirical applications. These applications, whose primary objective is to respond to the issue of convergence, have given contradictory results. These can be explained by the fact that the authors often do not use the same convergence concepts and by the diversity of the methodological approaches and the test procedures used (cross section, panel data, temporal series).

Looking for a link between economic growth and reducing differences in standard of living is the object of an article by Wodon et al. (2002). The authors use two concepts of convergence: β- and σ-convergence. After showing where the majority of empirical work is lacking in the link between growth and convergence, they offer a new approach. In effect, the latter underlines that variance of the GPD logarithm used in the majority of empirical studies does not respect the expected properties of a measure of inequality. They show that β-convergence, generally defined as a reduction in worldwide growth, is nothing but a theoretical implication. The authors establish a link between β-convergence and σ-convergence while noting that the former does not necessarily imply the latter but that the opposite has been verified.

Diop (2002) uses β-convergence and σ-convergence to analyse nominal and real convergence of economies of the Economic Community of West African States (ECOWAS). This study establishes that there is an absence of real convergence of the zone's economies in which nominal convergence has experienced success. In this way, over the entire period analysed, nominal convergence did not lead to real convergence in ECOWAS countries. When limited to WAEMU member countries, the author finds per capita GDP convergence. He explains these differences in results by those in mobility of factors, diversification of production in the economies and price and wage flexibility.

Guetat and Serranito (2008) analyse income convergence in MENA region countries. They use the techniques to test for σ-convergence and polynomial β-convergence proposed by Chatterji. According to these authors, it appears that the process of σ-convergence is not uniform over time. In effect, there seems to be a movement of convergence among MENA zone countries towards the level of income found in southern European countries, and this is only between the two oil crises. The Chatterji-style estimation of convergence clubs leads to the rejection of the hypothesis of β-convergence for the period 1960–2000. Yet, by estimating the model for the sub-periods, the results show the existence of convergence clubs starting the second half of the 1990s.

Hakim et al. (2007) analyse income convergence in African RECs based on three kinds of convergence: β-, σ- and conditional convergence. Using the methodology described by Caselli et al. (1996) that uses the generalised method of moments (GMM) as a method for estimation, the authors arrive at the following results: the 14 SADC countries converge according to σ-convergence criteria. Probably one of the most interesting results is that for these countries, the rates of conditional and absolute convergence are near each other. This could mean that the countries of the Southern African Development Community (SADC) seem to be converging towards a single state of equilibrium. Following the example of the SADC and the Common Market for Eastern and Southern Africa (COMESA), the results show signs of convergence for ECOWAS countries.

However, the authors observe slow progression in the income convergence process in Africa. As a result, despite the importance of regional integration, they note that there is little progress and that the prospects of the integration process in Africa are not as promising as one would like to believe. In effect, they find the time it takes to catch up—around 20 years—to be a little long. This means that in all the RECs, one must wait at least 20 years to see the countries found at the bottom of the standard of living scale catch up with the others.

Beyaert (2007) uses an estimation of panel date to determine if and when European Union member countries constituted an economic convergence zone. To this end, he applied a process inspired by Evans and Karras (1996). By combining this procedure with bootstrap techniques, the author arrived at the conclusion that the European regional policy that had been led since 1987 produced the expected results because there was a reduction in inequalities (diversion) in standard of living among the member states. In effect, the three poorest countries in the region—Spain, Greece and Portugal—experienced per capita income convergence towards the regional average.

III   Methodology

Following the pioneering work done by Baumol (1986), considerable effort went into investigating the path to convergence in different national and regional samples, using two methodological approaches. The first, based on cross-sectional analysis, proposes two main concepts of the notion of convergence: one notion of catching up and one of homogenisation, while the second, which considers convergence to be a stochastic process, uses the properties of time series.

Econometric Specifications

Until recently, the procedure for testing convergence was β-convergence and consisted of reversing the rate of per capita GDP growth of countries on their initial level of per capita GDP and certain specific variables for the countries. The standard techniques of inference were then carried out to test the negativity of the coefficient of the initial per capita GDP level.

These analyses were based on the principle that all economies are similar and that growth dynamics are uniform. One of the weaknesses of these techniques is that they focus on explaining the average growth rate without taking into account deterioration of performance over time.[5]

The methodological approach developed by Evans and Karras[6] (1996) maintains the general framework of testing the hypothesis of convergence in panel data. It involves fewer restrictions on the data-generating process than the alternative approaches.[7] In this section, we will present this procedure and a few modifications drawing from Gaulier et al. (1999).

Let us consider N countries whose per capita income for each country i equals y_{it} at the given time t. In practice, these economies converge if and only if the expected values of per capita income differences $(y_{it} - \bar{y}_t)$ (where $\bar{y}_t$ is average income) are stationary for all the countries:

$$\lim_{P \to \infty} E_t\left(y_{it+P} - \bar{y}_{t+p}\right) = \mu_1$$

To be clear, the process of convergence takes place when income deviations relative to the average level approach a constant linked to each country when time leans towards infinity. Evans and Karras characterise the process as absolute or conditional on the basis of the individual effects μ_i: if these values are different from zero, the process of convergence is referred to as conditional.

In order to test the convergence hypothesis, Evans and Karras consider the following data-generating process:

$$\lambda_i(L)(y_{it} - \bar{y}_t) = \alpha_i + \varepsilon_{it}$$

This process has two advantages. First, unlike cross-sectional studies, all the differences between the economies are entirely controlled by the individual effects o_{ij}. In effect, given the major structural disparities between the countries,[8] we cannot suppose that the control and environmental variables usually used in cross- sectional analyses are able to capture all the impacts of these differences on individual dynamics. Secondly, this approach is less restrictive than that of Bernard et al. (1996) because it enables economies to have different self-reversing dynamic structures.

---

[5] In fact, Evans (1996, 1997) observes that this approach provides an invalid inference if, for example, the time dimension is not large enough.

[6] It is itself based on one modification of Levin and Lin's (1992) stationarity test in panel data.

[7] We could cite others, the cross-sectional tests.

[8] Technological gaps, idiosyncratic permanent shocks, etc.

Evans and Karras use the following overall form:

$$\Delta(y_{it} - \bar{y}_t) = \alpha_i + \rho_i(y_{it} - \bar{y}_t) + \sum_{j=1}^{p_i} \gamma_{ij}\Delta(y_{it} - \bar{y}_t) + \varepsilon_{it} \tag{3.7}$$

where all the parameters ρ_i are negative when all the N economies converge and zero when they diverge, and where the roots of the polynomial $\sum_{j=1}^{p} \gamma_{ij} L^j$ are outside the unit circle. The parameters α_i designate the individual effects, and the residuals ε_{it} are supposedly individually asymptomatically not correlated.[9] The test procedure consists of four steps: the first three test convergence, while the last characterises the process of convergence.

Step 1: Estimate the model (3.7) with OLS in order to recuperate the standard error $\hat{\sigma}_i$ for each country. Generate the series $\hat{z}_{it} = y_{it} - \bar{y}_t/\hat{\sigma}_i$. This leads to a model with a panel structure.

Step 2: The normalised model is:

$$\Delta \bar{z}_{it} = \delta_i + \rho \hat{z}_{it-1} + \sum_{j=1}^{p_i} \gamma_{ij} \Delta \hat{z}_{it-j} + \mu_{it} \tag{3.8}$$

$$\text{Or } \delta_i = \frac{\alpha_i}{\hat{\sigma}_i} \text{ et } \mu_{it} = \frac{\varepsilon_{it}}{\hat{\sigma}_i}$$

Contrary to Eq. (3.7), the parameter ρ is shared by all the countries, while the parameters associated with lagged differences remain specific to each country. Evans and Karras show that the test of $\rho_t = 0$ versus $\rho_t < 0$ in model (3.7) is equivalent to the test of $\rho < 0$ in model (3.8) with panel structure. Model (3.8) is then estimated by GMM (generalised method of moments) or by LSDVC.[10]

Step 3: Compare the t-statistic $t_{\hat{\rho}}$ associated with $\hat{\rho}$ to critical values obtained by Student statistics. If $t_{\hat{\rho}}$ is greater than the critical value for a significance level, then one rejects the null hypothesis $\rho = \rho_i = 0$ ($\forall_i$) in favour of the alternative $Pi < 0$ ($\forall_i$). If Ho is rejected, one concludes in convergence without being able to characterise it as being absolute or conditional. However, the rejection of Ho, with the resulting acceptance of the hypothesis of convergence, does not necessarily mean that all economies are convergent.[11]

---

[9] With regards to the choice of the delay order, Perron (1996) (cited in Gaulier et al. 1999) shows that this considerably affects the power of stationarity tests. In practice, the number of delays does not exceed 2.

[10] See Appendix for the details on this method.

[11] As highlighted by Evans and Karras (1996), it could occur that certain economies converge while others diverge.

Step 4: Characterisation of convergence

Under the hypothesis of conditional convergence, all the parameters α_i of Eq. (3.7) are different from zero. Thus, in order to test for absolute convergence, we calculate the following F-statistic:

$$F_{\hat{\delta}} = \frac{\sum_{i=1}^{N} t_{\hat{\sigma}_i}^2}{(N-1)} \tag{3.9}$$

We compare this statistic to the critical value of the Fisher statistic. In case of conditional convergence, one proceeds to explain the individual disparities (see below for the group of explicative variables).

Estimation Method

The choice of panel estimation methods depends on the nature of the chosen model. Here, we present a dynamic model along with the methods that apply to it. Thus, we consider the following model:

$$z_{i,t} = \rho z_{i,t-1} + \alpha_i + \beta x_{i,t} + u_{i,t} \tag{3.10}$$

with $u_{i,t} = \gamma u_{i,t-1} + \varepsilon_{i,t}(AR(1))$ or $u_{i,t} = \gamma u_{i,t-1} + \varepsilon_{i,t}(MA(1))$

The estimation of such a model necessitates estimation methods that are rather complex due to the presence of a correlation between fixed effects and the lagged dependent variable (Nickell 1981). To overcome this problem of correlation, the literature proposes two estimation methods: the least squares dummy variable corrected (LSDVC) and the generalised method of moments (GMM).

The efficiency of each of these methods depends on the size of the sample. In effect, Bruno (2005) shows that the LSDVC estimator is more efficient than the GMM estimator when the sample size is small. As a result, these two methods will be explored in this study depending on the size of the samples under consideration. For example, for the estimation of the community groups, the first method will be privileged in view of the number of countries found in each REC. On the other hand, for all the countries, the GMM method is a better choice.

The Data and Its Sources

We will be using two groups of variables: a first group related to the estimation of β-convergence from per capita GDP in purchasing power parity (GDPPPP) and per capita GDP in purchasing power parity lagged by one period (GDPPPP(−1)).

The second group is made up of control variables that enable one to take the specific characteristics of each country into account. These are investment ratio measured in terms of fixed gross capital formation in percentage of GDP (INV), public expenditure in percentage of GDP (GOV), rate of openness (OPEN), ratio of secondary schooling (SER), rate of population growth (POP) and the number of boys and girls registered in secondary school (MALE and FEMALE). Introducing these variables is inspired from the work of Barro and Sala-I-Martín (1992). Using this second group of variables, the authors were able to explain the specific structural characteristics linked to each country in a sample of 100 countries in the Organisation for Economic Cooperation and Development (OECD).

The data used in the framework of this study are annual and come from the World Bank's World Development Indicator (WDI 2007). They cover the period going from 1985 to 2005. This period was chosen due to the availability of data for the majority of the countries for the period of the study.

IV   Evaluation of the Convergence of African Economies

Analysis of σ-Convergence

The analysis of changes in per capita GDP standard deviation enables the assessment of the convergence process of the economies. In effect, the reduction of the distribution indicator (standard deviation) would tend to indicate the presence of a process of convergence.

Figure 3.1 retraces the evolution of the deviation in income levels among African countries over the 1985–2005 period. This figure shows a rise in the standard deviation of per capita GDP in African countries, which suggests an absence of real convergence of the continent's economies. In view of this result, it is important to look at the various regional economic communities (RECs) from a different

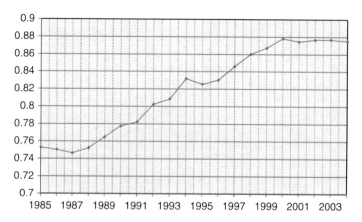

Fig. 3.1 Evolution of standard deviation of per capita gross domestic product (Source: WDI and authors' calculations)

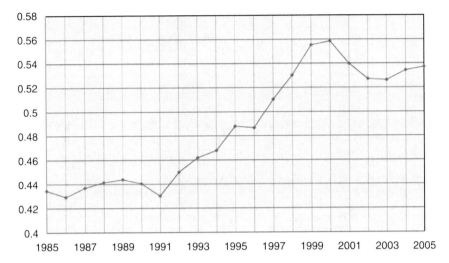

Fig. 3.2 ECOWAS: evolution of standard deviation of per capita gross domestic product (Source: WDI and authors' calculations)

perspective. In other words, it is a question of knowing if these economic groupings have, generally speaking, reached their key objective, that of reducing the differences in level between member countries.

Evaluation of σ-Convergence Within the RECs

This subsection evaluates the economic convergence process of the various African RECs based on the σ-convergence test.

ECOWAS Economies

Figure 3.2 enables the analysis of per capita GDP among ECOWAS countries through the evaluation of the standard deviation of this variable calculated for all of the community's countries, with the exception of Liberia due to a lack of data. One can note that, generally speaking, over the entire period of the analysis, the per capita income gaps between the member countries increased. This observation led us to conclude that there was an absence of convergence in per capita GDP within the ECOWAS. An analysis of economic convergence of WAEMU countries will allow for a more refined analysis.

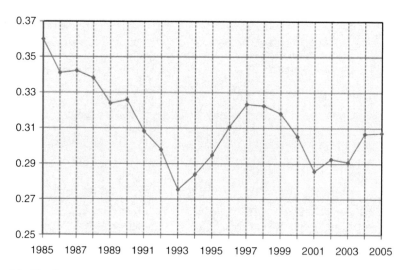

Fig. 3.3 WAEMU: evolution of standard deviation of per capita domestic product (Source: WDI and authors' calculations)

WAEMU Economies

In the WAEMU countries, one observes (Fig. 3.3) an overall trend towards a reduction in the standard deviation in the zone's per capita income, which indicates the presence of a process of σ-convergence in these economies for the analysed period. However, despite this overall evolution, one should note some contrasting changes over the following periods: 1985–1993, 1994–1997, 1998–2001 and 2002–2005. A lowering of the standard deviation is noted over the longest period (1985–1993) and for the period 1998–2001, while an increase in the indicator occurred for the periods 1994–1997 and 2002–2005. More in-depth analysis revealed that the reduction in the standard deviation observed was primarily due to a decrease in per capita GDP in the Côte d'Ivoire, which levelled up that of other Union countries, which had remained constant. Thus, the observed convergence would be more the result of a reduction over time of per capita GDP in the "richer" countries than that of the initially "poorer" countries catching up. One can note that the passage of the ECOWAS to the WAMU with the exclusion of Nigeria among others translated into a reduction of disparities and confirms the asymmetric effect exercised by this country on her neighbours in the subregion.

CEMAC Economies

A study of the evolution of per capita income standard deviation in CEMAC countries shows two major periods: 1988–1997 and 1998–2005 (Fig. 3.4). One observes a lack of convergence during the first period. In effect, increasing

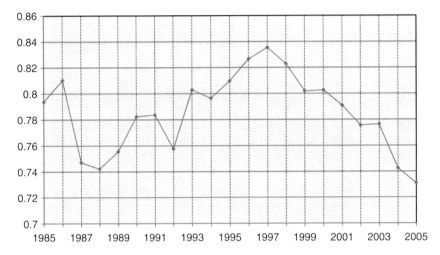

Fig. 3.4 CEMAC: evolution of standard deviation of per capita gross domestic product (Source: WDI and authors' calculations)

distribution in per capita income in CEMAC economies marks that period. Unlike during this first period, from 1998 to 2005, one sees a reduction in the standard deviation of the per capita GDP which signifies the existence of a process of economic convergence in the community. This outcome could be the result, among other things, of strong per capita GDP in Chad starting in the 2000s.

SADC Economies

SADC countries show a lack of convergence in standard of living (Fig. 3.5). In effect, over the entire period that was analysed, one can note a trend to a higher standard deviation in per capita income in the zone's countries. This result could be explained by, among other things, the low rate of growth in per capita GDP in countries such as Zambia, Zimbabwe, DRC and Madagascar, which recorded average growth less than zero over the period that was studied.

COMESA Economies

Like in the SADC, one also notes a trend of increased per capita income distribution in COMESA economies (Fig. 3.6) but with a slight decrease starting in 2002. In view of this result, we can conclude that there was an absence of σ-convergence.

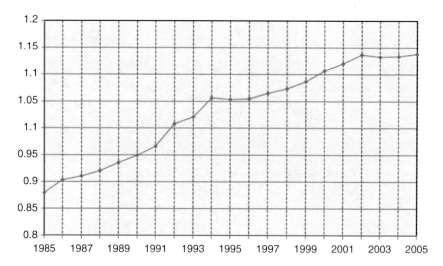

Fig. 3.5 SADC: evolution of standard deviation of per capita gross domestic product (Source: WDI and authors' calculations)

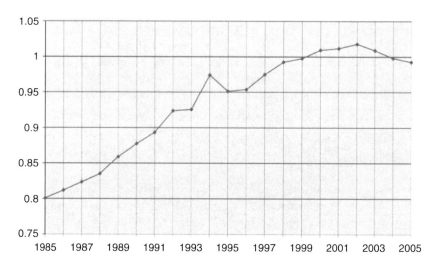

Fig. 3.6 COMESA: evolution of standard deviation of per capita gross domestic product (Source: WDI and authors' calculations)

Analysis of β-Convergence

The analysis of β-convergence covers changes in growth in relation to initial income in the studied countries.

Figure 3.7 shows the position of each country based on average per capita GDP growth over the 1985–2005 period and their initial income level (1985 GDP).

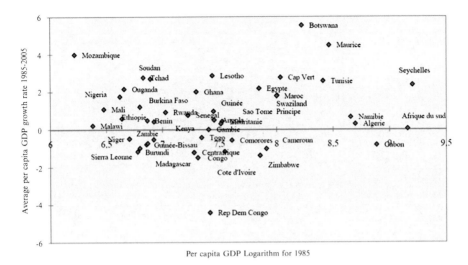

Fig. 3.7 Per capita income convergence, 1985–2005 (Source: WDI and authors' calculations)

Overall, one can note that for all the studied countries, it is somewhat difficult to establish with certitude the inverse relationship between per capita income growth and initial income (Fig. 3.7). However, it seems that certain poor countries tend to grow more rapidly than the rich countries. In effect, a close look at Fig. 3.7 shows clearly that certain low per capita income countries such as Mozambique, Lesotho and Swaziland experienced more rapid growth than South Africa.

We will take a more in-depth look at these analyses using econometric estimations in the following section.

β-Convergence Test

This test seeks to determine if the increase of the deviation of GDP to the African average is negatively linked to the level of these gaps observed in the previous period.

Following the first step, which consisted in determining the per capita GDP variable lag for each country so as to estimate the model (3.7) for each country, the result shows that all the per capita GDP series are first-order integrated (I(1)). This enabled us to obtain the standard errors for each estimation in order to constitute the series of z_{it} variables from model (3.8).

The implementation of the steps presented in Section III led to the results presented in Table 3.1 for the income convergence test for African countries.

These results show that the GDP (β) coefficient is significantly zero at a threshold of 5%. We therefore conclude in no real convergence among the African economies, and the test stops at the second step. This result is not surprising in view of the disparities among the countries. In effect, Barro and Sala-i-Martin (1992)

Table 3.1 Estimation results for Africa

$F(1.826)$		52.19
Prob $> F$		0
Variables	*GMM*	
Δz_{it}	Coefficient	*P*-value
z_{it-1}	0.001	0.54
	(−0.002)	
Δz_{it-1}	0.799***	0.005
	(−0.094)	
c	0.008	0.15
	(−0.058)	
Arellano-Bond	: AR(1) test	$z = -8.32***$
Arellano-Bond	: AR(2) test	$z = -3.01***$
Sargan test		chi2(17) = 5.53

*Significant at 10%; **significant at 5%; ***significant at 1%

Table 3.2 β-Convergence test results in RECs

Estimation method	ECOWAS	CEMAC	WAEMU	SADC	COMESA
GMM					
ρ	0.006 (0.315)	−0.001 (0.938)	−0.009 (0.541)	0.002 (0.508)	−0.001 (0.827)
Sargan test (*P*-value)	0.953	0.997	0.562	1	1
LSDVC					
ρ	−0.166*** (0.002)	−0.207** (0.026)	−0.123*** (0.208)	−0.2741** (0.000)	0.138 (0.141)

Source: WDI and authors' calculations
*Significant at 10%; **significant at 5%; ***significant at 1%

show that when one considers countries that are very different from each other, distribution in per capita GDP growth relative to the average level persists infinitely.

Non-convergence of income levels within African economies led us to study the convergence clubs. In the following section, we evaluate β-convergence within the various RECs. Even without this result, it would still have been particularly interesting to conduct the analysis by sub-region in order to understand the integration process.

REC Evaluations

The results of the β-convergence tests within the RECs are found in Table 3.2. In view of these results, we note income convergence in the economies of the various RECs. Within the ECOWAS area, the results of the LSDVC estimation, unlike those using the GMM method, show signs of per capita income convergence in the zone's economies. In effect, at a threshold of 1%, we reject the null hypothesis that ρ is not significantly different from zero. This result is not surprising

Table 3.3 Characterisation of convergence

REC	Fisher	Degree liberty	P-value
CEMAC	4.717	−4.97	0.0020
ECOWAS	3.224	−14.297	0.0000
WAEMU	3.012	−7.157	0.0010
SADC	5.3	−12.257	0.0000

Source: WDI and authors' calculations

based on the explanations given by Bruno (2005), which suggest that the LSDVC estimator is more efficient than the GMM method for small samples.

The same results are observed for the CEMAC, ECOWAS and SADC zones. In effect, in these three economic areas, one remarks real economic convergence in relation to the LSDVC estimation results.

In contrast, for the COMESA countries, the results of the two estimations (GMM and LSDVC) both confirmed the absence of convergence noted above based on the analysis of σ-convergence. We note that the hypothesis of income convergence in the four RECs (CEMAC, ECOWAS, WAEMU and SADC) is plausible without being able to characterise it. Is the convergence absolute or conditional?

Characterising the β-Convergence

The above sections demonstrated income convergence in the various RECs. One should now specify whether the convergence is absolute or conditional. The convergence is characterised using a test of homogeneity among the income levels (see the fourth step of the methodology). The results of this test can be found in Table 3.3.

A close look at this table shows that the p-value associated with the various Fisher statistics is less than 5%. As a result, one can admit that at a critical threshold of 5%, there is conditional convergence in the four RECs: CEMA, WAEMU, ECOWAS and SADC.

In other words, income level convergence in each of the RECs is linked to structural disparities in the various countries that form them. This means that these various RECs constitute convergence clubs. This result supports our expectations. In effect, Barro and Sala-I-Martín (1992) published similar results for various groups of countries, and Ghura and Hadjimichael (1996) did so for sub-Saharan African countries. Furthermore, the procedure stops at the second step for the COMESA, considering the fact that the convergence test is not conclusive for this REC. We have just noted that income level convergence in the various groupings is closely tied to the countries' economic and political structure. As a result, it is important to pinpoint the elements that could impede this absolute convergence in each of the RECs.

Table 3.4 Explanation of conditional convergence

	GDP rate		Period				1985–2005	
Dependent	ECOWAS		CEMAC		WAEMU		SADC	
Explanatory	Coef	t	Coef	t	Coef	t	Coef	t
C	4.465	0.59	14.673*	10.89	−8.86**	4.12	−1.643	0.46
	(7.622)		(1.347)		(2.47)		(3.57)	
OPEN	−0.026	0.80	0.043	5.93	0.049**	6.38	0.025	1.74
	(0.032)		(0.007)		(0.106)		(0.014)	
GOV	0.1043	0.84			1.76	3.32	−0.233***	3.86
	(0.124)				(1.84)		(0.06)	
INV	0.288**	2.60	−0.216*	6.60	0.56**	3.15	0.241**	2.790
	(0.11)		(0.032)		(0.89)		(0.086)	
LABOUR	1.011*	1.43			0.09*	5.03	0.0204	0.09
	(0.709)				(1.45)		(0.238)	
POP	−2.049*	0.92	−4.496*	8.18			0.0398	0.07
	(2.216)		(0.549)				(0.595)	
$Prob > F(5, 7)$	0.021		0.051		0.023		0.031	
R^2	80.15%		99.10%		72.60%		55.50%	
Observations	15		5		8		13	

All figures in parentheses are standard errors
*Significant at 10%; **significant at 5%; ***significant at 1%

Fixed-Effects Analysis

The Case of West African Economies

ECOWAS economies, and primarily that of the WAMU, are to a lesser extent characterised by a growth dynamic that has not experienced fundamental change in recent decades, despite the structural disparities among the countries. However, one notes that in view of the estimations (Table 3.4), only the private investment-to-GDP ratio seems to have had a positive impact on per capita income. In fact, its positive effect could have contributed to facilitating conditional convergence.

Other control variables seemed to not have any significant influence on growth convergence. But by reducing the space of these variables, one notes that the ECOWAS economies stimulate income growth by the accumulation of the labour force, with a negative effect on population growth rates. This could be justified by the population level in Nigeria, which increased by more than 50% in 20 years.[12]

By limiting to the WAEMU space, one observes the same effect of the investment-to-GDP ratio and the labour force on conditional convergence.

---

[12] Nigeria's population went from nearly 79 million in 1985 to more than 130 million in 2005 (see WDI 2007).

However, one notes that unlike in the ECOWAS, external trade by WAEMU countries supports economic growth and does so above and beyond income convergence.

Besides, the weak contribution made by investment levels and foreign trade to economic growth indicates that there exist a number of other factors that favour income convergence.

The Case of SADC Economies

For SADC economies, two key situations deserve to be highlighted. The subregion is, for the most part, driven by South Africa which experiences low (near zero) per capita income growth but a per capita income that is among the highest in Africa. Botswana, on the other hand, has a distinctly higher per capita GDP growth rate during the studied period (nearly 6%) and seems to support the theory according to which initially poor economies converge more quickly than those that are initially rich (see Solow 1956).

The empirical analysis of this region's convergence showed that the countries constitute a cluster of conditional convergence. This could in part be justified by free domestic trade, by South African transfers and, above all, by the slowed growth in South Africa.

Examination of the sources of structural disparities that impede absolute convergence brought to light a few different situations. First, one notes that investment rates have a significant and positive effect on the level of growth evolution (Table 3.4). Thus, because of the relative weakness of this indicator (21.9% on average in the subregion), there is little change in per capita GDP growth, which contributed to slowing the convergence process. Then, the estimation results show that how much public expenditure there is in the GDP has a very significant and negative influence on per capita GDP evolution. It stands at an average of 20.9% in the subregion with a lot of disparity among the countries (evolving from 11 to 37%). This result is not surprising if one refers to related work found in the literature (see, e.g. Barro 1991).

One can note that within the SADC, income convergence is somewhat boosted by the investment rate, while it is more or less diminished by governmental expenses.

The Case of CEMAC Economies

In the case of the CEMAC, considering the small size of the sample (five in our case), it was nearly impossible to judge at the same time the effect of all the control variables on economic growth.[13] However, to overcome this difficulty, we

---

[13] OLS estimations require that the number of variables be lower than the number of observations.

undertook a sequential estimation, whose main results are presented in Table 3.4. One can also note that for CEMAC economies, investment rates significantly influenced convergence.

However, one notes, rather, a negative impact, which appears somewhat paradoxical compared with the above results and those found in the literature. Also, we show a negative relationship between the rate of demographic growth and an evolution in income levels.

Trade openness in CEMAC economies did not impact the disparities that impede absolute income convergence. This result is not such as to create a controversy in comparison to the results found in the literature. Here, trade openness is used to try to explain the structural disparities that slow down absolute convergence. In the case at hand, such a result could be dependent on the concentration of trade with extra-regional countries. This is all the more edifying because intra-regional trade only constitutes about 2% of external trade.

V   Policy Implications and Recommendations

We have noted that four out of five of the groupings chosen for our study form conditional convergence clusters. The overall result of this analysis is that, overall, in the REC, the low level of income convergence is primarily due to disparities in the investment-to-GDP ratio. As a result, harmonisation of investment policies is an objective that could, if achieved, help boost absolute convergence in the RECs and particularly in the WAEMU.

With regards to trade with commercial partners, in nearly all of the RECs (with the exception of the CEMAC and the WAEMU), its impact proves to be insignificant, even though it is of the expected sign. As a result, one should favour intra-regional trade in order to facilitate subregional integration and above and beyond income-level convergence.

With the nonexistence of income convergence on an African level, it is important to implement policies that will ensure the actual take-off of the African Union, following the example of the European Union.

VI   Conclusion

The main objective of this study was to study per capita income convergence in African countries for the period from 1985 to 2005. There were two reasons justifying the choice of this period: on the one hand, data was available, and on the other hand, we needed to cover a large number of countries. The analysis is based on panel data convergence tests. It uses Evans and Karras' (1996) methodology. The originality of the latter is that it combines both panel data and a determination of the stochastic series dynamics for per capita income in each country. This methodology was used on data collection from the WDI base (2007).

The results of the analyses demonstrated the absence of income convergence among all the African countries. This non-convergence is primarily due to the pooling of a large number of heterogeneous countries (46 in our case). As a result, in order to highlight the similarities shared by certain RECs, we sought to verify whether the existence of convergence clubs was a plausible hypothesis. The study shows that out of five groupings, four form convergence clubs: the ECOWAS, CEMAC, WAEMU and SADC. The phenomenon of non-convergence was, however, observed by the COMESA. This cluster has per capita income that is nearly half that of the African level with a lot of heterogeneity. The presence in these groups of large countries such as South Africa, Botswana and Mauritius Island (in terms of per capita income) and of low-income-level countries contributes to increasing standard of living divergence, which could have contributed to income divergence on an African level.

For the RECs where conditional convergence was observed, we carried out a fixed-effects analysis. The results showed that investment rates are significantly linked to unobservable structural disparities. So, we deduced that the evolution of demographic growth has a slight influence on convergence of income level and that this is not the case for external trade. This situation is dependent on the weakness of intra-regional trade in the various RECs. In effect, the latter does not exceed 13% of external trade in any of the RECs.

One of the main limitations of this study is that it does not take into account human development indicators and the financial sector. Human development indicators were not taken into account due to a lack of data for nearly the entire period studied. Also, one could envision studying the average duration needed to absorb the imbalance for each of the RECs that form convergence clubs.

Appendices

Appendix 1: Regional Economic Community (REC) Member Countries

- *ECOWAS* (Economic Community of West African States): Benin, Burkina Faso, Cape Verde, Côte d'Ivoire, Gambia, Ghana, Guinea-Bissau, Guinea, Liberia, Mali, Niger, Nigeria, Senegal, Sierra Leone and Togo
- *CEMAC* (Economic and Monetary Community of Central Africa): Cameroon, Central African Republic, Chad, Congo, Equatorial Guinea and Gabon
- *COMESA* (Common Market for Eastern and Southern Africa): Angola, Burundi, Comoros, Democratic Republic of Congo, Djibouti, Egypt, Eritrea, Ethiopia,

Kenya, Madagascar, Malawi, Mauritania, Namibia, Rwanda, Seychelles, Soudan, Swaziland, Uganda, Zambia and Zimbabwe
- *SADC* (South African Development Community): Angola, Botswana, Democratic Republic of Congo, Lesotho, Madagascar, Malawi, Mauritania, Mozambique, Namibia, South Africa, Swaziland, Tanzania, Zambia and Zimbabwe
- *WAEMU* (West African Economic and Monetary Union): Benin, Burkina Faso, Côte d'Ivoire, Guinea-Bissau, Mali, Niger, Senegal and Togo

LSDVC Estimators: The Principle

Consider the following standard dynamic model with panel data:

$$y_{it} = \gamma y_{i,t-1} + x_{it}'\beta + \eta_i + \varepsilon_{it} \quad |\gamma| < 1 \; i = 1,\ldots,N \; et \; t = 1,\ldots,T \qquad (3.11)$$

where y_{it} is the dependant variable, x_{it} is a vector $((k-1) \times 1)$ explicative exogenous variables, η_i unobservable individual effects and ε_{it} an unobservable white noise. In compiling the observations over time and for individuals, one obtains the matrix form of model 3.11:

$$y = D\eta + W\delta + \varepsilon$$

where y and $W = [y_{-1} : X]$ are matrices of observation of order $(NT \times 1)$ and $(NT \times k)$, respectively, $D = I_N \otimes i_T$ is the individual dummy matrix (i_T is a vector $(T \times 1)$ composed of ones), η is the vector (of order $(N \times 1)$) of individual effects, white noise vector (of order $(NT \times 1)$) and $\delta = [\gamma : \beta']$ is the vector of order $(k \times 1)$ of the coefficients.

LSDV estimators of model 3.11 are non-converging and in general biased.[14] Bruno (2005) draws on the approach developed by Bun and Keviet[15] (2003), whose principle is described below.

The LSDV estimator of δ is given by:

$$\delta_{LSDV} = (W' MW)^{-1} W' My$$

where $M = I - D(D'D)^{-1}D'$ is a symmetric matrix enabling one to annul individual effects.

---

[14] See Nickell (1981).
[15] Cited by Bruno (2005).

Approximation of bias is given by:

$$c_1 = (T^{-1}) = \delta_\varepsilon^2 tr(\wedge)q_1$$
$$c_2(N^{-1}T^{-1}) = -\sigma_\varepsilon^2[Q\bar{W}' \wedge M\bar{W} + tr(Q\bar{W}' \wedge M\bar{W})I_{k+1}] + 2\sigma_\varepsilon^2 q_{11} tr(\wedge' \wedge \wedge)I_{k+1q_1}$$
$$c_3(N^{-1}T^{-2}) = \delta_\varepsilon^4\{2q_{11}Q\bar{W}'\wedge\wedge'\bar{W}q_1 + [(q_1'\bar{W}'\wedge\wedge'\bar{W}q_1) + q_{11}tr(Q\bar{W}'\wedge\wedge'\bar{W})$$
$$+ 2tr(\wedge'\wedge\wedge'\wedge)q_{11}^2]q_1\}.$$

where $Q = [E(W'MW]^{-1} = [\bar{W}'MW + \delta_\varepsilon^2 tr(\wedge\wedge')e_1e_1']^{-1}\bar{W} = E(W), e_1 = (1,0,....0)'$ vector $(k \times 1)q_1 = Q_{e_1}$ and $q_{11} = e_1'q_1L_T$ the matrix of order $(T \times T)$ made up of 1 under the diagonal and zeros everywhere else; $L = L_N \otimes L_T$, $\Gamma_T = (I_T - \gamma L_T)^{-1}$, $\Gamma = I_N \otimes \Gamma_T$ and the matrix $\wedge$ is then defined by $\wedge = ML\Gamma$. With an increase in the level of precision, the three approximations of bias are:

$$B_1 = c_1(T^{-1}), B_2 = B_1 + c_2(N^{-1}T^{-1}) \text{ and } B_3 = B_2 + c_3(N^{-1}T^{-2}) \quad (3.12)$$

LSDV corrector estimators of bias are obtained by subtracting any term of Eq. (3.12) from the LSDV estimator. In practice, consistent corrected estimators are obtained by looking for consistent estimators of δ_ε^2 and γ. This enables:

$$LSDVC_i = LSDV - \hat{B}_i, \quad i = 1, 2, 3 \quad (3.13)$$

The possible consistent estimators are the Anderson and Hsiao (1982) (AH) estimator, the Arellano and Bond (1991) estimator, and the Blundell and Bond[16] (1998) (BB) estimator. Depending on the choice of γ (from among the three earlier proposals), a consistent estimator of δ_ε^2 is given by:

$$\delta_h^2 = \frac{e'_h Me_h}{(N - k - T)} \quad (3.14)$$

where $e_h = y - W\delta_h h = AH, \ AB \ et \ BB.$

References

Anderson, T.W and Cheng Hsiao. (1982), 'Formulation and Estimation of Dynamic Models Using Panel Data', *Journal of Econometrics*, 18:47–82.

Arellano, M and S. Bond. (April 1991), 'Some tests of specification for panel data: Monte Carlo evidence and an application to employment equations', *The Review of Economic Studies*, 58:277–297.

Banque mondiale. (2000), 'Rapport sur le developement dans le monde: Combattre la Pauvrete'. Paris, Eska.

---

[16] All cited by Bruno (2005). For more details, see Bruno (2005).

Barro, Robert J. (1991), Economic Growth in a Cross Section of Countries. NBER Working papers 3120, National Bureau of Economic Research, Inc.

Barro, R.J. and X. Sala-I-Martín, (1992), 'Convergence', *Journal of Political Economy*, 100(2): 223–251.

Baumol, W. (1986), 'Productivity Growth, Convergence and Welfare: What the Long Run Data Show', *American Economic Review*, 76: 1072–1085.

Bernard, Andrew B. and Charles I. Jones. (1996), 'Comparing Apples to Oranges: Productivity Convergence and Measurement Across Industries and Countries', *American Economic Review*, 86(5): 1216–38.

Beyaert, A. (2007), TAR Panel Unit Root Tests and Real Convergence, *Review of Development Economics* Volume 12, Issue 3: 668–681.

Blundell, R. and S. Bond. (1998), 'Initial conditions and moment restrictions in dynamic panel data models'. *Journal of Econometrics*, 87(1): 115–143.

Bun, M.J. and J.F. Keviet. (2003), 'On the diminishing returns of higher order terms in asymptotic expansions of bias', *Economic Letters*, 79:145–152.

Bruno, G. S. F. (2005), 'Estimation and inference in dynamic unbalanced panel data models with a small number of individual', *Working Paper, No. 165*.

Caselli, F., G. Esquivel and F. Lefort, (1996), 'Reopening the convergence debate: a new look at cross-country growth empirics', *Journal of Economic Growth* (1): 363–389.

Diop, P. L. (2002), 'Convergence nominale et convergence réelle: une application des concepts de σ-convergence et de β-convergence aux économies de la ECOWAS', *Note d'Information et Statistiques*, BCEAO, No. 531.

Evans, P. (1996), 'Using panel data to evaluate growth theories', *International Economic Review*, 39 (2): 295–306.

Evans, P. (1997), 'How Fast Do Economies Converge? Review of Economics and Statistics', 79:219–225.

Evans, P. and G. Karras (1996), 'Convergence Revisited', *Journal of Monetary Economics*, 37: 249–265.

Galor O. (1996), 'Convergence? Inferences from Theoretical Models', *CEPR Discussion Papers* 1350, C.E.P.R. Discussion Papers.

Gaulier, G, C. Hurlin and P. Jean-Pierre, (1999), 'Testing Convergence: A Panel Data Approach', *Annales d'Economie et de Statistiques*, 55–56: 411–427.

Ghura, D and Hadjimichael, M.T. (1996), 'Growth in Sub-Sahara Africa', *IMF Staff papers*, 43(3), September.

Guetat, I. and F. Serranito, (2008), 'Convergence des pays de la région de MENA vers les niveaux de revenu des pays du Sud d'Europe: une évaluation empirique', *Document du Travail du CEPN No. 2008-17*, Centre d'économie de l'Université Paris Nord.

Hakim, B. H., N. Stephen, A.E. Karingi and N.M.S Jallab, (2007), 'Why doesn't Regional Integration Improve Income Convergence in Africa', African Trade Policy Center, United Nations Economic Commission for Africa.

Islam, N. (1995), 'Growth Empirics: A Panel Data Approach', *Quarterly Journal of Economics*, 110: 1127–1170.

Levin, A. and C.F. Lin. (1992), 'Unit Root Test in Panel Data: Asymptotic and Finite Sample Properties', *University of California at San Diego*, Discussion Paper 92–93.

Nickell, S.J. (1981), 'Biases in Dynamic Models with Fixed Effects', *Econometrica*, 49 (2): 1417–1426.

Solow, R. (1956), 'A Contribution to the Theory of Economic Growth', *Quarterly Journal of Economics*, 70: 65–94.

Wodon, Quentin T. and S. Yitzhaki, (2002),' Growth and Convergence: An Alternative empirical Framework', March 2002, World Bank and Hebrew University.

World Bank (2005), World Development Report, *Publications and Reports*

WDI (2007) World Development Indicators, World Bank.

Chapter 4
Has There Been Real and Structural Convergence in WAEMU Countries?

Nacisse Palissy Chassem

Abstract The goal of this study is to examine the process of real and structural convergence in the WAEMU from 1970 to 2005. This is undertaken using σ-convergence, smoothing spline regression and β-convergence. Demand-side structural convergence is measured by real gross capital formation per capita and supply-side structural convergence by total factor productivity or the Solow residual (1957). Real convergence is assessed by real per capita GDP. The data used are annual WAEMU observations that come from the World Bank 2007 CD-ROM. The results of the study bring to light the presence of real and structural convergence respectively for the periods 1976–1991 and 1975–1991. In contrast, there was an absence of structural convergence for the periods 1970–1975 and 1992–2005 and of real convergence for the periods 1970–1974 and 1992–2005. β-Convergence helps show that structural convergence is a necessary condition for real convergence for the period 1975–1991 and a sufficient condition for the period 1992–2005. So, in the WAEMU, by evaluating structural convergence, one also evaluates real convergence. We also noted economic foundations such as investment and demographic growth do little to feed growth in WAEMU countries, where growth depends rather on total factor productivity or the Solow residual, generally assimilated with labour organisation and with production techniques that can be influenced by institutional and macroeconomic frameworks.

I   Introduction

The WAEMU[1] was created to promote economic growth and improve the standard of living of the populations residing in its member countries via economic integration. The WAEMU, which was set up in 1994, has undertaken reforms

---

[1] WAEMU currently groups together eight countries: Benin, Burkina Faso, Côte d'Ivoire, Guinea-Bissau, Mali, Niger, Senegal and Togo.

N.P. Chassem (✉)
Institute for Statistics and Applied Economics (ISSEA), Yaoundé, Cameroon
e-mail: nchassem@yahoo.fr

E.T. Ayuk and S.T. Kaboré (eds.), *Wealth Through Integration*, Insight and Innovation   69
in International Development 4, DOI 10.1007/978-1-4614-4415-2_4,
© International Development Research Centre 2013

that have contributed to improving trade relations among its member states. In effect, trade between WAEMU member states grew continually after 1996. Intra-WAEMU exports increased from 11.6% of total Union exports to 13.8% in 2004.

However, overall economic growth in WAEMU countries for the period 1994–2005 remained lower than the level (around 8%) that was hoped for in order to substantially absorb poverty. In effect, the scope of poverty in the WAEMU remains a concern. According to the WAEMU Commission (2006), around 45% of the population in the Union is poor.

Nevertheless, effective economic integration could contribute to reducing poverty and to improving health and education in the WAEMU directly via migratory movements by using funds sent by migrant workers for productive activities (CNUCED 2009) and indirectly through economic growth from an increase in technological progress and foreign direct investment (FDI). Indeed, economic integration brings with it the advantages of new opportunities for trade, larger markets and increased competition (Venables 2000; World Bank 2000). Technological spillovers sometimes accompany trade as a country can import from outside its borders or can export. FDI also results in transfers of technology and know-how across borders (ECA 2004a).

II   Problem Statement and Objectives

Review of the Literature

From Economic Integration to Economic Convergence

The approach to economic integration adopted within the WAEMU consists of implementing several programmes and policies that aim to ensure economic convergence. In economics, convergence refers to the progressive decrease in differences among several countries for certain economic indicators. There are three main forms of convergence: nominal convergence, real convergence and structural convergence.

Nominal convergence relates to macroeconomic stability variables such as inflation, debt, budget deficit, interest rates, etc. while real convergence concerns standard of living, which is generally approached via the real GDP per capita. Structural convergence covers structural characteristics such as demand structure, which is sometimes approached through consumption or investment rates and population growth, and offer structure, which can be evaluated through production technology.

Nominal convergence in the WAEMU is regularly assessed by monitoring the convergence criteria.[2] This study will look at real and structural convergence, whose monitoring is not yet done regularly as is the case with nominal convergence and whose evaluation depends on a variety of techniques economists often use for its measurement.

Bamba (2004) reviews the literature related to methods for the empirical measurement of convergence, presenting the advantages and disadvantages of each. The majority of methods are based on statistical inferences. One notes that they generally complement rather than oppose each other. In our study, we will use Barro and Sala-i-Martin's (1990) techniques for sigma (σ)- and beta (β)-convergence. These are the two most used techniques in the literature to apprehend real and structural convergence.

Real and Structural Convergence in the WAEMU

Very few authors have approached the question of real convergence in the WAEMU, and there are hardly any studies of structural convergence. Lamine (2002) uses data from the Central Bank of West African States (BCEAO) and σ-convergence and β-convergence techniques to demonstrate that there is real convergence in the WAEMU. He also notes that this convergence is perverse because it results more from a decrease in GDP in the "rich" countries rather than a phenomenon of catching up by the countries that were initially "poorer". Ben Hammouda et al. (2007a, 2007b) also show that there is real convergence in the WAEMU countries. The ECA (2008) uses co-integration tests to demonstrate the existence of a shared per capita GDP trend in WAEMU countries. It also establishes real convergence in the WAEMU using regression of per capita income distribution on the trend. These studies, however, remain silent when it comes to analysing the dynamics of the convergence. In other words, they do not say whether or not, punctually speaking, there is convergence. In this study, we will use smoothing cubic spline regression to identify the periods of convergence and divergence for WAEMU countries.

---

[2] The convergence criteria are divided into two groups. Primary criteria are (1) the ratio of the basic fiscal balance to nominal GDP $\geq 0\%$, (2) the average annual inflation rate of $\leq 3\%$, (3) the ratio of outstanding domestic and foreign debt to nominal GDP $\leq 70\%$ and (4) nonaccumulation of domestic and external payment arrears in the current financial period. The so-called secondary criteria are (5) the ratio of the wage bill to tax revenue $\leq 35\%$, (6) the ratio of domestically financed public investment to tax revenue $\geq 20\%$, (7) the ratio of current exterior balance outside grants to nominal GDP $\geq -5\%$, and (8) the tax-to-GDP ratio $\geq 17\%$.

The Link Between Real and Structural Convergence

In the Solow growth model (1956), real convergence among several countries occurs if they have the same path to long-run equilibrium. For that to occur, they simply need to have the same structural characteristics, because these characteristics, according to the Solow model, determine the paths to long-run equilibrium.

Using the neoclassical analytical framework, Desdoigts (1997) highlights that initial differences in terms of per capita income tend to disappear if, and only if, they do not stem from differences in technologies, preferences, savings ratios, population growth ratios or market structures. Elmslie (1995) states that real convergence could be induced by technology transfer.

Ondo (1999) concludes, following an analysis of integration in sub-Saharan Africa, that integration cannot really take shape in places where macroeconomic policies are divergent. He adds that these policies can only converge if the economies react in the same way to shocks, which supposes that their systems and structures are similar.

According to Linder (1961), countries that have a relatively comparable standard of living are more likely than others to do trade, on the condition that their economies are diversified enough. The founding EU countries are an example of this. In effect, they shared characteristics (development, diversified production and efficient infrastructure), which led to strong market integration. WAEMU countries, on the other hand, have relatively heterogeneous characteristics[3] and little economic diversity.

In this study, in addition to analysing the process of real and structural convergence in the WAEMU, we will also examine whether or not structural convergence is a sufficient condition for there to be real convergence in the WAEMU.

Research Questions, Hypotheses and Study Objectives

Research Questions

In the course of this research the questions that were the object of our attention were the following:

1. Has there been structural convergence in the WAEMU?
2. Has there been real convergence in the WAEMU?

    a. If so, is it absolute or conditional to structural convergence?
    b. If not, could one have it to be conditional to structural convergence?

---

[3] The level of infrastructure development in Côte d'Ivoire and Senegal is markedly different from that found in the other WAEMU countries.

Research Hypotheses

Hypothesis 1. There was no structural convergence in the WAEMU over the entire period studied. This hypothesis is based on the intuition that, since independence, the infrastructure gaps between the "rich" countries and the "poor" countries in the WAEMU have not decreased. We will validate this hypothesis using σ-convergence and smoothing cubic spline regression.

Hypothesis 2. There was no real convergence in the WAEMU over the entire period studied. This hypothesis stems from hypothesis 1 and from the conclusions drawn by Solow (1956) and Desdoigts (1997). It will be tested using σ-convergence and smoothing cubic spline regression and absolute and conditional β-convergence.

Hypothesis 2.a. Real convergence in the WAEMU depends on the existence of structural convergence.

Hypothesis 2.b. Structural convergence is a sufficient condition for there to be real convergence.

Study Objectives

The objective of this study is to examine the processes of real and structural convergence in WAEMU countries over the period 1970–2005. The study also analyses the link between the two forms of convergence, and then it will attempt to indicate the policy measures to take to accelerate the process of economic integration among WAEMU countries.

The rest of the study is organised as follows: Section III presents the methodology, the analytical variables and the data used. Section IV analyses the results obtained. Section V gives the economic policy implications and makes recommendations. Section VI presents conclusions.

III   Methodology and Data

σ-Convergence

The goal is to assess how the gaps in economic indicators evolve. Its analysis is based on the distribution of the considered variables. There is convergence when dispersion diminishes over time. If $X_{i,t}$ is the value of the variable of interest X for the country i in year t, the dispersion indicator often chosen is given by the following formula:

$$D(t) = \sqrt{\frac{1}{N} \sum_{i=1}^{N} (X_{i,t} - \mu_t)^2}; \quad 0 \leq t \leq T, \tag{4.1}$$

where $\mu_t = \frac{1}{N} \sum_{i=1}^{N} X_{i,t}$, N is the number of countries and T is the number of years minus 1. There is convergence for the period $[0, T]$ if:

$$D(t+1) < D(t), \quad \forall t \in [0,T]. \tag{4.2}$$

The disadvantage of this approach is that the $D(t)$ index is sensitive to disruptions. Lazarev and Gregory (2007) propose an approach to overcome this disadvantage, which consists of supposing that the $D(t)$ index is the sum of a trend and the disruptions.

$$D(t) = d(t) + \varepsilon_t, \quad \varepsilon_t \sim N(0, \sigma_\varepsilon^2), \quad \forall t \in [0,T]. \tag{4.3}$$

Convergence is defined relative to the trend, and there is convergence over the period $[0,T]$, if the first derivative of the trend is significantly inferior to zero.

$$\frac{d'(t)}{dt} < 0, \quad \forall t \in [0,T]. \tag{4.4}$$

On the other hand, it is said that there is divergence if it is significantly higher than zero.

The advantage of this approach is that it enables one to identify periods of convergence and of divergence. However, no recommendation is made concerning the functional form that the trend should take or concerning its estimation. Lazarev and Gregory (2007) use a non-parametric smoothing method, notably the smoothing cubic spline regression, to estimate $d(t)$.

β-Convergence

β-Convergence applies to showing that poor countries are possibly catching up with rich countries. It consists of regressing the average annual growth rate over the initial level of the chosen variable. There is convergence if the countries whose initial level of the chosen variable was low is evolving more rapidly. So, the coefficient of the initial variable of interest in the regression should be significantly below zero.

The regression models used in this study are those used by Barro and Sala-i-Martin (BSM) in 1995. There is *absolute* β-convergence when the β coefficient is significantly less than zero in the following model:

$$\log(y_{i,t}) - \log(y_{i,t-1}) = \beta \log(y_{i,t-1}) + \mu_i + \eta_{it}. \tag{4.5}$$

There is *conditional* β-convergence when the *β*-coefficient is significantly less than zero in the following model:

$$\log(y_{i,t}) - \log(y_{i,t-1}) = \beta \log(y_{i,t-1}) + \sum_{k=1}^{K} \pi_k \log(x_{k,i,t}) + \mu_i + \eta_{it}, \qquad (4.6)$$

where $1 \leq i \leq N$, $1 \leq t \leq T$, with N, the number of countries and T, the end of the study period. $y_{i,t}$ is the level of the variable of interest for the country i during year t. $x_k(1 \leq k \leq K)$ are control variables. β and $\pi_k(1 \leq k \leq K)$ are parameters to estimate. $\eta_{it}\left(\eta_{it} \sim N\left(0, \sigma_{\eta}^2\right)\right)$ are supposedly independent errors. $\mu_i\left(\mu_i \sim N\left(0, \sigma_{\mu}^2\right)\right)$ is the country's heterogeneity.

Using classic methods (OLS or within estimation) for the estimation of (4.5) and (4.6) gives non-converging estimators due to the correlation between the lagged variable and the dependent variable $\log(y_{i,t})$ with the country heterogeneity μ_i.

Following Anderson and Hsiao (1981), Arellano and Bond (1991), Arellano and Bover (1995) and Ahn and Schmith (1995), Blundell and Bond (1998) propose an estimation method that guarantees the convergence of the parameter estimators. Their method is based on the general method of moments (GMM). They also demonstrate that it not only improves precision of the estimators but also reduces the finite sample bias (Baltagi 2001).

The instrumental variables used in the Blundell and Bond (1998) estimation method are defined as follows:

1. If $x_{k,i,t}$ are endogenous variables, then the instrumental variables will be $y_{i,t-j}$, $x_{k,i,t-j}, j \geq 2$.
2. If $x_{k,i,t}$ are predetermined variables, then the instrumental variables will be $y_{i,t-j}$, $j \geq 2$, $x_{k,i,t-j}, j \geq 1$.
3. If $x_{k,i,t}$ are exogenous variables, then the instrumental variables will be $y_{i,t-j}, j \geq 2$, $x_{k,i,t-j}, j \geq 0$.

Data and Choice of Analytical Variables

The data used are WAEMU's annual country observations for the period 1970–2005. They come from the World Bank's 2007 CD-ROM.

Real convergence will be determined from per capital GDP at constant prices for the year 2000, while structural convergence will be approached with the real per capita gross capital formation (GCF) at constant prices for the year 2000 and the level of technology measured by total factor productivity. According to the Solow growth model (1956), these two last variables determine the path to an economy's long-run equilibrium.

In effect, if we suppose that the Solow Cobb-Douglass production function and or the technical progress (A) is neutral, production is given relative to the following:

$$Y = AK^{\alpha}L^{1-\alpha}; \quad 0<\alpha<1, \qquad (4.7)$$

where Y is production, K capital,[4] L labour and A the level of technology still called total factor productivity (TFP) or Solow residual. By dividing the relation (4.7) by L, one gets the following equation:

$$\frac{Y}{L} = A \left(\frac{K}{L} \right)^{\alpha}. \tag{4.8}$$

It shows that production by labour unit Y/L depends on capital divided by labour unit K/L and on TFP. In other words, with the hypothesis that labour L evolves at the same pace as the population, relation (4.8) shows that changes in per capita production are ensured by increased per capita capital and the level of technology.

In this case, the TFP is given by the following:

$$\text{TFP} = A = \left(\frac{Y}{L} \right) \left(\frac{K}{L} \right)^{-\alpha} \tag{4.9}$$

IV   Results and Discussions

Was There Structural Convergence in the WAEMU?

Figure 4.1 shows the evolution of the first derivative of the real per capita GCF distribution trend. It highlights WAEMU country structural convergence on the demand side for the period 1976–1993 and shows that these countries diverged for the periods 1970–1975 and 1994–2005. These results suggest that the establishment of WAEMU did not enable member countries to bring their demand structure onto the same path of growth. They reveal that policies that favour mobility of capital and people have not yet reached their objective and call on the WAEMU to also adopt and implement shared investment and demographic policies.

Why then do we observe convergence of demand structures in WAEMU countries for the period 1976–1993? In effect, a close look at Fig. 4.6 in the Appendix shows that this convergence could result from real per capita GCF in the Côte d'Ivoire and Togo getting closer to that of the other countries, which had remained relatively constant over the studied period. Figure 4.7, which is not discussed further in the present study, refers to supply-side structural convergence.

A look at first derivative of the per capita GCF deviation trend for each country relative to the WAEMU average (Fig. 4.9 in the Appendix) shows that (1) the countries that contributed to the 1976–1993 convergence were Benin, Burkina Faso, Côte d'Ivoire, Guinea-Bissau, Mali and Togo, which represent three quarters of the WAEMU countries; (2) the countries that did not converge during the 1970–1975 period are Burkina Faso, Côte d'Ivoire, Guinea-Bissau, Mali, Senegal

---

[4] Capital at the moment t is given by $K_t = I_t + (1-\delta)K_{t-1}$, where I is gross fixed capital formation and $\delta [\approx 0,07$ see Benhabib and Spiegel (1994)] is the capital depreciation rate. Initial capital is given by $K_0 = I_0/(g + \delta)$ where g is the average annual growth rate of I.

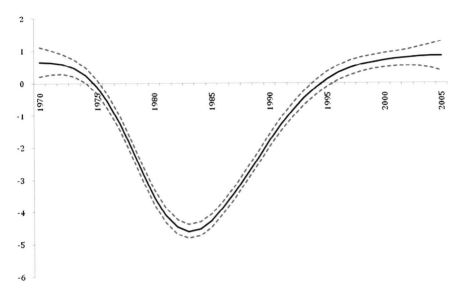

Fig. 4.1 First derivative of real per capital gross capital formation distribution trend (WAEMU) – *dotted lines* are 95% confidence interval points of the continuous curve

and Togo, or a total of three quarters of the WAEMU countries and (3) the divergence over the period 1994–2005 results from Benin, Burkina Faso, Guinea-Bissau, Mali, Senegal and Togo, or three quarters of the WAEMU countries.

Figure 4.2 gives the evolution of the first derivative of the TFP distribution trend or Solow residual. There was structural convergence in WAEMU countries on the offer side for the period 1976–1991 and divergence for the periods 1970–1975 and 1992–2005. The Solow residual is generally assimilated with labour organisation and production processes. In this way, TFP divergence in WAEMU countries implies divergence in labour organisation and in production processes. These do not fully explain the results in that the WAEMU countries are agricultural and have nearly the same production processes. However, if we consider that the Solow residual is endogenous, which implies that it is influenced by certain variables, notably those related to the institutional framework (quality of the bureaucracy, degree of corruption, etc.), to the macroeconomic situation (inflation, non-productive state expenditure, etc.) and to the political instability (coups, revolutions, strikes, etc.), then the divergence that is observed for the period 1992–2005 is merely the reflection of the divergence observed in nominal convergence criteria. Here, we should note that on average, fewer than three countries out of a total of eight respected the criteria for the 1997–2008 period.

The behaviour of TFP convergence that one observes from 1976 to 1991 is perhaps due to the economic crisis that occurred during that period, which resulted from a decrease in export income following the fall in prices of the main cash crops (cacao, cotton, coffee, etc.) and which impacted nearly all the WAEMU countries.

The analysis of the first derivative of the TFP distribution trend for each country relative to the WAEMU average (Fig. 4.10 in the Appendix) shows that (1) the

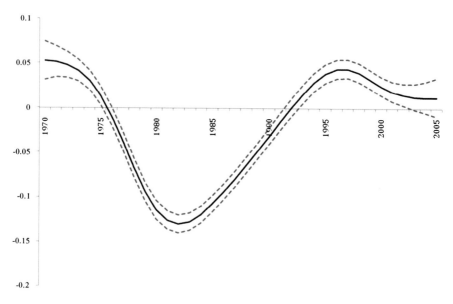

Fig. 4.2 Evolution of the first derivative of the total factor production distribution trend (WAEMU) – *dotted lines* show the 95% confidence intervals of the continuous line

observed TFP convergence for the period 1976–1991 results from Burkina Faso, Côte d'Ivoire and Guinea-Bissau, or fewer than half of the WAEMU countries; (2) the countries that contributed to the TFP divergence from 1970 to 1975 are Niger, Burkina Faso, Côte d'Ivoire and Togo, or half of WAEMU countries and (3) the divergence observed over the 1992–2005 period results from the divergence of the following countries: Benin, Burkina Faso, Côte d'Ivoire, Guinea-Bissau, Niger, Senegal and Togo, or seven out of eight WAEMU countries.

To sum up, in terms of structural convergence in WAEMU countries, we conclude that hypothesis 1, which states that "there was no structural convergence in the WAEMU", is verified for the periods 1970–1975 and 1992–2005. However, it was not verified for 1976–1991.

Was There Real Convergence in the WAEMU?

Figure 4.3 shows first-derivative changes in real per capita GDP distribution. It shows real convergence among WAEMU countries from 1975 to 2005 and that these countries diverged from 1970 to 1974.

A close look at Fig. 4.5 in the Appendix shows that real per capita GDP of the Côte d'Ivoire moved closer to that of the other WAEMU countries that remained relatively constant. Thus, the real convergence that is observed could merely represent Côte d'Ivoire's levelling up. A close look at real σ-convergence of

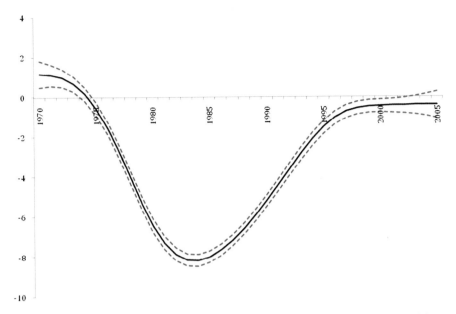

Fig. 4.3 First-derivative plot of per capita GDP distribution trend (WAEMU) – the *dotted lines* show the 95% confidence interval of the continuous line

WAEMU countries outside of Côte d'Ivoire over the period 1970–2005 (Fig. 4.4) shows that these countries converged from 1970 to 1991 but diverged over the period 1992–2005. As a result, by comparing Figs. 4.3 and 4.4, one could deduce that real per capita GDP in WAEMU countries got closer during the 1975–1991 period but moved apart during the periods 1970–1974 and 1992–2005. These results coincide perfectly with those obtained for structural convergence, which conforms to the conclusions drawn by Solow (1956) and Desdoigts (1997).

Hypothesis no. 2 by which "there was no real convergence in the WAEMU" is verified for the periods 1970–1974 and 1992–2005, but not verified for the period 1975–1991.

A closer look at the first-derivative plot showing a tendency towards deviation in per capita GDP for each country relative to the WAEMU average (Fig. 4.8 in the Appendix) shows that (1) the countries that contributed to real convergence for the period 1975–1991 are Benin, Burkina Faso, Côte d'Ivoire, Guinea-Bissau and Mali, or five of eight WAEMU countries; (2) the countries that did not show real convergence for 1970–1974 are Benin, Côte d'Ivoire, Guinea-Bissau and Niger, or a total of half the WAEMU countries and (3) real divergence for the period 1994–2005 results from Benin, Guinea-Bissau, Niger, Senegal and Togo, or five of eight WAEMU countries.

The σ-convergence technique combined with smoothing cubic spline regression, despite the possibilities it offers to analyse the process of convergence, is not entirely satisfactory, because it does not enable us to establish a link between real and structural convergence. This is why we used β-convergence to test hypotheses 2.a and 2.b.

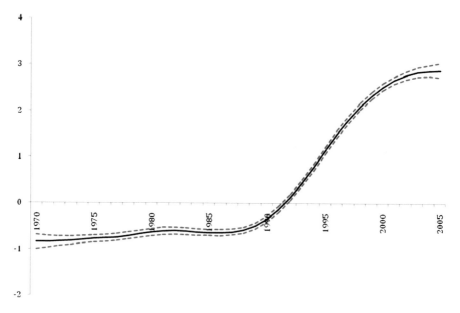

Fig. 4.4 First-derivative plot of per capita GDP distribution trend (WAEMU with the exception of Côte d'Ivoire) – the *dotted lines* show the 95% confidence interval of the continuous line

Through hypothesis 2.a, we wish to determine if the real convergence observed for the period 1975–1991 results from the structural convergence, while with hypothesis 2.b, we want to know if under the hypothesis of structural convergence, one could have real convergence in WAEMU countries for the period 1992–2005.

For this, we estimated four equations. The first is Eq. (4.5). The second is Eq. (4.6) using LGCF as the control variable. The third is Eq. (4.6) with the control variable being LTFP. The fourth is Eq. (4.6), including LGCF and LTFP as control variables. All these equations enable us to test if there was real convergence under the condition of structural convergence. If not the case, they enable one to find the structure responsible for real convergence.

Table 4.1 shows the results of these estimations. A close look at Eq. (4.5) shows that there is no absolute real convergence. Thus, the observed real convergence is conditional. In view of the results of overall significance (Fisher), of non-autocorrelation of residuals (AR(2)) and of instrument validity (Sargan), the Eqs. (4.6b) and (4.6c) are interpretable, although only Eq. (4.6b) accords with the real observed convergence (with the help of σ-convergence) for this period.

It shows that the observed real convergence was conditional to structural convergence and more specifically to TFP convergence. Hypothesis 2.a is, therefore, verified: "The real convergence observed among WAEMU countries for the period 1975–1991 was the result of structural convergence". This also means that, considering the absence of absolute real convergence, structural convergence was required for there to be real convergence during the 1975–1991 period.

Table 4.1 Results of β-convergence equation estimations

Variable	Equation (4.5)		Equation (6.a)		Equation (6.b)		Equation (6.c)	
Period 1975–1991								
$LGDP_{i,t-1}$	−0.358	[0.261]	NA		−0.495**	[0.175]	−0.412	[0.441]
$LGCF_{i,t}$			NA				0.027	[0.096]
$LTFP_{i,t}$					0.922**	[0.317]	0.574***	[0.167]
Fisher	1.870	[0.208]	NA		8.070**	[0.012]	7.350**	[0.011]
AR(1)	−1.600	[0.110]	NA		−1.390	[0.165]	−1.010	[0.312]
AR(2)	−1.960*	[0.050]	NA		−1.090	[0.278]	−1.570	[0.117]
Sargan	90.730	[0.855]	NA		122.650	[0.787]	130.860	[0.921]
Period 1992–2005								
$LGDP_{i,t-1}$	0.110	[0.700]	−0.095	[0.166]	−0.731***	[0.178]	−0.982*	[0.459]
$LGCF_{i,t}$			0.102*	[0.051]			0.011	[0.054]
$LTFP_{i,t}$					0.735***	[0.135]	0.998*	[0.483]
Fisher	0.160	[0.700]	2.450	[0.156]	29.320***	[0.000]	11.25***	[0.005]
AR(1)	−1.560*	[0.118]	−1.660*	[0.097]	NA		1.420	[0.156]
AR(2)	−0.810	[0.420]	−0.800	[0.426]	NA		1.610	[0.108]
Sargan	76.490	[0.399]	84.310	[0.817]	87.130	[0.754]	90.030	[0.937]

Note: The estimations for the period 1975–1991 cover all eight WAEMU countries, while those for 1992–2005 cover WAEMU countries with the exception of Côte d'Ivoire. As all the variables were considered as endogenous in the model, the instruments are $y_{i,t-j}, x_{k,i,t-j}$ and $j \geq 2$. The numbers between the parentheses are White heteroscedasticity-robust standard errors. Those between square brackets are the *p*-values. ***, ** and * indicate, respectively, a 1, 5 and 10% significance. The Sargan test null hypothesis is "exogeneity of the instruments". So, the larger the *p*-value, the more exogenous the instruments. The autocorrelation test has a null hypothesis of "absence of autocorrelation" and is applied to differentiated residuals $\Delta\varepsilon_{i,t}$. The AR(1) test rejects, generally speaking, the null hypothesis because $\Delta\varepsilon_{i,t} = \varepsilon_{i,t} - \varepsilon_{i,t-1}$ and $\Delta\varepsilon_{i,t-1} = \varepsilon_{i,t-1} - \varepsilon_{i,t-2}$ share $\varepsilon_{i,t-1}$. The AR(2) test is more important because it enables the detection of autocorrelation of the $\varepsilon_{i,t}$. *NA* means "not available". The variance-covariance matrix of the explicative variables is not defined as positive

For the period 1992–2005, Eq. (4.5) confirms that there was no absolute convergence for this period because the β-coefficient is not significant, and in addition, it is positive. The results of tests for significance, non-autocorrelation of residuals and instrument validity show that Eqs. (4.6a) and (4.6c) are interpretable. Thus, in Eq. (4.6a), the β-coefficient is negative but not significant. This result suggests that real per capita GCF convergence contributes to real convergence in WAEMU countries. However, the non-significance of the β-coefficient shows that real per capita GCF convergence is not sufficient. In Eq. (4.6c), the β-coefficient is negative and significant, which confirms hypothesis 2.b: "Structural convergence was a sufficient condition for real convergence in WAEMU for the period 1992–2005".

Based on Eq. (4.6c) estimated for the period 1992–2005, one also notes that economic growth in WAEMU countries does not depend on the real per capita GCF (its coefficient is not significant) but rather on the TFP or the Solow residual. This implies that economic basics such as investment and demography do little to feed economic growth in WAEMU countries, which depends more on TFP or Solow residual, thus explaining how vulnerable these economies are to external shocks, natural shocks and terms of trade.

V   Policy Implications

Regional integration could help WAEMU countries to increase their market size, to strengthen their power of negotiation and their image on the world stage, to pool their resources in order to find joint solutions, to make the most of their comparative advantages, to implement more in-depth and lasting reforms and to prevent and resolve conflicts through stronger economic bonds (ECA 2004b).

According to Linder (1961), real convergence could promote integration across countries by stimulating trade. The countries that have comparable standards of living are more likely to trade than those with different standards of living. Yet, we have just empirically established that structural convergence was a necessary and also sufficient condition for there to be real convergence respectively for the periods 1975–1991 and 1992–2005. Thus, by evaluating structural convergence, one also evaluates real convergence.

We have also established that economic growth in WAEMU countries does not rely on the basics such as investment and demography, but rather on residual elements related to labour organisation and production techniques, which could be influenced by the institutional framework and the macroeconomic framework. So, WAEMU country economic growth could be unstable because it is based on not very stable residual elements, left at the mercy of exogenous shocks, natural shocks and variations in terms of trade. It follows that WAEMU country economic convergence could be unstable, because all it takes is one economy reacting differently than the others to a shock in order for convergence to be disturbed.

VI   Conclusions and Recommendations

The objective of this study was to examine the process of real and structural convergence in the WAEMU over the period 1970–2005. We did this using σ-convergence, smoothing spline regression and β-convergence. Demand-side structural convergence was observed through real per capita gross capital formation and supply-side structural convergence by total factor productivity or Solow residual (1957). The data used in this study are annual observations that come from the World Bank 2007 CD-ROM.

The results of the study showed the presence of structural and real convergence respectively for the periods 1976–1991 and 1975–1991. On the contrary, they demonstrate the absence of structural convergence for the periods 1970–1975 and 1992–2005 and of real convergence for the periods 1970–1974 and 1992–2005.

Absolute and conditional β-convergence demonstrated that the structural convergence was a necessary and also sufficient condition for real convergence respectively for the periods 1975–1991 and 1992–2005. Consequently, in the WAEMU, evaluating structural convergence also evaluates real convergence.

We also noted that growth in WAEMU countries relies very little on economic fundamentals such as investment and demography, but rather on total factor productivity or the Solow residual, which is generally assimilated with labour organisation and production techniques, which can be influenced by the institutional and macroeconomic environment. As a result, growth in WAEMU countries could be an unstable one and left to the mercy of exogenous shocks, natural shocks and variations in terms of trade. It follows that economic convergence of WAEMU countries would be unstable, because all it takes is for one economy to react differently than the others to a shock in order for convergence to be greatly disturbed.

In terms of recommendation to accelerate economic integration in the WAEMU, one should promote the convergence of institutional frameworks and put more emphasis on respecting nominal convergence criteria in order to improve labour organisation and production processes. In addition, it is very important that the economies in WAEMU countries rely on fundamental variables such as per capita investment and demographic growth rates and that these be identical for all. With this in mind, it would be the proper time to also define convergence criteria for real annual per capita investment and annual population growth rates.

Appendices

Smoothing Cubic Spline Regression

Given that $\lambda > 0$, a smoothing cubic spline is a third-order polynomial function solution of the following minimisation problem:

$$\underset{(f \in W^2[0,T];\ \lambda)}{\text{Min}} \left\{ \sum_{t=0}^{T} [y_t - f(t)]^2 + \lambda \int_0^T [f''(t)]^2 dt \right\}, \qquad (4.10)$$

where $W^2[0, T]$ refers to all the functions defined over $[0, T]$ such that f and f' be absolutely continuous and integrable squares and that f'' be an integrable square, λ is called the "smoothing parameter". It establishes a compromise between data proximity (controlled by the term $\sum_{t=0}^{T} [y_t - f(t)]^2$) and the total function regularity (controlled by the term $\int_0^T ([f''(t)]^2 dt)$). For a very high λ value ($\lambda \to \infty$), the term $\int_0^T ([f''(t)]^2 dt)$ must be equal to zero, which leads to a smooth and regular f^* estimator that could be biased. On the other hand, for a low λ value ($\lambda \to 0$), the term $\int_0^T ([f''(t)]^2 dt)$ must be very high and one gets an f^* estimator that interpolates the data, less biased but with greater variance.

There are, in general, two different approaches for choosing the λ parameter: the subjective choice and the automatic method based on data. We opted for the latter approach.

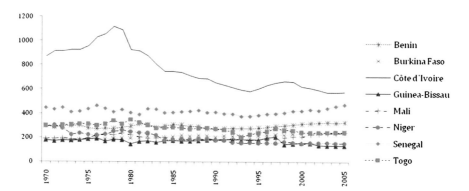

Fig. 4.5 Evolution of real per capita GDP in WAEMU countries

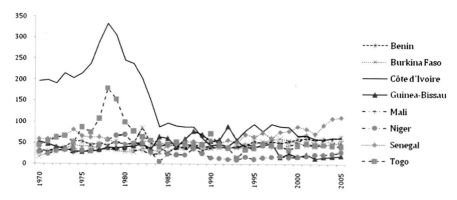

Fig. 4.6 Evolution of real per capita GCF in WAEMU countries

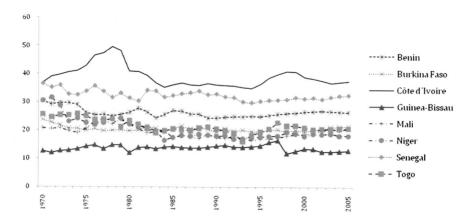

Fig. 4.7 Evolution of TFP in WAEMU countries

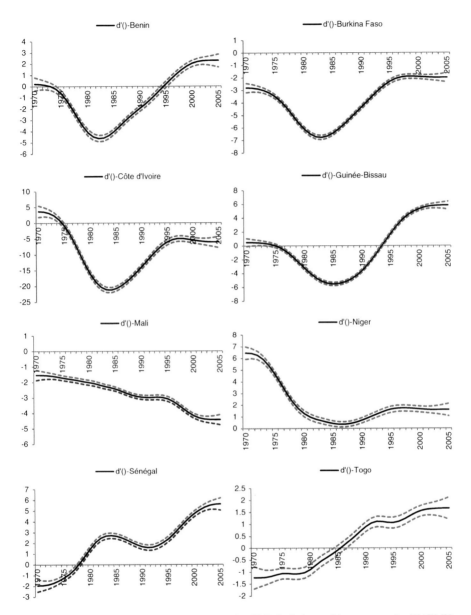

Fig. 4.8 Changes in first-derivatives of per capita GDP deviations with respect to the WAEMU average

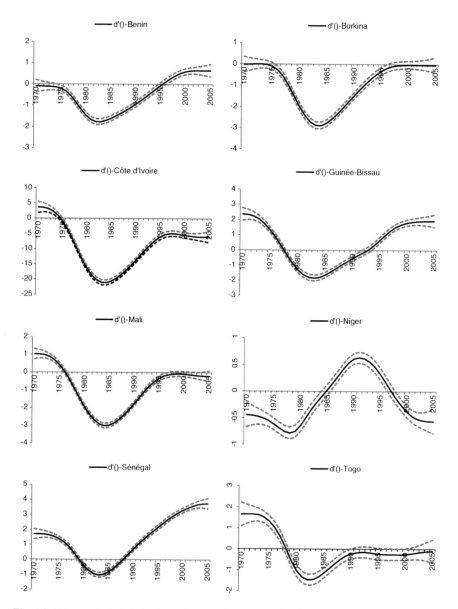

Fig. 4.9 Changes in first-derivatives of per capita gross capital formation (GCF) deviations with respect to the WAEMU average

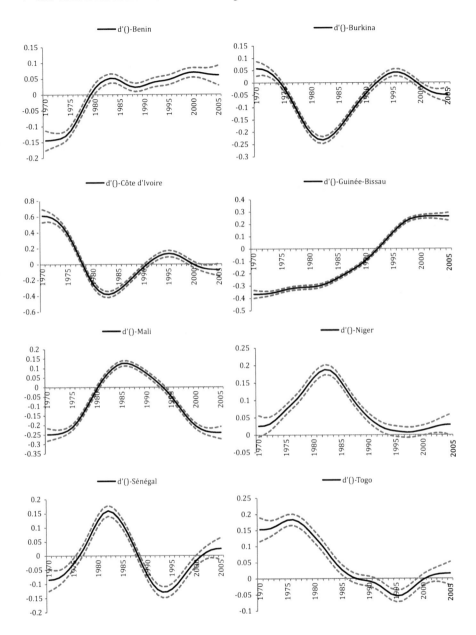

Fig. 4.10 Changes in first-derivatives of total factor productivity (TFP) deviations with respect to the WAEMU average

References

Anderson, T.W. and C. Hsiao (1981), 'Estimation of dynamic models with error Components', *Journal of the American Statistical Association* 76, 598–606.

Ahn, S.C. and P. Schmidt, (1995), 'Efficient estimation of models for dynamic panel data, *Journal of Econometrics* 68, 5–27.

Arellano, M. and S. Bond (1991), 'Some tests of specification for panel data: Monte Carlo evidence and an application to employment , *Review of Economic Studies* 58, 277–297.

Arellano, M. and O. Bover (1995), 'Another look at the instrumental variables estimation of error component models', *Journal of Econometrics* 68, 29–51.

Baltagi, B. (2001), *Econometric analysis of panel data*. Chichester, John Wiley.

Bamba, L. (2004), 'Analyse du processus de convergence dans la zone UEMOA', *World Institution for Development Economics Research, Research Paper no. 2004/18*.

Barro, R and X. Sala-I-Martin (1990), 'Economic Growth and convergence across the United States', *NBER Working Papers* 3419, National Bureau of Economic Research, INC

Barro, R. and X. Sala-I-Martin, (1995), *Economic Growth*. McGraw-Hill, New-York.

Desdoigts, A. (1997), 'Vers une convergence globale ou locale ?' *Economie Internationale, no. 71, 3ème trimestre.*

Ben Hamouda, H., S. Karingi, A Njuguna and M. Sadni-Jallab, (2007a), 'Why Doesn't Regional Integration Improve Income Convergence in Africa?'Paper prepared for the African Economic Conference, 15-17 November 2007, United Nations Conference Centre, Addis Ababa, Ethiopia

Ben Hamouda, H., S. Karingi, A Njuguna and M. Sadni-Jallab, (2007b), 'Does Macroeconomic convergence Lead to Growth? The Case of Africa', African Trade Policy Centre, Economic Commission for Africa.

Benhabib, J. and M. Spiegel (1994), The role of human capital in economic development: evidence from aggregate cross-country data, *Journal of Monetary Economics* 34(2):143–173.

Blundell, R. and S. Bond (1998),'Initial conditions and moment restrictions in dynamic panel data models', *Journal of Econometrics* 87, 115–143.

Conférence des Nations Unies sur le Commerce et le Développement, (2009), 'Le Développement Economique en Afrique Rapport 2009: Renforcer l'Intégration Economique Régionale pour le Développement du l'Afrique', United Nations, New York and Geneva.

Economic Commission for Africa, (2004a), 'Rapport économique sur l'Afrique 2006: Libérer le potentiel commercial de l'Afrique'. *Commission Economique pour l'Afrique des Nations Unies, Addis-Abeba.*

Economic Commission for Africa, (2004b), 'Etat de l'intégration régionale en Afrique'. *Commission Economique pour l'Afrique des Nations Unies, Addis-Abeba.*

Economic Commission for Africa (2008), 'Assessing Regional Integration in Africa: Towards Monetary and Financial Integration in Africa', *Commission Economique pour l'Afrique des Nations Unies, Addis-Abeba.*

Elmslie, B. (1995), 'The convergence Debate between David Hume and Josiah Tucker'. *Journal of Economic Perspectives,* 9(4): 207–16.

Lamine, D. (2002), 'Convergence nominale et réelle: une application des concepts de la σ-convergence et de la β-convergence aux économies de la CEDEAO'. *Banque Centrale des États de l'Afrique de l'Ouest, Note d'information statistique n°531.*

Lazarev, V. and P. Gregory, (2007), 'Structural convergence in Russia's economic transition, 1990–2002'. *Econ Change,* 40: 281–304.

Linder, S. (1961), *An Essay on Trade and Transformation*. Uppsala: Almqvist and Wiksells.

Nations Unies, (2009), Le Développement Economique en Afrique Rapport 2009: Renforcer l'intégration économique régionale pour le développement de l'Afrique. *Nations Unies, New York et Génève.*

Ondo O. A., (1999), 'La problématique de l'intégration en Afrique Subsaharienne (le cas de l'Afrique centrale)', *Economie et Gestion*, vol. I, n° 2, janvier-juin.

Solow, R., (1956), 'A Contribution to the Theory of Economic Growth', *The Quarterly Journal of Economics*, 70(1): 65–94

Venables, A., (2000), 'International Trade: Regional Economic Integration', *International Encyclopedia of Social and Behavioural Sciences. [www.iesbs.com]*

World Bank (2000), Trade Blocs, Washington, DC

Chapter 5
The Impact of the Convergence, Stability and Growth Pact in the WAEMU

Adama Combey and Komla Mally

Abstract In the WAEMU area, nominal convergence is regularly monitored and is the object of increasing interest. However, few studies have focussed on the real convergence of WAEMU countries, and in particular the contribution the Convergence, Stability and Growth Pact (CSGP) has made to the dynamics of real convergence. The goal of this study is to analyse the effect of the pact on the dynamics of real convergence. After examining the concept of sigma-convergence and convergence in distribution, we use the beta-convergence approach with panel data in order to take into account the differences of technological state that exist among the countries. We use the GMM system to correct for the endogeneity bias, and the results suggest that one cannot reject the hypothesis of conditional convergence and that the pact triples the speed of levelling the gap of real per capita GDP in WAEMU member countries for the period 1997–2008. So, adopting the CSGP improved the overall standard of living in the Union's member countries. The study has, however, some limitations, notably the reduced time dimension and the fact that it did not take into account non-monetary aspects of poverty.

I Introduction

During the 1980s, the West African Monetary Union (WAMU) experienced poor internal performance and external shocks that had huge repercussions in the member countries' economies. The drop in international prices for raw materials, the main source of export income, and the appreciation, in real terms, of the CFA franc had a negative impact on the key macroeconomic indicators, leading to a

A. Combey (✉) • K. Mally
Centre for study, research and training in Economics and Management
of the University of Lomé, Togo
e-mail: adama.combey@gmail.com

E.T. Ayuk and S.T. Kaboré (eds.), *Wealth Through Integration*, Insight and Innovation
in International Development 4, DOI 10.1007/978-1-4614-4415-2_5,
© International Development Research Centre 2013

serious economic crisis that resulted in lower production and a worsening of living conditions for the populations.

To relieve this situation, in the 1990s it became necessary to deepen economic integration further by coordinating the joint monetary policy with the national budget policies in order to ensure the Union's cohesion and to stimulate economic growth. As a result, on January 10, 1994, seven countries[1] signed a treaty to form the West African Economic and Monetary Union (WAEMU) to complete that instituted by the WAMU, with a goal of creating a truly integrated economic space.

On December 8, 1999, an additional act to the WAEMU treaty was voted concerning the Convergence, Stability, Growth and Solidarity Pact (PCSC) among WAEMU members, along with a community ruling dated December 21, 1999, concerning the convergence pact's implementation. This pact aims to meet the following objectives: strengthening economic convergence, macroeconomic stability, accelerating economic growth and creating more solid bonds among member states.

The pact makes reference to the convergence of a group of macroeconomic indicators (*nominal convergence*). It imposes specific conditions for the convergence of these indicators, notably in terms of budget deficit, inflation rate and public debt. There are eight indicators divided into two categories (see Appendix 1).

An analysis of the main indicators in the Union for the 1997–2008 period is as follows. Real GDP increased annually for the period 1997–2008, but at a decreasing rate. In effect, the growth rate varied from 7.6% in 1997 to −0.2% in 2000, the year from which it begins to increase to reach 4.4% in 2008.

Furthermore, primary indicators for the 1997–2008 period are described below. The number of countries that respected the basic fiscal balance went from 4 in 1997 to 0 in 2005 and 2 in 2008. The inflation rate compared to the norm of 3% was more respected by the countries, because the number of countries that respected this criterion sometimes reached seven out of seven and was generally around six and five for the entire period. Even if the outstanding public debt did not respect the norm in 2004–2005, it evolved favourably during the period. The majority of countries had a debt ratio of less than 70% for the period. Efforts can also be noted in the area of payment arrears. Appendix 2 presents the achievements in terms of criteria during these three final years of the period.

According to the BCEAO (2003) "the pace of convergence slowed in Union states. It also appears that during the period 2000–2002, macroeconomic convergence of Union member states was insufficient on the whole to ensure passage into the stability phase initially foreseen for 2003". The WAEMU Commission (2004), noting that it was unlikely that convergence would be achieved in 2005, emphasised: "A year away from the deadline for convergence, it is urgent for the States' authorities to take the measures necessary to ensure consolidation of the macroeconomic framework for convergence".

---

[1] Benin, Burkina Faso, Côte d'Ivoire, Mali, Niger, Senegal and Togo; Guinea-Bissau joined the Union in 1997.

II   Statement of the Problem and Justification

For the last few decades, monetary unions have been adopting joint objectives for their economic aggregates (especially fiscal and monetary objectives). These indicators are chosen for their importance to or their impact on economic activity. Convergence of the indicators is important for the viability of a union (Akanni-Honvo 2003). Recently, a number of economists have focussed their attention on the question of which economic structure is the best for a monetary union. From there, the analysis of the issues surrounding budgetary policy and its impact on a union's economic activity has become of major importance in the economic literature. More emphasis has been placed on the importance of macroeconomic or budgetary externalities that lead to monetary integration. Four theoretical solutions have been proposed to reduce these negative externalities: (1) the merging of national governments, (2) the coordination of national budgetary policies, (3) the budgetary federalism and (5) the rules of supranational stability such as a stability pact. Stability pact-like rules are often adopted both for monetary unions of developed countries and those of developing countries.

What is at stake with the rules for a monetary union is that they impede the stabilising function of national budgetary policies and therefore contribute to better coordination between the joint monetary policies and the decentralised budgetary policies. Respecting the rules will lead to nominal convergence and economic integration, which in turn will stimulate trade and promote economic growth (Frankel and Rose 2002).

The stability pact adopted would then have the role of making the governments to aim, in the medium term, for a deficit nearing equilibrium or a surplus, allowing the automatic stabilisers the responsibility to limit the effects of cyclical fluctuations. The monetary control mechanism would be enough to stimulate development in maintaining key equilibriums (Ary Tanimoune et al. 2005).

Since the adoption of the pact, nominal convergence has been monitored regularly in the WAEMU space and has been the object of increasing interest. Several empirical studies have looked into nominal convergence. However, very few have explored real convergence and, above all, the effect of the pact on the dynamics of real convergence. A possible justification for this is that unlike nominal convergence, which seems to be a prerequisite for the creation of a monetary union, it is generally admitted that real convergence is not a required condition for adopting a single currency. However, although different income levels are compatible with participation in a monetary union, real convergence is also sought after, in that it promotes economic cohesion within the union and enables the minimisation of negative effects of asymmetric shocks, thus reducing the needs for adjusting the exchange rate and improving the capacity the various countries have to observe the discipline implied by the efficient implementation of a single monetary policy (Diop 2002).

The basic underlying hypothesis for setting convergence criteria is that respecting them will boost activity and economic growth and that the signature of the pact is a "response to the need to accelerate economic growth at a regional level, to support macroeconomic stability and strengthen solidarity among countries" (BCEAO 2003). Although the primary objective of the pact is to establish a real integrated economic area, it should also contribute to the dynamics of real convergence.

Achieving virtuous real convergence enables real economic growth that is necessary to reduce poverty (Dollar and Kray 2000). Yet, Lombardo (2008) shows that growth determines poverty, even if the elasticity of poverty to growth varies with each region and depends on initial conditions in terms of inequality and level of development. In addition, Roemer and Gugerty (1997) prove that increasing real per capita GDP "can be and is also a powerful force for reducing poverty". So, to what extent does respecting the criteria contribute favourably to reducing poverty in the Union?

III Objectives

The main objective for this chapter is to study the link between nominal convergence and real convergence. Two other specific objectives can be derived from this main one: (1) re-examining the process of real convergence within the WAEMU and (2) analysing the effect of the pact on the dynamics of real convergence.

The rest of the chapter is organised as follows: Section IV presents the methodology with a brief review of the theoretical justifications for the pact along with the various tests used to analyse convergence. Section V presents results and discussions. Further research needs are identified in Section VI. The implications of economic policies and recommendation are presented in Section VII. Section VIII provides conclusions with comments and research for the future.

IV Methodology

Theoretical Basis for the Stability Pact

Why is it necessary to impose constraints on national fiscal policies in a monetary union's member countries? The answer the various theories provide to this question turns around the free-rider behaviour of fiscal authorities. In effect, imposing fiscal constraints depends on the commitment of the monetary authority relative to its political future. Temporal incoherence in administering monetary policy leads to free-rider behaviour in the administration of fiscal policies. A monetary authority without any commitment tends to increase inflation rates when the level of the states' outstanding debt is high and to reduce the inflation rate in the opposite situation. Yet, when the fiscal authority of a member state wants to make a decision regarding its level of outstanding debt, it recognises that by increasing its level of indebtedness, the monetary authority will increase the inflation rate.

Thus, it introduces the cost of inflation induced by the debt into its programme and ignores the cost of this induced inflation imposed on other member states. This "free-rider" behaviour will lead to a level of indebtedness that cannot be sustained and to high inflation. This is the point of view of Chari and Kehoe (2007). Their model gives the following results: if the monetary authority can make a commitment, then the fiscal regulations imposed on the various member states will not lead to increased welfare; however, if it cannot make a commitment, then constraints will improve welfare in the member states.

Beetsma and Uhlig (1999) find that, in general, tax authorities have a short-term vision of the administration of fiscal policies, and as a result, the main source of debt is policy distortion by the member state governments. Furthermore, Bertola and Drazen (1993) analyse the effect of fiscal austerity and suggest that high fiscal deficit could be the sign of upcoming high fiscal pressure. This anticipation could discourage private investment, which could have negative effects on growth. Giavazzi and Pagano (1996) then developed this analysis from another perspective. The authors used international evidence to demonstrate the non-Keynesian effect of budget deficit. In a monetary union, the fiscal structure is more linked to the general price level and therefore, to the inflation rate than it is to monetary policy. A high deficit generally requires high prices in order to decrease real debt and enable fiscal authorities to respect upcoming budget constraints (Woodford 2001). More long-term budget balancing would then be the source of macroeconomic stability by reassuring investors of the fact that taxes and general interest rates will not increase to finance future budget imbalances.

A number of economists think that the first advantage of a monetary union is lowering inflation with its advantages, notably promoting economic integration and economic growth, and that the costs reside in the effects decentralised fiscal policies have on monetary policy. Herzog (2005) uses a dynamic model to demonstrate the role the pact plays in fiscal policy discipline. This model is interesting because it uses a dynamic approach based on differential equations, unlike other models that use game theory. This model brings the following points to light: (1) fiscal policy interacts with monetary policy; (2) budgetary decisions relative to deficit and debt impact price stability and, therefore, monetary policy; (3) fiscal policies interact among themselves in competing for the public good "price stability" and (4) the pact is a third institution necessary to discipline fiscal policy, reduce "free-rider" behaviour and help monetary policy to achieve its objective of price stability. The main result is the inability of or the limitations of the monetary policy to discipline fiscal policies without the pact.

Through fiscal policy discipline and price stability, the pact enhances trade in the Union and could accelerate real convergence therein (Diop 2002).

Economic Convergence Tests

In the empirical literature, several methods have been used to analyse per capita income convergence. The differences are related to the type of data used (cross-section, time series, panel data) to carry out the tests as well as the information that is generated (absolute convergence, conditional convergence, club convergence).

The property of convergence, referred to as absolute convergence, results from the implications of traditional representations of growth in the Solow-Swan model. In their model, the steady state stability implies that two economies with the same structural characteristics other than their level of per capita income converge towards each other on the same steady path. But, new theories of growth highlight the endogenous nature of growth. They identify the accumulation of knowledge, the role of human capital, the accumulation of technological capital through research and development and the public expenditure on infrastructure (Muet 1997, and Montoussé 1999) and as a result tend to predict per capita income divergence or conditional income convergence. As a result, several tests have been proposed in the literature to lead empirical investigations of convergence.

The starting point is β-convergence, stemming from the work of Barro and Sala-i-Martin (1990, 1992), to test how income in developing countries catches up to that in developed countries. The test procedure consists of regressing the growth rate over its initial level in a cross section, such that

$$\ln(y_{i,t}) = \alpha + \beta \ln(y_{i,0}) + \mu_{i,t} \qquad (5.1)$$

One can conclude that there is β-convergence when the β coefficient is negative and statistically significant. This test has been criticised a lot in the literature. The criticisms concern, on one hand, the interpretation of the β coefficient and, on the other, the information about per capita income distribution. In effect, if poor countries grow more quickly than rich countries, they could overrun rich countries. In addition, the test ignores information concerning per capita income distribution. Quah (1993) demonstrated that even with growing distribution, the β parameter could still be negative. Furthermore, estimation of the β parameter by classic econometric technique (notably ordinary least squares) is biased because it does not take into account unobserved heterogeneity among the countries and other growth determinants.

Another test has therefore been proposed: σ-convergence. The procedure consists of analysing changes in per capita income distribution over time. There is evidence of σ-convergence when the distribution decreases over time. Only panel data-based convergence tests provide better precision in the estimation of β because these tests resolve the problems of omitted variables by taking into account unobserved heterogeneity (Islam 1995). The fixed effects are interpreted as the reflection of technology, and therefore these are conditional convergence tests. Another test known under the name of convergence in distribution is a lot more adapted to determining the existence or not of club convergence. Bernard and Durlauf (1994) provide a methodology based on unit root tests or co-integration of series differences.

Recent empirical studies undertaken on developing economies, notably those of the Economic Community of West African States (ECOWAS), WAEMU and the Economic Community of Central African States (CEMAC), emphasise income convergence or real GDP and/or convergence indicators defined by zones.

Akanni-Honvo (2003) concludes that, on the whole, the zones are in a process of beta-convergence conditional on structural transformations structural development and that the process is longer in Africa.

Diop (2002) tests for sigma-convergence and beta-convergence using data from the ECOWAS and finds that, overall, economies converge nominally but are not in a process of real convergence. He recognises that convergence is both nominal and real in the subsample of WAEMU countries. Using the same methods, Jones (2002) arrives at the conclusion that the ECOWAS countries form a convergence club with per capita income convergence process or trend and a decrease in standard deviation over time. Ndiaye (2006) shows that the conditional convergence hypothesis appears more robust than that of absolute convergence, which gives poor results. In the same line of thought, Bécart and Ondo-Ossa (1997), on the basis of criteria from an optimal monetary zone and convergence tests using the basic Solow model and its extensions, demonstrated that the economies in the African franc zone tend to converge with greater homogeneity in the WAEMU compared with the Monetary Union of Central Africa (UMAC). In addition, these authors support that measures to harmonise national economic policies had a favourable impact on conditional economic convergence. Finally, Dramani (2007) used the Barro and Sala-i-Martin (1992) model and find that nominal convergence leads to real convergence and adds that the criteria and institutions are efficient.

Research Strategy

Following this brief review of the literature, three methods were used successively: sigma-convergence, convergence in distribution and beta-convergence.

Sigma-Convergence

The analysis of σ-convergence will enable to determine if real per capita GDP in the various WAEMU countries tended to get closer together or farther apart over the analysed period. This analysis is based on the sigma distribution analysis of the GDP according to the following formula:

$$\sigma_t = \left[\frac{1}{n} \sum_{i=1}^{n} \left(y_{i,t} - \bar{y}_{\bullet,t} \right) \right]^{1/2} \tag{5.2}$$

where $y_{i,t}$ and $\bar{y}_{\bullet,t}$, respectively, designate the GDP logarithm per inhabitant i at the date t and its average level, and n is the number of countries. One can conclude that there is convergence when distribution diminishes over time and that there is divergence if the opposite case is valid.

Plane and Tanimoune (2005) suggest, to be on the safe side, to undertake an analysis of σ-convergence by a Wilcoxon non-parametric test. "The latter is particularly well adapted to small samples and has the characteristic of being non-restrictive on error normality hypotheses imposed in the Carree and Klomp (1997) test. From the calculated σ-convergence, a test of the significance of the rank differences between the sub-periods" is performed.

Convergence in Distribution

The principle of convergence in distribution is based on the comparison over time of real per capita GDP distribution in the member countries. The advantage of this technique is that it enables the researcher not only one to detect convergence when distribution tightens up over time but also to detect the existence of convergence clubs when the distribution is multimodal. This tests the hypothesis that member countries do not converge at an identical pace but distinguish themselves by a different growth pattern.

Conditional Convergence

The specification that was chosen is that of the classic formulation of models that have been used to test for the conditional convergence or divergence phenomenon among regions, following the research done by Caselli et al. (1996). Thus

$$\log(Y_{i,t}) - \log(Y_{i,t-1}) = \beta^* \log(Y_{i,t-1}) + \phi X_{i,t} + \mu_i + \theta_t + \varepsilon_{i,t} \tag{5.3}$$

where $Y_{i,t}$ is the proxy indicator for the level of monetary poverty measured by real per capita GDP in country i for the period t, $X_{i,t}$ all the other growth determinants (share of investment in GDP, primary schooling ratio, size of government measured in government expenditure in the GDP, ratio of economic openness measured by the sum of exports and imports in the GDP), μ_i the specific country effect which makes it possible to control for the technological differences and other growth determinants that are not covered in $X_{i,t}$, θ_t the specific study period effect and $\varepsilon_{i,t}$ the error term.

If $\beta = 0$, then the hypothesis of conditional convergence is rejected. However, if $\beta < 0$, then there is conditional convergence among the countries.

The speed of convergence will be calculated in accordance with neoclassical convergence models, that is, $\beta = -[1 - \exp(-\lambda t)]$, where λ is the speed of convergence or the rate of convergence towards steady state or the levelling up of the economies among themselves. The transformation gives $\lambda = -[\log(1 + \beta)]/t$.

By setting $y_{i,t} = \log(Y_{i,t})$ and by rearranging, Eq. 5.3 becomes

$$y_{i,t} = (1 + \beta)y_{i,t-1} + \lambda x_{i,t} + \mu_i + \theta_t + \varepsilon_{i,t}. \tag{5.4}$$

To analyse the effect of CSGP on the dynamics of real convergence, we integrated into Eq. 5.4, $n_{i,t}$ the number of convergence criteria respected by a country i at a date t and its interaction with the logarithm of lagged per capita GDP. Equation 5.4 becomes

$$y_{i,t} = (1 + \beta)y_{i,t-1} + \alpha n_{i,t} + \rho n_{i,t}y_{i,t-1} + \lambda x_{i,t} + \mu_i + \theta_t + \varepsilon_{i,t} \tag{5.5}$$

The intuition behind our reasoning is the following. Suppose, for example, two countries A and B with $y_{A,t}$ and $y_{B,t}$, respectively, their real per capita GDP in log such that $y_{B,t-1} > y_{A,t-1}$. "All else being equal", according to Eq. 5.5, we obtain

$$\frac{y_{A,t} - y_{B,t}}{y_{A,t-1} - y_{B,t-1}} = \beta + \rho^* \left(n_{A,t} - n_{B,t} \right) \tag{5.6}$$

So, the interpretation of the coefficient ρ depends on its sign. If $\rho < 0$, then it represents the variation in real convergence dynamics if and only if the logarithm of per capita GDP is increasing relative to the number of criteria respected, that is, that α is positive.

Two panel data estimation techniques were used successively to estimate the Eqs. 5.4 and 5.5. The first is the Within estimator. This method poses the hypothesis that the specific country effects are fixed or stable over the period that was studied. These effects enable one to control for the unobservables in explaining growth, notably the differences in the technological state of the countries and all the other growth determinants that could have been omitted in the specification. This technique presents certain limitations because the equation estimated by the Within estimator is the following:

$$y_{i,t} - \bar{y}_{i,\bullet} = (1 + \beta)\left(y_{i,t-1} - \bar{y}_{i,\bullet}\right) + \lambda\left(x_{i,t} - \bar{x}_{i,\bullet}\right) + \left(\varepsilon_{i,t} - \bar{\varepsilon}_{i,\bullet}\right) \tag{5.7}$$

Besides, by construction, $\bar{y}_{i,\bullet}$ is correlated with $\bar{\varepsilon}_{i,\bullet}$, and thus $y_{i,t-1} - \bar{y}_{i,\bullet}$ is correlated with $\left(\varepsilon_{i,t} - \bar{\varepsilon}_{i,\bullet}\right)$. As a result, the coefficient $(1 + \beta)$ is biased downwards. The correction of this endogeneity bias problem requires instrumentation of $y_{i,t-1} - \bar{y}_{i,\bullet}$. Thus, another estimation technique must be used, the instrumental variables technique, but the greatest difficulty encountered in the application of this technique resides in the choice of the right instruments.

Certain authors, based on Arellano and Bond (1991), have used the generalised method of moments (GMM) technique to resolve this problem linked to the addition of supplementary moment conditions. The basic principle of their method consists of instrumenting the lagged value of the dependent variable in the equation in first difference by its lagged p-order values. But the Arellano and Bond first difference estimator does not function well in the following two cases: (1) when there is persistence in the $y_{i,t}$ and (2) when variance of the fixed effects is relatively larger than variance of the idiosyncratic error (Wooldridge 2002).

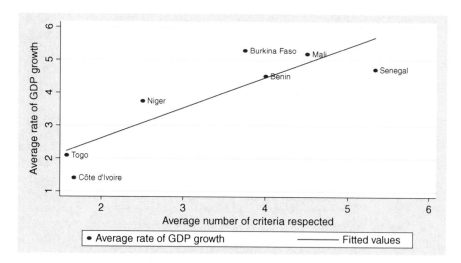

Fig. 5.1 Real GDP growth rate and average number of criteria respected (1997–2008) (Source: Authors' calculation)

The second method that is more appropriate is the GMM estimator in the Blundell and Bond (1998) system. The advantage of this technique is that it combines the moment conditions of the equation in first differences, using as instruments level lagged variables, and the moment conditions of the level equation using as instruments the difference in past values in order to respond to the weaknesses of the Arellano and Bond (1991) technique. But before establishing the definitive list of instruments, one must ensure the absence of second-order autocorrelation of disturbances in the model and the Sargan test allows one to validate the instruments.

Figure 5.1 illustrates the link between economic growth and the number of criteria respected for the 1997–2008 period. One notes a positive correlation between respecting the nominal convergence criteria and economic growth within the WAEMU. In effect, Senegal is the country that respected the most criteria over the period, while the Côte d'Ivoire and Togo, which were characterised by political instability, were the worst offenders.

Data Source

The data cover seven WAEMU countries (except Guinea-Bissau) for the period from 1997 to 2008. These data come from WAEMU Commission statistics "Selected Statistics on Africa Countries" 2008 Volume XXVII of the African Development Bank's statistics department.

V   Results and Discussions

Analysis of Sigma-Convergence

Figure 5.2 retraces changes in distribution in the logarithm of real per capita GDP for the 1997–2008 period.

This figure shows an overall trend towards a decrease in the standard deviation of real per capita GDP in WAEMU countries, suggesting that there was real convergence of the economies for the 1997–2008 period. However, despite this overall evolution, it is possible to detect contrasting evolutions for the following periods: a decrease in standard deviation is noted for the periods *1997–1998, 2000–2003* and *2005–2007*, while there is an increase in this indicator for the periods *1998–2000* and *2003–2004*.

The Wilcoxon non-parametric test was applied for the two following periods: before the pact (1997–1999) and under the pact before the period of entry into a phase of stability (2000–2007). This test rejects the null hypothesis H0 ($Z = 2,126; Prob > |z| = 0,0335$) of variance equality at a threshold of 5% in favour of the alternative hypothesis that there was real convergence of the economies under the CSGP.

This overall convergence can be qualified as perverse convergence if it is the rich countries of the Union that move closer to the poor countries. So, our analysis was completed by Fig. 5.3, which traces the evolution of real per capita GDP.

One notes that the reduction of distribution over the 1997–2008 period is due primarily to real per capita GDP growth in Senegal, Benin, Burkina Faso and Niger, catching up with that of Côte d'Ivoire, which remained relatively constant. This observation suggests that the observed convergence is largely due to the real per capita GDP of the poorer countries catching up with that of the rich countries.

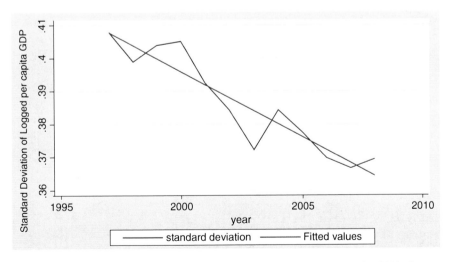

Fig. 5.2 Evolution of distribution of the log of real per capita GDP for 1997–2008 (Source: Authors' calculation)

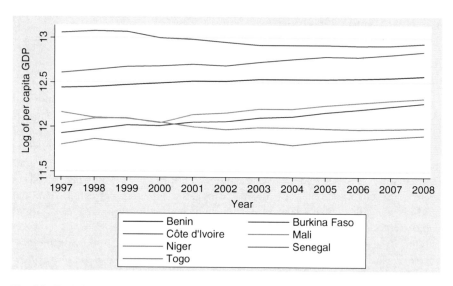

Fig. 5.3 Evolution of the log of real per capita GDP for WAEMU countries from 1997 to 2008 (Source: Authors' calculation)

Analysis of Convergence in Distribution

The sigma-convergence analysis is completed by a convergence in distribution assessment that takes into account the results of the latest studies of the Union. Figures 5.4 and 5.5 retrace the non-parametric distribution estimations of the logarithm of per capita GDP for two sub-periods: 1997–1999, 3 years before the CSGP was adopted and executed, and the 2005–2007 period. The distribution in Fig. 5.4 represents the initial distribution. By definition, there would have been real convergence of WAEMU economies when this distribution gets closer together over time, that is, if all the elements of the distribution converge to the same level. The sub-period 2005–2007 represents that from which the Union is supposed to return during the stability phase. Figure 5.5 suggests a distribution that not only gets closer together over time but also that evolves towards a non-unimodal distribution. This result suggests that beyond an overall convergence of all the WAEMU countries for the 1997–2007 period, one notes the existence of "convergence clubs". One distinguishes the "rich" countries whose level of convergence is above the average (Côte d'Ivoire, Senegal and Benin) and the "poor" or disadvantaged countries whose level of convergence is lower than average (Burkina Faso, Mali, Niger and Togo).

Analysis of Beta-Convergence

The various estimation techniques used are the Within estimation (EF1 to EF3) and the GMM system (GMM1 to GMM3) as shown in Eqs. 5.4 and 5.5. The results are presented in Table 5.1. Concerning the three first columns, the objective was,

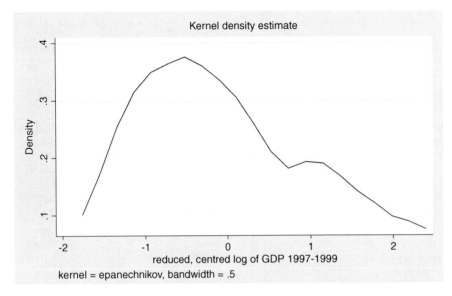

Fig. 5.4 Distribution of the log of per capita GDP for the period 1997–1999 (Source: Authors' calculation)

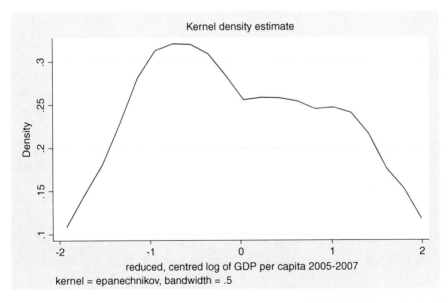

Fig. 5.5 Distribution of the log of per capita GDP for the period 2005–2007 (Source: Authors' calculation)

Table 5.1 Fixed effects and GMM system results

Variables	Within			GMM system		
	EF1	EF2	EF3	GMM1	GMM2	GMM3
$y_{i,t-1}$	0.830***	0.827***	0.703***	0.965***	0.99***	0.99***
	(0.071)	(0.074)	(0.119)	(0.027)	(0.001)	(0.008)
$n_{i,t}$		0.0193	−0.0299		0.0592***	0.0321**
		(0.0320)	(0.0385)		(0.022)	(0.013)
$n_{i,t}\,y_{i,t-1}$		−0.00223	0.007		−0.0091**	−0.0039*
		(0.0056)	(0.007)		(0.0038)	(0.0024)
Ouv			−0.113*			0.019
			(0.058)			(0.0311)
Inv			0.081			−0.122**
			(0.081)			(0.053)
ConGouv			0.462**			0.226*
			(0.197)			(0.118)
Scol			0.0003			−0.0001
			(0.0004)			(0.0002)
Constant	0.971**	0.964**	1.631**	0.210		
	(0.399)	(0.416)	(0.661)	(0.152)		
Speed of convergence	0.18	0.19	0.35	0.04	0.01	0.01
Square-R	0.804	0.817	0.85			
Fisher test	4.94***	5.03***	5.12***			
Wald test				0.00	0.00	0.00
AR(2)				0.42	0.41	0.45
Sargan				0.46	0.84	0.98
Nb of instruments				61	78	86

Robust standard errors in parentheses
Significance: *** $p < 0.01$, ** $p < 0.05$, * $p < 0.1$
The reported values for AR(2), the Sargan test and the Wald test are critical probabilities

among other things, to test the hypotheses of conditional convergence and the effect of the pact on convergence dynamics with or without the control variables. Columns 4–6 present the results of the GMM estimation based on the hypothesis that the control variables are endogenous. The latter corrects for the problems of bias in the Within estimator results. All the estimations were obtained by applying a correction to the disturbance variance-covariance matrix (heteroscedasticity-robust standard deviations).

The quality of the adjustment is good because the determination coefficient is very high, with 80% of the per capita GDP logarithm variation being explained by the model. The Fisher significance test of the fixed effects indicates that the hypothesis of joint nullity of all the fixed effects is rejected for a risk threshold equal to 5%. To test for the robustness of our result, we have introduced other growth determinants.

Whether it applies to the hypothesis of real convergence or that of the effect of the CSGP on convergence dynamics, the results differ depending on the estimation techniques used. The coefficient of the GDP logarithm is higher in GMM than in Within, which confirms the downward bias with the Within estimator.

As for the hypothesis of conditional convergence, the results concord with the expected sign, irrespective of the technique used, and with or without control of the other growth determinants. The convergence coefficient is negative and statistically significant with the Within estimator $\hat{\beta} = -0.17$ representing $((0.83-1)$ column 1). To test the effect of the CSGP on convergence dynamics, we introduced the number of respected criteria in interaction with the lagged GDP logarithm (column 2) and the control variables (column 3). Introducing the control variables did not modify the sign, or the order of magnitude or the significance of the convergence coefficient. In effect, the CSGP has an effect on the convergence dynamics because the coefficient is of the expected sign, but this result is not satisfactory from a statistical point of view because the coefficient is not significant.

The convergence coefficient becomes -0.30 following the introduction of control variables. The sign of the coefficient of the number of criteria respected in interaction with the lagged GDP logarithm are inverted but still remain insignificant.

The Results indicate that the logarithm per capita GDP for WAEMU countries converges at an annual speed that is between 18 and 30%, a speed that is overestimated due to the bias introduced in the estimation of $\hat{\beta}$. The speed of convergence is reduced to between 1 and 4% a year with the GMM estimator.

The Within estimator result indicates that the effect of the CSGP on convergence dynamics is neither of the expected sign nor statistically significant. However, this effect becomes statistically significant and of the expected sign with the GMM estimator. The tests of instrument validity show that these seem to be valid. Similarly, the Arellano and Bond statistics test does not allow one to reject second-order autocorrelation of the model's disturbance. This result suggests that conditional to CSGP, real convergence accelerated over time by 0.0039, or a speed that tripled over the period (0.0039*10, or around 4%).

The number of criteria respected has a positive and statistically significant effect at a threshold of 10% on the increase of growth; this result concords with Fig. 5.1. The results demonstrate the important role regional integration plays in promoting economic growth. In effect, the efforts member countries make at nominal convergence and in reducing free-rider behaviour induce economic growth in the Union. WAEMU member countries therefore benefited from the virtuous behaviour of respecting nominal convergence criteria because the latter led the Union onto a path of homogenization of standard of living in the region.

Furthermore, we note that the control variables, the ratio of primary schooling and that of openness, did not have significant effect on economic growth in the region. These results are not surprising because empirical research, notably that of Islam (1995), has shown that unlike what is observed in cross-section estimations, the various human capital indicators, especially primary schooling, cease to have a significant impact on economic growth as soon as the temporal dimension is taken into account.

On the other hand, whatever the estimation method used, government consumption exerts a positive and statistically significant effect on economic growth. Increasing government consumption has a considerable impact on economic growth. This effect is contrary to the theory defended in the literature concerning public consumption. According to the literature, accrued budget deficits are an obstacle to private investment due to the increase in real interest rates. Similarly, accrued public expenditure gives a glimpse of future fiscal obligations and, as a result, dampen the incentive measures and reduces growth. Thus, we can interpret this result to be a composition effect of public expenditure engendered by the pact, which stimulated growth. But, the investment rate has a negative and statistically significant effect on economic growth. We interpret this as a consequence of inadequate private investment in WAEMU.

In order to test the robustness of our interpretation, we split the sample in two: the relatively rich countries of Benin, Côte d'Ivoire and Senegal on one hand and Burkina Faso, Mali, Niger and Togo on the other. The results indicate that private investment has a positive effect on growth, regardless of estimation technique used, in the first group of countries, that is, the relatively rich countries. However, the impact becomes negative and statistically significant in the second group or the relatively poor countries.

VI   Gaps for Future Research

The results and interpretations of this study show some weaknesses that should be mentioned. These weaknesses can be grouped into two categories: the lack of data and methodological weaknesses. Due to a lack of data for the period, certain economic growth determinants such as terms of trade instability and political instability were not controlled. From a methodological point of view, there is no good counterfactual allowing us to carry out an analysis in which adopting the pact would be represented by a dummy variable. Furthermore, as poverty is also a non-monetary phenomenon, one could envision using a more appropriate variable that reflects this. A microeconomic approach incorporating various poverty indicators could be used. In addition, one could use a large sample covering other integration zones that did or did not adopt a pact. In this sample, the countries that had not adopted a pact would be treated as counterfactuals. Finally, real convergence being a long-term phenomenon, it would be preferable to redo the study over a long period of time. Our future work will take these weaknesses into account so as to gain a better understanding of the link between economic convergence and poverty in the Union.

VII   Policy Implications and Recommendations

This section has a two goals: first, to highlight the link between our results and poverty reduction and then to present the policy implications and recommendations.

Regarding poverty reduction, our results suggest that the CSGP is a factor that promotes real economic growth and accelerates real convergence in the zone. It is therefore a source of poverty reduction and of levelling of standard of living in the WAEMU states.

Regarding economic policy implications, this report shows that the pact is a good instrument to promote growth and thus in the process of fighting poverty. The convergence criteria are therefore relevant. The economic policy actions taken as part of the CSGP are effective. But, the CSGP's effectiveness depends on the "credibility" of the multilateral monitoring system and the sanctioning procedures.

We recommend that decision-makers (1) boost the multilateral monitoring system in place in the WAEMU and (2) set up and apply a system of sanctions based on the number of criteria that have been violated.

VIII   Conclusion

This study set out to reconcile two school of thoughts found in the literature. One defends the benefits of nominal convergence in a union and the other focuses on the levelling of GDP in the economies (real convergence). We have examined the link between the CSGP adopted within the WAEMU and real convergence in the member countries. This relationship has been examined using the "beta-convergence" approach and estimated using panel data. After sigma-convergence analysis, complemented by analysis of convergence in distribution and of beta-convergence, the hypotheses of conditional convergence and of convergence clubs cannot be rejected for the period studied. The pact has considerably reduced free-rider behaviour in member countries and has made a positive contribution to real convergence in the Union. The acceleration was 0.39% per year, or around a 4% gain in convergence speed. Adopting the pact has thus tripled the speed of real convergence for the period. Thus, promoting regional integration through adopting the CSGP is favourable for economic growth, real convergence and therefore for poverty reduction in the subregion.

Appendices

Appendix I Convergence criteria

Primary criteria	Norms	Secondary criteria	Norms (%)
Basic fiscal balance	≥ 0	Wage bill as percentage of tax revenue	≤ 35
Inflation rate	$\leq 3\%$	Domestically financed public investment to tax revenue	≥ 20
Ratio of outstanding domestic and foreign debt to nominal GDP (%)	$\leq 70\%$	Tax to GDP ration	≥ 17
Domestic and external payment arrears in the current financial period	$= 0$	Current exterior balance outside grants to nominal GDP	≥ -5

Appendix 2 Achievement of Convergence Criteria in WAEMU Countries from 2006 to 2008

Convergence criteria (based on additional convergence indicators)	Achievement of criteria in 2008[a] by state and review of performance in 2006 and 2007 in the WAEMU								Number of countries having respected the criteria		
	Benin	Burkina Faso	Côte d'Ivoire	Guinea-Bissau	Mali	Niger	Senegal	Togo	2008	2007	2006
1 Basic fiscal balance[b] to nominal GDP (norm ≥ 0)	1.6	−1.2	1.2	−2.0	−0.1	5.0	−0.9	−0.7	3	3	3
2 Underlying inflation rate (norm ≤3%)	7.0	10.7	6.3	10.4	9.2	11.3	5.3	8.7	0	7	1
3 Total outstanding debt to nominal GDP (norm ≤ 70%)	19.1	23.2	71.5	219.3	37.5	20.1	25.8	62.4	6	5	5
4 Non-accumulation of payment arrears (in billions)	0	0	292.1	20.7	0	0	0	0.8	5	5	5
4.1 Domestic payment arrears	0	0	80.3	10.7	0	0	0	0	6	4	3
4.2 Foreign payment arrears	0	0	402.5	21.8	0	0	0	0.8	5	5	5
5 Wage bill to tax revenue[b] (norm ≤ 35%)	35.0	44.7	43.9	106.7	35.8	29.8	29.0	33.3	4	4	4
6 Domestically financed public investment to tax revenue[b] (norm ≥ 20%)	23.7	43.7	14.9	12.4	23.5	42.4	30.7	12.9	5	2	4
7 Current exterior balance outside grants to nominal GDP (norm ≥ −5%)	−10.3	−11.9	0.7	−19.9	−8.6	−15.1	−11.2	−8.9	1	1	1
8 Tax revenues (norm ≥ 17%)	17.2	12.2	15.5	10.8	13.3	11.7	18.3	14.6	2	1	1
Number of criteria respected by countries 2008	6	3	2	0	3	5	5	2			
2007	5	4	2	0	5	6	6	3			
2006	3	4	2	2	6	6	6	2			

Source: WAEMU Commission (2009, June)

[a]Shaded areas show respected criteria

[b]Corrected for budget grants and HIPC resources

References

Akanni-Honvo, A., (2003), 'Intégration régionale, effets frontières et convergence oudivergence des économies en développements'. *Revue Région et Développement* n° 17: 109–143.

Arellano, M. and S. Bond, (1991), 'Some tests of specification for panel data: Monte Carlo evidence and an application to employment equations', *Review of Economic Studies*, 58: 277–297.

Ary Tanimoune, Nasser, Jean-Louis Combes and Patrick Plane (2005), 'Les effets non linéaires de la politique budgétaire: le cas de l'Union Economique et Monétaire Ouest Africaine', Working papers 200520, CERDI

Barro, R. and X. Sala-I-Martin, (1992), 'Convergence', *Journal of Political Economy*, 100 (2): 223–251.

Barro, R. and X. Sala-I-Martin, (1990), 'Economic Growth and Convergence across The United States', *NBER Working Papers* 3419, National Bureau of Economic Research.

bceao (2003), 'Evolution de la convergence macroéconomique au sein de l'Union Economique et Monétaire Ouest Africaine (UEMOA)', 29 January 2003, http://www.bceao.int/internet/bcweb.nsf/pages/cm001

Bceart, A.and A. Ondo-Ossa, (1997), 'Zone monétaire optimale et convergence dans les unions monétaires en Afrique',Congrès de Porto et Evora, 28–31 May

Beetsma, R. and H. Uhlig, (1999), 'An analysis of the Stability and Growth Pact', *The Economic Journal*, 109 (October): 546–571.

Bernard, A. and S. Durlauf, (1994), 'Interpreting test of convergence hypothesis'. *NBER Technical Working Paper*, 159.

Bertola, G. and A. Drazen, (1993), 'Trigger Points and Budget Cuts: Explaining the Effects of Fiscal Austerity', *American Economic Review*, vol. 83(1) (March):11–26.

Blundell, R. and S. Bond, (1998), 'Initial conditions and moment restrictions in dynamic panel data models', *Journal of Econometrics*, 87:115–143.

Caselli F, Esquivel G and Lefort F, "Reopening the Convergence Debate: A New Look at Cross-Country Growth Empirics", Journal of Economic Growth, no. 1, 1996: 363–389.

Carree M. A. and L. Klomp (1997): Testing the Convergence Hypothesis : a Comment, The Review of Economies and Statistics, 4, vol. LXXXIX, : 683–686.

Chari, V. and P. Kehoe, (2007), 'On the need for fiscal constraints in a monetary union', *Journal of Monetary Economics*, Vol. 54: 2399–2408.

Diop, P., (2002), 'Convergence nominale et convergence réelle: une application des concepts de σ-convergence et de β-convergence aux économies de la CEDEAO', *UMOA, Notes d'informations statistiques de la BCEAO*. December.

Dollar, D., and A.Kray, (2000), 'GROWTH is good for poor', *Journal of Economic Growth*, Vol. 7, no. 3, September:187–212,

Dramani, L., (2007),'Convergence et intégration économique en Afrique : cas des pays de la zone Franc', *MPRA*, Université Cheick Anta Diop de Dakar, April.

Frankel, J. and A. Rose, (2002), 'An Estimate of the Effect of Common Currencies on Trade and Income', *Quarterly Journal of Economics*, Vol. 117, No. 2: 437–466.

Giavazzi, F. and M. Pagano, (1996),'Non-Keynesian Effects of Fiscal Policy Changes: International Evidence and the Swedish Experience', *NBER Working Papers*, No. 5332.

Herzog, B. (2005), 'Modelling Fiscal-Monetary Interaction and the Stability and Growth Pact in a Complex European Framework A New Approach with Differential Equations', February, mimeo.

Islam, N. (1995),'Growth Empirics: A Panel Data Approach', *Quarterly Journal of Economics* 110:1127–1170.

Jones, B. (2002),'Economic Integration and Convergence of Per Capita Income in West Africa', *African Development Review*, Vol. 14: 18–47

Lombardo, V. (2008), 'Growth and inequality effects on poverty reduction in Italy'. University of Naples Parthenope, Italy. *MPRA Paper* No. 14351

Muet, A. (1997), 'Le conseil d'analyse économique ou l'anti-consensus', L'économie politique no. 1 janvier

Montousse, M. (1999), Théories économiques. 3rd edition Bréal, Collection Grand Amphi Economie, Paris

Ndiaye, M. (2006),'UEMOA: une intégration à deux vitesses à travers les clubs de convergence'Université Check Anta Diop de Dakar, Sénégal. Journées sur « Intégration, développement économique et transition », Paris, September. AUF, PEP, and DIAL.

Plane, P. and N. Tanimoune (2005), 'Performance et convergence des politiques économiques en zone franc', Revue française d'économie, V.20, No.1 : 235–268

Quah, D. (1993),'Empirical Cross-section dynamics in Economic Growth', European Economic Review, 37: 426–434

Roemer, M. and M.K. Gugerty (1997), 'Does economic growth reduce poverty?'Technical Paper. Harvard Institute for International Development. March

WAEMU (1999 to 2008), "Rapports semestriels d'exécution de la surveillance multilatérale 3", WAEMU Commission

WAEMU (2009), Rapport semestriel d'exécution de la surveillance multilaterale Juin

Woodford, M (2001), 'Fiscal Requirements for Price Stability', Journal of money, Credit and banking, Vol. 33 No. 3: 669–728.

Wooldridge, J. (2002), Econometric Analysis of Cross Section and Panel Data, MIT Press.

Chapter 6
Real Convergence in the WAEMU Area: A Bayesian Analysis

Claude Wetta and Antoine Yerbanga

Abstract The objective of this study is to understand the process of development of Union countries by analysing real convergence. To reach this goal, it analyses absolute and conditional convergence on one hand and sigma convergence on the other. The data used comes from several sources: the World Bank, Penn World Tables, the ADB and the BCEAO.

In analyzing absolute and conditional convergence, the study uses the Bayesian estimation method to determine the speed of (absolute and conditional) convergence for each country. This study chose not to use the stacked method because it does not enable one to obtain the speed of convergence for each country. This latter method determines a single speed for all the countries. Analysis of sigma convergence is done using a graph. The idea is to represent and analyse the per capita GDP variance ratio. This ratio is the relation between per capita GDP variance at year t and at year 1994. The year 1994 was chosen because it is the year the Union was founded. The results of the study show that there is weak absolute convergence within the Union and that the educational policies, just as the openness policies, could accelerate growth and convergence in these countries.

The study also notes the presence of sigma convergence for the periods 1980–1994 and 2000–2008. Note that the first period is a "before-integration" period and the second an "after-integration" period. For the latter, one can say that the countries are in the process of economic integration. The absence of sigma convergence during the 1994–2000 period does not in any way bring into question the positive impact of integration on sigma convergence. In effect, it is possible that a policy does not produce immediate effects. Generally, there is a time-lag between when a policy is put into place and when the effects of the policy can be felt.

C. Wetta (✉) • A. Yerbanga
UFR/SEG (Research and Training Centre in Economics and Management) at the University of Ouagadougou II, Ouagadougou, Burkina Faso
e-mail: claude.wetta@univ-ouaga.bf

E.T. Ayuk and S.T. Kaboré (eds.), *Wealth Through Integration*, Insight and Innovation in International Development 4, DOI 10.1007/978-1-4614-4415-2_6,
© International Development Research Centre 2013

111

That could be the case in this study. Countries often take time to adapt to the new rules and measures, and as a result, the date the treaty comes into effect does not coincide with the practical application of its measures.

The heterogeneity of data sources is a limitation of this study. In addition, there was no data for Guinea-Bissau for the entire study period and was therefore excluded from the analysis of absolute and conditional convergence. Other equally important variables were not integrated into the analysis. These are variables that measure the quality of institutions such as democracy, good governance, property rights protection, etc. Future research could take these aspects into account.

I Introduction

Convergence is defined as the reduction of the gap between a given set of countries for selected indicators. This concept covers two different notions: nominal convergence that studies the evolution of price variables and real convergence that is defined by the levelling up of standard of living and/or a reduction in structural differences among the countries (Ekomie 1999). Real convergence covers three major concepts: absolute convergence, conditional convergence and sigma convergence. The first two are grouped together under β-convergence. From a general viewpoint, the notion of β-convergence refers to the speed at which the economies tend to approach their steady state, that is, a state of balanced growth.

Absolute convergence seeks to verify if standards of living in the various countries under consideration tend to come closer over time. The question that arises is: have the initially poor countries experienced per capita growth that is higher than that experienced in the initially rich countries? This approach supposes that the countries exhibit similar characteristics and that, in their development, they converge from a specific initial situation towards a single steady state.

Conditional convergence takes into account the various differences in structural characteristics found among the countries. Thus, these structural characteristics determine the paths to long-run equilibrium. In this case, each economy will converge towards its own long-run equilibrium level.

To measure the possibility of there being a convergence phenomenon, another method tries to observe if the spread in revenue has decreased. The goal in this case is to verify if per capita income approaches the average level of the observed countries or regions. Convergence can be analysed using a normative or a statistical approach. The normative approach will evaluate convergence on the basis of explicit harmonisation of policies and announced objectives. This harmonisation is also considered to be a precursor and an obligatory path towards real convergence (Mosse 2000). The statistical approach poses convergence as a postulate. The method consists of empirically and quantitatively measuring the gap in relation to this postulate.

An econometric analysis based on models, using secondary macroeconomic data from the Penn World Tables, the ADB, the World Bank and the BCEAO, made it possible to answer the first two questions. Statistical analysis was used to answer the third. The study uses variables such as per capita GDP, the degree of economic openness, investment and primary schooling rate.

II   Problem Statement and Justification

It seems that one can partially explain the mixed results experienced by past attempts at African integration by the lack of convergence among the economies on this continent. As a result, the treaty establishing WAEMU affirms in its preamble "the need to enhance complementarity of the states' production apparatuses and to reduce the disparities among the member states' level of development" (WAEMU 2003). In order to avoid past errors, the WAEMU set up a Convergence, Stability and Growth Pact that states what is at stake and the objectives.

Respecting these stakes and objectives should lead to real economic convergence among the WAEMU member states (Ouedraogo 1999). However, the standard of living of the majority of the people living in the Union remains very low. The United Nations ranking based on the sustainable Human Development Index (HDI) not only places nearly all of the Union's states at the bottom of the list but their socio-economic indicators are also ill-matched. Only three countries—Benin, Côte d'Ivoire and Senegal—had a per capita GDP higher than the Union average for the period 1998–2000 (UNDP 2002).

Such income inequality is a source of instability and incessant movement of populations that are always seeking a better life. The consequences are an aggravation of the unequal distribution of populations across the community area and conflicts between native populations and immigrants.

If it is agreed that the main economic objective of a country, and more generally of the entire political space that has been granted economic competence, is to ensure that all of its inhabitants have a high and growing standard of living, then one should also look into the evolution of standard of living disparities or, in other words, at the problem of real convergence in national and infra-national spaces.

The general question we raise is the following: does the process of development in Union countries obey a mechanism of economic catching up or a mechanism of divergence in terms of per capita GDP?

In effect, there are major variations in the Union's production of wealth. The Côte d'Ivoire alone contributed 41% of the community's GDP for the 1995–2000 period. It was followed by Senegal (18%). The two states accounted for about 60% of the community's GDP. Senegal was followed by Mali, Burkina and Benin (10%), Togo and Niger (6%) and Guinea-Bissau (1%) (WAEMU Economic Policy Department, 2001, cited by Yerbanga 2004).

Such disparities are not conducive to favouring or facilitating integration. It is necessary for integration to enable an increase in the level of economic development and, as a result, of the contribution each state makes to the Union's GDP. This will not only enable growth and consolidation of its economic weight but also safeguard it from greater individual and collective vulnerability.

From the point of view of the countries that are behind, regional integration's economic legitimacy lies in its contribution to "real convergence". But, for the richer countries, the expected convergence also contributes to achieving more explicit objectives: political stability for the less developed countries, cohesion in the zone and slowing migratory flows. A very high level of diversity could require huge and lasting financial intervention on the part of the region's richer countries.

The competitiveness of a union as a whole not only depends on its enterprises and on its higher-performing countries. It also depends on the coherence and the cohesion of the whole (Barnier 2001). The question of real convergence of the economies is therefore necessary for economic and monetary unions. In order for the union to reap the expected benefits of integration for its population, it should support the actions that can contribute the most to reducing socio-economic and territorial disparities.

The economic literature concerning convergence shows that early research done on per capita income convergence covered industrialised countries. Then, studies took into consideration developing countries in so-called representative samples. The economic and monetary unions became fields of study for convergence. However, these studies are more focussed on nominal convergence. A few studies covering real convergence were carried out for the economic and monetary unions of Europe and Central Africa. However, each union has its specific characteristics, which explains the basis of our study: "Real convergence in WAEMU economies: a Bayesian Analysis". The main concern is to determine the state of real convergence in the Union's economies, along with the factors that explain growth of the economies towards their long-run equilibrium.

Alongside the coordination of monetary policy, which has been ensured since 1972 in the framework of WAMU, the countries that signed the WAEMU treaty set up a process of multilateral monitoring in order to coordinate their economic policies as foreseen by articles 64–75 of the Treaty. This coordination must ensure compatibility between maintaining decentralised economic policies and the requirements that arise from the joint monetary policy. The WAMU convergence council set up the budgetary convergence criteria in 1993. These criteria serve to strengthen the nominal convergence of the economies; but respecting the criteria does not mean that there is real convergence. So, the question arises as to whether or not one can speak of real convergence within the WAEMU.

What are we talking about?

The idea is to analyse absolute convergence within the WAEMU. Here, the hypothesis is that the only difference between the Union's economies is the initial GDP level. Are the WAEMU countries converging towards their steady state and, if so, at what speed? It is necessary to know the growth dynamics of the Union's economies. The speed of convergence could enable one to have an idea about the time needed for a country to reduce by half the gap separating its current per capita GDP level and that of its long-run equilibrium level.

Considering that the only difference between the countries is the per capita GDP is a strong hypothesis for the Union's countries. In effect, within the Union, we have the Sahelien countries on one hand and on the other the coastal countries excluding Senegal. The latter has a specific status because it is both Sahelien and coastal. In the first group of countries, agriculture is subject to very high climatic variations. This situation compromises rapid economic growth in this sector. In the coastal countries, agriculture is less subject to climatic variations. This leads us to emit the hypothesis of different fixed growth factors.

As there are different countries in the WAEMU, the constancy of the intertemporal utility and production function, which suppose that economic and social structures do not evolve and that the economies are protected from internal and external shocks, is overridden. It seems that the difference in growth rate could be explained by the differences in structural characteristics.

There are disparities in access to education in Africa in general and especially in the WAEMU countries. In addition, whereas the minimum required to promote development and trade is to have a road network density reaching at least 20–25 km of roads for every 100 sq km, the WAEMU has only an average of 4.75 km. This leads to a clear blockage in production and trade, because many zones are not served. Seventy-one percent of this highly unbalanced network is found in the coastal countries that cover only 20% of the community area. The Sahelian countries, which occupy 80% of the space, only have 29% of the network (WAEMU 2003). These realities lead us to raise the question of whether or not the zone will be able to catch up. This study aims to determine the factors that could influence the countries' economic growth towards their long-run equilibrium.

Migrations, be they internal or external, are greatly influenced by the economic development of the Union's states. They can contribute to a truly spatial redistribution of the population by reducing the congestion in overpopulated zones, but they can also bring to the surface or crystallise conflicting relations in the subregion and between certain states if the development gap is left to increase. The difference of development between the states leads to population flows from one country to another.

We will also measure the dispersion in the average of the variance of in per capita GDP in the Union's countries and pinpoint the trend over time. In effect, intertemporal measuring of distribution indices is supposed to explain the effectiveness of harmonisation policies (Mosse 2000). Far from being an academic exercise, the statistical observation of economic convergence is a democratic obligation (art. 109J of the EU treaty). It has therefore become a stake in the quest for economic and monetary union. Finally, the study will seek to understand the impact economic integration has on sigma convergence in the Union countries.

The process of integration undertaken by WAEMU aims to ensure its member states experience sustained economic growth and a balanced joint development of their countries and their populations (WAEMU 2003). This study aims to supply decision-makers with information that could help them formulate policies in view of boosting subregional integration.

Previous studies (Barro 1991; Barro and Sala-I-Martin 1990, 1991) use cross-section comparisons stemming from a panel of countries. Although the main evidence of the principle of convergence comes from cross-section variations between countries, we have chosen an analysis based on time-series data, due to the small size of the sample of WAEMU countries. In addition, Simoes (2000) used cross section, time-series and mixed data to study real convergence within the European Union and reached different results. This explains the use of panel data in our study, because the information they provide seems to be better, in particular for the variables that show a lot of variation over time within a country. The WAEMU, which is the spatial framework of the study, is a space particularly suitable from an empirical point of view (in terms of data comparability) and from a theoretical point of view.

III   Objective of the Study

The main objective of the study is to determine the state of real convergence in the economies of the Union for a chosen period and the factors that could favour the countries' march towards long-run equilibrium. To reach this main objective, the following specific objectives were chosen: (a) analyse absolute convergence of the Union's economies, (b) analyse conditional convergence of the Union's economies and (c) analyse sigma convergence.

IV   Methodology

The Iterative Bayesian Estimation Method

This section sets out to justify the choice of the iterative Bayesian estimation method and to provide a description of the estimation technique.

Justification for the Choice of Method

With panel data, a model that has become linear can be estimated by applying several methods. Let us mention two of them that are considered to be "extremes". Either the data are stacked and one obtains a single estimation for each coefficient for all the countries or one estimates the model separately for each country.

In the first case, the basic hypothesis is that of inter-individual homogeneity and the parameters that are specific to the process of convergence will then be common to all the countries included in the sample. Yet, based on the conclusion of convergence analyses, the hypothesis of inter-individual homogeneity is rejected in the majority of cases (Anna 2003). The reasonable hypothesis for the WAEMU countries is to think that the countries do not have the same speed of convergence. It is therefore not necessary to stack the data. If, however, one proceeds with the estimation of the coefficients specific to each country, their values risk to be excessively dispersed and, furthermore, they could possibly have theoretically unexpected signs. The implicit hypothesis is that the economies considered draw their sources of growth in a completely heterogeneous manner, which is not a reasonable supposition either. The economies that accept to join a Union share the same market, the same road infrastructures and the same trade laws, under the condition that the rules of free circulation of people and goods are respected. We think it is the case in the WAEMU and, as a result, the hypothesis of heterogeneity must be set aside. In other words, separately estimating the coefficients cannot be envisioned either. These two observations lead us to envisage another estimation method. The latter should be a synthesis of the first two. One of the recommended solutions is to try to approach the overall stacked estimation by shrinking the estimators obtained separately for each economy. This explains the use of the Bayesian method in this study. In effect, the problem posed by the first two methods is that they are both based on extreme hypotheses. If the data are stacked, one admits that the coefficients are identical for all the countries. If, on the other hand, one calculates different estimations for each country, you admit that the coefficients differ for each one. According to Anna (2003), the truth is found between these two extremes. The parameters are probably not perfectly identical, but there is a certain similarity among them (Maddala et al. cited by Anna 2003). One way to take this similitude into account is to admit that the parameters come from a joint distribution, from the same expectation and non-null variance-covariance matrix. The authors show that the resulting estimations are a weighted average of the estimation on a stacked sample and separate estimations on time-series proper to each individual. Thus, each individual estimation is "shrunk" to get closer to the overall stacked estimation.

Iterative Bayesian estimators are members of the shrinkage estimator family. Their use is preferred if the model contains dynamic endogenous variables, which is the case with this study. Anna (2003) applied this estimation method to the panel of European Union and Eastern European countries for the period 1987–2001. Canova and Marcet (1995), cited by Coulombe Serge (1997), also used this estimation method to analyse conditional convergence of European regions.

Iterative Bayesian Estimation Technique

Technically, it is the iterative Bayesian procedure that enables the calculation of shrinkage estimators in dynamic models of heterogeneous panels even if the temporal dimension is relatively short, as is the case of our analysis. We will present the procedure step by step below.

The first step consists of calculating the OLS estimators of the ordinate at the origin (constant), the coefficient before $(y_{i,t-1})$ and the coefficients associated with other explanatory variables (if needed[1]) separately for each country:

$$\hat{b}_i = (X'_iX_i)^{-1} (X'_iY_i).$$
$$\scriptstyle [k\times 1] \qquad [k\times k] \qquad [k\times 1]$$

The first iteration is based on the calculation of the simple arithmetical average of the individual estimators:

$$\hat{u} = \frac{1}{N} \sum_{i=1}^{N} \hat{b}i$$
$$\scriptstyle [k\times 1] \qquad [k\times 1]$$

N designates the number of countries. In our case, it equals eight (8).

The estimation of the a priori variance is obtained based on the difference between the coefficients relative to the average:

$$\hat{\sum}_{[k\times k]} = \frac{1}{N-1}_{[k\times k]} \left(R + \sum_{i=1}^{N} (\hat{b}_i - \hat{u})(\hat{b}_i - \hat{u})' \right)$$

R designates a diagonal dimension matrix $[k \times k]$ whose non-null terms take on very small values (0.001 in most cases) (Anna 2003). The R matrix is then added to improve the convergence of the iterative procedure. The estimator of σ_i^2 is a priori calculated from the sum of the squares of the residuals based on the estimation by the ordinary least squares (OLS) method.

$$\hat{\sigma}_i^2 = \frac{1}{T-k} (Y_i - X_i\hat{b}_i)'(Y_i - X_i\hat{b}_i).$$

k designates the number of explanatory variables other than the constant term, and T designates the number of years.

The estimators of the parameters $u, \Sigma, \hat{\sigma}_i^2$ enable the calculation of the shrinkage estimators:

$$b_i^* = \left[\frac{1}{\hat{\sigma}_i^2} X'_iX_i + \hat{\Sigma}^{-1} \right]^{-1} \left[\frac{1}{\hat{\sigma}_i^2} X'_iX_ib_i + \hat{\Sigma}^{-1}\hat{u} \right].$$

The second iteration is based on the estimators b_i. These estimators give:

The average a posteriori $u^* = \frac{1}{N} \sum_{i=1}^{N} b_i^*$ (N designates the number of countries), estimation of the variance a posteriori

---

[1] It is in the analysis of conditional convergence that in addition to the variable $\log(y_{i,t-1})$, there are other explicative variables such as degree of openness and schooling ratio.

$$\sum_{[k \times k]}^{*} = \frac{1}{N-1} \left(R + \sum_{i}^{N} \left(b_i^* - u_i^* \right) \left(b_i^* - u_i^* \right)' \right)$$

and the estimation of $\hat{\sigma}_i^2$ a posteriori

$$\sigma_i^{*2} = \frac{1}{T-k} \left(Y_i - X_i b_i^* \right)' \left(Y_i - X_i b_i^* \right).$$

T designates the number of years and k the number of explanatory variables other than the constant.

These parameters enable one to deduct the distribution a posteriori of the coefficients

$$b_i^{**} = \left[\frac{1}{\sigma_i^{*2}} X'_i X_i + \Sigma^{*-1} \right]^{-1} \left[\frac{1}{\sigma_i^{*2}} X'_i X_i b_i^* + \Sigma^{*-1} u^* \right].$$

The third and following iterations are identical to the second. To stop the procedure, we use the calculation of the standard deviation of shrinkage estimators. As soon as the latter is less than or equal to 0.001, the procedure stops, because we consider that the estimators are sufficiently "shrunk" to the average. The choice of criteria is delicate because it is important for the results in that heterogeneity of the estimators has to be sufficiently reduced but not "erased" by the pending iterations.

The iterative Bayesian estimators will thus be less dispersed and, according to Li et al. (1996), they will have more reasonable values than individual estimators. We propose to use this iterative procedure to estimate the speed of convergence specific to each country in order to be able to analyse and compare them.

V   Results, Discussion and Future Research

Results of the Absolute Convergence Estimation

The results are presented in Tables 6.1 and 6.2, the former containing the parameters and the latter the speeds of absolute convergence.

From Table 6.1, we can deduce the speeds at which the economies converge towards equilibrium. The speed of convergence is obtained by identification. Where b_i is the coefficient of the variable $\ln y_{it-1}$, T the number of years and β_i the speed. We get: $\beta_i = -1/T \ln(1 + b_i)$.

The analysis of absolute convergence shows that there is convergence within the WAEMU. But such convergence is weak taking into account the fact that the speed of convergence is lower than the value that one frequently finds in convergence

Table 6.1 Parameters of the absolute convergence model using the Bayesian method

	Variables	Parameters	Standard deviation
Benin	Constant	1.0135	0.21
	$\ln y_{it-1}$	−0.227	0.025
Burkina	Constant	1.1238	0.042
	$\ln y_{it-1}$	−0.2097	0.048
Côte-d'Ivoire	Constant	1.2566	0.11
	$\ln y_{it-1}$	−0.1886	0.013
Guinea-Bissau	Constant	1.1178	0.049
	$\ln y_{it-1}$	−0.2106	0.05
Mali	Constant	1.1423	0.021
	$\ln y_{it-1}$	−0.2068	0.025
Niger	Constant	1.2570	0.12
	$\ln y_{it-1}$	−0.1890	0.014
Senegal	Constant	1.2264	0.075
	$\ln y_{it-1}$	−0.1935	0.088
Togo	Constant	1.1744	0.0487
	$\ln y_{it-1}$	−0.2018	0.014

Source: Results of the estimations using the Bayesian method

Table 6.2 Speeds of absolute convergence

Country	Benin	Burkina	Côte d'Ivoire	Guinea-Bissau	Mali	Niger	Senegal	Togo
Speed of convergence (%)	1.43	1.30	1.16	1.31	1.287	1.163	1.194	1.25

studies.[2] The speed of absolute convergence in the Union countries is between 1.16 and 1.43%. We infer that the time needed to reduce by half the gap that separates their per capita GDP level from the long-run equilibrium level is between 48.47 and 59.75 years.[3] The countries converge towards their cruising speed in low gear. So, it is necessary to accelerate the countries' movement towards their long-run income level. The analysis of conditional convergence will enable us to identify policies that could accelerate convergence among the Union countries towards their level of long-run equilibrium.

Analysis of Conditional Convergence by the Bayesian Method

Table 6.3 presents the parameters and the speeds obtained. By taking into account the variables of degree of economic openness (0), investment (*I*) and primary school ratio (*P*), it was possible to obtain higher convergence speeds. These higher

---

[2] Convergence literature shows that the majority of studies arrive at values nearing 2%.

[3] One just needs to resolve the equation $\ln(1/2) = \ln e^{-\beta t}$ with t as unknown.

Table 6.3 Parameters and speeds of conditional convergence

Country	Variable	Parameter	Speed of convergence (%)
Benin	Constant	1.67	6.09
	In ln Y_{it-1}	−0.67	
	ln I_{it-1}	0.067	
	ln O_{it-1}	0.149	
	ln P_{it-1}	0.23	
Burkina Faso	Constant	2.786	6,51
	ln y_{it-1}	−0.69	
	ln I_{it-1}	0.062	
	ln O_{it-1}	0.145	
	ln P_{it-1}	0.178	
Côte d'Ivoire	Constant	4.78	7.3
	ln y_{it-1}	−0.73	
	ln I_{it-1}	0.0375	
	ln O_{it-1}	0.137	
	ln P_{it-1}	0.084	
Guinea-Bissau	Constant	5.34	7.5
	ln y_{it-1}	−0.74	
	ln I_{it-1}	0.036	
	ln O_{it-1}	0.135	
	ln P_{it-1}	0.058	
Mali	Constant	3.99	6.98
	ln y_{it-1}	−0.72	
	ln I_{it-1}	0.046	
	ln O_{it-1}	0.14	
	ln P_{it-1}	0.122	
Niger	Constant	5.1	7.47
	ln y_{it-1}	−0.739	
	ln I_{it-1}	0.034	
	ln O_{it-1}	0.136	
	ln P_{it-1}	0.069	
Senegal	Constant	4.69	7.28
	ln y_{it-1}	−0.731	
	ln I_{it-1}	0.039	
	ln O_{it-1}	0.137	
	ln P_{it-1}	0.089	
Togo	Constant	5.47	7.6
	ln y_{it-1}	−0.747	
	ln I_{it-1}	0.031	
	ln O_{it-1}	0.134	
	ln P_{it-1}	0.052	

Source: Results of estimations use Bayesian method

convergence speeds consequently reduce the time needed to reduce by half the gap that separates the per capita GDP from the steady state. This time it falls between 9.11 and 11.55 years.

What about the connection between convergence and poverty reduction?

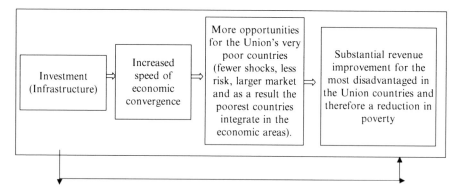

A direct connection can be established between investment and poverty reduction. By supposing that investments create new jobs and that the latter are occupied by the poorest members of the population that had been excluded from the labour market, one can deduce that investments reduce poverty.

The second link between investment (in infrastructure) and poverty reduction necessarily passes through economic convergence. It is therefore a question of a link between convergence and poverty reduction. The study establishes that the investments have a positive impact on economic convergence. By observing attentively the investment variable, one realises that it contains expenditure on infrastructure that supports production (roads, bridges, etc.). The infrastructure explains very broadly the regional differences in poverty within not only the countries but also within the union. For Willoughby (2003), its impact on disadvantaged populations can be understood in three ways:

- On one hand, the infrastructure extends local and national markets by integrating them into larger markets, broadening the spectrum of economic opportunities that the poor members of the population can seize. As a result, it reduces the costs of transactions, which enables markets to function more efficiently. In other words, the author means simply that completing infrastructure will promote convergence (broadening local and national markets) that, in turn, will increase the economic opportunities, especially for the poor. It is then these opportunities that will allow them to escape from poverty.
- On the other hand, setting up infrastructure and reliable basic services (transport, healthcare, energy, irrigation, etc.) reduces the vulnerability of populations to shocks and crises. It has been shown that the latter constitute a major obstacle to economic development. Thus, reducing these risks could unlock the potential of entire regions. These shocks and crises are minimised in the presence of economic convergence.
- Finally, infrastructure significantly improves agricultural productivity and, as a result, household income, nutrition, health, education and also their use of family

planning. Each dimension of human development is directly or indirectly concerned by one or several types of infrastructure and therefore potentially favoured by this kind of investment.

In addition to absolute and conditional convergence, the analysis of sigma convergence could provide significant added value to this investigation.

Analysis of Sigma Convergence

The most intuitive convergence concept is undoubtedly sigma convergence. This is simply the reduction over time of the dispersion of per capita GDP (Gaulier and Frédéric 2001). For there to be sigma convergence, one first needs the presence of absolute convergence. The analysis of absolute convergence among the Union countries led to the conclusion that there was absolute convergence. This raised the question of the existence of sigma convergence in the Union. This analysis will enable a better understanding of the impact of economic integration on sigma convergence.

After calculating the variance and the variance ratio, the latter will be represented graphically:

$$\text{Or,} \quad \sigma_t^2 \frac{1}{n} \sum_{i=1}^{8} (y_{it} - \bar{y}_t)^2 \quad \text{with} \quad \bar{y}_t = \frac{1}{n} \sum_{i=1}^{8} y_{it}.$$

n designates the number of countries. Here, $n = 8$; y_{it} designates the real per capita gross domestic product of the country I at the period t.

To observe the evolution of the disparities, we have divided the variance of each year by the variance of 1994. The year 1994 was chosen because it marks the beginning of economic integration between Union countries. The results are presented in Fig. 6.1. A close look at the figure shows a decrease in the variance ratio until 1994. After this date, this ratio tended to increase until 1999. After that date, a new trend downwards was observed until 2006.

When we observe the curve represented by the evolution of σ_t^2/σ_0^2, we can isolate three phases:

- The first phase corresponds to the 1980–1994 period. During this period, the gaps in relation to the Union average decreased. One can talk about sigma convergence for this period. It is important to note that this period is before economic integration. Even if one notes the existence of sigma convergence, one should remember that this period, unlike the others, was also characterised by large variations in per capita GDP in the Union.
- The second phase corresponds to the period 1994–1999. This period shows that the gaps between countries tended to increase. This period corresponds to the period that followed economic integration. However, it is a period of weak variation in per capita GDP within the Union. We can therefore say that,

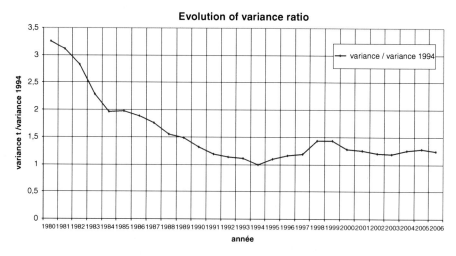

Fig. 6.1 Evolution of the variance ratio (Source: Established by the authors using WBI data, 2008)

during this period, economic integration did not promote sigma convergence. The countries did not converge towards the Union average during the 1994–1999 period. A change of policy does not always go immediately where it hopes to go. One must often wait for a long time in order to experience the effects of a policy.

• The third phase corresponds to the 1999–2008 period. Overall, the curve tended to decrease, expressing the presence of a sigma convergence during the period. How can this be explained? One could say that integration began to have an effect. Another explanation of the observation could be found in the crisis that struck Côte d'Ivoire starting in 1999, which meant that the country recorded very weak and even negative growth.

How can we explain the presence of β-convergence and the absence of sigma convergence for the 1994–1999 period? We could explain this situation by the existence within the Union of asymmetrical regional shocks. If large-scale asymmetrical regional shocks take place, distribution of per capita GDP could not decrease despite the presence of β-convergence (Gaulier and Frédéric 2001). Strong β-convergence does not impede an increase in the variance ratio: the countries change their ranking during the 1994–1999 period without a reduction in the dispersion. These results are similar to those found by Gaulier and Frédéric (2001) in their study of the regions of France. Before 1980, there was sigma convergence in the regions' productivity and, after this date, the tendency was to diverge. There is reason to strengthen the convergence criteria in order to promote steady growth among Union countries.

Future research could use variables related to institutions such as democracy, protection of property rights, good governance, etc. More and more, the no less important effect of these variables has been recognised on growth and poverty reduction. A future study could broaden the sample to include ECOWAS countries that are not members of the WAEMU.

VI   Policy Implications and Recommendations

The rate of primary schooling has a positive impact on the growth of countries towards their steady state of per capita GDP. That means that in order to attain the long-run level of production per inhabitant, the WAEMU countries should institute a policy of sustained growth that consists of improving human capital, that is, developing worker skills. Thus, a policy supporting education and vocational training (school infrastructure, hiring and training teachers) could be envisioned. The countries should boost active measures in favour of youth insertion, and young people represent a major portion of the population. On the scale of the Union, a workforce-upgrading policy could be envisioned by creating joint training units. This policy supporting education should, above all, privilege the countries that have a low schooling rate, to enable them to develop rapidly and catch up with the others. Generally, the low rates of schooling are in part linked to a lack of education infrastructure. Five of the six French-speaking African countries in which the rate of schooling is the lowest in West Africa are members of the WAEMU: Burkina Faso, Guinea-Bissau, Mali, Niger and Senegal.[4] It is, therefore, in these countries that the education efforts should be focussed. Higher education should not be forgotten either. Constant improvement in productivity comes through the acquisition of knowledge. Secondary and higher education could represent a solution.

The economic growth of the countries towards their steady state can be explained by economic openness. The uneven distribution of road infrastructure within the community could be a handicap to growth, particularly in the disadvantaged countries, but also for the others to the extent that the latter cannot penetrate the markets of the countries that are not served by the infrastructure. One cannot assimilate economic openness with a policy of free trade. As Rodriguez and Dani (1999) and Siroen (1996)[5] highlighted, the states determine their trade policy but not their degree of openness, which also depends on the structural characteristics of the economies (size, development, resources, geography, etc.). The link between trade and growth that has been shown (convergence here) only has clear implications in terms of economic policy if the states are able to act significantly on their international insertion.

The coefficient of the investment rate is positive. This means that, in accordance with the growth theory, investment favours countries' growth towards their long-term equilibrium level. The states should undertake a policy to develop public infrastructure (roads, bridges, urban networks), because investment and public services contribute to growth. At the scale of the Union, balanced territorial development should be envisioned. The key property of the public infrastructures is that each user fully benefits from their effects while only paying a fraction of their cost. Foreign direct investments (FDI) should be encouraged within the

---

[4] UNESO Africa Department (2001).

[5] Cited by Gaulier and Frédéric (2001).

Union. That could be done by adopting flexible and simple laws code within the Union. These should encourage foreign investors through an attractive fiscal policy. The Union should work to create a good climate for business. Foreign investors are very adverse to risk. Political instability and weak laws linked to property rights do not encourage foreign investors.

The coefficient of the degree of openness variable is positive. It is clear that the states cannot act on their insertion. It is for the WAEMU Commission to improve the economic openness of member countries by setting up communication infrastructures (roads, bridges, airports), particularly in the countries where they are nearly inexistent.

The following economic policy recommendations have been formulated:

The development of an educational system to stimulate sustained growth within the Union: measures that will improve the educational system could have a non-negligible impact on the reduction of per capita GDP disparities, and all the more so if the investments in education are directed towards the countries with very low per capita GDP. These are the countries that generally have the lowest schooling rates. A lack of qualified personnel is clearly an obstacle to modernisation of the Union's economies and to the reduction of inequalities.

The development of infrastructures to promote trade that have a positive impact on convergence: from this perspective, and particularly in relation to the openness policy, investment in both physical and social infrastructure seems to us to be necessary to facilitate communication and dissemination of technical progress between countries, notably the interland countries with the rest of the Union. Considering the constraints that insufficient infrastructure places on trade of goods and capital, improving its quality and extending it seems to be necessary to benefit from the efficiency gains that come from openness.

Taking indicators that favour real convergence into account in the convergence criteria. The Union should make sure the countries respect not only the existing criteria but also those that could be added.

VII General Conclusions

Growth has always preoccupied economists. The study of real convergence within the West African Economic and Monetary Union has led us to reflect on the following questions:

- What is the state of real convergence of the gross domestic product within the Union? In other words, at what speed are the countries converging towards their steady state?
- What are the factors that could influence the countries' movement towards their long-run equilibrium level?
- What is the impact of economic integration on the Union's sigma convergence?

- The conclusions we reached were the following:
- Weak absolute convergence exists within the WAEMU. The speed of convergence estimated for each country is lower than 1.5%, and the time needed for a country to reduce by half the gap that separates its current per capita GDP level from that of its steady state is around 50 years. This indicates that the countries are very far from their steady state.
- The analysis of sigma convergence shows that disparities in terms of per capita GDP tended to decrease for the period 1982–1994. Starting in 1994, one sees an increase in dispersion that continues until 1999. Starting in 1999, one notes a trend towards smaller deviations. The absence of sigma convergence during the 1994–1999 period does not in any way bring into question the positive impact of integration on sigma convergence. In effect, a policy cannot produce immediate effects. Generally, one has to wait 2–3 years after it has been set up to hope to experience the effects. That could be the case of this economic integration. Countries often take time to adapt and respect the new rules or measures, and as a result, the date the treaty comes to effect does not coincide with the application of practical measures.
- The degree of economic openness, the rate of investment and the primary schooling rate proved to have a significant positive impact on the countries' march towards their level of long-run equilibrium. Thus, policies favouring education, trade and investment could accelerate growth in Union countries.

The heterogeneity of data sources constitutes a limitation of this study. In addition, no data was available for Guinea-Bissau for the entire study period and had to be excluded from the analysis of absolute and conditional convergence. Other variables that are equally important were not integrated into the analysis. These are variables that measure the quality of institutions such as democracy, good governance, protection of property rights, etc. Future research could seek to take these aspects into account.

Appendices

Appendix 1: Absolute convergence

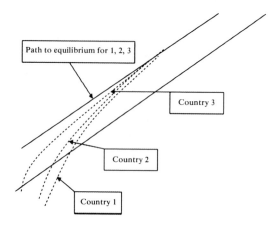

Source: Bensidoun and Laurence Boone (1998)

Appendix 2: Sigma convergence

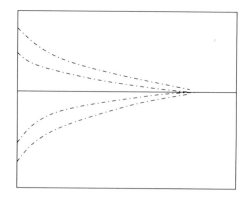

Source: Bensidoun and Laurence Boone (1998)

Appendix 3: Convergence conditionnelle

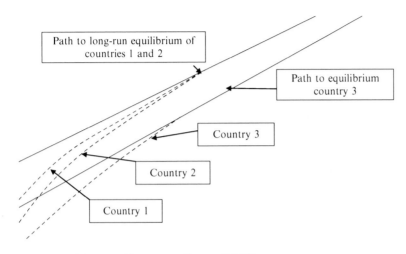

Source: Bensidoun and Laurence Boone (1998)

References

Anna, Tikhonenko (2003), Une étude de convergence appliquée au panel des pays de l'UE et des pays de l'Europe de l'Est candidats à l'adhésion. Université de Nice Sophia-Antipolis ATER CEMAFI

Barnier, Michel (2001), Deuxième rapport sur la cohésion économique et sociale.

Barro, R. J. (1991),'Economic growth in a cross-section of countries', *Quarterly Journal of Economics, vol. 106, 2: 407–443.*

Barro, R.J. and X. Sala-I-Martin (1990), 'Economic Growth and convergence across the United States', *Working Papers, no. 3419, National Bureau of Economic Research, may*

Barro, R.J. and X. Sala-I-Martin (1991), 'Convergence across states and regions' *Brooking Papers on Economic Activity no. 1:107–182*

Bensidoun, Isabelle and Laurence Boone (1998) *L'économie mondiale.* P. 94–103. Edition La Découverte, collection Repère, Paris.

Canova, Fabio and Marcet, Albert (1995), 'The Poor Stay Poor: Non-convergence across countries and regions', *CEPR Discussion Paper No 1265.*

Coulombe, Serge (1997), 'Les disparités régionales au Canada: diagnostics, tendances et leçons pour la politique économique', *Document de travail no. 18, Université d'Ottawa.*

Ekomie, Jean Jacques (1999), 'La Convergence des économies d'Afrique Centrale', *Revue d'Economie LEA Volume 1 Numéro 2.*

Gaulier, G. and Frédéric Carluer (2001), 'Productivité des régions françaises pour moyenne période : Une convergence de façade', *Revue économique. Volume 52, Numéro 1 janvier 2001:147–166.*

Li H., G.S. Maddala and R.P. Trost (1996), 'Estimation des élasticités de court et de long termes de la demande d'électricité sur données de panel à partir d'estimateurs à rétrécissement', *Economie et Prévision, no. 126(5) :127–137.*

Mosse, Philippe (2000), 'Les théories de la convergence appliquées à l'analyse économique des réformes des systèmes hospitaliers', Communication présentée au Congrès 2000 de l'Association française de Science Economique.

Ouedraogo, Tambila (1999), 'La convergence des politiques macroéconomiques au sein de la zone UEMOA'. Mémoire, UFR/SEG, Université de Ouagadougou,

Rodriguez, Francisco, and Dani Rodrik (1999), Trade Policy and Economic Growth: A Skeptic's Guide to cross-National Literature,' NBER Working Paper 7081

Simoes, Marta Cristina (2000), La convergence réelle Selon la Théorie de la Convergence : Quelles explications pour l'Union Européenne ? *Estudo Do Gemf* (2) : 1–38

Siroen, Jean-Marc (1996), 'L'intégration entre pays inégalement développés dans la régionalisation de l'économie mondiale : Une analyse comparative' rapport de synthèse final, commissariat général du plan.

UNPD (2002), Rapport mondial sur le développement humain 2002. Paris, De Boeck et Larcier

WAEMU (2003), Document-cadre d'orientations générales de la politique d'aménagement du territoire.

Willoughby, Christopher (2003), *Infrastructure and Pro-Poor Growth: Implications of Recent Research*, United Kingdom Department for International Development.

Yerbanga, Antoine (2004), '*La convergence réelle des économies de l'UEMOA*', Mémoire de DEA/PTCI. Université de Ouagadougou.

Chapter 7
The Effects of Credit Constraints on Economic Convergence: The Case of the WAEMU Countries

Abdoulaye Diagne and Abdou-Aziz Niang

Abstract This study sets out to analyse the effects of a weak financial system on WAEMU country convergence to the global frontier growth rate. To do so, we have used a Schumpeterian growth model with technology transfer that was initially developed by Aghion et al. (Q J Econ 120:173–222, 2005). This brought to light the fact that credit is a constraint that prevents these countries from fully benefiting from technology transfer and pushes them farther away from the growth frontier by considerably slowing their speeds of convergence. Our results have also demonstrated that there is a critical level of private credit and that the WAEMU countries, which record a level of credit lower than this threshold, tend to diverge.

I Introduction

In the debate around economic convergence, the literature has focused on a certain number of aspects in order to explain the gap between per capita GDP levels in poor countries and those in rich countries. As highlighted by Easterly and Levine (2001), technology seems to be the most plausible explanation. According to these authors, 60% of the variations in per capita GDP growth rates can be explained by the difference in the growth of productivity. The farther behind a country is from the leading country in terms of technology, the easier it is for that country to progress by emulating the innovator countries. This should contribute to reducing or at least stabilising the gap between the countries. However, although it is becoming a more or less standard approach for growth models to take technology into account, the

A. Diagne (✉)
Consortium for Economic and Social Research (CRES), and Cheikh Anta Diop University (UCAD) Dakar, Sénégal
e-mail: cres@ucad.sn

A.-A. Niang
Department of Economics, University of Bourgogne, Dijon, France

E.T. Ayuk and S.T. Kaboré (eds.), *Wealth Through Integration*, Insight and Innovation in International Development 4, DOI 10.1007/978-1-4614-4415-2_7,
© International Development Research Centre 2013

manner of introducing technology transfer and the differences in technological levels into multi-country models differs greatly.

For this study, we use the Schumpeterian growth model with technology transfer that was developed by Aghion et al. (2005). This model puts the emphasis on the fact that a lack of access to credit constitutes a constraint that keeps poor countries from fully benefiting from technology transfer and distances them from the frontier growth rate. The countries that have a level of financial development that is higher than a certain threshold should converge in the long run to the same frontier growth. And those that have financial development that is below this critical threshold in the long run record a growth rate that is below the frontier growth rate. Researchers advocate three main reasons. The first is that adopting technology that was developed elsewhere involves major financial means enabling agents to readapt it to the country's specific environment and to implement it. Thus, as underlined by Aghion et al. (2005), even if this expenditure does not constitute investment in research and development (R&D) in the classical meaning of the term, it plays a similar role to the extent that it enables the acquisition of new technological possibilities. The second reason is that the farther away the technological frontier, the more difficult it is to adapt the technology to the local context. Finally, the third cause is linked to the fact that innovators can defraud their creditors by dissimulating positive results of their innovation projects at a cost that positively depends on the level of financial development. And as a result, the credit multiplier is lower for poor countries with a low level of financial development.

In recent years, a certain amount of research has focused on the role financial development plays in economic growth. However, the majority of the theories that have been proposed emphasise the role that financial development plays in the process of technology transfer and as a result, they do not explain why, despite technological diffusion, economies do not manage to reach parallel long-run growth paths. The authors that have looked into the link between financial development and economic convergence include King and Levine (1993), Calderon and Liu (2003), Blackburn and Hung (1998), Kahn (2001), Morales (2003), Beck and Levine (2004), Levine (2005), Djankov et al. (2007), Rousseau and Wachtel (1998), and Roubini and Sala-i-Martin (1992).

With this study, we will attempt to show that a less-developed financial system constitutes a major handicap that constrains the WAEMU countries' process of convergence to a global growth frontier. Given the economic history between France and the WAEMU countries, we will consider, on one hand, the case in which France is the leading country whose economic growth rate represents the growth frontier for WAEMU members, and on the other hand, we will analyse the case of the United States as the "frontier country".

The first part of this work will focus on presenting the issue, the justification for the study and its objectives. Then, we will present the Schumpeterian growth model and the econometric methodology based on the GMM system approach in a dynamic panel that was developed by Blundell and Bond (1998). And finally, we will conduct an empirical analysis using a sample made up of the eight WAEMU countries for the period 1984–2004.

II   Problem Statement and Justification

In recent years, the debate about the analysis of economic convergence has experienced unprecedented growth, both in the high number of theoretical and empiric analyses and in practical implications in terms of economic policy decisions. With the West African Economic and Monetary Union being an economic integration model in Africa, it is important to understand what factors influence member countries growth and economic convergence. Supporting economic growth has often been one of the major concerns of the authorities in the member countries and, faced with low internal resources, external aid has been considered a prime recourse. But the weight of external debt has ended up creating serious macroeconomic imbalances. In recent years, attention has focussed on internal development strategies, notably through the development of access to credit. A large number of initiatives have been undertaken in this direction by trying to raise the level of financial intermediation, in the hope of supporting economic growth. The theory shows that financial intermediaries reduce the search costs for potential investment opportunities, by enabling risk management, mobilisation of savings, and facilitating trade. As Levine et al. (2000) highlighted, by supplying economic services, financial intermediaries influence savings and allocation decisions and as a result modify the long-run growth rate.

A huge amount of empirical literature has looked into the link between economic convergence and financial development, as well as between financial development and growth in productivity. Generally speaking, this research concludes in favour of a significant link more or less sensitive to the variable used to capture the level of financial intermediation. By considering interest rates as an indicator, Mattesini (1996) underlines a negative relationship between real interest rates and economic growth. On the other hand, Arestis et al. (2001) bring to light the positive role that banks play in stimulating growth.

These authors also highlight that this can be assimilated with the influence stock markets have on the evolution of the growth rate. As for Demetriades and Hussein (1996), they detect a bidirectional relationship between financial development and growth. Fisman and Love (2004) demonstrate that in the short term, financial development benefits high growth-potential firms, while in the long term, it allows for a better allocation of resources towards sectors looking for external financing. One can also note that the conclusions of the empirical analyses in these areas are very diverse. Furthermore, there is a lot of confusion concerning the various transmission channels that link finance to economic growth. In general, studies lean towards liberalising financial flows when they study this link. In effect, there is a relative controversy over the question of knowing if liberalising the capital account produces important effects on long-term growth. Obstfeld (1994) supports that this favours the reallocation of resources from countries with abundant capital towards those where it is less abundant. In addition, free flows of capital boost growth in productivity due to a greater international diversification of risks.

According to Aghion et al. (2005), the level of private credit constitutes the most relevant indicator to measure the level of financial development, because it proves to be more than a simple measure of the size of the financial sector. Furthermore, as we are dealing with African countries, empirical studies on the link between convergence and financial development show a mixed impact on the latter. This effect varies with the sample that is considered, more precisely depending on the economic and financial history of the group of countries under study. Dufrénot et al. (2007) explain that this is due in part to the use of poorly adapted econometric methodology. The authors use as a basis the hypothesis that there are various channels by which financial development affects economic growth. These channels include the effect of liquidity, the role of financial intermediaries and the reduction of information costs. Thus, in the analysis of the impact of financial intermediation on the real sector, it is important to consider the possibility that the finance-growth link acts differently depending on the country. As a result, one must take these specific characteristics into account in the use of an adapted econometric approach.

Thus, the interest of this study is to take into consideration the specific nature of the WAEMU regarding the impact the level of access to credit has on economic convergence. One should note that what is at stake is not only the theory, because it is important to be able to verify that financial development can impact growth and convergence in member countries, but the economic policy stakes are also considerable. What is the impact of credit constraints on the convergence of WAEMU countries, and is there a critical level of financial development for these countries?

III Study Objectives

This study is part of the empirical verification of the hypothesis of economic convergence for WAEMU countries. It focuses on one of the points targeted by economic integration policies at the level of the WAEMU space: financial development. The idea is to verify if a weak financial system influences growth and economic convergence of these countries. Previous research (Levine and Zervos 1998; Rousseau and Wachtel 1998) demonstrated that the level of financial development constitutes a good indicator to predict economic growth. However, as we have just highlighted in the previous section, financial development indicators considered by previous research differ between authors. In referring to the Schumpeterian growth model with technology transfer developed by Aghion et al. (2005), we will specifically attempt to verify if a credit constraint can impede the process of convergence in Union countries.

Methodologically speaking, we use the generalised method of moments (GMM) approach in dynamic panel in order to control the potential biases linked to simultaneity, to omitted variables and to unobserved specific effects. In addition, the combination of the inter-individual dimension with the temporal dimension provides additional information about the variation of the growth rate and its determinants over time, and making it possible to obtain more precise estimations.

As a result, the study will focus on three specific objectives: (1) presenting the theory on the link between credit constraint and economic convergence, (2) presenting the econometric methodology used and its relevance to the WAEMU countries and (3) implementing these econometric tools in order to empirically analyse the finance-convergence link for WAEMU countries over the 1984–2004 period.

IV Methodology

The Model

We use a Schumpeterian growth model developed by Aghion et al. (2005). We consider that there is a group of n countries among which the trade of goods and factors is insignificant, yet there exists a high level of technology transfer among them. Thus, each country has the possibility of using any idea discovered elsewhere. We also suppose that in each country, the individuals live between two periods and only have two work units consecrated essentially to services and acquired exclusively during the first period. The utility function of each individual living in a given country is in the form $U = c_1 + \varphi c_2$ where $0 \prec \varphi \prec 1$. Considering that the population of each country is equal to the unit and that the work produces a "general" multifunctional good and a continuum of specialised intermediary goods, the production function for the general sector is

$$Z_t = \int_0^1 (A_t(i))^{1-\beta}(Z_t(i))^\beta di, \quad 0 \prec \beta \prec 1 \tag{7.1}$$

where $Z_t(i)$ is the input of the last version of the intermediary good i. β and $A_t(i)$ correspond respectively to elasticity and the productivity parameter, which are connected to it. The general good is used for consumption, as an input to R&D and also as input to production of intermediary goods.

For each given sector, the profit of a successful innovator will be equal to $\pi_t(i)$, while a failed innovator will have a profit that equals zero for the following period. Within the general sector, the added value corresponds to salaried income, while the added value in the intermediary sectors corresponds to profit. As for per capita GDP, it is equal to the sum of the added values in all the sectors.

$$Y_t = w_t + \mu_t \pi_t \tag{7.2}$$

where w_t is the salary rate that is equal to the marginal product of labour serving to produce the general good in a perfectly competitive framework and μ_t the probability of success. Thus, K_{t-1} is the quantity of the general good that has to be invested. At equilibrium, in each sector, the quantity of investment in R&D required to innovate is determined by the cost function

$$K_{t-1} = \tilde{k}(\mu_t)\bar{A}_t \tag{7.3}$$

where $\tilde{k}$ is the R&D-to-technology investment and $\bar{A}_t$ the global technology frontier that increases at a constant speed $g \succ 0$. One can note that the farther the frontier, the harder it is to innovate. For each sector subject to a credit constraint, the net expected benefit will be maximised based on μ_t and can be written

$$\varphi\mu_t\pi\bar{A}_t - \tilde{k}(\mu_t)\bar{A}_t \tag{7.4}$$

So, the behaviour of agents varies depending on whether or not there are credit constraints.

In the Case of Unlimited Access to Financing

Aghion et al. (2005) show that in this case, all the economies should converge to the same rate of growth. The level of the economies' growth path should be different, due to the specific nature of each economy, but their long-term growth rates will be equal. In effect, supposing that each innovator can have access to financing in an unlimited manner at a rate $r = \varphi^{-1} - 1$ that he commits to reimbursing even if the project fails, one can choose μ_t in order to maximise (7.4) without constraints. The per capita GDP at equilibrium will increase at the same rate g as the technological frontier $\bar{A}_t$.

In the Presence of Credit Constraints

Now let us suppose that the credit markets are imperfect and that each entrepreneur at the end of the period t has access to a salaried income w_t and to invest the quantity k_t in an R&D project, he has to borrow $k_t - w_t$. Let us suppose that he pays a cost of ck_t, he could defraud his creditors in the case of the project being successful. There is a credit constraint if the optimal level of non-constrained credit is strictly higher than the innovators' capacity for innovation.

Aghion et al. (2005) consider that a very developed financial system protects creditors by rendering it more difficult to use fraudulent practices that consist of masking the project's success with the goal of not reimbursing the financing. Thus, one can reasonably measure the financial development of the cost parameter c. In such a case, credit constraints are less persistent if the cost parameter is high, that is, if the development of the financial system has reached a level that is high enough to induce high costs for those who fraud. In addition, Aghion et al. (2005) show that the farther away a country is from the technology frontier, the more its firms are likely to have credit constraints.

Ultimately, the major implication of this theory is that the probability that a country converges to the frontier growth rate increases with its level of financial development. In addition, financial development will have a positive or null effect on the per capita GDP of each of the converging countries (in growth rate) if the coefficient is higher than or equal to zero. On the other hand, if the coefficient is negative, financial development will have a negative effect on the countries that are closer to the leader in terms of per capita GDP.

Econometric Approach

Convergence Equation

Using a cross-sectional approach, Aghion et al. (2005) propose a standard convergence equation to which a term is added for the interaction between the initial per capita GDP and the level of financial intermediation

$$g_i - g_1 = \phi_0 + \phi_f F_i + \phi_y(y_i - y_1) + \phi_{int} F_i(y_i - y_1) + \phi_x X_i + \varepsilon_i \qquad (7.5)$$

where g is the average per capita GDP growth rate, F private credit, y the level of per capita GDP in logarithm, X a collection of control variables, and ε_i is the error term. Another difference with the standard models is the fact that the per capita GDP logarithm is taken relative to the leading country, which explains the presence of the variables g_i and y_i that refer to the leading country. We use a panel data approach to estimate this convergence equation for the WAEMU countries. And in order to add a temporal dimension, we have considered the period 1984–2004, divided into 4-year sub-periods in such a way as to have five temporal observations: 1984–1988, 1988–1992. . ., 2000–2004. As we are using per capita GDP, the five observations correspond to 1988, 1992, 1996, 2000 and 2004. So if, for example, $t = 2{,}004$, $t\text{-}1 = 2{,}000$. For private credit and the other variables, the observations at instant t correspond to the averages between t and t-1. In this way, the equation can be written

$$\begin{aligned} g_{it} - g_{1t} = \phi_0 + \phi_f F_{it} + \phi_y(y_{i,t-1} - y_{1,t-1}) + \phi_{int} F_{it}(y_{i,t-1} - y_{1,t-1}) \\ + \phi_x X_{it} + \varepsilon_{it} \end{aligned} \qquad (7.6)$$

After development, expression (7.6) can be reformulated as follows:

$$\begin{aligned} y_{it} - y_{1,t} = \phi_0 + \phi_f F_{it} + \gamma(y_{i,t-1} - y_{1,t-1}) + \phi_{int} F_{it}(y_{i,t-1} - y_{1,t-1}) \\ + \phi_x X_{it} + \varepsilon_{it} \end{aligned} \qquad (7.7)$$

where $\gamma = 1 + \phi_y$.

The steady state levels[5] that corresponds to zero growth is

$$\hat{y}_{i,t-1}^* = -\frac{\phi_0 + \phi_f F_{it} + \phi_x X_{it} + \varepsilon_{it}}{\phi_y + \phi_{int} F_{it}} \qquad (7.8)$$

With λ_i the convergence parameter of the economy i, it will depend on the level of financial development and at the period t, this convergence parameter is given by the following relation

$$\lambda_i = \phi_y + \phi_{int} F_{it} \qquad (7.9)$$

If one considers the entire study period, one can define the convergence parameter for each economy in the following way:

$$\bar{\lambda}_i = \phi_y + \phi_{int} \bar{F}_{it} \qquad (7.10)$$

λ enables one to verify if the growth rate converges to a growth rate that corresponds to that of the leading country. In this case, it takes a negative value. So, the development of the financial sector of a country can make it possible to increase its probability of converging if and only if $\phi_{int} \prec 0$. Thus, it is possible to define convergence clubs given that one country could converge towards the frontier growth rate if its level of private credit exceeds the critical value $F^c = -\phi_v/\phi_{int}$. From (7.8), the result is that the long-term effect of financial development on relative production is

$$\frac{\partial \hat{y}_{i,t-1}^*}{\partial F_{it}} = \frac{\phi_f + \phi_{int} \hat{y}_{i,t-1}^*}{-(\phi_y + \phi_{int} F_{it})} \qquad (7.11)$$

Besides, if $\lambda \succ 0$, this implies that a country below its steady state will experience a level of economic growth that tends to distance it from that of the leading country.

Estimation Using Dynamic Panel Generalised Moments

The use of panel data as part of the study of the impact of financial development on economic convergence in the WAEMU zone offers the advantage of taking into account both interstate and the time-related variability, which are, in general very strong in these countries. This can manifest itself econometrically by the existence of specific individual effects that are not treated in a cross-sectional regression where these phenomena are incorporated into the error term. This is exactly what raises the bias constraint that we are attempting to remove by the use of panel data econometrics.

---

[5] «$\hat{y}_{i,t-1} = y_{i,t-1} - y_{1,t-1}$. It is noted at a stationary state as $\hat{y}_{i,t-1}^*$.»

To do so, the generalised method of moments (GMM) will be implemented as a result of the dynamic aspect of our theory, which could leave room for a possible problem of endogeneity. This type of bias can be interpreted as the part of innovation in the error, both on growth and on finance. This could, in turn, lead to endogeneity of the interaction term. By using the GMM method developed by Arellano and Bond (1991) and Arellano and Bover (1995), we can at least control part of this endogeneity by using instruments relative to the lagged variable.

Let us note, however, that even if the differentiated form presents a certain advantage, using the GMM method under this form could, nevertheless, give rise to problems. And in this case, the effectiveness of GMM estimators depends on the validity of the instruments. Arellano and Bover (1995) show, in effect, that in a dynamic panel, the lagged variables often constitute weak instruments for the differentiated form. And as a result, this could lead to biased coefficients. Thus, following Blundell and Bond (1998), we are using a system that combines the difference equation and the level equation in order to obtain a better estimator

$$\begin{cases} y^r_{it} = \gamma\, y^r_{i,t-1} + \phi_f\, F_{it} + \phi_{int}\, W_{it} + \phi_x X_{it} + \upsilon_i + \xi_{it} \\ y^r_{it} - \gamma\, y^r_{i,t-1} = \gamma\left(y^r_{i,t-1} - y^r_{i,t-2}\right)\phi_f(F_{it} - F_{i,t-1}) \\ \qquad\qquad + \phi_{int}\left(W_{it} - W_{i,t-1}\right) + \phi_x\left(X_{it} - X_{i,t-1}\right) + \left(\xi_{it} - \xi_{i,t-1}\right) \end{cases} \qquad (7.12)$$

where $y^r_{it} = y_{it} - y_{1t}$ et $W_{it} = F_{it}\, y^r_{i,t-1}$. We will also implement the Sargan test to ensure the validity of the instruments. This is a test that follows a law of χ^2 and under the null hypothesis, the validity of the instruments is accepted.

V   Empirical Results

We have estimated the dynamic system (7.12) by considering, on one hand, the United States as the leading country, and on the other, considering France as the leading country. Based on a worldwide sample covering 71 countries, Aghion et al. (2005) carry out a cross-sectional regression of Eq. (7.5) with the United States as the "frontier country" that determined the rhythm of innovations. Taking France into account in our analysis can be explained by the existence of strong political, economic and, notably, financial cooperation between this country and the WAEMU countries. This means that these countries are more likely to record a growth rate that converges to the frontier growth represented by France than to the one represented by the United States.

The Data

As highlighted in the presentation, the level of financial development is theoretically measured by the cost necessary to defraud the financial system. However, because this cost is not directly measurable, we follow Aghion et al. (2005) and use the level of private credit. This variable is obtained from IMF statistics and corresponds to the credit granted to the private sector relative to the GDP. It excludes credit granted to the public sector and that granted by the central banks and the development banks. One should note that this source only contains values from the beginning and end of the period, so following Levine et al. (2000), we have calculated private credit in the following way:

$$\text{CREDIT} \equiv \frac{\frac{1}{2}\left(\frac{F_t}{P_t^e} + \frac{F_{t-1}}{P_{t-1}^e}\right)}{\frac{Y_t}{P_t^a}} \tag{7.13}$$

where F is the credit granted by the deposit banks and other private sector financial institutions, Y is the GDP. The consumer price indices P^e and P^a correspond respectively to the end-of-period value and the average for the entire period. The interaction term noted as INTER will thus be equal to the product of the CREDIT variable and the logarithm of the initial level of the relative per capita GDP. Next to this interaction term, we will introduce two other control variables into our convergence equation, which are consumption over GDP noted as CONS, and inflation INFL, measured by the average growth rate of the consumer price index. The per capita GDP and the CONS variable come from the Penn World, Table 6.2. while INFL comes from IMF statistics. See Table 7.1 for descriptive statistics.

Convergence to American Frontier Growth

The results of the dynamic system estimation are presented in Table 7.2. These results confirm the theory when we use the United States as a lead country. The interaction term records a negative and significant effect at the 5% threshold, which the implicit effect ϕ_y of the initial per capita GDP on growth is positively significant with a value of 0.2698. Table 7.2 also provides results of the Sargan test with, as a null hypothesis, an absence of correlation between the instruments and the errors. With a marginal probability of $p = 0.6173$, the null hypothesis is easily accepted.

The fact that ϕ_y is positive implies that there is at least one WAEMU member country whose rate of economic growth does not converge to that of the United States. Furthermore, one also notes that at equilibrium, the credit variable has a negative impact on GDP. Thus, at equilibrium, the WAEMU countries that record a relatively high per capita GDP, which are closer to the lead country, will experience a negative effect of financial development.

These results enable the calculation of the convergence parameter for each country based on relation (7.10) and also the definition of the critical level F^c of financial development which, according to our estimations, is equal to 13.77% of the GDP. The WAEMU member countries that have a very low level of credit (under F^c)

will not be able to join the convergence club, given that the convergence parameter is equal to $\bar{\lambda}_i = \phi_y + \phi_{int}\bar{F}_i$ remains positive if F is relatively low. Thus, during our study period, Burkina Faso, Guinea-Bissau and Niger diverge due to their low levels of private credit, which are respectively 11.49, 12.29 and 9.74%. All the other countries in our sample show negative convergence parameters and have growth rates that converge to that of the so-called leader country (the United States). Thus, the Côte d'Ivoire, Senegal, Togo, Benin and Mali, which have the largest percentages of private credit for this period, show negative convergence parameters that equal, respectively, -0.2480, -0.1718, -0.1092, -0.0656 and -0.0314. This corresponds to respective speeds of convergence of 7.13, 4.71, 2.89, 1.70 and 0.80% (Table 7.3).

Convergence to French Frontier Growth

Table 7.3 presents the results of the estimation carried out using France as the lead country. The Sargan test gave a critical probability of $p = 0.1431$, enabling us to accept the validity of the instruments. The interaction term is negative and significant at the 5% threshold; in addition, the implicit effect of the lagged variable is positive and $\hat{\phi}_y = 0.3012$. As a result, with an interaction term coefficient equal to -0.0265, the critical level of private credit this time is equal to 11.37%. And this time, only Niger, which has the lowest level of private credit (9.74%), diverges from the French growth frontier. Table 7.5 gives the speed of convergence for each of the countries in our sample. It is 12.73% for the Côte d'Ivoire, which has the highest level of credit, and 0.08% for Burkina Faso, which is the converging country that records the lowest level of financial development.

Furthermore, one also notes that the minimum level of private credit needed to converge to the American growth frontier is clearly higher than that needed to converge to the French growth frontier. Outside of the fact that the American technological frontier is farther away, the basic reason for this we can highlight at this point is linked to a strong relationship of dependence that exists between France and the WAEMU countries. In effect, France being a member of the franc zone maintains an important level of economic, and notably financial, cooperation with the WAEMU countries. The measures taken as part of this cooperation, and whose ultimate goal is to create a favourable banking and monetary framework, also specifically facilitate economic relations between France and the WAEMU. In addition, migratory flows and technical cooperation that result from this relationship also constitute a good channel for transferring know-how and technology, whose acquisition occurs both through practical application and theoretical training. In this way, the efforts carried out as part of this cooperation seem to have a decisive effect on the convergence process of these countries.

Finally, we should mention that estimations were also carried out considering a local leader: Nigeria. The results are presented in Table 7.6, and none of the variables included in the estimation had a significant effect at the standard 5% threshold.

VI   Policy Implications and Recommendations

Our results show that the economic integration policies initiated as part of the WAEMU should be accompanied by a good financial integration policy that makes it possible to promote financial development within the Union. According to Levine et al. (2000), better financial development could be obtained by strengthening the efficiency of rules linked to the legal framework, such as those related to the rights of creditors. And even if implementing these policies implies costs that could be high, the results show that the advantages in terms of gains in growth for the WAEMU countries seem to be certain. For example, according to the results we got, an improvement of 2.28 percentage points in the level of private credit in Burkina Faso would enable the latter to converge to the growth frontier represented by the French economy, while Niger and Guinea Bissau need respective increases of 1.49 and 4.3 percentage points. The goal of economic integration within the WAEMU should, therefore, be accompanied by the implementation of policies that enable greater harmonisation of regulations on the credit market in order to ensure that all the member countries—and particularly Niger, Burkina Faso and Guinea-Bissau, which have the Union's lowest levels of credit—have better access. Djankov et al. (2007) emphasise that the countries that are closest in terms of the regulations that bind creditors tend to experience similar levels of financial development. In addition, in the long run, an integrated and open financial system is likely to be more competitive, transparent and effective.

Besides, given that innovation is recognised as one of the most important factors in economic growth, all policies in favour of financial intermediation could also enable better performance in terms of economic growth largely because of their positive impact on productivity R&D. The presence of financial intermediaries reduces the asymmetry of information and decreases the constraints linked to the appropriation process of external R&D effects (Morales 2003). This promotes, in turn, the private production of innovation.

VII   Conclusion

This study focussed on the effects of a weak financial system on economic convergence in WAEMU countries. This analysis shows that credit constraint prevents these countries from fully benefiting from technology transfer and distances them from the growth frontier by considerably reducing their speeds of convergence. Thus, the WAEMU countries that have the lowest levels of financial development record relatively slow or even null speeds of convergence. These empirical investigations confirm the theory presented and highlight the important role financial services play in economic growth within the Union. An effective intermediation service facilitates access to private credit and makes it possible for there to be technological innovation and increases the rate of capital accumulation (King and Levine 1993). The results enable one to say that within the WAEMU, all policies that aim to improve access to credit will have ramifications on growth and convergence of the member countries' economies.

Appendix

Table 7.1 Descriptive statistics (panel (1984–2004))

Country	Per capita GDP (US$)		CREDIT (%)		CONS (%)		INFL (%)	
	Average	Stand. err.	Average	Stand. err.	Average	Stand. err.	Average	Stand. err.
Benin	1185.07	66.7	17.11	8.71	87.48	2.60	17.23	19.41
Burkina Faso	914.44	99.01	11.49	2.25	88.97	4.06	11.00	14.43
Côte d'Ivoire	2155.38	86.48	26.42	1.24	78.11	1.31	13.93	18.32
Guinea Bissau	616.6	11.61	12.29	7.68	89.85	18.11	120.00	91.36
Mali	993.59	133.55	15.37	3.59	89.10	2.01	8.37	17.10
Niger	863.82	82.3	9.74	5.20	64.19	7.73	8.09	22.41
Senegal	1445.38	95.54	22.53	6.18	95.67	4.31	11.76	15.17
Togo	840.76	50.60	19.34	3.21	80.29	5.10	13.53	20.15

Note: See sections IV and V for description of the data

Table 7.2 WAEMU country convergence speeds (country 1: United States)

Country	Convergence parameter	Speed of convergence (%)
Benin	−0.0656	1.70
Burkina Faso	–	–
Côte d'Ivoire	−0.2480	7.13
Guinea Bissau	–	–
Mali	−0.0315	0.80
Niger	–	–
Senegal	−0.1718	4.71
Togo	−0.1093	2.89

Table 7.3 Estimation results (country 1: United States)

DEP.: *LN RELATIVE GDP*	"System GMM" estimation 1984–2004			(N=40)
	Coef.	Std. err.	z-stat	Prob.
ln relative initial GDP	1.2698	0.2587	4.91	0.000
CREDIT	−0.0581	0.0261	−2.23	0.026
INTER	−0.0196	0.0084	−2.34	0.019
CONS	0.0075	0.0036	2.08	0.037
INF	−0.0010	0.0007	−1.48	0.140
Constant	0.2160	0.8125	0.27	0.790
Instruments (Sargan test)				
Value	8.1180			
Prob.	0.6173			

Table 7.4 Estimation results (country 1: France)

DEP.: *LN RELATIVE GDP*	"System GMM" estimation 1984–2004			(N=40)
	Coef.	Std. err.	z-stat	Prob.
ln relative initial GDP	1.3012	0.3352	3.88	0.000
CREDIT	−0.0748	0.0360	−2.08	0.037
INTER	−0.0265	0.0124	−2.14	0.032
CONS	0.0068	0.0039	1.75	0.080
INF	−0.0002	0.0007	−0.25	0.803
Constant	0.2435	0.9438	0.26	0.796
Instruments (Sargan test)				
Value	14.7081			
Prob.	0.1431			

Table 7.5 WAEMU country convergence speeds (country 1: France)

Country	Convergence parameter	Convergence speed (%)
Benin	−0.1522	4.13
Burkina Faso	−0.0033	0.08
Côte d'Ivoire	−0.3989	12.73
Guinea Bissau	−0.0245	0.62
Mali	−0.1061	2.80
Niger	–	–
Senegal	−0.2958	8.77
Togo	−0.2113	5.93

Table 7.6 Estimation results (country 1: Nigeria)

DEP.: *LN RELATIVE GDP*	"System GMM" estimation 1984–2004			(N=40)
	Coef.	Std. err.	z-Stat	Prob.
ln initial relative GDP	0.1974	0.5406	0.37	0.715
CREDIT	0.0004	0.0071	0.06	0.955
INTER	0.0029	0.0171	0.17	0.863
CONS	0.0007	0.0052	0.14	0.892
INF	0.0002	0.0015	0.18	0.857
Constant	0.2879	0.4003	0.72	0.472
Instruments (Sargan test)				
Value	14.2221			
Prob.	0.1631			

References

Aghion P, P. Howitt, and D. Mayer-Foulkes (2005), 'The effect of financial development on convergence: Theory and evidence' *Quarterly Journal of Economics*, 120(1):173–222.

Arellano, M. and S. Bond (1991), 'Some tests of specification for paneldata: Monte Carlo evidence and an application to employment equations', *Review of Economic Studies*, 58(194)277–297.

Arellano, M. and O. Bover (1995), 'Another look at the instrumental variable estimation of error-components models', *Journal of Econometrics*, 68(1):29–51.

Arestis, P., P.O. Demetriades, and K.B. Luintel (2001), 'Financial Development and Economic Growth: The Role of Stock Markets', *Journal of Money, Credit, and Banking*, 33(1):16–41.

Blackburn, K., and V. Hung (1998), 'A Theory of Growth, Financial Development and Trade', *Economica*, 65(257):107–124.

Beck, T., and R. Levine (2004), 'Stock markets, banks and growth: Panel evidence', *Journal of Banking and Finance*, 28(3): 423–442.

Blundell, R., and S. Bond (1998), 'Initial conditions and moment restrictions in dynamic panel-data models', *Journal of Econometrics*, 87(1): 115–143.

Calderon, C., and L. Liu (2003), 'The direction of causality between financial development and economic growth', *Journal of Development Economics*, 72(1): 321–334.

Demetriades, P.O., and K. A. Hussein (1996), 'Does Financial Development Cause Economic Growth? Time-Series Evidence from Sixteen Countries',*Journal of Development Economics*, 51(2): 387–411.

Djankov, S., C. McLiesh, and A. Shleifer (2007), 'Private Credit in 129 Countries', *Journal of Financial Economics*, 84(2): 299–329.

Dufrénot, G., V. Mignon, and A. Péguin-Feissolle (2007), 'Testing the Finance-Growth Link: Is there a Difference between Developed and Developing Countries?', Centre d'Etudes Prospectives et d'Informations Internationales, No 2007–24.

Easterly, W., and W. Levine (2001), 'It's Not Factor Accumulation: Stylized Facts and Growth Models', *World Bank Economic Review*, 15(2): 177–219.

Fisman, R., and I. Love (2004),'Financial Development and Growth in the Short and Long Run', *NBER Working Paper*, 10236.

Kahn, A. (2001), 'Financial Development and Economic Growth', *Macroeconomic Dynamics*, 5(3): 413–433.

King, R., and R. Levine (1993), 'Finance and Growth: Schumpeter Might Be Right', *Quarterly Journal of Economics*, 108(3): 717–737.

Levine, R. (2005), 'Finance and growth: theory and evidence', in Philippe Aghion Steven Durlauf (Eds.) Handbook of Economic Growth (chapter 12: 865–934)

Levine, R., N. Loayza, and T. Beck (2000), 'Financial Intermediation and Growth: Causality and Causes', *Journal of Monetary Economics*, 46(1): 31–77.

Levine, R., and S. Zervos (1998), 'Stock markets, banks, and economic growth', *American Economic Review*, 88(3):537–558.

Mattesini, F. (1996), 'Interest Rate Spreads and Endogenous Growth',*Economic Notes*, 25(1): 111–29.

Morales, M. (2003), 'Financial Intermediation in a Model of Growth through Creative Destruction', *Macroeconomic Dynamics*, 7(3): 363–393.

Obstfeld, M. (1994), 'Risk-Taking, Global Diversification, and Growth', *American Economic Review* (December):1310–1329.

Roubini, N., and X. Sala-I-Martin (1992), 'A Growth Model of Inflation, Tax evasion, and financial Repression', *NBER working paper No.* 4062.

Rousseau, P.L., and P.Wachtel. (1998), 'Financial intermediation and economic performance: historical evidence from five industrial countries', *Journal of Money, Credit, and Banking*, 30(4): 657–678.

Chapter 8
Free Movement of Goods in WAEMU and the European Union: Community Law a Comparative Study from the Perspective of Trade

Ousmane Bougouma

Abstract Free movement of goods is one of the four community freedoms defined by the EC and the WAEMU treaties that constitute the four "pillars" of a common market. Articles 4 and 77–81 of the WAEMU treaty are the counterparts of articles 28–37 of the Treaty on the Functioning of the European Union (formerly articles 23–31 of the EC treaty). These two texts stem from the same movement and share the same ambition, that of liberalising trade among the member states in order to establish a principle of free movement of all products with monetary value and therefore likely to be the object of commercial transactions. The free movement of goods is, in effect, a key community freedom. Community freedoms have a daily impact on the lives of the citizens, and no community progress could be made without free movement regimes. They interest both member states and enterprises, which are the economic players. In this contribution, we propose to examine primarily the WAEMU framework for the free movement of goods, both in terms of the legal texts and the practice through the successful experience of the European Union.

I Introduction

"Nature unites people . . . because of their mutual interest. The spirit of trade, which is incompatible with war, sooner or later gains the upper hand in every state".[1] This spirit of trade that promotes the union of people evoked by I. Kant as early as the eighteenth century resonates like a prophecy in view of the large number of trade-

---

[1] I. Kant, *Perpetual Peace: A Philosophical Sketch*, 1st ed. 1795, Coll. Bibliothèque des textes philosophiques, éd. Vrin, Paris, 2002, p. 81.

O. Bougouma (✉)
UFR/SJP (Research and Training Centre in Law and Political Sciences),
University of Ouagadougou, Ouagadougou, Burkina Faso
e-mail: oussouboug@yahoo.fr

E.T. Ayuk and S.T. Kaboré (eds.), *Wealth Through Integration*, Insight and Innovation in International Development 4, DOI 10.1007/978-1-4614-4415-2_8,
© International Development Research Centre 2013

147

and economy-related groupings of countries we see today. Europe and west Africa both have taken the approach of trade and economic union.

The economic Europe stemmed from the Paris convention of 18 April 1951 that established a common market in coal and steel,[2] a common market that would be prolonged and broadened with the Rome treaty of 25 March 1957[3] and is today upheld by the European Union (EU). The goals were the promotion of trade among the people of Europe and the liberalisation of national economies within the community.

The wind of integration also blew over west Africa, albeit for slightly different reasons. The subregion has even become a veritable test laboratory in terms of economic integration, as so many community organisations have followed one another since the emergence of nationally sovereign states.[4] The most recent economic integration organisation to date is the West African Economic and Monetary Union (WAEMU). It is certainly "a new old enterprise",[5] but it is an exception when compared with the repeated failures of economic groupings among west African states. It is an organisation for economic and legal integration,[6] and the determination to build a unified market is not without similarities to the European Union (EU) economic integration movement.

---

[2] The European Coal and Steel Community (ECSC) was established between six western European countries: France, Germany, Italy and Benelux (Belgium, Netherlands, Luxembourg). It was concluded for 50 years and disappeared in 2002.

[3] Two treaties were signed on 25 March 1957 in Rome, between the ECSC members creating two new communities: the European Atomic Energy Community (EAEC or EUROTOM) and the European Economic Community (EEC).

[4] We can mention the Conseil de l'Entente (30 May 1959), the Union Douanière de l'Afrique de l'Ouest (UDAO) (1959–1966), the Union Douanière des États de l'Afrique de l'Ouest (UDEAO) (1966–1973), the West African Economic Community (WAEC) (1966–1994), the Economic Community of West African States (1975). See E. Cerexhe and L. le Hardy de Beaulieu, "Introduction à l'Union économique ouest africaine", publ. CEEI., Ed. DE Boeck, 1997, pp. 16, ss.; L. M. Ibriga, « L'UEMOA, une nouvelle approche de l'intégration économique régionale en Afrique de l'ouest », *Annuaire africain de droit international*, Vol. 6, 1998, pp. 23–64 ; D. B. BA, « Le problème de la compatibilité entre l'UEMOA et l'OHADA », in *La libéralisation de l'économie dans le cadre de l'intégration régionale : le cas de l'UEMOA,* Actes du colloque de Ouagadougou, 16 and 17 December 1999, Publication du CEEI, p. 157s.

[5] D. B. Ba, « Le problème de la compatibilité entre l'UEMOA et l'OHADA », in *La libéralisation de l'économie dans le cadre de l'intégration régionale : le cas de l'UEMOA,* Actes du colloque de Ouagadougou 16 and 17 December 1999, Publication du CEEI, p. 157s.

[6] The legal integration led by the WAEMU finds itself, according to J. Issa-Sayegh, more and more "on equal footing and even in competition with that of other international organisations responsible for the same mission in the same legal areas". These would be the African Intellectual Property Organisation (AIPO), the Conférence Interafricaine des Marchés d'Assurance (CIMA), the Conférence Interafricaine de Prévoyance Sociale (CIPRES), the Organisation pour l'Harmonisation du Droit des Affaires en Afrique (OHADA) and the Economic Community of West African States (ECOWAS). (CEDEAO). Concerning conflicts in standards between the WAEMU and the OHADA, see D. B. Ba, « Le problème de la compatibilité entre l'UEMOA et l'OHADA », op. cit p. 157s; for conflicts in standards between the WAEMU and the ECOWAS, see L. M. Ibriga "Le problème de la compatibilité entre l'UEMOA et la CEDEAO", in *La libéralisation de l'économie dans le cadre de l'intégration régionale : le cas de l'UEMOA*, op. cit., p.197–227.

The WAEMU was largely inspired by the successful EU system.[7] Their resemblance is both institutional[8] and material.

From a material point of view, the two communities have the goal of creating a common market based on an economic and monetary union. Indeed, article 2 of the Treaty on the European Communities (EC treaty) stipulates that the "community shall have as its task, by establishing a common market and an economic and monetary union and by implementing common policies or activities referred to in Articles 3 and 4, to promote throughout the community a harmonious, balanced and sustainable development of economic activities". Article 4 of the WAEMU treaty goes in the same direction by stipulating that the union aims to establish a common market "based on the free movement of people, goods, services and capital and the right for people with an independent or salaried activity to settle, along with establishing a common external tariff and a joint trade policy".

In the common market, free movement of goods occupies a central position in both treaties. In view of all these symmetries, it would be very interesting to undertake a comparative study of the two community systems of free movement of goods. In effect, in the two integration systems, the free circulation of goods by eliminating port duties and opening the markets to competition aims at the optimal allocation of resources among the member states and subsequently increasing taxpayer income. Generally speaking, due to its socio-economic objectives, developing countries such as those in the WAEMU rightly perceive economic integration to be a panacea for the problem of development and poverty reduction.[9] In this way, free movement is a veritable instrument for reducing poverty.

---

[7] J. Issa Sayegh, "L'ordre juridique de l'UEMOA et l'intégration juridique africaine", op. cit. p.804 et s and P. Viaud, "Union européenne et Union économique et monétaire de l'Ouest africain", *op cit*, p. 15.

[8] From an institutional point of view, it is easy to make the connection between the conference of heads of state and of government, the council of ministers and the commission as the WAEMU's managerial bodies and the European Council, the Council of the European Union and the European Commission. It is edifying in more than one way to compare the competences of the WAEMU's Council of Heads of State and Government with those of the Council of the European Union. In effect, according to the terms of article 17 of the WAEMU treaty, the conference defines the union's major policy orientations. Article 4 of the Treaty on European Union is no different in that it stipulates, "The European Council shall provide the union with the necessary impetus for its development and shall define the general political guidelines thereof. The European Council shall bring together the heads of state or government and the president of the commission." Note however that unlike in the EU where the president of the commission is a rightful member European Council in virtue of the Treaty on European Union, the president of the WAEMU Commission attends conference meetings, but in no way does the treaty make it compulsory for heads of state or government. Also, the conference has a hierarchical relationship with other WAEMU institutions and in this way is the keystone of the entire system, while that is not the case for the European Union. V. P. Viaud, "Union européenne et Union économique et monétaire de l'Ouest africain", *RMCUE*, no. 414, Jan. 1998, p. 15.

[9] L. M. Ibriga, « L'état de la mise en œuvre de l'union douanière dans l'espace UEMOA », in *Sensibilisation au droit communautaire de l'UEMOA, Actes du séminaire sous-régional*, Ouagadougou-Burkina Faso du 6–10 October 2003. Paris, éd. Giraf, 2003, p. 111.

In view of the institutional and material similarities between the two communities' institutions, should we conclude in a phenomenon of normative importation on the part of the WAEMU? In other terms, what is the degree of symmetry between the two systems of free movement of goods? Do WAEMU laws concerning free movement of goods contain any specific characteristics? Highlighting this issue serves a twofold purpose. Indeed, it raises the question of real impact and of the effectiveness of WAEMU's free circulation of goods. It also raises the question of the opportunity and relevance of liberalising trade, particularly in the WAEMU space.

Finally, in order to respond to these questions, we will use a normative approach comparing the basic texts the two economic integration organisations have concerning free circulation of goods, putting an emphasis on their differing approaches. At the heart of this analysis, we will look closer at the question of dismantling barriers to the free circulation of goods (I).

Beyond the analysis of the theoretical and normative framework, the work will also consist, thereafter, of analysing the implementation of free movement of goods by examining the litigation mechanisms and the policies for harmonising or standardising national legislation (II).

I   Prohibiting Barriers to Free Movement of Goods in the EC and the WAEMU: A Symmetric Approach

The free movement of goods is a fundamental community liberty.[10] It is the basis of the WAEMU and the EU common markets. That is why the EC and the WAEMU treaties prohibit any barriers to exercising this freedom, even though this prohibition is tempered with exceptions.

A – The principle: the prohibition of barriers to free movement of goods

Prohibiting barriers is central to the principle of free circulation of goods. A barrier is any measure that impedes, interferes with, handicaps or limits the entry or exit of merchandise in a community member state. There are a variety of barriers. It is therefore necessary to identify (2) them, but first one must define the goods that are protected by the principle of free movement (1).

---

[10] Gavalda (C.) and Parleani (G.), *Droit des affaires de l'Union européenne*, Paris, Litec, 4th edition, 2002.

[11] Neither the EC treaty nor the WAEMU treaty defines the notion of merchandise. The CJEC fills this gap in its ruling *Commission v/Italy,* 10 Dec. 1968, case 7/68, REC. P. 617.

1. Identification of Protected Goods

In EU law, goods are considered to be "products that can be valued in money and that are capable, as such, of forming the subject of commercial transactions".[11] This definition encompasses both agricultural and industrial products. The CJEC has developed a broad, pragmatic and mercantile conception of the notion of goods. Free movement applies to "products originating in member states and to products coming from third countries which are in free circulation in member states".[12] A good is considered to originate in a member state when it has been wholly obtained or produced there or when it has undergone its last substantial process or operation that is economically justified there.[13] This definition therefore excludes products that come from "screwdriver plants" whose activity consists of simple packaging or product presentation operations without truly creating a new product or contributing some substantial added value.[14]

In WAEMU law, article 4 discusses free movement of goods, and paragraph II and title III of the treaty cover free movement of merchandise. Are these two terms identical? The treaty does not define the notion of good or the notion of merchandise.

A good is a civil notion, while merchandise is a purely commercial notion. A good is any thing that can be appropriated. All merchandise is therefore a good, but the contrary is not always true. Should we conclude that the scope of free movement foreseen by the WAEMU treaty is broader than that foreseen by the EC treaty? Nothing could be less certain. Here, the two terms are used interchangeably, and do not reveal a true difference in approach from the WAEMU legislator.

In any case, in the WAEMU, for a product to be able to benefit from free movement, it must originate in the community and be accredited. The originating products are classified as home-grown products, traditional crafts and industrial products.

In the terms of article 4 of the supplementary law no. IV, the following are considered to be home-grown products originating in WAEMU member states:

---

[12] Art. 23 of the EC treaty.

[13] Regulation (EEC) no. 802/68 of the Council 27 June 1968, on the common definition of the concept of the origin of goods, OJ L 148, 28 June 1968, pp. 1–5, article 24 of the Community customs code, Regulation (EEC) no. 2913/92 of the Council, dated 12 October 1992, establishing the community customs code, JO L 302 dated 19 October 1992.

[14] See, notably, CJEC ruling 26 January 1977, *Gesellschaft für Uberseehandel c/ Handelskammer Hamburg*, aff. 49-76, *Rec.*, I, p.41.; Gavalda (C.) and Parleani (G.), *Droit des affaires de l'Union européenne*, Paris, Litec, 5th edition, 2006, p. 54.

[15] See article 4 of additional act no. 04/96, WAEMU official bulletin June 1996; additional protocol no. III/2001, WAEMU official bulletin no. 24 third quarter 2001V. Article 4 of the additional act no. 04/96, mentioned above.

[16] See article 6 of the above-mentioned additional act no. 04/96.

[17] Before 1 January 2003, in order for an industrial product to be considered to originate in the WAEMU, at least 60% of its raw material had to come from the union. If the raw materials came from outside the union, there had to be an added value of at least 40% of the ex-factory price before tax.

animal, mineral and plant products that have not been subject to industrial transformation, even if they have undergone finishing that will ensure their conservation.[15] The craft products are hand-made articles or those made without the aid of tools, instruments or other measures operated directly by the artisan.[16]

Since 1 January 2003,[17] an industrial product is considered to have originated in the WAEMU when it is wholly manufactured there or when it has undergone sufficient transformation there, under the condition that this transformation resulted in either a change in tariff classification in the tariff and statistics nomenclature or a community added value greater than or equal to 30% of the ex-factory cost before tax.[18]

Industrial products, in addition to respecting the rules regarding their origins, must also be accredited for free movement. The accreditation takes the form of a certificate of origin granted by the competent national authorities. The accreditation decisions are sent to the WAEMU Commission, which plays an auditing and monitoring role. Although simplification of the procedure is to be welcomed, one must nevertheless fear the delivery of accreditations of convenience. To date, 2,136 industrial products of origin that have been accredited, produced by 489 firms, circulate freely within the union.[19] This is a noteworthy achievement for the WAEMU. One should note, however, that the WAEMU has not established specific marking as in the case in EU where "EC" conformity marking on a product materialises the product's conformity to community requirements that are the responsibility of the product's manufacturer.[20] Marking in the WAEMU consists simply of recording the accreditation number on the certified product. The "EC" marking is justified for reasons of consumer health and safety. Without such marking, the WAEMU should establish a quality control procedure for products that benefit from free movement. This will make it possible to protect consumers and to decrease the circulation of all kinds of counterfeit products throughout the WAEMU space.

In terms of paragraph 2 of article 23 of the EC treaty, free movement of goods also applies to "products coming from third countries which are in free circulation in member states". Free practice is done by a customs declaration and after import duties have been paid. Once in free practice, community legislation regarding free movement of goods is applicable to imported merchandise. It confers on merchandise originating in third countries the status of community merchandise. Thus, merchandise that is lawfully imported from a third country, in principle, moves freely in the community that is part of the single EU trade area.

---

[18] See article 5 of the additional protocol no. III/2001, mentioned above.

[19] See the WAEMU website: www.uemoa.int.

[20] See Decision no. 93/465/EEC dated 22 July 1993 concerning the modules for the various phases of the conformity assessment procedures and rules for affixing and use of the CE conformity marking, which are intended to be used in the technical harmonisation directives., JO L 220 dated 30 August 1993, COM/93/144-02 ; modified by Regulation no. 765/2008 dated 06 February 2008 on accreditation and market surveillance, non-published in the OJ.

Unlike in the EU, the WAEMU does not apply the principle of free practice. So, a good from a third country imported into the community will be subject to the CET as many times as it will be re-exported. This exclusion of the principle of free practice in the WAEMU can be explained by a determination to fight trade deflection. The WAEMU is therefore not a single trade area. The absence of free practice in the WAEMU is a stumbling block in negotiations between the WAEMU and the EU.[21] The EU considers that the WAEMU should establish free practice to enable merchandise to move freely. Setting up free practice will have economic advantages, yet runs the risk of increased fiscal competition among the member states and trade deflection that would be prejudicial to high-tax countries. Should one, however, close the door on free practice in the WAEMU? The fear of losing tax and customs revenue, particularly in interland member states, explains the hostility to free practice in the WAEMU. In effect, in a traditional set-up, it is recommended to collect harbour duties at the first entry customs offices, even if they are then paid over to the merchandise's destination country. Although this set-up has the advantage of simplicity in duty collection, it also has the disadvantage of the burden of paying over the same duties to the destination countries and of creating liquidity problems and recovery deficits. Considering this situation, one could recommend that the WAEMU envisage putting in place specific accompanying measures such as advanced fiscal harmonisation.

To summarise, whereas in the EU all goods produced in and legally imported into the community can move freely, in the WAEMU, only products that originated in the community areas can move entirely freely. To ensure this free movement, the two community areas have banned barriers to this freedom.

2.   Identifying Barriers to Prohibit

There are many barriers to free movement of goods, and they take many forms. One can, however, divide them into tariff and non-tariff barriers. One should note, however, that although both of these types of barriers continue to impede free movement of goods in the WEAMU, only non-tariff barriers continue to be an issue in the EU, since tariff barriers have been more or less removed.

a)   Tariff Barriers

Pecuniary interference, still referred to as tariff barriers in international economic law terminology, comprises compulsory levies. These levies consist of customs duties, of taxes equivalent in effect to customs duties and of taxes of all kinds that have a protective or discriminatory effect.

Customs duties are classic harbour duties collected by states at the time of import or export of merchandise. Eliminating these customs duties has been the object of the customs union both in the EU and in the WAEMU, and of

---

[21] See the 2008 report from the WAEMU Commission regarding the functioning and evolution of the union.

differentiation of community space by the establishment of a common external tariff (CET) or a common customs duty (CCD). The six founding states of the EEC formed the customs union as early as 1 July 1968, a full 18 months before it was initially planned.[22] In the WAEMU, the customs union was established progressively. In effect, as early as 1996, a zone of preferential trade was set up, with a 30% reduction in entry duties. This rate increased to 60% in 1997, and then to 80% in 1999. On 1 January 2000, the reduction became total, making the WAEMU a customs union.[23]

Since 1 January 1993, the member states of the European Community have removed their borders and the customs service diminished within the states. In the WAEMU, customs borders have been maintained, but one is seeing their merger through adjacent control posts at the borders. Maintaining these posts may be amply justified; however, control procedures are a real barrier to the free movement of goods.

In the image of the EU, the WAEMU community customs union has its roots in international instruments such as WTO rules.[24] Both communities have also developed customs codes.[25] EU customs law is part of its history, its achievements; WAEMU customs law, however, is still being built. L. M. Ibriga would say that although the WAEMU customs union is to a large extent underway, it remains an unfinished work.[26] Yet, if customs laws are easy to identify, they remain more insidious obstacles that are truly discreet areas of state protectionism.[27] A typical example can be found in charges having an equivalent effect as the customs duty.

The notion of a levy equivalent in effect was not defined in either the EC or the WAEMU treaties. Indeed, article 76 of the WAEMU treaty and articles 23 and 25 of

---

[22] On European Community customs law, see, among others C. J. Berr "Introduction au droit douanier", Economica, new ed. Paris, 2008, 73 p; (J.-C.) Berr, and (E.) Natarel, "Union douanière", *RTD eur*, no. 3, Jul-Sep. 2006, p. 463 and "Union douanière", *RTD eur*, no. 4, Oct-Dec. 2007, pp. 665–677. On WAEMU customs law, see among others F.-X, Bambara, "La réglementation douanière communautaire de l'UEMOA", in *Sensibilisation au droit communautaire de l'UEMOA, Actes du séminaire régional sur l'Ordre communautaire de l'Union Economique et Monétaire Ouest Africaine (UEMOA)*, Ouagadougou, 1er – 5 November 2004. pp. 101–116; (L. M.) Ibriga "L'état de la mise en œuvre de l'union douanière dans l'espace UEMOA", in *Sensibilisation au droit communautaire de l'UEMOA, Actes du séminaire sous-régional*, Ouagadougou-Burkina Faso du 6–10 October 2003. Paris, ed. Giraf, 2003, pp. 111–124.

[23] Bambara (F.-X.), "La réglementation douanière communautaire de l'UEMOA", in *Sensibilisation au droit communautaire de l'UEMOA, Actes du séminaire régional sur l'Ordre communautaire de l'Union Economique et Monétaire Ouest Africaine (UEMOA)*, Ouagadougou, 1er – 5 November 2004. pp. 101–116.

[24] See article 23 of the EC treaty and article 77 of the WAEMU treaty.

[25] For the WAEMU, see the regulation no. 09/2001/CM/UEMOA of 26 November 2001 on adoption of the WAEMU customs code.

[26] L. M. Ibriga, "L'état de la mise en œuvre de l'union douanière dans l'espace UEMOA", mentioned above.

[27] Dubouis (L.) and Blumann (C.), *Droit matériel de l'Union européenne*, Domat, Droit public, 5th ed., Montchrestien, 2009, P. 236.

the EC treaty forbid equivalent-effect taxes without actually defining them. It is the CJEC that, after some exploration, defined equivalent-effect charges as "any pecuniary charge, however small and whatever designation and mode of application, which is imposed unilaterally on domestic or foreign goods when they cross a frontier, and which is not a customs duty in the strict sense, constitutes a charge having equivalent effect, even if it is not imposed for the benefit of the state, is not discriminatory or protective in effect or if the product on which the charge is imposed is not in competition with any domestic product".[28]

So, to be considered to be equivalent to a customs duty, the charge must be pecuniary in nature, no matter how small, other than the actual customs duty, imposed by a member state or by the state's competent authority, even as part of a purely internal framework,[29] no matter what it is called and no matter its mode of application. They are different from internal fees and taxation.[30]

A levy is qualified as a charge with an equivalent effect when it applies to national or foreign merchandise exclusively because they are crossing a border. It does not matter that it has no discriminatory or protective effect. Similarly, it cannot be justified for social, environmental or cultural (or other, for that matter) reasons. Charges of equivalent effect are entirely banned. The only exception concerns the pecuniary charge that aims strictly to "pay for a service that is clearly identified and effectively carried out by an economic operator".[31] It does not benefit from free movement of goods derogations.[32]

The ban on charges of equivalent effect being absolute, unconditional and objective,[33] unduly collected charges must be fully reimbursed. In WAEMU community law, the regime for charges of equivalent effect remains to be clarified, and there are yet to be community laws and jurisprudence exploring this notion, to our knowledge.

---

[28] CJEC, 1 July 1969, *commission c/Italie*, aff. 24/68,*Rec*. P. 193; 7 July 1994, *Lamaire NV*, aff. 130/93, *Rec*. P. 3215.

[29] CJEC, 9 September 2004, *Carbonati Apuani c/ Comune di Carrara*, aff. C-72/03, Rec., I-8027; *Europe* Nov. 2004, no. 350, note A. Rigaux; J. Cavallini, Chronique de jurisprudence de la Cour de justice, *RMCUE* no. 491, September 2005, p. 535 ; *RDUE* 2/2004, p. 323.

[30] On the distinction between charges of equivalent effect to customs duties and other categories of fees, see Joël Molinier, Nathalie De Grove-Valdeyron (N.) *Droit du marché intérieur européen*, 2ème LGDJ, Paris, 2008. p. 230.

[31] CJEC, 26 February 1975. *W. Cadsky SpA contre Istituto nazionale per il Commercio Estero*, aff. *Rec*. 1975 p.281.

[32] See infra point B.

[33] Louis Dubouis and Claude Blumann, *Droit matériel de l'Union européenne*, Domat, Droit public, 5th ed., Montchrestien, 2009, p. 262.

The ban on charges of equivalent effect as customs duties has the goal of keeping member states from deflecting customs powers. But taxation is a barrier just as effective as customs duties.

b) Non-tariff Barriers

It is difficult and even impossible to give a nomenclature to non-tariff obstacles since they come in so many forms. However, one does distinguish quantitative restrictions (QR) and measures that have equivalent effect of quantitative restrictions (MEEQR). In the terms of articles 28 and 29 of the EC treaty and article 76 a) of the WAEMU treaty, QR and the MEEQR are forbidden both for import and for export. Both positive and negative measures, such as a state's simple abstention, can constitute a QR or an MEEQR.[34] The MEEQR calls for more development. The WAEMU and the EC treaties have remained laconic both on the notion of what an MEEQR is and the form it can take.

In European Community law, the ban on MEEQR is found in article 28 of the EC treaty. Like the notion of the charge of equivalent effect, the MEEQR stems from jurisprudence. In effect, the CJEC defines them in its famous Dassonville case as "any trade regulation between member states that could directly or indirectly, currently or potentially, impede intra-community trade".[35] It applies both to import and export. The measures of equivalent effect to quantitative restrictions are disparate and difficult to list. One can, however, cite the measures that concern sales conditions and modalities, which regulate the circumstances of time and place related to the sale of a good, etc.[36] They primarily target quotas. A European Commission green paper gives a summary (see the green paper on the completing of the internal market dated 14 June 1985). In reality, there are three categories of MEEQR, which are:

- Blatant discriminatory measures that target products imported from another member state

---

[34] CJEC, 9 December 1997, *Commission contre France*, aff. C-265/95, *Rec.*, I-6959. This refers to an impediment due to French famers demonstrating against the import of fruit and vegetables from Spain.

[35] Sur la notion de mesures d'effet équivalent à des restrictions quantitatives voir notamment, CJCE, 11 juillet 1974, *Dassonville*, aff, 8/74, Rec. P. 834 ; 24 novembre 1993, *Keck et Mithouard*, aff. 267 et 268/91, Rec. P. 6097 ; M. A. DAUSES, « Mesures d'effet équivalant à des restrictions quantitatives à la lumière de la jurisprudence de la Cour de justice des Communautés européennes », *RTDE*, 1992, n° 4, p. 607.

[36] For a closer look at the different measures of equivalent effect to quantitative restrictions, see Joël Molinier, Nathalie De Grove-Valdeyron, *Droit du marché intérieur européen*, 2ème LGDJ, Paris, 2008. p. 59 et ss.

[37] Mattera (A.), "Libre circulation des marchandises et articles 30 à 36 du traité CEE", *RMC*, 1976, p. 500.

– Measures that appear to apply indiscriminately but in reality disguise discrimination
– Measures that apply indiscriminately but are not justified for reasons of general interest

A broad definition of the notion of MEEQR covers "all state interventions dissimilated in the most disparate regulations that, under the veil of legitimacy, often contain effects that are restrictive to the free movement of goods. . ."[37]

In the WAEMU, measures of equivalent effect are just as varied. They are forbidden by article 76 a) of the treaty. In its 2008 annual report on the functioning of the union, the WAEMU Commission drew up a list of impediments equivalent to quantitative restrictions. These include technical and administrative barriers imposed on community products such as inspection formalities prior to embarking, imposed minimum import quantities, subordination of the import of origin products to the purchase of national products and retaining declarations prior to import. There are also physical barriers such as escorts, undue tax collection and the multiple roadblocks along the union's transport corridors. In effect, illicit tax collection and long delays due to multiple controls of transport corridors are the key barriers to the free movement of goods within the WAEMU. Yet, there is no worse obstacle to the free movement of goods than time. It may be true that "it is the ordinary destiny of laws to be far from practices"[38]; it is also true that in the WAEMU, the practice of the free movement of goods is far from the community regulations. The reality offers nothing but impediments and red tape of all kinds.[39]

To fight these restrictions, the WAEMU Commission, in collaboration with ECOWAS, has set up an observatory of abnormal practices (APA) on the interstate roads in order to monitor and uncover the dysfunctions in the goods transport system. The goal is to take corrective measures as part of the fight against practices that constitute measures equivalent to quantitative restrictions and even to tariff barriers. Actions should be carried out, particularly in the direction of member states, to remove the multiple control posts and to abolish the various illicit tax collections. The commission should also implement action in event of failure to comply with articles 5, 6 and 7 of additional protocol number I against states that do not respect community prescriptions. One should note to this effect that building the community cannot take place without litigation. Sanctions are more effective than political discourse. The WAEMU would benefit from strengthening its mechanism for recourse for failure to comply by making it stricter. In addition, making economic players more aware of their rights should not be neglected. Ignorance feeds corruption and red tape of all kinds related to the police, the customs and the

---

[38] Abarchi (D), Problématique des réformes législatives en Afrique : le mimétisme juridique comme méthode de construction du droit, *Revue Trimestrielle de droit africain (Penant)*, Jan-Mar 2003, no. 842, P. 88 et ss.

[39] See, notably, the eighth report of the Observatoire des Pratiques Anormales, published on 8 September 2009 and the Country no 4402 dated 07 July 2009 p. 8.

roads. The commission should also act directly to raise the awareness of economic players. Nobody is better placed to defend rights than the holder of the rights himself or herself.

B   Exceptions: Admitting Barriers to the Free Movement of Goods

Like all rules of law, there are some exceptions to the principle of free movement of goods. These exceptions are stipulated in the EC and the WAEMU treaties. The CJEC has defined a strict legal regime for these exceptions.

1.   Identifying Allowable Barriers

In the terms of article 79 of the WAEMU treaty, a state can restrict or forbid import, export or transit of merchandise in its territory for reasons of public morality; public order; public security; protection of health or the lives of people or animals; preservation of the environment; protection of national treasures with artistic, historic or archaeological value; and protection of industrial or commercial property. These reasons for restricting free movement are restrictively listed. In addition, the treaty leaves member states the liberty of invoking or not invoking any reasons to restrict the free movement of goods.

This measure repeats word for word article 30 of the EC treaty. But what justifies and motivates repeating this article? In effect, "west Africa is not western Europe",[40] and two so dissimilar economic systems should not adjust to the same rules. In effect, even if the WAEMU Commission monitors the restrictions, one should be concerned that the member states may be tempted to broadly interpret this list. The risk is all the more real because the regime of justifications for the restrictions has not yet been specified by the WAEMU, as is the case in the EU.

2.   Justifying the Barriers to Admit: The General-Interest Test

Neither the WAEMU nor the EU treaty defines the legal framework of justifications of barriers to free movement of goods. But as exceptions, they should be interpreted strictly, because they impinge upon a fundamental community freedom. For a measure to be accepted, it must also meet the twofold test of necessity and proportionality. Proportionality is judged in view of the goal of general interest that motivates the measure in question. This general interest has a twofold dimension. On one hand, interference is only allowed if the business sector in question requires state organisation or intervention. This is the test of necessity. On the other

---

[40] See Sossouvi (M.), *La libre circulation des marchandises et des capitaux dans la Communauté Economique des États de l'Afrique de l'Ouest (CEDEAO) à travers l'expérience de la Communauté Economique européenne (CEE)*, Thèse, 1989. p. 18.

hand, interference can neither be made into a general measure nor can it excessively impede the free movement of goods. The measure must be particular. That is the test of proportionality. Between two restrictive measures, the one that restricts free movement of goods the least, earns the favour of the CJEC. In brief, to be justified, the legislation must not go beyond what is necessary to reach the sought-after goal. A member state that has to adopt legislation that restricts the free movement of goods must demonstrate its necessity for the restrictive measure along with that measure's relevance to the sought-after objective.

In the WAEMU, states may, in virtue of article 79 of the treaty, be held to communicate the restrictive measures they have, but no obligation to justify them is mentioned. Also, the treaty does not mention measures that could later be adopted by the member states, and even less so the nature of the restrictions that are allowed. In effect, contrary to article 30 of the EC treaty that limits undermining free movement of goods only to the quantitative restrictions and the MEEQR mentioned in articles 28 and 29 of the same treaty, the WAEMU treaty is silent regarding application of article 79's restrictive measures. During this period of economic crisis, when the states are tempted by all types of protectionist measures, it is recommended to define an adequate regime for exceptions to the principle of free movement of goods in the WAEMU.

III   Mechanisms for Implementing Free Movement of Goods in the EU and the WAEMU: An Asymmetrical Approach

Achieving economic integration necessarily requires effectiveness in terms of community freedoms, including the free movement of goods. But the strict application of repressive measures, which are more often than not curative, is not sufficient to eliminate barriers to the free movement of goods. Preventive measures have been implemented both in the WAEMU treaty and the EC treaty. They consist of reconciling member states legislations. In effect, the EU and the WAEMU, aware that free movement of goods can only be achieved in a healthy legal environment, have anticipated support policies that include reconciling national legislations. The scope of harmonisation is quite broad, but it is the area of taxation that is of particular interest when it comes to the free movement of goods. The techniques deployed here and there are, however, divergent.

---

[41] See the 14 June 1985 white paper on completing the internal market.

A. National Legislation Harmonisations Techniques Impacting the Free Movement of Goods: New Approach and European Standardisation vs. WAEMU Regulations

In its white paper on completing the internal European market,[41] the European Union Commission recommends no fewer than 300 measures, three-quarters of which concern the free movement of goods. This document represents a decisive turning point in attempts to reconcile national legislations because it recommends a *new approach* to harmonisation modalities and methods. In effect, the commission, using as a basis EC article 30 forbidding technical barriers, had set up a programme to eliminate these barriers. This programme consisted of the council adopting more than a 150 directives to eliminate technical barriers to the free movement of goods that result from disparities in legislative, regulatory and administrative requirements in the member states. These directives, that aimed to be very detailed, harmonised the national measures relative to a product (vertical harmonisation) or to a group of products (horizontal harmonisation). Long months of negotiations blocked this process, and the expected results were not attained. As usual, it was the CJEC that unblocked the European Community machinery in the famous *cassis de Dijon* case.[42] The court, responding to a prejudicial question of the *Finanz Gerichtshof* of the Hessen Land, included the technical barriers in the MEEQR and concluded that harmonisation is not a prerequisite for the free movement of goods.

The consequences of the Cassis de Dijon ruling consisted of simplification of standards.[43] The commission generalised the principle of equivalence and mutual recognition, thus reducing the scope to which harmonisation of national requirements applies. Thereafter, harmonisation was confined to principles and key requirements such as health, safety, environmental and consumer protection, the rest being delegated to the standards developed by European and international standardisation bodies. In this way, standardisation becomes complementary to the regulations and as a result integrates the economic players in the community's technical harmonisation circuit. This is the "new approach" that was set up in the European Union.

In the WAEMU, harmonisation belongs to a rival area. According to article 60 of the treaty, the conference establishes the guiding principles and identifies the

---

[42] CJEC, 20 February 1979, *Rewe-zentral AG c/ Bundesmonopolverwaltung für Branntwein- Q. P. Hessisches Finanzgericht* known as the *"Cassis de Dijon"* case, Aff. 120/78, *Rec.* 649.

[43] See the commission's communication on the ruling pronounced by the Court of Justice of the European Communities Journal official no. C 256 dated 03/10/1980 p. 0002–0003.

[44] See opinion no. 001/1997 of the WAEMU Court of Justice dated 20 May 1997.

[45] Article 61 of the WAEMU treaty.

[46] Use of the term *"measures"* supposes a free choice of law on the part of the lawmaker. The CJEC confirms this analysis in the ruling United Kingdom v European Parliament and Council dated 6 December 2005, aff. C-66/04, Rec. I-10555, *Europe* no. 30.

priorities for harmonisation. It is then up to the council, upon proposition of the commission, to adopt the directives and regulations[44] needed for harmonisation.[45] As in the EU, the commission has a monopoly over taking initiatives. But this initiative is dependent upon the prior intervention of the conference in order to define the areas of harmonisation. In the WAEMU, having recourse to a directive or regulation is left to the judgement of community institutions, unlike in the EU, which for so long privileged directives for harmonisation. Yet, one should note that article 95 of the new EC treaty also allows recourse to a regulation to achieve harmonisation.[46]

Unlike in the EU, which favoured unanimity for harmonisation, the authors of the Dakar treaty chose the flexible path of a two-thirds majority.[47] One should note, however, the absence of the WAEMU parliamentary committee in the process of harmonisation, unlike in the EU, where the parliamentary body plays a joint decision-making role with the council.

Thus, the WAEMU prefers to decree harmonisation rules, that is, to have recourse to rules that will be transposed (directives) or applied directly in the member state legal systems (regulations). The principle of equivalence or mutual recognition is, nevertheless, provided for in article 76 e) and article 80 of the treaty. The lack of a spirit of litigation among economic operators combined with illegal practices (such as arrangements outside the law), which result in there being little jurisprudence within the community, does not promote a reconciliation of national legislations such as that proposed by the *new approach*, which is a litigation-based path to harmonisation. In effect, WAEMU law remains the prerogative of a few legal specialists. As Copernic said, "mathematics is written for mathematicians". In the WAEMU, the law seems to have been written for legal specialists and helped along by illiteracy in the general population, "proletarians of knowledge rarely call upon the law".[48] These are the sociological limits to the WAEMU's approach to integration in general and to the effectiveness of free movement of goods.

B. Harmonisation of Taxation: The Impact of Taxation on Free Movement of Goods

The free movement of goods would be vain if the member states could establish discriminatory internal taxation to the detriment of imported products. If one is not careful, taxation could constitute a real barrier to achieving free movement of goods. Achieving a common market depends on reconciliation of tax legislations. Free movement of goods litigation also contributes.

---

[47] See above-mentioned article 61.

[48] J. Koutaba, "Les limites sociologiques à l'application du droit", in *Sensibilisation au droit communautaire de l'UEMOA : actes du séminaire sous-régional des 6–10 octobre 2003*, Ouagadougou-Burkina Faso, éd. Giraf, p. 201.

[49] See article 4 e) of the WAEMU treaty.

1. Reconciliation of Tax Legislations

The principle of subsidiarity[49] is used both in the EU and the WAEMU when it comes to tax harmonisation, a kingly area par excellence and the last bastion of member state sovereignty. This principle postulates that community bodies intervene "only if and in so far as the objectives of the proposed action cannot be sufficiently achieved by the member states and can therefore, by reason of the scale or effects of the proposed action, be better achieved by the community".[50]

So, the EC and the WAEMU treaties do not entirely amputate the member states fiscal sovereignty. In effect, the EC treaty recognises a reserve of fiscal competence for EU member states. Exercising this sovereignty should not impinge upon the free movement of goods. "The authors of the treaty were from the start aware of the necessity of anticipating a few measures in this area".[51] Thus this way, the community whose founding fathers aimed to make it an economic community[52] did not ignore completely issues related to taxation. Potentially, the treaty contained measures that enable it to intervene in the area of taxation. The principle of tax neutrality has not, however, removed tax borders within the community. It became quickly clear that the states could replace customs barriers by a consumption tax and thus entirely undo the determination to build a common market. It was therefore necessary that indirect taxes, and particularly tax on business turnover, not undermine fiscal neutrality. As a result, very early on harmonisation became necessary.

Indirect taxes were more easily harmonised. In effect, as early as 1967, two directives[53] from the council upon proposal of the commission lay the basis for harmonisation of the VAT. These two directives were then followed by a third voted in 1969[54] that introduced the community VAT system into the national tax systems. Several other directives have completed the picture.[55] Following the VAT, excise duties as special consumption taxes were harmonised.[56]

Unlike indirect taxes, direct taxes were not harmonised. With the exception of article 87 (former article 92) of the EC treaty that forbids state assistance with respect to taxes, the treaty remains silent on the question, because harmonisation of direct taxes does not seem to be essential. But, it became progressively obvious that

---

[50] See, among others, article 5 of the EC treaty; Louis Dubouis and Claude Bluman, *Droit institutionnel de l'Union européenne*, Paris, Litec, 2^d edition, 2005. p. 323.

[51] D. Calleja, D. Vignier, R. Wägenbaur, *Dispositions fiscales-rapprochement des législations*, commentaires Megret, le droit de CEE, ULB ed., 2nd ed., 1993, p. 3.

[52] C. Blumann and L. Dubouis, *Droit Institutionnel de l'Union européenne*, 2nd ed., Litec, p. 1s.

[53] Directive dated 14 April 1967 no. 67/227, JOEC no. 71, 14 April 1967, p. 1301 et 1303.

[54] Directive no. 69/463/CEE, JOEC L 320 dated 20 December 1969, p. 34.

[55] Directive dated 17 May 1977 no. 77/388/CEE, also called the sixth VAT directive, JOEC L 145 dated 13 June 1977, p. I. Directive 2004/7, JO L 27, dated 30 January 2004.

[56] Excise duties were harmonised by the directive 92/12, JO 1 76, dated 23 March 1992 and directive 2004/106, JO L 359, dated 04 December 2004.

for community freedoms to have their full effect, there needed to be a minimum of harmonisation of direct taxes. The treaty recognises the council's competence to adopt directives in this area if needed.

Hence, article 90 of the same treaty forbids discriminatory or protective internal taxation. A member state cannot impose higher or protectionist taxes on products from another member state that are similar to products that are legally sold on its territory. By higher taxes, one should interpret as the application of a higher rate, a broader tax base or heavier tax penalties. This ban also applies to products that are found to be circulating freely in the community. The goal is to establish fiscal neutrality for internal taxation in order to promote competition among national and imported products.

The measures found in the WAEMU treaty are not as detailed in the area of taxation, and that is fair enough. With the exception of article 4 e), which provides for tax harmonisation if necessary, the treaty is silent about the fiscal powers of member states in the area of free circulation of goods. There is not even a general community measure similar to article 90 of the EC treaty. Yet, does this mean that the free movement of goods in the WAEMU is fiscally vulnerable? Absolutely not. In effect, the treaty provides the community institutions with legal instruments to confront the possible abuse of fiscal powers by member states.

Aware of the impact taxation has on achieving a common market, the authors of the WAEMU treaty provided for the harmonisation of fiscal policies. In effect, according to article 65 3) §1, "the member states shall harmonise their fiscal policies according to the procedure provided for in articles 60 and 61 to reduce excessive disparities in the structure and size of their tax levies". Unlike in the EU, harmonisation of tax rules in the WAEMU requires a qualified majority. It is important to point this out, because member states could see their taxation modified without its own consent, while in the EU, unanimity is still required for fiscal harmonisation.[57]

In addition, article 79 of the WAEMU treaty forbids all arbitrary discrimination and disguised restrictions. The fact that this measure does not specifically concern free movement of goods notwithstanding, it could be applied. Thus, the member states remain free in their tax practices on the condition that they conform to the principle of non-discrimination. A whole chapter of taxation has already been

---

[57] See article 93 of the EC treaty.

[58] See Directive No. 02/98/CM/UEMOA dated 22 December 1998 on harmonisation of Member State legislation concerning value added tax (VAT).

[59] See directive no. 03/98/CM/UEMOA dated 22 December 1998 on harmonisation of Member State legislation concerning excise duties.

[60] See Alain Faustin Bocco, *Politique commerciale commune et rôle de l'UEMOA dans les négociations commerciales* in Rencontre communautaire d'échange sur "la politique commerciale commune de l'UEMOA et les négociations commerciales", Bamako, 13 to 15 February 2007.

[61] See directive no. 01/2008/CM/UEMOA on harmonisation of modalities for determining the taxable income of legal entities within the WAEMU.

harmonised in the WAEMU. This is the case for indirect taxation such as the VAT[58] and excise duties.[59]

More recently, the WAEMU implemented a development tax policy, centred on a harmonisation programme for direct domestic taxation.[60] There is harmonisation at the WAEMU level concerning how to determine the taxable income of legal entities.[61] It is unfortunate that this harmonisation is limited to legal entities when we know that individual traders are the most numerous. Yet, this exclusion can be justified by the often informal nature of individual activities and testifies to the distrust community authorities have with regard to this type of business. There has also been harmonisation of the taxable equivalent basis rate. The maximum rate is 30%. The WAEMU has also established a tax convention that aims to avoid double taxation.[62]

2. Litigation Concerning Free Movement of Goods

Law without the right to legal action is an empty shell. Free movement of goods, a community freedom recognised by the economic operators, cannot be achieved without adequate protection both from the justice system and from the community authorities. Yet, can one bring a state to court for disrespect of the free movement of goods? This question raises the issue of community controls and the means of recourse offered to those brought to trial in virtue of the principle of free movement of goods.

The free movement of goods has a "self-executing" effect, which means that it completes the legal heritage of nationals of community, according to Denys Simon.[63] This effect, which is attached to all supranational rules, was defined by the CJEC in its well-known Van Gend en Loos ruling in 1963.[64] Free movement of goods can thus be invoked before national jurisdictions. No restrictions can oppose this right.[65] In the WAEMU, litigation concerning free movement of goods follows the traditional community litigation channels. So, additional protocol no. 1 concerning WAEMU control bodies, in its article 12, provides that cases can be filed with the court with a preliminary ruling from a national jurisdiction. However, preliminary rulings are rare in the WAEMU. According to article 5 of the same protocol, the Court of Justice recognises, upon recourse by the commission or any member state, member state's negligence of their obligations in virtue of the union

---

[62] See ruling no. 08/CM/UEMOA dated 26 September 2008 concerning adoption of rules aimed at avoiding double taxation in the WAEMU and tax support rules. This ruling took force on 1 January 2009 and can therefore be invoked by union taxpayers.

[63] Denys Simon, *Le système juridique communautaire*, 3rd ed. PUF, Paris, p.387.

[64] CJEC, 5 February 1963, *van Gend en Loos*, 26/62, p. 1- G.A., T. 1, no. 29.

[65] CJEC, 21 June 1974, Jean Reyners v/Etat Belge, aff. 2-74, Rec. 631.

[66] See article 6 of the protocol.

treaty. This procedure could certainly be used for negligence in terms of free movement of goods, but we know that the states are not prone to bringing each other to court, as can be seen from European experience. Also, the negligence procedure in the WAEMU is not restrictive vis-à-vis the states. Strictly speaking, it is more a procedure of cooperation than a legal procedure.[66]

IV   Conclusion

The Dakar treaty strongly resembles the Maastricht treaty, and that is fair enough. Legal mimicking is not bad in and of itself. Yet, European legal material should not be seen as one-size-fits-all for the WAEMU. It is certainly true that legal relations between the economic agents are moving towards globalisation and a symbiosis in the business world would enable economic operators in the two community spaces to not be legally disoriented when they change their geographic location.[67] But the WAEMU has to import and repackage EU legal products in order to take into account the specific nature of its common market because "borrowing...from western experiences and transposing them to French-speaking African republics is to have a poor understanding of the reality".[68] National laws in the WAEMU space are related to French law, yet one should avoid establishing a symmetrical lineage between WAEMU and EU law. WAEMU adaptations of the community free movement of goods system are necessary to take into account the specific nature of the community space. In effect, trade trends are very different from the European model. In the EU, it is a question of good use and good distribution of available resources, while in the WAEMU, the problem is the actual development of these resources.[69]

The WAEMU is resolutely turned towards open markets on a regional level. Achieving this common market requires, however, a certain number of actions. It is first of all necessary to improve the regulatory framework by adding derivative laws and by making them more restrictive. The WAEMU should also work on reducing the time lag that exists between the resolutions and their implementation. In effect, the states do not hesitate to marginalise the rights to free movement of goods, particularly when it leads to loss of income. The commission should, therefore, make sure that community law deploys all its effects (primacy, direct

---

[67] D. Abarchi, Problématique des réformes législatives en Afrique : le mimétisme juridique comme méthode de construction du droit, *Revue Trimestrielle de droit africain (Penant)*, Jan.-Mar 2003, no. 842, P. 88 and following.

[68] F. Perroux, L'économie des jeunes nations, Paris, PUF, 1962, p. 168, cited by L. M. Ibriga in *Sensibilisation au droit communautaire UEMOA*, mentioned above.

[69] André Watteyne, « Une intégration économique africaine à l'image de l'intégration économique européenne : le cas de l'UEMOA », *Revue burkinabé de droit*, no. 39–40, special issue, 2001, p. 83 and following.

and immediate applicability) throughout the WAEMU space. This will also enable the community jurisdiction to play its part in building the community space, because in the EU, where policies have hesitated, the CJEC has made decisions, allowing the European community machine to make progress.

It is then necessary to act upon member states by establishing a schedule to eliminate the barriers to free movement of goods, following the full analysis of tariff and non-tariff barriers that persist within the community space.

Finally, it is necessary to act upon the economic operators by involving them more in the standardisation process. The economic players are, in effect, poorly prepared for liberalisation of trade. Is this not what causes the most fear in the WAEMU integration process?[70] Trade integration must also come with rapid industrialisation. Did not the European Community first focus on the production of coal and steel and then on atomic energy in order to finally embrace its entire economy?

In any case, strengthening the common market in general and free movement of goods in particular is a basic condition for economic development within the WAEMU space. The member states seem to have understood that "Today, the voice of a single state cannot be heard".[71]

References

Abarchi, D., (2003), ' Problématique des réformes législatives en Afrique : le mimétisme juridique commeméthode de construction du droit', *Revue Trimestrielle de droit africain (Penant)*, Jan. –Mar. 2003, no. 842, P. 88 et ss.

BA (D. B.), « Le problème de la compatibilité entre l'UEMOA et l'OHADA », in La libéralisation de l'économie dans le cadre de l'intégration régionale: le cas de l'UEMOA, Actes du colloque de Ouagadougou des 16 et 17 décembre 1999, Publication du CEEI, p. 157

BAMBARA (F.-X.), « La réglementation douanière communautaire de l'UEMOA », in Sensibilisation au droit communautaire de l'UEMOA, Actes du séminaire régional sur l'Ordre communautaire de l'Union Èconomique et Monétaire Ouest Africaine (UEMOA), Ouagadougou, 1er – 5 novembre 2004. pp. 101–116

BERR (C. J.), « introduction au droit douanier », Economica, nouvelle éd. Paris, 2008, p 73.

BERR (J.-C.), et NATAREL (E.), « Union douanière », RTD eur, n° 3, Juil-Sept. 2006, p. 463 et « Union douanière », RTD eur, n° 4, oct-déc. 2007, pp. 665–677.

BLUMANN (C.) et DUBOUIS (L.), Droit Institutionnel de l'Union européenne, 2ème éd., Litec, p. 1s.

BOCCO (A. F.), politique commerciale commune et rôle de l'UEMOA dans les négociations commerciales in Rencontre communautaire d'échange sur « la politique commerciale commune de l'UEMOA et les négociations commerciales », Bamako, du 13 au 15 février 2007.

---

[70] L. M. Ibriga, A.S. Coulibaly, D. Sanou, *Droit communautaire ouest-africain*, col. Précis de droit burkinabé, PADEG, 2008, p. 197.

[71] See European Union report by the Belgian prime minister cited by Etienne Cerexhe, *in* preface by Luc Marius Ibriga, Saïd Abou Coulibaly, Dramane Sanou, *Droit communautaire ouest-africain*, col. Précis de droit burkinabé, ed. Presses Africaines PADEG, 2008, p. I.

CALLEJA (D.), VIGNIER (D.), WÄGENBAUR (R.), dispositions fiscales-rapprochement des législations, commentaires Megret, le droit de CEE, éd. de l'ULB, 2ème ed., 1993, p.3

CEREXHE (E.) et HARDY de BEAULIEU (L. le), « Introduction à l'Union économique ouest africaine, publ. CEEI., Ed. DE Boeck, 1997, pp. 16.

Dubouis, L. and C. Blumann (2009), 'Droit matériel de l'Union européenne' Domat, Droit public, 5th ed., Montchrestien, 2009, 752 p.

Gavalda, C. and G. Parleani (2006), Droit des affaires de l'Union européenne, Paris, Litec, 5th edition, 2006, 570 p.

Mattera, A. (1988), Le marché unique européen : ses règles, son fonctionnement, Jupiter, Paris, 1988, pp. 598.

Olinier, J. and N. De Grove-Valdeyron (2008), Droit du marché intérieur européen, 2nd LGDJ, Paris, 2008. 230 p.

Colloque de Ouagadougou, La libéralisation de l'économie dans le cadre de l'intégration régionale: le cas de l'UEMOA, 16–17 December 1999, Publications du CEEI, no. 3.

Burgorgue-Larsen, L. (2004), 'Prendre les Droits communautaires au sérieux ou la force d'attraction de l'expérience européenne en Afrique et en Amérique Latine', in Mélanges J.C GAUTRON, Les dynamiques du droit européen en début de siècle, Paris, Pedone, 2004, pp.603 et s.

Diarra, E. (2004), 'Coopération ou intégration fiscale au sein de l'Union Economique et Monétaire Ouest Africaine (UEMOA) 'Revue burkinabé de droit, no. 45, September 2004

IBRIGA (L. M.), « L'UEMOA, une nouvelle approche de l'intégration économique régionale en Afrique de l'ouest », Annuaire africain de droit international, Vol. 6, 1998, pp. 23–64.

Ibriga, L.M. (2003), ' L'état de la mise en œuvre de l'union douanière dans l'espace UEMOA' in Sensibilisation au droit communautaire de l'UEMOA, Actes du séminaire sous-régional, Ouagadougou-Burkina Faso du 6–10 October 2003. Paris, ed. Giraf, 2003, pp. 111–124.

« La problématique de la juridictionnalisation des processus d'intégration en Afrique de l'Ouest », Colloque de Rouen du 11 mai 2006, voir : www.institut-idef.org

IBRIGA (L. M.), COULIBALY (A. S.), SANOU (D.), droit communautaire ouest-africain, col. Précis de droit burkinabé, PADEG, 2008, p. 197.

Issa Sayegh, J. (2004), 'L'ordre juridique de l'UEMOA et l'intégration juridique africaine' in mélanges J.C Gautron, Les dynamiques du droit européen en début de siècle, Paris, Pedone, 2004, pp.804 et s.

Kabore, H. T. (2003),'La libéralisation des échanges intracommunautaires et leur impact sur le développement des États membres', in Sensibilisation au droit communautaire de l'UEMOA, Actes du séminaire sous-régional, Ouagadougou-Burkina Faso du 6–10 October 2003. Paris, ed. Giraf, 2003, pp. 79–102.

Kant, E. (2002), Projet de paix perpétuelle, 1ere éd. Vrin, Paris, p. 81

Koutaba, J. (2003), 'Les limites sociologiques du droit', in Sensibilisation au droit communautaire de l'UEMOA: actes du séminaire sous régional des 6-10 octobre 2003, Ouagadougou -Burkina Faso, éd. Giraf, p. 201.

Mattera, A. (1988), Le marché unique européen: ses regles, son functionnement, Jupiter, Paris, pp 598.

Molinier, J and Grove-Valdeyron, N. De. (2008) 'Droit du marché intérieur européen', 2eme LGDJ, Paris, p. 230.

Rigaux, A. and Cavallini, J. (2005) Chronique de jurisprudence de la Cour de justice, RMCUE No 491

Sawadogo, F.M. and L.M. Ibriga (2003), ' L'application des droits communautaires UEMOA et OHADA par le juge national', in Sensibilisation au droit communautaire de l'UEMOA, Actes du séminaire sous-régional, Ouagadougou-Burkina Faso du 6–10 October 2003. Paris, ed. Giraf, 2003, pp. 155–176.

Sossouvi, M. (1989) 'La libre circulation des marchandises et des capitaux dans la Communauté Economique des États de l'Afrique de l'Ouest' (CEDEAO) à travers l'expérience de la Communauté Economique européenne (CEE), Thèse, 1989.

Sow, G. (2003),' La construction de l'union douanière : aspect fiscaux et contentieux douanier', in *Sensibilisation au droit communautaire de l'UEMOA, Actes du séminaire sous-régional*, Ouagadougou-Burkina Faso du 6–10 Octobre 2003. Paris, ed. Giraf, 2003, pp. 125–137.

Toe, J.Y. (2003), ' Quel ordre juridique dans les États de l'Afrique de l'Ouest ? ', in *Sensibilisation au droit communautaire de l'UEMOA, Actes du séminaire sous-régional*, Ouagadougou-Burkina Faso, 6–10 October 2003. Paris, éd. Giraf, 2003, pp. 15–32.

Viaud, P. (1998), ' Union européenne et Union économique et monétaire de l'Ouest africain', *RMCUE*, no. 414, Jan. 1998, p. 15.

Watteyne, A. (2001), 'Une intégration économique africaine à l'image de l'intégration économique européenne : les cas de l'UEMOA', *Revue burkinabé de droit*, no. 39–40, special issue, 2001, p. 83 et ss.

Yehouessi, D. Y. (2004), 'L'ordre juridique communautaire de l'UEMOA', in *Sensibilisation au droit communautaire de l'UEMOA, Actes du séminaire régional sur l'Ordre communautaire de l'Union Economique et Monétaire Ouest Africaine (UEMOA)*, Ouagadougou, 1ᵉʳ – 5 November 2004 : 13–29.

Part II
Regional Financing Instruments and Fighting Poverty

Chapter 9
The Role of Cash Transfers from Migrants in Promoting the Financing of Economic Development in WAEMU Countries

Ameth Saloum Ndiaye

Abstract This study demonstrates that cash transfers from migrants promote economic growth and that these resources contribute to increasing domestic investment. The fundamental stake of these cash transfers is that these resources are perceived as a new source for financing development. By focussing on the WAEMU countries for the period 1974–2006, our results show that productive investment is a major channel through which cash transfers influence growth. An econometric analysis also shows that cash transfers act de facto as a substitute for financial services in promoting productive investment and, as a result, growth in the zone. This result demonstrates, consequently, that the influence of cash transfers on investments occurs in a shallow financial system marked by limitations in liquidity, notably where there are few deposits and limited access to credit. The main implication is that it is essential to channel cash transfers more towards productive investments, first by boosting the number of migrants using banks, thus enabling the financial system to offer savings products and entrepreneurial loans, and secondly by setting up financial and non-financial support structures. In light of this, the study recommends the creation of a regional diaspora investment support fund that could be responsible for identifying promising migrant projects and could provide financial and technical support in order to improve their entrepreneurial capacity and ability to manage their productive activities.

I Introduction

The problem of cash transfers is not new, in view of data from the International Monetary Fund (Balance of Payments Statistics 2008c) that show increasing volumes of transfers since the 1970s. There are several explanations for the

A.S. Ndiaye (✉)
Faculty of Economics and Management (FASEG), Cheikh Anta Diop University (UCAD), Dakar, Senegal
e-mail: asandiaye@yahoo.fr

E.T. Ayuk and S.T. Kaboré (eds.), *Wealth Through Integration*, Insight and Innovation in International Development 4, DOI 10.1007/978-1-4614-4415-2_9,

171

increasing interest shown for these flows of private capital. First, cash transfers have become a progressively more important channel for meeting the need for external funding in developing countries. As a result, what is primarily at stake with these payments is that these resources are perceived as a new source of development funding (Ratha 2003; Spatafora 2005). Secondly, empirical evidence shows that cash sent by migrants is less volatile and therefore more stable and reliable than other financial flows such as official development aid and foreign direct investment (Ratha 2003; Buch and Kuckulenz 2004; Gupta et al. 2007). Thirdly, the resources sent by migrants play an ever more important role in the balance of payments for many developing countries and can significantly contribute to containing the vulnerabilities of their external positions (Bouhga-Hagbe 2006). And finally, recent studies demonstrate that migrant transfers are a useful and effective means to reduce poverty and income inequality (Baruah 2006; Gupta et al. 2007; Chami et al. 2008).

There is a vast amount of empirical literature on the effect of cash transfers, particularly on economic growth. However, to our knowledge, very few studies (Giuliano and Ruiz-Arranz 2005) have done an econometric analysis of the channels through which the cash transfers impact growth. Our study analyses this research question that has not yet been sufficiently explored in the literature by focussing on the channel of productive investment in WAEMU countries for the period from 1974 to 2006. In effect, the growth impact of cash transfers depends greatly on the existence of structures capable of attracting these resources and directing them towards productive activities. As a result, this study contributes to a better under-standing of the impact of cash transfers on the economic development of this union. In addition, the study contributes to a better understanding of the role of the financial system in directing these cash transfers towards productive investment circuits.

This study is structured as follows. The first section presents the issues and justification for the study. The second section outlines the study's objectives. The third section highlights the methodology used. The results, discussions and future research are presented in the fourth section. Policy implications and recommendations are found in section V.

II Problem Statement and Justification

Cash transfers from migrants, perceived as a new source of development funding (Ratha 2003; Spatafora 2005), are generating increasing interest. The importance of this issue for the WAEMU countries can be explained on several levels. First, from 1974 to 2005, the seven top-ranking countries to record the highest volumes of cash transfers in the franc zone (FZ) were members of the WAEMU (cf. Fig. 9.1a). A closer look at the cash transfer-to-GDP ratio shows that WAEMU countries are among the top nine countries receiving cash transfers in the FZ (cf. Fig. 9.1b). Furthermore, according to Gupta, Pattillo and Wagh (2007), in 2005, the majority of WAEMU countries were among the top ten countries benefiting from cash transfers in sub-Saharan Africa.

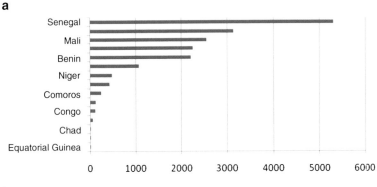

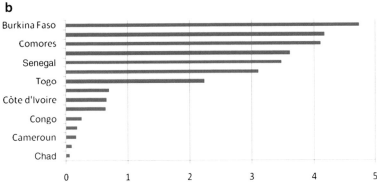

Fig. 9.1 Cash transfers in the franc zone (FZ), 1974–2005 (million US\$ and % of GDP) (**a**) Total cash transfers in FZ, 1974–2005 (millions of US\$) (**b**) Total cash transfers in FZ in % of GDP, 1974–2005 (Source: The author uses data issued by the International Monetary Fund 2007 (CD-ROM))

Table 9.A.1 in Appendix 1 shows cash transfers as a total, on average and as a percentage of the GDP for all the WAEMU countries for the period 1974–2006.

There is a strong upward trend in cash transfers from migrants in the WAEMU (cf. Fig. 9.2). Indeed, over 33 years (1974–2006), these transfers only decreased ten times. Overall, these periods of decrease were not regular. They were only successive between 1981 and 1982, between 1993 and 1994 and from 1996 to 1997; the last year with a decrease was 2005. Over the entire period from 1974 to 2006, WAEMU countries received a total volume of around US\$18.2 billion in resources sent by migrants, representing an average of US\$79.8 million per year (see Table 9.1).

The fund transfers also are slightly above foreign direct investment but are lower than foreign aid (see Fig. 9.2). However, it clearly appears that these cash transfers are less volatile and therefore more stable than other flows of entering capital. This stability of money transfers could enable the governments of WAEMU countries to reduce their need to access international capital.

Furthermore, we can observe major differences between the levels of cash transfers to the extent where, over the entire period, the lowest amount sent by

---

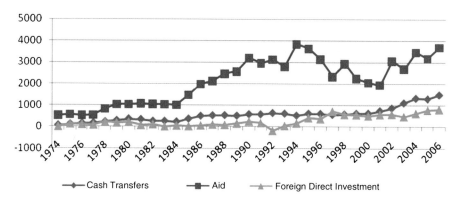

Fig. 9.2 Cash transfers, aid and foreign direct investment in the WAEMU, 1974–2006 (million US$) (Source: The author used data from the World Bank 2008b; the International Monetary Fund 2008c)

Table 9.1 Descriptive statistics of cash transfers in the WAEMU, 1974–2006 (millions of US$)

Statistics	Cash transfers
Total	18188.14
Average	79.77
Median	60
Minimum	2
Maximum	633
Standard deviation	91.30
Variation coefficient	114.45%

Source: The author's calculations use data from the International Monetary Fund (2008c)

migrants was US$2 million, while the ceiling of transferred cash was US$633 million. These results thus demonstrate the broad dispersion of cash transfers, reaching 114.45%. This distribution in cash transfers enables the relative containment of "Dutch disease"[1] effects (Gupta et al. 2007).

Finally, there are a number of stakes involved in cash transfers that are highly strategic for the economies of the WAEMU countries. The impact indicators chosen

---

[1] The Dutch disease is a concept that designates the difficulties that the Dutch encountered following the discovery and exploitation of vast reserves of domestic natural gas. The literature divides the effects of the Dutch disease into the "effect of resource movements", "effect of expenditure" and "effect of exchange rate" (Corden 1984; van Wijnbergen 1984; Neary et van Wijnbergen 2000; Carneiro 2007). The effect of resource movements is observed when the lucrative sector of natural resources attracts resources (talent, capital, public expenditure, etc.) coming from other sectors, contributing in this way to decreasing their growth. The effect of expenditure is present if the income from the natural resources creates increasing demand (and therefore inflation) in other sectors of the economy. The effect of the exchange rate that has been observed with a large internal flow of foreign currency coming from petrol and natural gas exports causes an appreciation of real exchange rate.

Table 9.2 Cash transfer impact indicators in the WAEMU, 1974–2006

	CT/ GDP	CT/ AID	CT/ DEBT	CT/ EXP	CT/ ICOR	CT * ILCR	CT per capita	GDP per capita	AID per capita
Benin	0.84	6.34	2.88	7.90	629.50	0.64	271.08	324.1	42.78
Burkina Faso	0.85	3.65	2.78	8.45	742.56	0.92	221.32	261.52	60.64
Côte d'Ivoire	0.23	9.59	0.17	0.33	276.94	0.23	127.21	555.01	13.27
Guinea-Bissau	0.63	1.71	0.20	1.24	−26.34	0.11	85.69	135.14	50.03
Mali	0.67	2.84	1.63	9.49	372.26	0.38	195.70	289.82	68.97
Niger	0.24	1.37	0.68	1.84	94.08	0.27	40.03	168.38	29.21
Senegal	0.98	7.19	2.99	4.11	1088.62	0.63	491.47	499.2	68.33
Togo	0.82	16.06	0.70	3.47	122.70	0.22	197.10	240.26	12.27
WAEMU	0.66	6.09	1.50	4.60	3300.33	3.42	1629.60	2473.43	345.49

Source: Author's calculations using data from the World Bank (2008a, b), International Monetary Fund (2008a, c)

Note: *CT/GDP* is the cash transfer-to-GDP ratio, *CT/AID* is the cash transfer-to-foreign aid ratio, *CT/DEBT* is the cash transfer-to-external debt ratio, *CT/EXP* is the ratio of cash transfers to exports, *CT/ICOR* is the ratio of cash transfers to the incremental capital output (in millions of US$); CT*ILCR is the product of cash transfers and the incremental capital-to-labour ratio (in millions of jobs); CT per capita designates the cash transfers per capita (in US$); AID per capita indicates the amount of foreign aid per capita (in US$). The per capita GDP is expressed in US$

Note: The period covered is 1974–2006 for all the sample countries, with the exception of Guinea-Bissau (1998–2006), which became a member of the WAEMU on 2 May 1997, and Mali (1985–2006), which joined the WAEMU on 1 June 1984

in Table 9.2 highlight what is at stake for the economies of these countries with migrant cash transfers.

This table, which covers the 1974–2006 period, shows that cash transfers represented more than half the WAEMU 2006 GDP (66%). However, the main limitation of the ratio of cash transfers to GDP is that it does not answer the following question: How much production gain was generated in the economy as a result of reinvesting this transferred cash into productive circuits? To answer this question, we highlight the cash transfer-to-incremental capital output ratio (ICOR).[2] The results indicate that use of transferred cash in productive activities in the economies in the WAEMU countries generated additional production evaluated at US$3300.33 million. This result shows that the resources transferred by migrants from WAEMU countries to their home families could be sources of increased production and thus of economic growth in the union.

As for official development assistance (ODA), our calculations reveal that cash transfers represent more than six times the ODA received by WAEMU countries in 2006. In addition, it appears that the cash transfers exceeded 1.5 times the external debt contracted by the WAEMU countries during the same year. These results imply that, thanks to the market of migrant cash transfers, the WAEMU countries

---

[2] ICOR (incremental capital-output ratio) indicates the production gains generated per unit of capital. It is equal to the relationship between the variation in capital (investment) and the variation in production (GDP) (Beja et al. 2004).

can significantly reduce their development aid needs and their external debt and, as a result, can reduce their dependence on bilateral and multilateral cooperation.

Another indicator that underlines the importance of the cash transfer market is the ratio of cash transfers to total exports. Our estimations indicate that cash transferred by migrants in the WAEMU space represents around 4.6 times the overall exports recorded in this zone in 2005. This conclusion suggests that cash transfers play a very large role in the balance of payments for WAEMU countries and make a significant contribution to limiting the external vulnerability of these countries.

Furthermore, if the cash transfers are reinvested in productive activities, they generate addition employment in the economy. So, how can we evaluate the number of additional jobs that could be created in this way? To do this, we define an indicator that is equal to the product of the cash transfers and the incremental labour-to-capital ratio (ILCR).[3] The results, listed in Table 9.2, show that reorienting the cash transfers to productive circuits could have created 3,420,000 additional jobs throughout all the WAEMU country economies for the period of the study, 1974–2006.

A closer look at Table 9.2 shows that, for the 1974–2006 period, the cash transfers per capita reached US$1629.6 for all the WAEMU countries. If we interpret these cash transfers per capita as being additional income available to each person who receives money transfers, then we can deduce that these resources transferred by migrants increased per capita GDP by an amount equivalent to the pre capita fund transfers.[4] By analogy, official development aid brings the per capita income to a level equal to per capita official development aid plus per capita GDP. Our calculations indicate that, thanks to cash transfers, each person in the WAEMU space could have an income of US$4,103.03, which is higher than the US$2,818.92 that could be obtained, thanks to official development aid. Thus, in the WAEMU zone, the microeconomic impact of cash transfers is more important that the microeconomic impact of official development aid.

The results of the above estimations therefore show that there are many stakes related to cash transferred by migrants for the economies of the WAEMU countries. These can be summarised as follows:

- Cash transfers are a source of growth in production and therefore of economic growth in the WAEMU.
- Cash transfers reduce the WAEMU countries' dependence on bilateral and multilateral cooperation.
- Cash transfers improve the WAEMU countries' external position.

---

[3] ILCR (incremental labour-to-capital ratio) refers to the number of additional jobs created per unit of capital. It is equal to the relationship between the variation in employment and the variation in capital (investment) (Beja et al. 2004).

[4] Because the calculation of per capita GDP does not take into account per capita cash transfers, it is clear that one person who also benefits from cash transfers will have an overall income equal to the sum of per capita GDP and the per capita cash transfer.

– Cash transfers create additional jobs in WAEMU country economies.
– Cash transfers reduce poverty in the WAEMU by increasing the income of all the individuals who receive them.

Nonetheless, these economic impacts are based on the basic hypothesis that the fund transfers are used primarily for financing productive investments. In other words, the challenge for political decision makers in WAEMU countries is to channel the cash transferred by migrants towards productive jobs.

III   Study Objectives

The overall objective of this study is to explore how cash transfers from migrants affect economic development in WAEMU countries. The specific goals consist of (a) analysing the impact of cash transfers on economic growth, (b) exploring how cash transfers impact investment to verify if productive investment is an important channel through which cash transfers impact economic growth and (c) analysing the role the financial system plays in guiding the cash transfers towards productive investment circuits. We will use an econometric methodology, as outlined below, to address these various issues.

IV   Methodology

This section proposes an econometric investigation of the influence cash transfers have on economic growth and on domestic investment. In addition, we will make an econometric examination of the role the financial system plays in the use of cash transfers for productive investment.

The Economic Growth Model

To assess the effects of cash transfers on economic growth, we use the following basic equation:

$$\text{TCP}_{it} = \delta_0 + \delta_1 \, \text{TCP}_{i,t-3} + \delta_2 \text{TFP}_{it} + \delta_3 X_{it} + u_i + v_t + \varepsilon_{it} \qquad (9.1)$$

where TCP is the real rate of GDP growth; TFP designates the ratio of cash transfers to GDP; X represents the vector of control variables including the inflation rate (INF) measured by the annual variation of the consumer price index, investment

(INV) and the quality of institutions (QINST) measured by the limitations placed on executive power with these taking on values ranging from 1 (unlimited executive power) to 7 (parity or executive subordination) (cf. Polity IV Project database); u is the specific country effect; v is the specific time effect; ε is the error term; i indicates a given country and t indicates a year.

In the econometric regressions, we use the two-stage least squares approach. The choice of this method can be explained by the existence of potentially endogenous variables. In effect, theoretically, cash transfers could increase when the rate of economic growth increases. Thus, cash transfers could appear as an endogenous variable in the model. As a result, the orthogonality error hypothesis is violated by ordinary least squares (Kpodar 2005). This is why we treat this problem of endogeneity by using the two-stage least squares approach. To this end, we instrument this endogenous variable with its lagged values.

To understand if productive investment constitutes an important channel through which cash transfers influence economic growth, in the next section, we will examine the impact of cash transfers on domestic investment.

The Domestic Investment Model

The basic domestic investment equation is as follows:

$$INVP_{it} = \eta_0 + \eta_1 INVP_{i,t-1} + \eta_2 TFP_{it} + \eta_3 Y_{it} + u_i + v_t + \varepsilon_{it} \qquad (9.2)$$

where INVP is the ratio of domestic investment to GDP; TFP is the ratio of cash transfers to GDP; Y represents the vector of control variables including the inflation rate (INF) measured by the annual variation of the consumer price index, the rate of real GDP growth (TCP) and the quality of institutions (QINST) measured by the limitations placed on executive power with these taking on values ranging from 1 (unlimited executive power) to 7 (parity or executive subordination) (cf. Polity IV Project database); u is the specific country effect; v is the specific time effect; ε is the error term; i indicates a given country; and t a year.

We use the two-stage least squares approach to deal with issues of endogeneity to the extent that the cash transfers could prove to be endogenous in the investment model. To this end, we instrument this endogenous variable by its lagged values.

As we indicated above, the major challenge for policy makers in WAEMU countries is to channel the cash sent by migrants towards productive investment. Therefore, in the following model, we will be analysing how the financial system influences the impact that cash transfers have on domestic investment.

Financial System, Cash Transfers and Domestic Investment

To grasp the role the financial system plays in using cash transfers for productive investment, we specify the basic model in the following way:

$$
\begin{aligned}
\text{INVP}_{it} = {} & \psi_0 + \psi_1\text{INVP}_{i,t-1} + \psi_2\text{TFP}_{it} + \psi_3\text{DEFI}_{it} + \psi_4(\text{TFP}_{it} * \text{DEFI}_{it}) \\
& + \psi_5 Z_{it} + u_i + v_t + \varepsilon_{it}
\end{aligned} \tag{9.3}
$$

where INVP is the ratio of domestic investment to GDP; TFP is the ratio of cash transfers to GDP; DEFI indicates financial development measured using two indicators, notably the private sector credit to GDP ratio (CPP) and the deposits to GDP ratio (DEP); the term (TFP*DEFI) is a measure of the interaction between the cash transfers and the financial system[5]; Z represents the vector of control variables including the inflation rate (INF) measured by the annual variation of the consumer price index, the rate of real GDP growth (TCP) and the quality of institutions (QINST) measured by the limitations placed on executive power with these taking on values ranging from 1 (unlimited executive power) to 7 (parity or executive subordination) (CF. Polity IV Project database); u is the specific country effect; v is the specific time effect; ε is the error term; i indicates a given country; and t a year.

To handle the endogeneity problems that can arise in the model, we use the two-stage least squares approach by instrumenting the potential endogenous variables (cash transfers, financial development and their interaction) by their lagged value.

The results of the econometric regressions are examined in the following section.

V   Results, Discussions and Future Work

Effects of Cash Transfers on Economic Growth in the WAEMU

The results of the effect of cash transfers on economic growth in the WAEMU are found in Table 9.3. The cash transfer coefficient is positive and statistically significant, suggesting that migrant cash transfers make a significant contribution to promoting economic growth in the WAEMU. These results remain true even after being controlled for other variables, notably macroeconomic variables (investment and inflation) and institutional variables (quality of institutions).

---

[5] In addition to the interaction variable (TFP*DEFI), we separately considered cash transfers and financial development as independent variable in Eq. 9.3 to ensure that the interaction term was not a proxy variable for either cash transfers or financial development (Giuliano and Ruiz-Arranz 2005).

Table 9.3 The impact of cash transfers on economic growth in the WAEMU

Explicative variables	(1)	(2)	(3)	(4)
Migrant cash transfers (TFP)	0.249	0.293	0.229	0.248
	(2.02)**	(2.42)**	(1.82)*	(1.76)*
Rate of economic growth (TCP$_{-3}$)	0.113	0.093	0.114	0.071
	(1.96)*	(1.47)	(1.98)**	(1.16)
Inflation rate (INF$_{-6}$)		−0.106		
		(3.12)***		
Quality of institutions (QINS)			0.000	
			(2.26)**	
Investment (INV)				0.163
				(2.11)**
Constant	0.019	0.025	0.020	−0.008
	(3.14)***	(3.83)***	(3.24)***	(0.65)
Observations	209	163	209	202
R^2	0.023	0.095	0.033	0.07

Robust z statistics in parenthesis

Note: The dependent variable is the rate of economic growth. The regressions are done using the two-stage least squares approach. The endogenous variable, cash transfers (TFP), is instrumented by its value lagged by a year in the regressions (1), (2) and (3) and by its value lagged by 2 years in regression (4). The definitions and sources of each of these variables are found in the appendix (Table 9.A.3)

* Significant at 10%; ** significant at 5%; *** significant at 1%

Effect of Cash Transfers on Domestic Investment in the WAEMU

The results presented in Table 9.4 show that cash transfers have a positive and significant impact on domestic investment in the WAEMU. This result implies that an increase in the amount of cash sent by migrants contributes to raising the level of domestic investment in this zone. This result remains true even when controlling for other variables, notably macroeconomic variables (investment and inflation) and institutional variables (quality of institutions). Furthermore, this result shows that productive investment constitutes a major channel through which cash transfers influence economic growth in this union.

The coefficients for cash transfers reported in Table 9.4 go from 0.174 to 0.444 for an average of 0.309. Because cash transfers and investment are measured as a percentage of the GDP, the result is that a dollar transferred by migrants generates about 31% productive investment in the WAEMU. This shows that a small part of the cash-transferred is used to finance productive investment in the union, revealing the full scale of the challenge policy makers face in order to channel more the resources sent by migrants towards productive activities so as to more effectively promote economic growth.

Table 9.4 Impact of cash transfers on domestic investment in the WAEMU

Explicative variables	(1)	(2)	(3)	(4)
Migrant cash transfers (TFP)	0.174	0.301	0.213	0.444
	(1.66)*	(2.99)***	(1.77)*	(2.11)**
Investment (INV$_{-1}$)	0.804	0.747	0.800	0.720
	(10.06)***	(10.56)***	(9.81)***	(8.92)***
Inflation rate (INF$_{-5}$)		−0.044		
		(1.82)*		
Quality of institutions (QINS$_{-1}$)			0.000	
			(3.31)***	
Rate of economic growth (TCP)				0.148
				(1.77)*
Constant	0.029	0.036	0.028	0.028
	(2.48)**	(3.28)***	(2.43)**	(2.63)***
Observations	214	164	206	182
R^2	0.65	0.71	0.67	0.69

Robust z statistics in parentheses

Note: The dependent variable is the rate of domestic investment. The regressions are done using the two-stage least squares approach. The endogenous variable, cash transfers (TFP), is instrumented by its value lagged by a year in the regressions (1) and (2), by its value lagged by 2 years in regression (3) and by its value lagged by 5 years in regression (4). The definitions and sources of each of these variables are found in the appendix (Table 9.A.3)

* significant at 10%; ** significant at 5%; *** significant at 1%

Role of the Financial System in Using Cash Transfers for Productive Investment in the WAEMU

Table 9.5 presents the results related to the influence the financial system has on the impact of cash transfers on domestic investment. The results reveal that whatever the indicator used to measure financial development (private sector credit or deposit), there is a negative and significant interaction between cash transfers and financial instruments; this suggests that cash transfers promote investment in a shallow financial system. Thus, there is a relationship of substitutability between cash transfers and financial instruments; cash transfers act de facto as a substitute for financial services to promote productive investment and, as a result, economic growth in the WAEMU. This result remains true, even when we control for other variables, including economic growth, inflation and the quality of institutions.

From another angle, this result reveals the existence of constraints linked to liquidity that lead to an inefficient financial system. The liquidity constraints can stem from the fact that the financial system does not help potential entrepreneurs to start up productive activities due to a lack of guarantee and to high interest rates on loans (Giuliano and Ruiz-Arranz 2005). As a result, the financial market does not fully fulfil its role, which is to meet the financial needs of economic agents, to the extent that cash transfers tend to substitute for the domestic banking system's capacity to meet market needs. As a result, the shallow financial system does not

Table 9.5 Financial system, cash transfers and domestic investment in the WAEMU

	Private sector credit				Deposits			
	(1)	(2)	(3)	(4)	(5)	(6)	(7)	(8)
INV_{-1}	0.624	0.563	0.621	0.616	0.699	0.705	0.695	0.705
	(9.00)***	(4.57)***	(9.08)***	(7.65)***	(9.19)***	(8.78)***	(9.12)***	(8.22)***
TFP	2.014	2.663	1.971	1.789	0.612	0.682	0.590	0.501
	(2.15)**	(2.55)**	(2.06)**	(1.91)*	(3.11)***	(3.48)***	(2.99)***	(2.21)**
CPP	0.109	0.059	0.104	0.099				
	(1.01)	(0.73)	(0.94)	(0.96)				
CPP*TFP	−8.231	−10.556	−8.070	−7.543				
	(1.80)*	(1.93)*	(1.75)*	(1.66)*				
DEP					0.041	0.044	0.040	0.034
					(2.52)**	(2.56)**	(2.48)**	(2.03)**
DEP*TFP					−0.455	−0.487	−0.446	−0.71
					(2.50)**	(2.57)**	(2.46)**	(1.98)**
INF_{-2}		−0.018						
		(0.50)						
INF_{-1}						−0.008		
						(0.28)		
QINS			0.000				0.000	
			(1.04)				(1.86)*	
TCP				0.199				0.142
				(2.85)***				(1.65)*
Constant	0.022	0.037	0.024	0.022	0.025	0.024	0.027	0.025
	(0.87)	(2.04)**	(0.91)	(1.00)	(2.56)**	(2.37)**	(2.68)***	(2.41)**
Observations	174	132	174	174	182	167	182	182
R^2	0.45	0.56	0.46	0.52	0.68	0.72	0.68	0.70

* significant at 10%; ** significant at 5%; *** significant at 1%

Robust z statistics in parentheses

Note: The dependent variable is the rate of domestic investment. The regressions are done using the two-stage least squares approach. The endogenous variable, cash transfers (TFP), private sector credit (CPP) and their interaction (CPP*TFP) are instrumented by their value lagged by 6 years in the regressions (1), (3) and (4) and by their value lagged by 10 years in regression (2). The endogenous variables, cash transfers (TFP), deposits (DEP) and their interaction (DEP*TFP) are instrumented by their value lagged by 5 years in regressions (1), (2), (3) and (4). The definitions and sources of each of these variables are found in the appendix (Table 9.A.3)

offer migrants enough financial services, such as savings products and entrepreneurial loans, so that the resources that are transferred be channelled more towards productive investments in order to stimulate economic growth.

This econometric exercise enabled us to demonstrate that the volume of investment constitutes an important channel by which cash transfers from migrants promote economic growth. It would be interesting, for future studies, to also econometrically explore other potential channels that could include investment efficiency, investment in human capital, and even the multiplying effects from saving and a higher internal demand (Giuliano et Ruiz-Arranz 2005).

VI   Policy Implications and Recommendations

The results from the econometric regressions showed that cash transfers from migrants contribute to boosting the volume of domestic investment and therefore to promoting economic growth in the WAEMU. However, we have found that the influence of cash transfers on investment works in a shallow financial system marked by the presence of liquidity constraints, with notably few deposits and limited access to credit. As a result, any policy aiming to stimulate the volume of investment and to improve growth must take into account the necessity of promoting the financial system and also how to better channel migrant cash transfers. In this context, two approaches to economic policy could be chosen.

The first is related to the use of the cash transferred by the migrants. It has been well established in the literature that productive investment occupies a bare bones portion of the transferred cash in terms of its use; the majority of the resources sent by migrants serve to help the family or to finance real estate (African Development Bank 2008). Yet, to improve the impact of cash transfers on economic development, it is essential to use the cash sent more efficiently by channelling it more to productive investment (Gupta et al. 2007).

To do so, it is important to strengthen the use of banks by migrants.[6] Hence the financial system could more efficiently contribute to promoting productive investment coming from the cash transfers by offering financial services such as savings products and entrepreneurial credit. Then, it is important to set up financial and non-financial support measures to favour migrants with investment projects. Thus, it is absolutely necessary to create structures that can attract and channel cash transfers towards productive activities. In this way, it is important to set up a regional diaspora investment fund in the WAEMU area that could be a novel basic regional instrument for financing economic development in this zone. This regional fund could function by identifying promising projects led by migrants from WAEMU countries and helping them to improve their technical capacities to start their

---

[6] This is the Hispanic approach to cash transfers.

business and to manage productive activities, and also to fund their projects. This fund could provide either credit or guarantees to migrants.

Other than the use of cash transfers for productive investments, the other economic policy that could improve the impact of cash transfers on productive investment and on growth is to ensure that the resources that are sent by migrants come through formal channels. To do this, it is first necessary to stimulate competition on the cash transfer market,[7] considering that one of the results brought to light by the African Development Bank (2008) was that the more this market is competitive, the more the cash transfers use formal channels. In effect, increased competition on the money transfer market has the advantage of significantly decreasing transaction costs and of progressively absorbing informal transfers.[8] Table 9.A.2 in the Appendix reports the charges of major cash transfer agencies for an amount of 300 euros sent from France. This table reveals the competition between money transfer companies that contributes to decreasing the costs of cash transfer costs. Secondly, a strategy of increasing bank use among migrants could lead to a more formal way of transferring money.

VII   Conclusion

In this study, we have analysed the role played by cash transfers by migrants in promoting economic development in the WAEMU countries. For the entire period from 1974 to 2006, these countries recorded a total cash transfer volume of around US$18.2 billion, which represents an average of US$79.8 million per year. According to our estimations, these cash transfers represent several stakes of strategic importance for the WAEMU country economies. These transfers provide opportunities for reducing their dependence on external sources by lessening their need for development aid and external debt, boosting their production, creating jobs, improving their external position and reducing poverty as a result of increasing the income of each individual that benefited from these money transfers.

Using the two-stage least squares approach used to handle problems of endogeneity, we have found that cash transfers promote economic growth in the WAEMU and that these resources sent by migrants contribute considerably to increasing the level of domestic investment in this zone. This result shows that the volume of productive investment constitutes an important channel through which cash transfers influence economic growth in this union. The econometric

---

[7] According to the approach to cash transfers in the English-speaking world, one can stimulate competition on the cash transfer market with looser regulations.

[8] Nevertheless, the study by the African Development Bank (2008) found that the transaction costs have a secondary influence on the choice of how the resources are sent by migrants; this choice is primarily determined by the beneficiaries, who focus on the criteria of speed and fund accessibility.

analysis also indicates a negative interaction between the cash transfers and the financial development indicators (private sector credit and deposits), revealing a relationship of substitutability between cash transfers and financial instruments; the cash transfers act de facto as a substitute for financial services in promoting productive investment and, thus, economic growth in the WAEMU. Consequently, this result shows that the influence of cash transfers on investment operates within a shallow financial system marked by the presence of liquidity constraints, with notably few deposits and limited access to credit.

Thus, to improve the impact of cash transfers on economic development, it is essential to channel the transfers more towards productive investments by increasing bank use among migrants, thus enabling the financial system to contribute more effectively to guiding money transfers to productive sectors with the offer of financial services such as savings products and entrepreneurial credit. In addition, it is important to set up structures that can attract and channel money transfers towards productive activities. The study recommends the creation of a regional diaspora investment support fund that could identify promising projects for migrants from WAEMU countries and provide financial and technical support to improve their capacity to start their businesses and manage productive activities.

Appendix

Table 9.A.1 Cash transfers in the WAEMU, 1974–2006 (*million* US$ and % of GDP)

Country	Total	Annual average	In % of GDP
Benin	2,374.6	71.9	4.2
Burkina Faso	3,178	96.3	4.6
Côte d'Ivoire	2,406	75.2	0.7
Guinea Bissau	141	15.7	3.5
Mali	2,342.2	106.5	3.6
Niger	549.9	16.7	0.7
Senegal	5,933	179.8	3.6
Togo	1,263.5	38.3	2.4
WAEMU	18,188.1	75.0	2.9

Source: Calculations by authors using data from IMF (2008c) (Edition CD-ROM)

Table 9.A.2 Cost of cash transfer for a sum of 300 euros sent from France

Mode of transfer	Cost (euro)	Time
Western Union	29	10 min
Money Gram	23	10 min
I bank transfer[a]	10	2 days
I cash transfer[a]	20	3 days
Ordinary postal money order	10.60	3–5 days
Express postal money order	16.70	12 h

Source: African Development Bank (2008)
[a]m-banking Société Générale

Table 9.A.3 Definition of sources of variables

Variable	Definition	Source
CPP	Private sector credit-to-GDP ratio	World Bank (2008b)
DEP	Deposits-to-GDP ratio	International Monetary Fund (2008b)
INF	Inflation rate measured by variation in consumer price index	World Bank (2008b)
INV	Investment-to-GDP ratio	World Bank (2008b)
TCP	Rate of real GDP growth	World Bank (2008b)
TFP	Cash transfer-to-GDP ratio	International Monetary Fund (2008a)
QINS	Quality of institutions measured by limitations on executive power, with these limitations being given values ranging from 1 (unlimited executive power) to 7 (parity or executive subordination)	Polity IV Project's database

References

African Development Bank (2008), Les transferts des fonds des migrants, un enjeu de développement

Baruah, N. (2006), 'Les rapatriements de fonds à destination des pays les moins avancés (PMA): la circulation des fonds et les politiques en la matière', *Organisation Internationale pour les Migrations (OIM)*, Papier présenté à la Conférence ministérielle des Pays les Moins Avancés concernant le renforcement de l'impact des rapatriements de fonds sur le développement, Cotonou, Benin, February 2006

Beja, E. L., P. Junvith and J. Ragusett (2004), 'Capital Flight from Thailand', in Gerald Epsein, ed., *Capital Flight and Capital Controls in Developing Countries*, Edward Elgar Publishing

Bouhga-Hagbe, J. (2006), 'Altruism and Workers' Remittances: Evidence from Selected Countries in the Middle East and Central Asia', *International Monetary Fund*, Working Paper 06/130

Buch, C. and A. Kuckulenz (2004), 'Worker Remittances and Capital Flows to Developing Countries', Discussion Paper No. 04–31, Mannheim: *Centre for European Economic Research*

Carneiro, F. G. (2007), 'Development Challenges of Resource-Rich Countries: the Case of Oil Exporters', *World Bank-Africa Region*

Chami, R., A. Barajas, T. Cosimano, C. Fullenkamp, M. Gapen and P. Montiel (2008), 'Macroeconomic Consequences of Remittances', *International Monetary Fund*, Occasional Paper 259

Corden, W. M. (1984), 'Booming sector and Dutch Disease economics: Survey and consolidation', *Oxford Economic Papers*, vol. 36

Giuliano, P. and M. Ruiz-Arranz (2005), 'Remittances, Financial Development, and Growth', *International Monetary Fund*, Working Paper 05/234

Gupta, S., C. Pattillo and S. Wagh (2007), 'Impact of Remittances on Poverty and Financial Development in Sub-Saharan Africa', *International Monetary Fund*, Working Paper 07/38

International Monetary Fund (2007), *Balance of Payments Statistics (2007)*

International Monetary Fund (2008a), *Direction of Trade Statistics (2008)*

International Monetary Fund (2008b), *International Financial Statistics (2008)*

International Monetary Fund (2008c), *Balance of Payments Statistics (2008)*

Kpodar, K. (2005), 'Manuel d'initiation à Stata (Version 8', *Centre d'Etudes et de Recherches sur le Développement International (CERDI), Centre National de la Recherche Scientifique (CNRS)*

Neary, J. and S. van Wijnbergen (2000), 'Natural Resources and the Macroeconomy: A Theoretical Framework', in P. Stevens (ed.), *The Economics of Energy*, Edward Elgar

Ratha, D. (2003), 'Workers' Remittances: An Important and Stable Source of External Development Finance', *Global Development Finance, 2003*-Striving for Stability in Development Finance, (Washington: World Bank)

Spatafora, N. (2005), 'Two Current Issues Facing Developing Countries' in *World Economic Outlook, 2005*, (Washington: International Monetary Fund)

van Wijnbergen, S. (1984), 'The Dutch Disease: A disease after all?', *Economic Journal*, vol. 94 (373)

World Bank (2008a), *Global Development Finance (2008)*

World Bank (2008b), *World Development Indicators (2008)*

Chapter 10
Efficiency of Credit That Targets the Poor: Measures and Application of Agricultural Credit in Burkina Faso

Samuel Tambi Kaboré

Abstract Micro-credit has become a frequently used a tool to reduce poverty by targeting the poor through a variety of indicators. The efficiency of this type of micro-credit is not measured in the literature. This study proposes an efficiency index for credit programmes that target the poor, calculated based on the effectiveness of the target indicators. The efficiency index, which is calculated for agricultural credit, measures the percentage of the total envelope that reaches the poor. The results indicate that targeting farming has the potential of enabling agriculture credit to reach at least 89% of the monetarily poor households, with an efficiency index of less than 42%. This eligibility of the poor falls to 13.2% of poor households in 1998 and 22% in 2003 when targeting actual applicants for agricultural loans. Ultimately, agricultural credit reaches fewer than 11% of the monetarily poor households, with an actual efficiency of at most 42%. The large gap between potential and real eligibility indicates the eviction of the poor due to a variety of implicit indicators whose in-depth analysis will allow credit programmes to be better adapted to the target group. Targeting on the basis of other indicators, such as the major grains (e.g. sorghum), small ruminant breeding or the possession of farmland, is effective when it comes to the eligibility of poor households but inefficient in eliminating those who are not poor, which yields an efficiency index of at most 42%, even if the financial administration is effective in transferring the funds to the poor. To reach many more of the poor, agricultural credit still needs to be adapted to the conditions of the poorest, while agrarian reform that would give legal value to land, would offer the poor greater access to credit.

S.T. Kaboré (✉)
UFR/SEG (Research and Training Centre in Economics and Management),
University of Ouagadougou II, Burkina Faso
e-mail: stkabore@yahoo.fr

E.T. Ayuk and S.T. Kaboré (eds.), *Wealth Through Integration*, Insight and Innovation in International Development 4, DOI 10.1007/978-1-4614-4415-2_10,

I Introduction

Micro-finance and particularly micro-credit is being used more frequently by international financial institutions and local development actors as a tool[1] to reduce poverty. Financial institutions, the state and civil society organisations have developed a variety of micro-finance programmes to improve the access by the poor to financial services. Since analytical studies[2] have shown that poverty in Africa tends to be rural and agricultural in nature, agricultural credit initiatives have been developed or reinforced. To reach the poor, micro-finance service promoters, particularly those providing micro-credit, have proposed a variety of conditions, which we will discuss hereafter. Within the WAEMU, several initiatives have been launched, such as the Banque Régionale de Solidarité (BRS), the Regional Integration Aid Fund (RIAF), the Regional Agricultural Development Fund (RADF) and the Development and Cohesion Fund (FDC). The various access requirements constitute, in reality, implicit or explicit targeting indicators that influence the impact of credit as a tool to fight poverty.

In the analysis of the impact of credit programmes aimed at the poor, a distinction is generally made between efficiency and effectiveness[3] of credit (Ribe et al. 1990). The change in the beneficiaries' standard of living (effectiveness) has been the object of numerous analyses, unlike efficiency, which has been little analysed (cf. the below section on the issue).

Measuring the efficiency of the funds spent therefore deserves some attention, and this study contributes to analysing this issue. Measuring efficiency, however difficult, enables an evaluation of how the effects of poverty-reduction efforts shift from their initial target to the benefit of those who are not poor. This shift can have favourable indirect consequences on the poor (job creation, transfers, etc.) but in the short term contributes to reducing the impact of poverty-reduction strategies, because the poor in African countries are primarily self-employed farmers. This efficiency depends on errors in targeting linked to the targeting indicator and to performance in terms of cost of the institution that administers the credit (state project, NGO, credit institution in partnership with the state or development partners).

---

[1] The Poverty Reduction Strategy Documents (PRSD) of Benin (2002), Burkina Faso (2000 et 2004), Ghana (2003), Cameroon (2003), Guinea (2000), Mali (2002), Niger (2002) and Senegal (2002) provide for the development of financial services and notably micro-finance as a poverty-reduction tool (MEDEV (2004), MEF (2000, 2002), MF (2003), MINEPAT (2003), SP/CNDLP (2002) and SP/SRP (2002)).

[2] We can cite the INSD (1996, 2000a, 2000b, 2003) in Burkina Faso, Grootaert and Kanbur (1990), Grootaert (1996) in Côte d'Ivoire, Geda et al. (2001) in Kenya, Datt and Jolliffe (1999) in Egypt and the Poverty Reduction Strategy Documents (PRSD) developed between 2002 and 2006 (cf. see above notes and the references for more details).

[3] The efficiency of credit refers to the percentage of the overall expenditure (envelope) that reaches poor households, while the effectiveness measures how much the beneficiaries' standard of living increases.

The question of the effectiveness of credit institutions has been discussed at length in the literature but only from the perspective of micro-economic agents who wish to maximise their profits and who, to do so, can exclude the poor from credit or give them more expensive credit. Berger and Humphrey (1997) summarise 130 studies on credit institution effectiveness in 21 countries. The approach consists generally of using parametric or non-parametric analysis to estimate a cost or production function and to measure effectiveness by the relative difference in relation to the frontier that symbolises the best practice. At least five methods belonging to the two types are used and discussed by Berger and Humphrey (1997), and certain variants by Mester (1996) and McKillop et al. (2002). These approaches can be used to inspire methods to evaluate the effectiveness of targeting indicators. However, these methods are not apt for measuring the efficiency of credit targeting the poor as defined by Ribe et al. (1990) as the percentage of the credit that reaches the poor.

This study proposes a measure of the efficiency of credit based on the effectiveness of targeting indicators used to reach the poor. The efficiency indices are illustrated through agricultural credit programmes in Burkina Faso and then with the help of alternative targeting indicators—activities and sustained assets owned by households—in order to broaden the scope for assessing the targeting options capable of improving the efficiency of credit that targets the poor.

Section II focuses on the statement of the problem and is followed by the objectives of the analysis (Section III). The conceptual framework and the methodology are presented in Section IV. In Section V, the sources of the data are presented, along with the distribution of households in Burkina in relation to the potential targeting indicators. The results will be discussed in Section VI and will enable the formulation of the conclusion.

II   Problem Statement and Justification

Granting credit to a poor household to carry out a given activity has two effects: (1) its efficiency, i.e. the percentage of the overall expenditure that reaches the poor household, and (2) its effectiveness, i.e. the percentage by which the beneficiary's standard of living increases (Ribe et al. 1990). The credit's contribution to reducing poverty will be assessed by these two effects, which are components of its impact on poverty. Figure 10.1 should facilitate this discussion. At point A, the targeting policy reaches few poor (targeting indicators with a low level of efficiency) but high effectiveness, i.e. it greatly increases the standard of living of those who receive it (high K investment per poor person or higher profitability of the financed activity or both). At point A, if those who are reached are among the extremely poor, then the poverty severity index will be the most impacted.

Point B is the ideal point corresponding to a good targeting policy that reaches both a lot of poor and increases their standard of living greatly. In this case, the incidence, depth and severity of poverty will all decrease. Point C corresponds to a

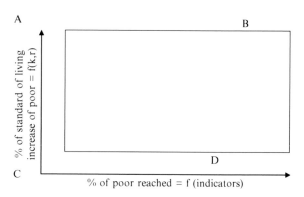

Fig. 10.1 Analysis of targeting policies (Source: Author)

poor targeting policy that reaches few poor and does little to increase the standard of living of the beneficiaries. At point D, the policy reaches a large number of poor but has only a small impact on their income levels.

From a strictly micro-economic point of view, the effectiveness of the targeting (ordinate axis) is, without a doubt, the most important measurement because it is linked directly to the standard of living and the well-being of the poor. Existing literature on the links between micro-credit and poverty reduction focuses primarily on this element (Zaman 2002; Olsen 2001; Todd 1998; Kaboré 2009). The main concern of the studies is how to be located on the right side (AB) of Fig. 10.1, without really knowing if one is close to A or to B, which nevertheless has different implications. Micro-finance institutions (MFI) use several tools and techniques to target poor clients in an effort to get closer to point B. These include simple and composite indicators, as well as those that are qualitative or quantitative and subjective or objective.

For example, the Grameen Bank of Bangladesh offers the credit to households that possess less than a half an acre of land. The BRAC Network in Bangladesh also targets the poor by requiring that beneficiaries have less than 0.5 acres of cultivated surface area and that they be manual farmers; this indicator enables the targeting of between 70 and 85% of primarily poor members (Zaman 2002). The CASHPOR (Credit and Saving for the Hard-Core Poor) in Asia has opted for targeting by housing type using a housing index that consists of rating the various characteristics of the house (size, structure, quality of the walls and of the roof) and of ranking households based on the average score. The SHARE and TPSI networks in India also use housing type to target by setting "threshold scores" for credit eligibility. The SEF (Small Enterprise Foundation) network in South Africa targets the poor using visual indicators of poverty (VIP) and a ranking called participatory wealth ranking (PWR)[4] (Simanowitz et al. 2000).

---

[4] The PWR index is built in a community meeting. The meeting participants are divided into three to five groups. Each group is responsible for placing the community's households into wealth and well-being categories. The poor category gets the highest score and the richest the lowest. The households are then ranked based on the average scores obtained by the three to five groups.

When poverty presents spatial concentrations, geographic targeting can be an effective tool by addressing the interventions and allocation of basic services to deprived or vulnerable zones or groups. The SKS (Swayam Krishi Sangam) network targets the untouchable caste in India using geographic targeting. The Maasai pastoral community in Kenya is also targeted in this way by the WEEC (Women Economic Empowerment Consort).

In the WAEMU space, national and regional support and/or credit fund initiatives use sector-based or social targeting. Those regional funds that use sector-based targeting include (1) the regional integration aid fund (RIAF), created in 1999 and targeting income-generating activities (IGA) in cross-border zones; (2) the regional agricultural development fund (RADF), which was created in 2006 and targets production and a common agricultural market, SME/SMIs and rural micro-enterprises (RME); and (3) the development and cohesion fund. In Burkina, sectorial targeting refer to agricultural credit and to certain funds like FAGRA that are destined for the agricultural sector. As for social targeting, we can cite the Banque Régionale de Solidarité (BRS), which targets the insertion of women and young people, reinsertion of workers, decentralised financial systems (DFS) and micro-enterprises. At the national level, we can cite the Fonds d'Appui aux Activités Rémunératrices des Femmes (FAARF).

Finally, there has been an increase in the development of more or less sophisticated statistical tools for targeting. The PAT (poverty assessment tool) developed by the IFPRI on behalf of the CGAP is a relevant example. It is based on an index or composite score for multidimensional poverty and can be implemented in five main phases[5] (Henry et al. 2003). When MFI clients are proportionally more numerous in the low-score class (the poorest), the intervention of the MFI is considered to be targeting the poor better. The PAT is not, in itself, a targeting tool but rather enables an evaluation of the degree to which the poor are reached by the MFI and also to make a comparison of several MFI. If we refer to Fig. 10.1, the PAT helps to evaluate if one is closer to A or to B but does not make it possible to pronounce on efficiency defined as the percentage of the overall expenditure that reaches poor households.

It is, however, important to have a tool for evaluating alternative targeting indicators that make it possible to more effectively reach the poor and, in this case, to determine the efficiency of credit granted according to these indicators. These are the questions that we will examine in this study. The empirical evaluation of efficiency

---

[5] The PAT is implemented in five steps: (1) carrying out a survey an a sample that includes MFI clients and non-clients who serve as a control, (2) generating a poverty index or score for each household by applying the analysis of the principle components, (3) dividing the control population into quantiles, the first of which corresponds to the poverty index within the population, (4) determining the "threshold scores" that enable a reproduction of the quantiles obtained in step 3 and (5) producing the frequencies of the MFI clients analysed in each class of scores identified in step 4.

is undertaken on agricultural credit in Burkina Faso. An analysis of the dynamics of poverty between 1994 and 2003 by socio-economic group shows that monetary and non-monetary poverty affects primarily farmers, who employ more than 80% of the active labour force; whereas the rural areas of Burkina Faso, composed essentially of farmers, contributed 96%, 93.9% and 92.2% to national poverty in 1994, 1998 and 2003, respectively (INSD 1996, 2000b, 2003). The emphasis on credit that is aimed at farmers means focussing on nearly 90% of national poverty.

III   Objectives

The overall objective of the study is to measure efficiency of credit that targets a poor population group. More specifically, the study aims at the following: (1) proposing a measurement of efficiency for credit that targets the poor, (2) measuring the efficiency of agricultural credit based on the proposed index and (3) determining the policy implications of credit that better targets farmers.

IV   Conceptual Framework and Methodology

The approach to evaluating the efficiency of credit targeting the poor will be discussed first and then applied to agricultural credit and to other alternative indicators for targeting credit.

Efficiency of credit targeting the poor is defined according to Ribe et al. (1990) as indicated above and depends on the effectiveness of the targeting indicators. Measuring the effectiveness of targeting indicators will be based on the economic concept of effectiveness. Effectiveness in its technical dimension represents the capacity to achieve a maximum result from a given volume of resources (Farrell 1957). In the analysis of effectiveness of firms, the maximum result is generally determined by a frontier function as mentioned in Section I above. Applied to a targeting indicator, the maximum number of poor people it can reach is the full population of poor people in the country or sub-population being studied. Its effectiveness will be measured by a degree of eligibility of the poor, i.e. the percentage of poor that the indicator makes it possible to reach. It is expected that the indicator will eliminate the non-poor. The percentage of non-poor eliminated using this indicator will be a measure of its effectiveness in discriminating the non-poor from the targeted beneficiaries.

For a given targeting indicator, we will discuss the targeting errors linked to it and will use them as the basis for defining its two effectiveness indices from which the efficiency index will be estimated. The choice of a targeting indicator is generally reflected in two types of errors (Lipton and Ravallion 1995).

The first type of error consists of considering a person as poor when he/she is not. From the perspective of targeting, this error will manifest itself by the fact that when using this indicator, the non-poor benefits from the effects of the targeting policy. When credit is granted according to indicator k, the effectiveness of discriminating the non-poor will be measured by the index $I_{np}(k)$ defined in Eq. 10.1. It measures the percentage of non-poor excluded from the benefits of targeting based on indicator k:

$$I_{np}(k) = 1 - \frac{\phi_{np}(k)}{(1 - P_0)\Phi} \qquad (10.1)$$

where $\phi_{np}(k)$ is the number of non-poor benefiting from the measure if no other indicator is associated with indicator k, P_0 is the numeric index of poverty within the population, and Φ is the total population. The reasoning can apply to the scale of the country or to whatever sub-group is considered (urban, rural, region, etc.). Similarly, the population can be defined as all the households or individuals.

When targeting indicator k is effective in discriminating the non-poor, no non-poor person will be reached, $\phi_{np}(k) = 0$ and $I_{np}(k)$ has the value of 1. $I_{np}(k)$, between 0 and 1, measures the percentage of non-poor eliminated from benefiting from the targeting measure.

The second type of error consists of wrongly eliminating poor people. With this type of error, poor people would not be benefiting from the targeted policy due to the fact that the targeting indicator is not discriminating enough. The effectiveness of taking the poor into account will be measured by the index $I_p(k)$ defined in Eq. 10.2, and that corresponds to the percentage of poor people reached by indicator k:

$$I_p(k) = \frac{\phi_p(k)}{P_0\Phi} \qquad (10.2)$$

The denominator measures all poor people. If the indicator is effective at the scale of the group being considered, all the poor people should be reached, which gives $I_p(k) = 1$. Generally, all the poor people of the group that have not been selected by indicator k, $I_p(k)$ measures the percentage of poor people reached by targeting based on indicator k. If indicator k is not observed among the poor, $\phi_p(k) = 0$ and the index $I_p(k) = 0$, representing total ineffectiveness in eligibility of the poor.

When the poor household is targeted by indicator k, a sum $K(k)$ is granted to them in the form of credit, which enables them to change their standard of living with a certain effectiveness. The "effectiveness of the credit" is not part of this study. The implementation of the measure for improving access to credit is referred to by an overall cost G divided into the budget consumed by the administration in charge of the implementation (GA) and an operational budget ($G0$). The operational budget will affect the poor ($G0_p$) and the non-poor ($G0_{np}$) based on the effectiveness of the target index discussed above. The administration will be all the more effective with a low budget uptake rate ($g = GA/G$), which corresponds to better governance in terms of costs. The administration's transfer effectiveness index will be measured by the value $1 - g$, corresponding to its capacity to transfer the overall budget to the beneficiaries.

Increasing access to credit is analysed here, supposing a set sum $K(k)$ of funding for each household. $K(k)$ can also be an average sum on the condition that the average be very significant, which corresponds to a situation in which the households receive similar (not very different) sums. We will discuss later the consequences of a large variation in the $K(k)$ given to households.

The efficiency index (EFICE) of the targeted investment $K(k)$ is measured by

$$\text{EFICE}(k) = \frac{\phi_{mp}(k) \cdot K(k)}{G} = \frac{I_{mp}(k) \cdot P_{m0}\Phi_m \cdot K(k)}{G}$$

$$= (1 - g)I_{mp} \cdot \frac{P_{m0}\Phi_m \cdot K(k)}{G0} \qquad (10.3)$$

where $\phi_{mp}(k)$ is the number of poor households who benefit from targeting on the basis of indicator k, $I_{mp}(k)$ is the poor household eligibility effectiveness index (cf. Eq. 10.2), P_{m0} is the numeric poverty index within the households, Φ_m is the total number of households and $(1 - g)$ measures the effectiveness of the transfer of the total budget in favour of the beneficiaries. $G0$ is the operational budget, i.e. the amount $(G0_p)$ that will go to poor beneficiaries and the amount $(G0_{np})$ that by mistake goes to the non-poor. It can be written as follows:

$$G0 = G0_p + G0_{np} = \Phi_m K(k)\lfloor I_{mp}(k)P_{m0} + \left(1 - I_{mnp}(k)\right)(1 - P_{m0})\rfloor \qquad (10.4)$$

in which $I_{mp}(k)$ is the effectiveness index in the eligibility of poor households (cf. Eq. 10.2), $I_{mnp}(k)$ is the percentage of non-poor households eliminated from benefiting from the targeting (cf. Eq. 10.1), P_{m0} is the numeric index of poverty within the households, and Φ_m is the total number of households. By replacing $G0$ by its expression obtained using Eq. 10.4 in Eq. 10.3, the efficiency index (EFICE) becomes

$$\text{EFICE}(k) = \frac{(1 - g) \cdot I_{mp}(k) \cdot P_{m0}}{I_{mp}(k)P_{m0} + \left(1 - I_{mnp}(k)\right)(1 - P_{m0})} \qquad (10.5)$$

Equation 10.5 demonstrates that the efficiency index of investment $K(k)$ targeted using indicator k is independent of the amount $K(k)$ given to each household but rather depends on the effectiveness of the financial administration transfer $(1 - g)$, the effectiveness of indicator k in the eligibility of the poor $(I_{mp}(k))$ and in the elimination of the non-poor $(I_{mnp}(k))$ and of the numeric index of poverty (P_{m0}). As we did not have relevant data to estimate g, we parameterised it at 10, 20 and 50%, which made it possible to discuss its influence on overall efficiency.

The above reasoning applies to households because $K(k)$ is given to each household but could also apply to individuals if the investment $K(k)$ is the average amount given to each person.

When the amount of the credit differs greatly among households and one uses the average as an approximation of $K(k)$, the impact on EFICE(k) will vary depending on whether the credit is pro-poor (a higher average amount going to poor households, i.e. the less well off) or pro-non-poor (a higher average amount going to non-poor households, i.e. the more well off). In general, the market conditions are pro-non-poor, because the amount depends on the stock of capital, i.e. the assets held by the household, which is more favourable to the non-poor. If the credit is pro-poor, EFICE(k) underestimates the part of the credit that reaches the poor because the average amount $K_p(k)$ is greater than $K(k)$. When the credit is pro-non-poor, EFICE(k) overestimates the part of the credit that reaches the poor because the average amount $K_{np}(k)$ that reaches each household is greater than K (k). To correct this bias, EFICE(k) must be calculated by integrating $K_p(k)$ and $K_{np}(k)$ into Eq. 10.5. This gives

$$\text{EFICE(k)} = \frac{(1-g) \cdot I_{mp}(k) \cdot P_{m0} K_p(k)}{I_{mp}(k) P_{m0} K_p(k) + \left(1 - I_{mnp}(k)\right)\left(1 - P_{m0}\right) K_{np}(k)} \qquad (10.6)$$

The quality of the correction depends on the quality of $K_p(k)$ and $K_{np}(k)$, which must be very representative of the poor and the non-poor, respectively.

The empirical estimation of EFICE(k) will be done on alternative targeting indicators k that are the following: (1) the fact of being a farmer, applying for or benefiting from agricultural credit, (2) the types of agricultural activities one does, (3) the types of goods and assets one owns. In general, this approach can serve to evaluate the effectiveness of a variety of targeting indicators used by MFIs, whether they be simple or composite, qualitative or quantitative and subjective or objective, and the efficiency of the credit targeted based on these indicators.

V   Sources of Data and Some Characteristics of the Households

The data comes from two sources: (1) the 1998 priority survey on household living conditions and (2) the Burkina survey of household living conditions (EBCVM) carried out in 2003. These surveys were carried out by the Institut National de la Statistique et de la Démographie (INSD) and covered 8,478 households in 1998 and 8,500 in 2003. The absolute poverty thresholds in expenditure per capita and per year were estimated to be 72,690 CFAF in 1998 and 82,672 CFAF in 2003. The surveys were carried out using a two-stage stratified sample. For the first drawing, the primary units or enumeration zones (EZ) were drawn without reopening, and for the second drawing, the households were drawn in each EZ. This sampling structure is taken into account in the extrapolation of the results to the entire country or to sub-groups of interest.

In these two surveys, the production module included questions on the demand and on the obtainment of agricultural credit[6] by the households for the 1997–1998

---

[6] Agricultural credit is primarily the realm of the Caisse Nationale de Crédit Agricole (CNCA), which was founded in 1980 and became the Banque Agricole et Commerciale du Burkina (BACB) in 2002. The Société des Fibres Textiles (SOFITEX) and the MFI also participate in providing agricultural credit. A farmer's access to credit is essentially linked to joint backing from the grouping to which he belongs. Generally, villages have at least one grouping that can provide backing.

and 2002–2003 campaigns, which made it possible to measure the efficiency of agricultural credit. Similarly, the analysis of efficiency can be extended to other alternative credit-targeting indicators that are supplied by the survey.

Table 10.A.1 (Appendix) gives the distribution of households according to some of the credit-targeting indicators. The data in Table 10.A.1 indicate that by targeting farmers, agricultural credit reaches at least 88% of the poor households in Burkina Faso (92.1% in 1998 and 88.6% in 2003) but also at least 65% of the non-poor households (65.7% in 1998 and 64.6% in 2003). These poor households are for the most part subsistence farmers. This kind of targeting would be effective in eligibility of the poor benefiting from the credit but inefficient in eliminating the non-poor.

If we consider the demand for agricultural credit during the surveys, the poor farming applicant households only make up 13.2% of the poor households in Burkina Faso in 1998 compared with 22% in 2003, which represents a gain of 7 percentage points. This increase in the demand for credit by poor households comes primarily from a rise in the demand among subsistence farmers whose rate went from 2.6% of poor farming households in 1998 to 15.3% in 2003, versus a decrease in the same rates among cotton producers (10.6% in 1998 to 6.7% in 2003). As a result, a minority of poor and non-poor apply for credit, which raises the issue of whether or not agricultural credit is adapted to the farmers' conditions. This kind of targeting would be inefficient in the eligibility of the poor to benefit from credit but efficient in eliminating the non-poor. Cotton farmers dominated the poor households applying for agricultural credit in 1998, but the structure changed in 2003 with a net increase in the demand by subsistence farmers.

If we consider the actual obtaining of credit, poor beneficiary farming households represented 10.0% of the poor households in Burkina Faso in 1998 versus 3.6% in 2003, or a decrease in 7 percentage points. This decrease in actual access of poor farming households to credit comes mostly from cotton farmers. The results in rural areas confirm these trends. In urban areas, the lower rate exemplify the low concentration of farmers in cities.

The results presented in Table 10.A.1 also enable an assessment of the potential results of targeting based on other indicators. For the activities of agricultural production, growing sorghum is the main activity of poor households (80.6% for all of Burkina in 1998 vs. 42.4% in 2003) but also of the non-poor (55.7% in 1998 and 28.5% in 2003). In animal production, goat rearing occupies more of the poor but also the non-poor. Possessing durable assets and goods also has the same distribution structure for the poor and as for the non-poor households. Farmland is the asset that is most held by poor families (93.7% in 1998, 95.4% in 2003) but also by non-poor households (82.4% in 1998 and 85.1% in 2003). Unfortunately, this is rural land that is not the object of legal title and that cannot serve as a guarantee for obtaining credit.

The assets that are real alternatives for obtaining credit are mainly ploughs and/ or carts (37.4% of poor households in 1998 and 42% in 2003) and draught animals (30.8% of poor households in 1998 and 39.6% in 2003). The other goods that can facilitate access to credit on the market are held by low percentages of poor households.

The above results show that to increase the impact of credit, be it agricultural or not, both targeting and access conditions need to be improved, which explains the important of the issues of effectiveness of indicators and the related efficiency of credit.

VI   Results and Discussions

We will first discuss the efficiency of agricultural credit in Burkina Faso and then the extension of credit targeting based on alternative criteria such as type of activity and household ownership of durable goods and assets.

The Efficiency of Agricultural Credit

We analysed the efficiency of agricultural credit at three levels of targeting: farmers without considering the demand (potential effect), farmers that demand credit and finally, the farmers benefiting from agricultural credit (observed real effect).

By targeting farmers without consideration of whether or not they applied for credit, the analysis highlights the potential effect sought after by decision makers and banking authorities that initiated the agricultural credit. The results in Table 10.1 show that by targeting farmers, agricultural credit proves to be pro-poor because the eligibility of the poor is, indeed, high, in the order of 92.1% of poor households in 1998 and 88.6% in 2003, or respectively 92.8 and 89.4% of poor individuals in 1998 and 2003. The effectiveness in eliminating the non-poor is, however, low, at 34.3% in 1998 and 35.4% in 2003, which corresponds respectively to 65.7 and 64.6% of non-poor families in 1998 and in 2003 who benefited from agricultural credit. Consequently, the overall efficiency of this kind of targeting is 38.2% in 1998 and 40.7% in 2003, even with the administration absorbing only 10% of the overall envelope for management expenses. In other words, 38.2 and 40.7% of the overall envelope reached the monetarily poor households in 1998 and 2003. This rate would be lower if the agricultural credit administrative services absorbed more than 10% of the overall budget. The results also show that if the agricultural credit were targeted only to subsistence farmers, it would reach fewer poor people (78.8% in 1998 and 72.5% in 2003), but it would have had a relatively better efficiency (39.3% in 1998 and 42.1% in 2003). The same trends can be observed when one focuses on rural and urban areas.

Let us now target farmers who apply for agricultural credit, which enables the analysis to take into account the reality of the financial market. The results in Table 10.1 show that the eligibility of the poor falls to 13.2% of poor households in 1998 versus 22% in 2003, which corresponds respectively to 15.5 and 21.1% poor individuals. This eligibility of the poor is worse yet if one targets cotton growers and subsistence farmers. Targeting farmers who are apply for agricultural credit

Table 10.1 Agricultural credit efficiency indices

Indicators (k)		Indicator effectiveness (%)		Credit efficiency indices (EFICE(k))			Poor people reached (%)
		$I_p(k)$	$I_{np}(k)$	$g = 10\%$	$g = 20\%$	$g = 50\%$	
Burkina Faso							
Analysis based on *farmers* without considering if they applied or not							
Farmers	1998	92.1	34.3	38.2	34.0	21.2	92.8
	2003	88.6	35.4	40.7	36.1	22.6	89.4
Cotton Growers	1998	13.2	87.9	32.7	29.1	18.2	15.7
	2003	16.1	85.0	35.3	31.4	19.6	17.9
Subsistence Farmers	1998	78.8	46.4	39.3	34.9	21.8	77.1
	2003	72.5	50.4	42.1	37.4	23.4	71.4
Analysis based on actual *applicants* for agricultural credit							
Farmers	1998	13.2	87.0	31.3	27.8	17.4	15.5
	2003	22.0	86.4	44.3	39.4	24.6	21.1
Cotton Growers	1998	10.6	90.0	32.4	28.8	18.0	12.5
	2003	6.7	94.7	38.7	34.4	21.5	6.9
Subsistence	1998	2.6	96.9	27.4	24.4	15.2	2.9
Farmers	2003	15.3	91.7	47.3	42.0	26.3	14.2
Analysis based on actual *beneficiaries* of agricultural credit							
Farmers	1998	10.9	89.1	31.1	27.6	17.2	12.6
	2003	3.6	95.5	29.1	25.9	16.2	4.5
Cotton Growers	1998	9.7	90.6	31.8	28.3	17.7	11.4
	2003	1.7	97.5	26.2	23.3	14.6	2.3
Subsistence Farmers	1998	1.2	98.5	26.1	23.2	14.5	1.2
	2003	1.9	98.0	32.5	28.9	18.0	2.2
Rural Area							
Analysis based on *farmers* without considering if they applied or not							
Farmers	1998	94.8	12.0	39.0	34.7	21.7	94.8
	2003	92.1	15.6	41.1	36.6	22.9	93.0
Cotton Growers	1998	14.0	82.7	32.9	29.2	18.3	16.7
	2003	17.4	79.2	35.3	31.4	19.6	19.2
Subsistence Farmers	1998	80.8	29.2	40.3	35.9	22.4	78.1
	2003	74.8	36.4	42.8	38.0	23.8	73.8
Analysis based on actual *applicants* for agricultural credit							
Farmers	1998	13.9	81.5	31.3	27.9	17.4	16.2
	2003	22.7	82.3	44.7	39.7	24.8	21.7
Cotton Growers	1998	11.4	85.6	32.4	28.8	18.0	13.3
	2003	7.2	92.6	38.7	34.4	21.5	7.4
Subsistence	1998	2.6	95.9	27.4	24.3	15.2	2.9
Farmers	2003	15.4	89.7	48.2	42.8	26.8	14.3
Analysis based on actual *beneficiaries* of agricultural credit							
Farmers	1998	11.5	84.5	31.2	27.7	17.3	13.2
	2003	3.6	94.1	28.6	25.5	15.9	4.5

(continued)

Table 10.1 (continued)

Indicators (k)		Indicator effectiveness (%)		Credit efficiency indices (EFICE(k))			Poor people reached (%)
		$I_p(k)$	$I_{np}(k)$	$g = 10\%$	$g = 20\%$	$g = 50\%$	
Cotton Growers	1998	10.4	86.5	31.8	28.3	17.7	12.1
	2003	1.9	96.5	26.1	23.2	14.5	2.3
Subsistence Farmers	1998	1.1	98.1	26.1	23.2	14.5	1.2
	2003	1.7	97.6	32.0	28.4	17.8	2.2
Urban Area							
Analysis based on *farmers* without considering if they applied or not							
Farmers	1998	54.1	84.1	25.2	22.4	14.0	61.5
	2003	48.3	85.3	32.4	28.8	18.0	46.7
Cotton Growers	1998	0.4	99.6	09.5	8.5	5.3	0.3
	2003	1.8	99.6	38.2	33.9	21.2	2.8
Subsistence Farmers	1998	53.6	84.6	25.6	22.7	14.2	61.2
	2003	46.5	85.7	32.2	28.6	17.9	44.0
Analysis based on actual *applicants* for agricultural credit							
Farmers	1998	3.1	99.1	26.8	23.8	14.9	4.0
	2003	14.8	96.6	38.5	34.2	21.4	15.4
Cotton Growers	1998	0.4	99.8	20.4	18.2	11.4	0.3
	2003	0.8	99.8	38.3	34.1	21.3	1.5
Subsistence Farmers	1998	2.7	99.3	28.2	25.1	15.7	3.8
	2003	14.0	96.8	38.5	34.2	21.4	13.1
Analysis based on actual *beneficiaries* of agricultural credit							
Farmers	1998	2.4	99.3	24.7	22.0	13.7	2.9
	2003	3.8	99.0	35.9	31.9	20.0	4.7
Cotton Growers	1998	0.4	99.8	20.4	18.2	11.4	0.3
	2003	0.3	99.9	40.8	36.3	22.7	0.5
Subsistence Farmers	1998	2.0	99.4	25.9	23.0	14.4	2.7
	2003	3.5	99.1	35.6	31.6	19.8	4.2

Source: Our calculations based on data from the 1998 Priority Survey no. 2 and the 2003 Burkina Survey on Household Living Conditions (EBCVM)

leads to an efficiency index of 31.3% in 1998 and 44.3% in 2003. The results are similar in rural areas but lower in urban areas, despite a better elimination of the non-poor.

To assess the efficiency of agricultural credit that was really observed, one needs to consider *the actual beneficiaries of the credit during the survey period*. When we look at the entire country, agricultural credit benefited 10.9% of the monetarily poor households in 1998 and 3.6% in 2003, or respectively 12.6 and 4.5% of the poor population. In rural areas, 11.5% of the monetarily poor households were beneficiaries in 1998 and 3.6% in 2003, or respectively 13.2 and 4.5% of the poor rural population. In urban areas, the figures are lower, which can be explained by the low concentration of farmers in cities. In 1998, the actual efficiency of agricultural credit was 31.1% on the national scale, 31.2% in rural areas and 24.7% in urban areas, under the hypothesis of a low-cost financial administration that would absorb only 10% of the overall envelope. In 2003, these figures were respectively 29.1% on a national scale, 28.6% in rural areas and 35.9% for the urban area.

There are, in the literature, evaluations of how well decentralised financial services reach the poor. The Consultative Group to Assist the Poor (CGAP) proposes a tool, the poverty assessment tool (PAT) to evaluate the capacity MFIs have at reaching the poor (Henry et al. 2003; Helms 2006). Evaluations done in Ghana and in Senegal using the PAT indicate that the capacity for reaching the poor does not depend on the type of institution but rather on where their offices and service points are located. In Senegal, the study indicated that in the Fenagie-Pech cooperative, two-thirds (67%) of the clients are among the poorest third of the population. In Ghana, the analysis shows that 26% of rural bank clients are among the poorest 20% of the population, in comparison to 16% of the micro-finance clients of NGOs. This is because the rural banks are located in the northern region where there is more poverty and where the NGOs are generally absent.

In 2003, the credits distributed by the MFI in Burkina Faso only represent 6.2% of the total volume of credit (MFB 2005). On the other hand, the MFIs accounted for 68.3% of the contact points, which indicates that these services address the poorest people who work with small amounts.

These results show the importance of geographic proximity indicators in the access poor people have to financial services.

The Efficiency of Credit That Is Targeted Using Other Criteria

We present the results of the efficiency analysis of credit using as targeting indicators the major activities of the poor (Table 10.A.2) and the most-held assets of the poor identified in Section V (Table 10.A.3).

The results in Table 10.A.2 indicate that the activities that enable one to reach a maximum number of poor are primarily growing sorghum/millet and raising goats. By targeting sorghum growing as an activity to support with credit, the total percentage of poor households concerned ranges from 80.6% in 1998 to 42.4% in 2003 for all of Burkina Faso, or respectively 82.4 and 42.6% of poor individuals. If the institution that administers the credit (project, NGO, etc.) absorbs 10% of the said envelope to cover various expenses, the credit efficiency index (EFICE) associated with sorghum is 38.9% for 1998 and 42.5% for 2003. This low index, despite the relative effectiveness of the administration's transfer, can be explained by the targeting error, which leads to the funds going to 55.7% $(1 - I_{np}(k))$ to non-poor households in 1998 and 28.5% in 2003. When the administration absorbs 50% of the budget, only 21.6% of the funds reach poor households in 1998 versus 23.6% in 2003.

In Burkina Faso, sorghum is considered to be a low-profit financial activity (producing less than 1 ton/ha and producer sales price being about 80 FCFA/kg during the harvest sales periods). The sorghum that is produced is primarily self-consumed, in such a way that its impact on the standard of living depends on the actual physical volumes consumed. A policy of targeting based on sorghum would lead to point D on Fig. 10.1 (Sect. II). To make sorghum an efficient activity for reducing poverty, the challenge would be to move it away from point D towards point B on Fig. 10.1. This kind of displacement can be obtained by increasing the amount $K(k)$ given to each household and/or the profitability of sorghum (increasing the physical yield or the net margin by a transformation or channel that would give it more added value). Such perspectives are not very obvious and/or realistic in the short term, thus making the exploration of other activities a necessity.

When the targeting indicators cover breeding activities, non-agricultural activities and market gardening, the percentage of poor people reached and the efficiency indices are generally lower than those found with sorghum. The results in rural areas are similar to those found for the entire country. In urban areas, income-generating activities (excluding salaried employment) are primarily non-agricultural activities. The choice of these activities as a targeting indicator would affect 58% of poor households (I_p) but would eliminate only 51.7% of non-poor households (I_{np}) in 1998.

The results found on Table 10.A.3 cover the targeting of assets and become interesting when viewed from the perspective of obtaining credit in the market that implicitly targets households with a certain number of assets. The major lesson that can be drawn from these results is that credit through the market could only become a key poverty-reduction tool if, through appropriate reform, one gave a legal value to farmland through some sort of titling arrangement. This would enable at least 90% of the poor households (93.7% in 1998 and 95.4% in 2003) to be able to apply for credit, which would reach at least 94% of poor individuals (94.7% in 1998 and 96.3% in 2003). The plough/cart as a target alternative would only affect at most 37.4% of poor households, or 46.4% of the poor in Burkina Faso in 1998. In 2003, 42% of the poor households and 49% of the poor are affected. In rural areas, the rates of eligibility are higher for poor families.

The results on Tables 10.A.2 and 10.A.3 can also be interpreted as the consequence or potential effects arising from a policy choice for targeting based on the said indicators. The choice based on the possession of farmland would affect more poor people. However, the efficiency of the credit would not exceed 42%, even with a good financial administration. In the image of agricultural credit, the eligibility indices for the poor and efficiency will be much lower after a demand has been expressed and after the actual credit has been granted.

In reality, for a variety of reasons, many poor presenting the k indicator will not benefit from credit. Olsen (2001) raised the issues of regional exclusion and the self-exclusion of minority groups and recommends targeting measures to correct these. The poor who take out small loans and who are sometimes located far from where the credit institutions are tend to cost the lender more money. Credit institutions are driven by the quest for cost effectiveness, as they are concerned about their short-term financial viability, and they apply higher interest rates to the poor and give more credit to less-poor borrowers that can borrow larger amounts. The concern credit institutions have for profitability can lead them to forget, in practice, the potential role credit can play as a tool for poverty reduction. Counts (2002), chairman of the Grameen Foundation USA, after having observed that the Grameen Bank makes nearly 1.2 billion transactions a year, recognises that this work is inefficient and recommends the use of modern means for automating transactions. In an environment that has poor means of communications, small financial institutions transfer these costs to the poor to avoid losing viability that would limit the poor's access to credit. There are also issues related to risk aversion, lack of information, etc.

One can use the results of Tables 10.A.2 and 10.A.3 to speculate on the overall targeting budget, but one is limited regarding the effects of poverty because households opt to finance a variety of different activities. Poor households tend to use a large part of the credit they receive for their consumption needs (Zaman 2002); this can increase the burden of debt because the residual sum generates lower income and therefore less capacity for reimbursing the loan. This author shows that in Bangladesh, the impact of micro-credit on poverty is based on loans that go beyond a certain threshold and on the initial depth of the poverty. So, the impact on poverty becomes significant when the moderately poor borrow over US $200 (10,000 taka) in accumulated credit. The analysis of such behaviour in poor households should make it possible to better determine the amounts of credit to grant households.

VII   Conclusions and Recommendations

In this study, we examine the efficiency of targeted credit based on the effectiveness of targeting indicators and the effectiveness of the financial administration in transferring the funds to the beneficiaries.

When agricultural credit targets farming, it proves to be potentially pro-poor because the eligibility of the poor is raised to around 92.1% of poor households in 1998, 88.6% in 2003, or respectively 92.8 and 89.4% of poor individuals in Burkina Faso. This targeting, however, is not very efficient in eliminating the non-poor (34.4% in 1998 and 35.4% in 2003), which corresponds respectively to 65.7 and 64.6% of non-poor households in 1998 and 2003 benefiting from agricultural credit. Consequently, the overall efficiency of this kind of targeting is 38.2% in 1998 and 40.7% in 2003, even with the administration absorbing only 10% of the overall envelope to cover management expenses. If we consider the demand for agricultural credit, eligibility of the poor falls to 13.2% of poor households and 15.5% of poor individuals in 1998 versus respectively 22 and 21.1% in 2003.

The actual number obtaining agricultural credit reached 10.9% of poor households in 1998 and 3.6% in 2003, or respectively 12.6 and 4.5% of the poor population in Burkina Faso. In rural areas, 11.5% of monetarily poor households were beneficiaries in 1998 and 3.6% in 2003, representing respectively 13.2 and 4.5% of the poor rural population. In urban areas, the figures are lower, given that there is a lower concentration of farmers in cities. In 1998, the actual efficiency of agricultural credit was 31.1% at the national level, 31.2% in rural areas and 24.7% in urban areas, under the hypothesis of a low-cost financial administration that absorbed only 10% of the overall budget. In 2003, these figures were respectively 29.1% at the national scale, 28.6% in rural areas and 35.9% in urban areas.

The comparison between the potential effect of agricultural targeting on credit (eligibility of at least 89% of poor households) and the real effect (eligibility of fewer than 11% of poor households) highlights the problem of implicit non-documented indicators linked to implementation and to the characteristics and preferences of the lenders and applicants that translate into the eviction of potentially targeted beneficiaries. This eviction can exceed 80% of the potential beneficiaries targeted using explicit indicators. To reach the poor (right of Fig. 10.1 (BD)), a more in-depth study of implicit indicators is necessary in order to reduce eviction and adapt the credit more to the target group.

Credit can also be targeted using other indicators. To reach the poorest, credit that targets activities should be granted, paying particular attention to grains, mainly sorghum, and small ruminants, especially goats. Given the low yield and rain-related risks linked to farming grains, raising small ruminants could be a pro-poor alternative for targeting credit. The credit could, nevertheless, reach more of the poor if the farmland, the asset most owned by the poor, could serve as a collateral via a reform that would give it a legal value through a title.

The analysis of efficiency shows that the percentage of the funds that reach the poor (efficiency index) cannot exceed 40%, taking into account the number of non-poor that share the same targeting indicators as the poor. The shift of funds to benefit the non-poor is high due to the socio-economic similarities that exist between the poor and the non-poor. In order for this shift to help reduce poverty, support measures should be linked to credit programmes so that the activities financed by the better-off households could create jobs.

Appendices

Table 10.A.1 Percentage (%) of poor and non-poor households based on a few targeting indicators

Types of targeting indicators	Burkina Faso				Rural zone				Urban zone			
	Poor		Non-poor		Poor		Non-poor		Poor		Non-poor	
	1998	2003	1998	2003	1998	2003	1998	2003	1998	2003	1998	2003
Agricultural credit												
Farmers	92.1	88.6	65.7	64.6	94.8	92.1	88.0	84.4	54.1	48.3	15.9	14.7
Cotton growers	13.1	16.1	12.1	15.0	14.0	17.4	17.3	20.8	0.4	1.8	0.4	0.4
Subsistence farmers	79.0	72.5	53.6	49.6	80.8	74.8	70.8	63.6	53.6	46.5	15.5	14.3
Applicant farmers	13.2	22.0	13.0	13.6	13.9	22.7	18.5	17.7	3.1	14.8	0.8	3.4
Applicant cotton growers	10.6	6.7	10.0	5.3	11.4	7.2	14.4	7.4	0.4	0.8	0.2	0.2
Applicant subsistence farmers	2.6	15.3	3.1	8.3	2.5	15.4	4.1	10.3	2.7	14.0	0.7	3.2
Farmer beneficiaries	10.9	3.6	10.9	4.5	11.5	3.6	15.5	5.9	2.4	3.8	0.7	1.0
Cotton grower beneficiaries	9.7	1.7	9.4	2.5	10.4	1.9	13.5	3.5	0.4	0.3	0.2	0.1
Subsistence farmer beneficiaries	1.2	1.9	1.5	2.0	1.1	1.7	1.9	2.4	2.0	3.5	0.6	0.9
Income-generating activities												
Sorghum (1998) et millet/ sorghum (2003)	80.6	42.4	55.7	28.5	83.2	45.0	74.6	38.2	43.7	13.2	13.4	4.1
Goats	66.8	39.3	44.1	30.9	70.3	42.2	60.7	41.5	19.2	6.8	07.1	4.2
Non-agricultural activities	41.9	–	42.3	–	40.7	–	39.6	–	58.0	–	48.3	–
Market gardening	5.9	8.8	5.4	8.4	5.8	9.0	6.9	10.8	7.0	6.0	2.2	2.2
Types of goods and assets owned												
Farmland	93.7	95.4	82.4	85.1	96.6	96.8	90.1	93.6	54.4	79.7	20.5	63.8
Plough (1998) and plough/ cart (2003)	37.4	42.0	26.7	32.2	39.0	44.0	36.2	40.2	14.2	19.0	05.5	11.9
Draught animal	30.8	39.6	22.5	31.4	32.2	41.7	30.4	41.1	11.1	16.0	04.7	7.1
Cart	24.7	–	19.1	–	25.0	–	23.5	–	20.1	–	09.4	–
Motorbike	14.6	12.0	29.3	29.7	14.4	11.4	18.8	19.4	17.5	19.4	52.5	55.6
Building plot	09.0	–	17.0	–	08.8	–	15.6	–	11.7	–	20.2	–

Source: Our calculations based on data from the 1998 Priority Survey no. 2 and the 2003 Burkina Survey on Household Living Conditions (EBCVM)

Table 10.A.2 Efficiency indices for credit targeted based on major activities of poor households

Indicators (k)		Effectiveness of indicators (%)		Credit efficiency indices (EFICE(k))			Poor individuals reached (%)
		$I_p(k)$	$I_{np}(k)$	$g = 10\%$	$g = 20\%$	$g = 50\%$	
Burkina Faso							
Sorghum (1998) and millet	1998	80.6	44.3	38.9	34.6	21.6	82.4
sorghum (2003)	2003	42.4	71.5	42.5	37.7	23.6	42.6
Goats	1998	66.8	55.9	39.9	35.5	22.2	72.4
	2003	39.3	69.1	39.0	34.7	21.7	42.6
Non-agricultural activities	1998	41.9	57.7	30.8	27.4	17.1	44.5
	2003	–	–	–	–	–	–
Market gardening	1998	05.9	94.6	32.7	29.0	18.1	06.8
	2003	8.8	91.6	34.8	31.0	19.3	9.4
Rural zone							
Sorghum	1998	83.2	25.4	39.8	35.4	22.1	79.2
	2003	45.0	61.8	42.8	38.1	23.8	45.1
Goats	1998	70.3	39.3	40.7	36.1	22.6	70.9
	2003	42.2	58.5	39.6	35.2	22.0	45.6
Non-agricultural activities	1998	40.7	60.4	38.0	33.8	21.1	40.7
	2003	–	–	–	–	–	–
Market gardening	1998	05.8	93.1	33.7	29.9	18.7	06.3
	2003	9.0	89.2	35.3	31.4	10.8	9.8
Urban zone							
Sorghum	1998	43.9	86.6	24.4	21.7	13.6	52.9
	2003	13.2	95.9	32.0	28.4	17.8	12.4
Goats	1998	19.2	92.9	21.1	18.8	11.7	25.7
	2003	6.8	95.8	19.7	17.5	10.9	7.2
Non-agricultural activities	1998	58.0	51.7	10.9	09.7	06.0	61.6
	2003	–	–	–	–	–	–
Market gardening	1998	7.0	97.8	24.2	21.6	13.5	08.2
	2003	6.0	97.8	28.2	25.0	15.6	5.3

Source: Our calculations based on data from the 1998 Priority Survey no. 2 and the 2003 Burkina Survey on Household Living Conditions (EBCVM)

Table 10.A.3 Efficiency indices for credit targeted based on sustainable assets and goods held by poor households

Indicators (k)	Effectiveness of indicators (%)		Credit efficiency indices (EFICE(k))			Poor individuals reached (%)	
	$I_p(k)$	$I_{np}(k)$	$g = 10\%$	$g = 20\%$	$g = 50\%$		
Burkina Faso							
Farmland	1998	93.7	31.5	37.7	33.5	20.9	94.7
	2003	95.4	14.9	36.2	32.2	20.1	96.3
Plough (1998) and	1998	37.4	73.3	38.2	34.0	21.2	46.4
plough/cart (2003)	2003	42.0	67.8	39.6	35.2	22.0	49.0
Draught animal	1998	30.8	77.5	37.7	33.5	21.0	39.1
	2003	39.6	68.6	38.8	34.5	21.5	46.2
Cart	1998	24.7	80.9	36.4	32.4	20.2	34.1
	2003	–	–	–	–	–	–
Motorbike	1998	14.6	70.7	18.7	16.6	10.4	22.0
	2003	12.0	70.3	17.6	15.7	9.8	15.7
Building plot	1998	9.0	83.0	19.6	17.4	10.9	10.2
	2003	–	–	–	–	–	–
Rural zone							
Farmland	1998	96.6	09.9	38.9	34.6	21.6	91.1
	2003	96.8	6.4	39.9	35.5	22.2	97.3
Plough (1998) and	1998	39.0	63.8	39.1	34.7	21.7	45.0
plough/cart (2003)	2003	44.0	59.8	41.2	36.6	22.9	97.3
Draught animal	1998	32.2	69.6	38.7	34.5	21.5	37.9
	2003	41.7	58.9	39.5	35.1	22.0	48.5
Cart	1998	25.0	76.5	38.8	34.5	21.6	32.3
	2003	–	–	–	–	–	–
Motorbike	1998	14.4	81.2	31.7	28.1	17.6	20.56
	2003	11.4	80.6	28.0	24.9	15.6	14.8
Building plot	1998	08.8	84.4	25.8	22.9	14.3	09.4
	2003	–	–	–	–	–	–
Urban zone							
Farmland	1998	54.4	79.5	21.0	18.6	11.6	03.6
	2003	79.7	36.2	15.9	14.1	8.8	83.8
Plough (1998) and	1998	14.2	94.5	20.5	18.2	11.4	01.4
plough/cart (2003)	2003	19.0	88.1	19.4	17.2	10.8	23.1
Draught animal	1998	11.1	95.3	19.2	17.1	10.7	01.2
	2003	16.0	92.9	25.0	22.3	13.9	19.5
Cart	1998	20.1	90.6	17.7	15.7	09.8	01.8
	2003	–	–	–	–	–	–
Motorbike	1998	17.5	47.5	03.3	02.9	01.8	01.5
	2003	19.4	44.4	5.1	4.5	2.8	26.9
Building plot	1998	11.8	79.8	05.6	05.0	03.1	00.8
	2003	–	–	–	–	–	–

Source: Our calculations based on data from the 1998 Priority Survey no. 2 and the 2003 Burkina Survey on Household Living Conditions (EBCVM)

References

Berger, A.N. and D.B. Humphrey (1997), 'Efficiency of Financial Institutions: International Survey and Directions for Future Research', *European Journal of Operational Research* 98: 175–212.

Counts, A. (2002),'Grameen Technology Center: Action to Reduce Poverty', Concept Paper, Grameen Foundation USA.

Datt, G. and D. Jolliffe (1999), 'Determinants of Poverty in Egypt : 1997'. *IFPRI, FCND Discussion Paper* No. 75. Washington, DC.

Farrell, M. J. (1957), 'The measurement of productive efficiency', *Journal of Royal Statistical Society*, Series A, Vol 120, Part III.

Geda, A., N. de Jong, G. Mwabu, M.S. Kimenyi (2001), 'Determinants of Poverty in Kenya: A Household Level Analysis', *Working Paper*. Institute of Social Studies (ISS) and Kenya Institute for Public Policy Research and Analysis (KIPPRA).

Grootaert, C. (1996), 'The determinants of poverty in Côte d'Ivoire in the 1980s', *Journal of African Economies*, Volume 6, Number 2 :169–196.

Grootaert, C. and R.Kanbur(1990), 'Analyse Opérationnelle de la Pauvreté et des Dimensions Sociales de l'Ajustement Structurel : Méthodologie et Proposition d'Application au Cas de la Côte d'Ivoire, 1985-88', Les Dimensions Sociales de l'Ajustement en Afrique Subsaharienne, *Document de travail No. 1*, Analyse socio-économique. World Bank, Washington, D.C.

Helms, Brigit (2006), 'Access for all: Building inclusive Financial Systems, capturing 10 yearsof CGAP experience', CGAP, World Bank.

Henry, C. And M. Sharma, C. Lapenu and M. Zeller (2003), 'Microfinance Poverty Assessment Tool', Consultative Group to Assist the Poorest (CGAP), the World Bank.

INSD (1996), 'Le Profil de Pauvreté au Burkina Faso',Ministère de l'Économie, des Finances et du Plan; Projet d'Appui Institutionnel aux Dimensions Sociales de l'Ajustement.

INSD (2000a), 'Analyse des Résultats de l'Enquête Prioritaire sur les Conditions de Vie des Ménages en 1998', Ministère de l'Économie et des Finances; Direction des Statistiques Générales, Étude Statistique Nationale, Première Édition, Ouagadougou, March 2000.

INSD (2000b), 'Profil et Évolution de la Pauvreté au Burkina Faso' Ministère de l'Économie et des Finances; Direction des Statistiques Générales, Étude Statistique Nationale, Première Édition, Ouagadougou, March 2000.

INSD (2003), 'Profil et Évolution de la Pauvreté au Burkina Faso', Ministère de l'Économie etdes Finances, Direction des Statistiques Générales, Ouagadougou.

Kaboré, T. S. (2009), 'Effectivité d'un crédit ciblé aux pauvres: le cas des microentreprises rurales du Burkina Faso',*Revue Canadienne d'Études du Développement* 29, No. 1–2 : 217–236

Lipton, M. and M Ravallion (1995), 'Poverty and Policy', in Berhman and T.N. Srinivasan (Eds) *Handbook of Development Economics*, Volume III, Elsevier Science B.V

McKillop, D.G., J.C.Glass, and C. Ferguson (2002), 'An Examination of the Efficiency of UK Credit Unions'

MEDEV (2004), 'Cadre Stratégique de Lutte contre la Pauvreté, Burkina Faso', Ministère de l'Economie et du Développement (MEDEV), January 2004. Ouagadougou, Burkina Faso.

MEF (2000), 'Burkina Faso: Cadre Stratégique de Lutte contre la Pauvreté', Ministry of Economy and Finance (MEF), Burkina Faso.

MEF (2000), 'Document Intérimaire de Stratégies de Réduction de la Pauvreté (DISRP)', Republic of Guinea, October 2000.

MEF (2002), 'Mali: Cadre Stratégique de Lutte contre la Pauvreté Final', Ministry of the Economy and Finance (MEF) Mali. Document prepared and voted by the government of Mali, May 2002.

MEF (2002), 'Document de Stratégie de Réduction de la Pauvreté, Sénégal', Ministry of the economy and Finance (MEF), Republic of Senegal, April 2002.

Mester, L.J. (1996), 'A Study of Bank Efficiency Taking into Account Risk-preferences', *Journal of Banking & Finance* 20:1025–1045.

MF (2003), 'Poverty Reduction Strategy 2003–2005: an agenda for growth and Prosperity', Ministry of Finance (MF) Ghana, February 2003.

MFB (2005),'Stratégie Nationale de Microfinance: document de politique et cadre logique de mise en œuvre', Ministry of Finance and Budget (MFB), Burkina Faso, November 2005.

MINEPAT (2003), 'Poverty Reduction Strategy Paper (PSRP)', Ministry of Economy, Programming and Development (MINEPAT), Cameroon, April 2003.

Olsen, W. (2001), 'Poverty and Access to Credit in Sri Lanka in the 1990s: A Multilevel Analysis', Development Studies Association, University of Bradford, Centre for International Development.

Ribe, H., S. Carvalho, R. Liebenthal, P. Nicholas and E. Zuckerman (1990), ,How Adjustment Programs Can Help the Poor: The World Bank's Experience', *World Bank Discussion Papers* 71. The World Bank, Washington, D.C.

SP/CNDLP (2002), 'Document de Stratégie de Réduction de la Pauvreté au Bénin 2003-2005', Secrétariat Permanent, Commission Nationale de Développement et de la Lutte contre la Pauvreté (SP/CNDLP), December 2002.

SP/SRP (2002), 'Document de Stratégie de Réduction de la Pauvreté, Niger', Prepared by the government of Niger, Secrétariat Permanent de la Stratégie de Réduction de la Pauvreté (SP/SRP).

Simanowitz, A. B. Nkuna, S. Kasim, and R.Gailey (2000), 'Overcoming the obstacles of identifying the poorest families: using participatory Wealth Ranking (PWR), the CASHPOR Housing Index (CHI) and other measurements to identify and encourage the participation of the poorest families, specially the women of those families', Microcredit Summit, 2000.

Todd, H. (1998), 'Women Climbing out of Poverty Through Credit or What do Cows Have to do With It?', *Livestock Research for Rural Development*; Volume 10, Number 3, 1998.

Zaman, H. (2002), 'Assessing the Poverty and Vulnerability Impact of Micro-Credit in Bangladesh: A Case Study of BRAC', The World Bank

Chapter 11
Performance and Effectiveness of the Decentralised Financial System and Poverty Reduction in Niger

Insa Abary Noufou

Abstract Reforms in the financial system have enabled WAEMU member countries to envision models other than the traditional models to assess credit risks and to ensure that credit contracts are respected, thus building trust between individuals who do not meet the requirements set by the classic banking system and financial institutions. This new approach, referred to as the decentralised financial system (DFS), should facilitate participation of the poor in economic activities via a savings and loan system that aims at being financially viable and profitable.

In Niger, this DFS continues to develop and to position itself as a tool to supply financial services to the most disadvantaged populations. As a result, after several years of experimentation with savings and loan micro-projects, it is important to attest on the performance of the microfinance sector and its contribution to economic and social development in Niger. These considerations have led us to raise the following questions: What is the system's capacity in terms of mobilising resources (collecting savings and refinancing)? Does the DFS have a significant reach in terms of the services offered to its clientele? Is the system able to reach its potential target, that is, the poor?

To answer these questions, our study proposes to analyse the performance and effectiveness of the financial system in Niger. The available data shows that development of the microfinance system is in full swing in Niger, with an increase in the number of Micro-Finance Institutions (MFI), in the volume of credit granted and in jobs created, and an increasing number of beneficiaries, which are primarily women. Despite the relatively high interest rates and usury for very short repayment periods, microfinance in Niger is striving to ensure financial self-sufficiency by developing a portfolio of savings and loan activities that have been increasing every year since 2000.

I.A. Noufou (✉)
Department of Economic and Financial Affairs, Office of the Prime Minister, Niger
e-mail: abary1@yahoo.fr

E.T. Ayuk and S.T. Kaboré (eds.), *Wealth Through Integration*, Insight and Innovation in International Development 4, DOI 10.1007/978-1-4614-4415-2_11,
© International Development Research Centre 2013

Despite some obstacles to long-term viability, micro-credit remains a financial possibility that is of vital importance to the poor and therefore is essential for poverty reduction in Niger. To make the DFS more effective, this study recommends targeting the poor and identifying their financial needs but also considering DFS clients not as people looking for charity but really as people who are trying to do business by accessing basic tools (capital and training).

I Introduction

Sub-Saharan Africa is one of the developing regions where the absolute number of poor people has been increasing continually, even if their proportion in relative terms fell from 47 to 41% of the total population between 1999 to 2004 (Chen and Ravallion 2007). Also, among the 4 billion poor people in the world, Sub-Saharan Africa (SSA) counted more than 250 million people living on less than a dollar a day in 1999,[1] and more than 21% of the young people, 7.6% of women and 9.1% of men lacked work in 2004.[2] This situation has led to the need to find an approach to provide services for the poor that is based on an innovative economic model that favours job and wealth creation, enabling the empowerment of the poor people in the face of poverty. This is what led to the development of new financial models to complement the traditional models in WAEMU member countries in order to facilitate the integration into the economy of those excluded from the classic banking system. This new approach, referred to as the DFS, is meant to facilitate poor peoples' participation in the economy by a financially viable and profitable savings and loan system. Yet, one cannot overlook the problem of sustainability and viability of microfinance institutions (MFI). This raises the question of the MFI's capacity to ensure long-term financial services for the poor. Two basic characteristics determine the system's conditions for viability. These are the credit institution's capacity to mobilise resources, on one hand, and to generate income through financial intermediation, on the other. As a result, a policy of MFI viability must be based on mobilising the local resources needed for operating, maintaining and increasing DFS activities. Although savings can be mobilised, the volume of credit the populations need is most often huge in relation to the volume of savings collected. The people targeted by the decentralised financial system are, in general, facing economic and social difficulty. Yet, the basic principle behind the system is based on the possibilities of lending the small sums that are needed to "buy a fishing net rather than giving away fish". One can question whether the poor can support the interest rates that will be applied to cover the costs of transactions and operations.

This issue, which arises in the system, hampers the MFI's financial approach. The problem is ambiguous, considering that the margin on the small loans is too

---

[1] Economic Commission for Africa (ECA), 2005 Report.
[2] 2004 world youth employment trends. ILO, 2004. ISBN 92-2-215997-7.

small to cover transaction costs and that the activities in question have very short cycles and the profitability rates, which are often high, can discourage the poor from carrying out the loan transactions. This is why this study raises the issue of this system's viability and its performance in the fight against poverty in Niger.

II   The Problem Statement and Study Objectives

Although the decentralised financial system is largely considered to be an effective tool in the fight against poverty, one question does arise: Is it viable and effective in the long-term fight against poverty?

The viability of micro-credit institutions, which should participate fully in achieving the objective of poverty reduction through savings and loans or even through grain banks, remains a concern. In effect, the performance, viability and effectiveness of the system to confront poverty can raise a real long-term problem if the management of the DFS is not guided by guarantee and security mechanisms that take into account its clientele's culture. This, however, could require a strict and transparent management of the system (savings/credit).

These considerations raise the following questions: What is the system's capacity in terms of mobilising resources (collecting savings and refinancing)? Does the DFS have a significant reach in terms of the services offered to its clientele? Is the system able to reach its potential targets, that is, the poor? Is the system financially viable and effective in contributing to poverty reduction in the long term?

To answer these questions, our study proposes to analyse the performance and effectiveness of the financial system in Niger.

III   Study Methodology

The main sources of data are the literature and existing data on the DFS and on poverty in general and more specifically in Niger. The analyses use documentation from National Microfinance Unit (NMU) and data from the household income expenditure survey (HIES III, 2007/2008) and the 2005 CWIQS.

As part of this study, the analysis of the effects of the DFS on the fight against poverty consists of (1) analysing the performance and viability of the DFS in Niger, (2) verifying if the credit granted is used for production or consumption, (3) identifying and quantifying the volumes of credit aimed at financing production and to determine the number of jobs generated using the socio-demographic characteristics of the beneficiaries, (4) analysing the loan requirements to ascertain whether the most disadvantaged have to access credit that finance income-generating activities and (5) analysing the proportion of poor households and the proportion of women that have access to credit in order to attest on the access poor people have to MFI services and to assess the contribution the DFS makes to reducing poverty in Niger.

This descriptive analysis will be accompanied by an econometric analysis of the relationships between the DFS variables and household poverty, using data from the CWIQS survey.

The logistic model can be used as an appropriate framework to analyse the relationship between the DFS variables and the status of poverty. In effect, it enables one to evaluate if the use of DFS services reduces the probability of being among the poor. These models enable the definition of all the possibilities in a multivariate binary context, defined by

$$P(y_{i=1}) = F(X_i \beta_i), i = 1, 2, 3, 4, \ldots n$$

where y_i is equal to a random sequence of the status of poverty defined based on the level of spending per capita, whose variables can take a value of 1 or 0, X_i is a **K** vector of exogenous variables related to the DFS, β_i is a vector of unknown parameters and **F** is a known function. The choice of **F** is acceptable as long as it remains a function of distribution. **F** can take on the following logistic application: $F(X) = \Phi(X) \cong e^x/1 + e^x$, which obeys the logistic law of density $f(t)$, with $f(t) = e^{-t}/(1 + e^{-t})^2$, where t is a real number. Its distribution is symmetrical and is the null average of the variance $\pi^2/3$. These models make it possible to reduce a complex and composite reality to a binary expression (0 and 1 or yes and no). This enables the analysis of the phenomenon of poverty from a static comparative perspective, based on this application. The estimation of such models is carried out by maximising the likelihood function:

$$log L = \sum \{Y_i log F(X_i \beta) + (1 - Y_i) log[1 - F(X_i \beta)]\}$$

The approximations are probabilities assigned by the model when an event occurs (in our case, being poor). The behavioural equation associated with the model can be presented in a linear $D_i = Z + \beta X_i + \varepsilon_i$, before exposing the logit model (proposed by Golberger in 1964) to explain the relationships between a binary variable (here, poverty) and the main explanatory variables, which in our case are the variables related to access to DFS services. The proposed model can be written in the form of

$\{Y_i = 1$ si $\beta \cdot X_i + \varepsilon_i < Z$, which means that the household is poor

$\{Y_i = 0$ if not

Y_i is the situation of a household being poor; β is the vector of coefficients or parameters to estimate; X_i is the vector of DFS variables, our primary choice being access to microfinance services, the interval of time for access to a microfinance service, the benefits of a loan and the degree of satisfaction with microfinance services. These variables are binary and dichotomous like the poverty variable in the model; ε_i represents the error term and Z the poverty threshold.

Before proceeding with this analysis, the following section gives a descriptive view of poverty and the characteristics of the DFS in Niger.

IV   Results, Discussions and Future Work

The Analysis of Performance and Viability Indicators for MFIs in Niger

To ensure the sustainability and the viability of the decentralised financial system, the various stakeholders in the system must be able to mobilise the local resources needed to operate and to develop long-term business. To do so, the MFIs must have the possibility of lasting over time.

MFI Impact Indicators in Niger

In Niger, the main indicators show the slow growth of microfinance activities despite the financial weaknesses of the sector. Between 2000 and 2007, the DFS was dynamic in its operations to mobilise deposits and had greater involvement of the populations. Deposits more than doubled and credit was multiplied by two and a half. The financial institutions showed a certain capacity for mobilising local savings, even if the volume of savings remained inferior to the credit needs.

Figure 11.1 shows that the capacities of the DFS to mobilise internal resources are inadequate to meet the financing needs of the beneficiaries. The reasons for this are simple; the clients of this system are individuals who do not have any resources

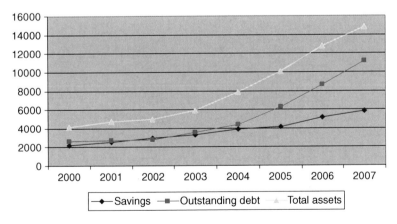

Fig. 11.1 Trend of impact indicators for MFI in Niger (in millions of CFA francs) (Source: Calculated based on NMU data)

to save. How can you expect an individual whose revenue does not allow him/her to cover their daily needs to participate in building up savings? The solution is to be sought from the angle of creating productive work that enables paying people who do not work and increasing the income of the primary sector producers, the majority of whom are poor.

To summarise, if the system does not have enough capacity to mobilise its resources, it is because the path has been poorly chosen. This system should be an instrument to support a policy of employment and/or intensifying production in primary industries.

MFI Performance and Financial Viability Indicators

Generally speaking, half of the MFIs have slightly positive financial results. But, this profitability is relative and still raises the issues of the existence of subsidies that improve the operating results of the MFIs. Without these subsidies, a large number of them would be indebted, notably those that are small in size (BCEAO 2004). Nevertheless, one should note that the rate of bad loans is relatively high, even if diminishing, with an average between 2000 and 2004 of 12.6% or around the proportion of the investments relative to total system assets. This constitutes a danger for the sustainability and viability of the MFIs, as well as for the performance of the DFS.

Nonetheless, the interest rate, the financial instrument that remunerates savings deposits, remains a problem. Savings must be remunerated in order to generate additional income so as to ensure the sustainability and viability of the MFI, that is, to grant new loans and to cover operational costs. In Niger, the interest rate in the DFS varies between 24 and 36%, depending on the institutions. The usury rate is set at 27% in accordance with ruling no. 0482/MF/RE/DGER/DMCE, dated 18 November 1999. The question remains whether or not the institutions should increase their credit rates further in order to survive without subsidies and to become financially self-sufficient.

A quarter of the operating costs of MFIs exceeds the deposits and savings of their clients. However, a lot of MFIs are too dependent on external resources and have reduced mobilisation of deposits, which signifies greater vulnerability with regard to the external financial assistance.

Ultimately, the performance and viability of the MFIs in Niger are problematic in the absence the subsidies. This is due to three main reasons:

- The persistence of financial dependence on external partners, which means that the deposits and savings do not cover the system's financial needs, when to be effective and viable, the system must be self-financing in the long term.
- The difficulties encountered in managing the resources received, which reduce their performance and effectiveness, make it harder to reach the system's set objectives.

Table 11.1 Performance and financial viability indicators

Year indicators	2000	2001	2002	2003	2004	2005
Operational costs (millions of CFAF)	1,168.0	990.0	1,026.0	1,158.0	1,416.0	21.2
Deposits (millions of CFAF)	2,169.0	2,565.0	2,981.0	3,325.0	3,856.0	4,186.0
Total beneficiaries	100,000.0	125,000.0	151,000.0	156,000.0	170,988.0	225,588.3
Number of women beneficiaries	33,576.6	39,858.8	73,178.4	78,104.9	85,609.0	118,111.0
Percent of women among the beneficiaries	33.6	39.9	48.5	50.1	50.1	52.4
Outstanding credit (millions CFAF)	2,649.0	2,748.0	2,829.0	3,586.0	4,380.0	6,289.0
Non-productive loans (millions CFAF)	322.0	406.0	431.0	405.0	415.0	–
Bad loans in % total credit Niger	12.2	14.8	15.2	11.3	9.5	–
Subsidies (millions of CFAF)	286.0	291.0	354.0	347.0	578.0	590.0
Subsidies in % of total assets	6.9	6.1	7.1	5.8	7.3	5.9
Investments (millions CFAF)	526.0	485.0	621.0	768.0	1408.0	–
Investment in % of total assets	12.7	10.2	12.4	12.9	17.9	–

Source: Calculation based on NMU data

- The poor profitability of the system linked to the high interest rates, the presence of non-productive loans and the capacity clients have to respect their financial commitments that lead to litigious or doubtful debts.

Table 11.1 illustrates the situation of MFI performance and viability indicators.

Effectiveness of the DFS in Reducing Poverty

The hypothesis is that when households have access to DFS services, one should see a reduction in poverty through the creation of jobs and through coverage of the economic activities of the most vulnerable populations through the use of credit. The question arises as to whether or not the DFS is accessible to the poor and to what extent it contributes to reducing poverty in Niger.

Access of Households to MFI Services Based on Area of Residence

In Niger, microfinance services are primarily aimed at rural areas in order to respond to the common needs of specific groups, such as rural producers, self-employed workers, inhabitants in disadvantaged neighbourhoods and, particularly,

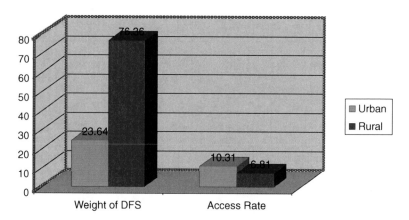

Fig. 11.2 Households with access to microfinance services (Source: Calculated based on CWIQS data from 2005)

farmers and stock breeders. This orientation is motivated by a concern for strengthening the organisational capacities of the rural populations, so they can get mobilised and carry out joint actions with the goal of undertaking and developing income-generating activities.

This process has made it possible to reach more than 7% of Nigerian households using microfinance services. Disparities have nevertheless been observed when looking specifically at area of residence. Among the households with access to the DFS, rural areas represent 76% and urban areas 24%. However, the rate of access that rural populations have is lower than the rate of access of urban households. Taken alone, only 7% of rural households have access to microfinance services, while this rate is estimated at more than 10% in urban areas (Fig. 11.2).

Poor Household Access to MFI Services

The poor households in Niger (53%) live for the most part in rural areas. In these areas, the intensity of household poverty was 56% according to 2005 CWIQS data. This leads one to believe that MFI intervention should be of greater interest in rural areas so as to create a rural financial market that is accessible to the poor. But as we can see in Table 11.2, the results of the 2005 CWIQS survey do not reflect this vision, which consists of giving a priority to poor and economically vulnerable people.

In effect, the DFS does not primarily target poor households but poor regions. Based on this survey, among the households that use micro-credit services, the proportion of poor people is relatively lower than the non-poor population (49% of poor vs. 51% of non-poor). This implies that inside the regions, the stakeholders operate without first conducting a situational analysis to specifically identify the poor within the targeted community.

Table 11.2 Proportion of poor people using DFS services by region (in %)

Regions	Proportion of poor with access to MFI services[a]	Percent (%) of poor using MFI services[b]	Incidence of poverty among households
Agadez	0.84	17.97	37.37
Diffa	0.37	6.63	14.67
Dosso	4.96	59.16	59.42
Maradi	7.79	69.12	72.31
Tahoua	1.49	21.40	37.96
Tillaberi	4.13	48.87	59.04
Zinder	2.87	56.33	62.00
Niamey	0.43	15.35	20.44
Niger	3.64	49.12	53.01

Source: Calculation based on 2005 CWIQS
[a]The number of poor households and beneficiaries of DFS services over the total number of households in Niger
[b]The number of poor households with access to DFS services over of the poor population in Niger

In Niger, the rate of access the poor have to MFI services is very low overall. In 2005 alone, 8% of the population used microfinance services, of which 3.6% were poor people (of the total population). This means that either the resources are very insufficient to serve the needs of a lot of poor people or that the services are not aimed at the poor.

The DFS and Targeting Women

The DFS as a whole is of particular interest for women in Niger, and one observes that women have increased access to the system's services. The number of women granted credit more than triples between 2000 and 2005. At the end of 2005, women represented around half of all the clients, compared with a third in 2000. As poor women develop their business activities, they become more self-sufficient, secured and confident to participate more actively in the economic, social and political life of their community. The participation of women in the system is judged to be a significant measure of the positive impact on the living conditions of the poor. It is in this spirit that the special programme of the president of the Republic of Niger grants credit to women that provides an institutional framework for women to group together at a local level. At the end of 2005, women had access to more than 177 MFI service points found in Niger, which represents around 90% of all the DFS sales points (Fig. 11.3).

Empirical Relations Between the Status of Poverty and DFS Variables in Niger

The effectiveness of the DFS is viewed here through the relations between certain basic variables related to the microfinance services and the status of poverty obtained from a logistic regression. The analysis of the relationship between the

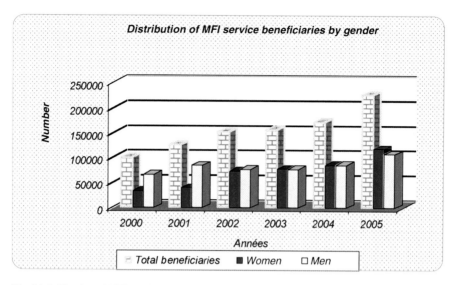

Fig. 11.3 Number of MFI service beneficiaries by gender (Source: Calculated based on data from the BCEAO)

DFS variables and the status of being poor or not, being taken from static data, puts us in a comparative static situation. However, the results can be interpreted in terms of the comparison of probabilities associated with different variables corresponding to the logistic regression results. The relationships are interpreted with odds ratios and estimated parameter signs.

The odds ratio is interpreted as a measure of association. If it is higher than 1, the relationship is increasing; it is decreasing if it is lower than 1. When it is equal to 1, there is no association. This interpretation could be corroborated by the signs of the estimated coefficients. In addition, the explanatory variables being dichotomous, the exponential of the variable coefficients can be interpreted as a measure of the associated odds ratio (OR) associated when going from one category to another. The model's constant is interpreted as "the effect" of the reference category. In other words, "C" enables the calculation of the probability of the *dependent variable y*, when all the co-variables $x1, x2, \ldots, xk$ are null.

$OR = \frac{P1}{1-P1} * \frac{1-P0}{P0} = e^{\beta i}$, with $P0$ as the probability that the individual presents the chosen modality, the reference being poor and $P1$ the probability associated with the modality that stems from the results of the regression. The codification of the explanatory variables is as follows:

- Use of Microfinance, 1 if yes the household uses the services and 0 if it does not.
- Satisfaction with Microfinance Services, 1 if yes the household is satisfied and 0 if it is not.

Table 11.3 Results of the logistic regression between poverty and DFS variables

DFS variables	B coefficients	Standard deviation	Probability of significance	Odds ratio	Confidence interval (Odds ratio)	
					Min	Max
Use of microfinance (yes)	−0.25	0.01	0	0.78	0.76	0.79
Satisfaction with microfinance services (yes)	0.43	0.01	0	1.54	1.50	1.57
Access time (less than 30 mins)	0.58	0.00	0	1.79	1.78	1.81
Take out loan (yes)	−0.56	0.01	0	0.57	0.56	0.58
Constant (C)	0.65	0.00	0	1.91		

Source: Calculation based on 2005 CWIQS; Meaning of the odds ratio and coefficients linked to the variables

- Access Time to MFI Services, 1 if access time is less than 30 minutes and 0 if it is more.
- Taking Out a Loan, 1 if the household has taken out a loan during the year and 0 if it has not.

Interpretation of the Logistic Regression Results

The variables are dichotomised, 1 if yes and 0 if no. Table 11.3 shows the results associated with the value 1 and the condition 0 is taken as a reference. To this effect, the observations respect the odds ratio formula and are interpreted in relation to the reference modality.

Poverty and Use of Microfinance Services

The use of microfinance services reduces the probability of being in the poor category. In effect, the odds ratio value (0.78) being less than 1 means that the probability that a user of microfinance services is poor is less than that of a non-user. So, one can say that microfinance is an effective way of making a lasting contribution to reducing monetary poverty in households. As a result, to make the effectiveness of the DFS sustainable, the public authorities and development partners should join efforts so that the system be exclusively at the service of the poor.

Poverty and Satisfaction with Microfinance Services

The poor are satisfied with microfinance services, with satisfaction being positive on the whole, the coefficient associated with the poor responding (yes) to satisfaction has a positive sign (0.43) and the corresponding odds ratio value is greater

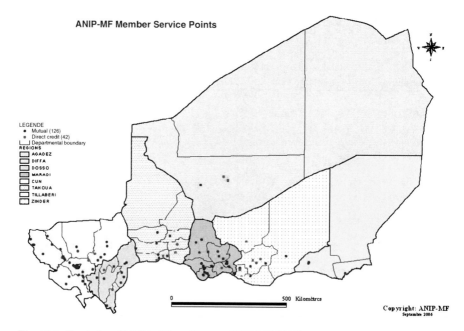

Fig. 11.4 Proximity of MFI in Niger (Source: ANIP-MF 2006)

than one. This means that the probability of a poor person declaring that they are satisfied with the microfinance services is greater than the probability that a poor person declares not being satisfied with microfinance services.

Poverty and Access Time to Microfinance Services

The time it takes to access the services measures how near or far one is to microfinance establishments in relation to the service beneficiaries' place of residence. When it takes too much time to access a microfinance service, this limits access and even the effectiveness of the system due to the resulting cost of the transaction.

In the specific case of this study, the system serves as a real neighbourhood service for the poor. In effect, the probability that a poor person declares that he has less than a 30 minutes walk to access a microfinance service is greater than those who are at a distance requiring more time than 30 minutes. The odds ratio (1.79) associated with the parameter of access in less than 30 minutes is greater than one. This means that the sign of the associated coefficient is positive (0.58). The effectiveness of the system is better understood when one looks at the associated confidence interval. The lower milestone is strictly higher than one and therefore all values associated with the odd will be higher than one (Fig. 11.4).

Loans and Poor People's Participation in Economic Life

The empirical results of this study show that, when the individuals have the possibility of taking out a loan to finance their debt, the probability of them falling in the class of the poor is less than the probability of those that do not take out a loan. The odds ratio associated with the "take out a loan" modality in a difficult situation is inferior to one (0.57), and the maximum value that it can take is 0.58, so therefore, it can never exceed one in this specific case. The loan is therefore a source of financing for the poor. Lending to the most disadvantaged enables them to be responsible when their initiatives are supported either by financing small activities or paying for education or healthcare or to a lesser degree consumption.

Ultimately, these results encourage initiatives that aim to lend money to farmers, breeders and small traders in rural areas. The poor need the DFS services to save small sums of money, to invest in their activities and to face major expenses and protect themselves from the risk of food-related insecurity.

However, future studies should focus on experimental data that allow for a concrete evaluation of the post-credit situation of beneficiaries in comparison with their initial situation.

V   The Limits of the Decentralised Financing System in Niger

The limits of the system can be seen mostly at the level of mobilising internal resources and failure in loans recovery. In effect, as micro-credit is practised in Niger, it must be reimbursed. The borrower must, therefore, be able to reimburse the loan, something that is weak given that the majority of the poor do not have reliable income-generating activities. Granting loans to this kind of persons may aggravate not only their debt burden and their poverty but also may compromise the viability of the lending institution.

The DFS often targets a variety of social problems: the victims of floods or other natural disasters, people with vocational training certification and the unemployed, all the types of individuals in precarious situations who the government and development institutions desire to assist with micro-credit. However, micro-credit programmes designed for this type of situation rarely work. They most often have very high rates of default or non-reimbursed debt.

It is hard to succeed with the directed use of microfinance to resolve development challenges in situations where people's main source of subsistence has been destroyed or is very precarious. Like in all institutions, MFI must survive over time and develop while serving the poor, which has many consequences due to the difficulty this category of the population has in providing a collateral to guarantee their financial solvency. The MFI must, therefore, set up instruments to control the financial risks, while integrating very low-income beneficiaries.

The interest rates applied in the DFS are somewhat higher than in the classic financial system because the cost of a small loan is proportionally higher than that of a large loan. The proportional cost of administration for micro-credits is also very high because they address a clientele that has no credit history and no collateral and that is often illiterate and located in isolated regions. It is costly for the MFI to go to these clients and ensure repayment.

VI Policy Implications and Recommendations

Despite the reticence that can be raised regarding microfinance, the reality in the field and experience show that microfinance helps the poor to (1) participate in the economy, (2) improve their level of monetary income, (3) boost the viability of family businesses and (4) acquire training and become productive to overcome poverty.

In addition, the DFS is an instrument of emancipation that enables the poor, and particularly women, to become agents of economic development. By providing access to financial services, microfinance plays an important role in fighting a numerous dimensions of poverty. For example, the income generated by an activity not only enables it to develop but also to contribute in improving the household's income level and therefore in improving their food security, in educating the children, and in covering healthcare costs, etc.

However, one should recall that micro-credit proves to be more useful for those who have identified an economic opportunity. In this way, the poor who work in stable or growing economies, who have shown their capacity to undertake the proposed activities in a spirit of enterprise and their commitment to repay their debts, are the best candidates for micro-credit. But as in any business, having financial products that cover expenses is very often what ascertains the sustainability of the MFI and an effective response to the financial needs of their clients.

In terms of recommendations, the authorities and the other stakeholders (MFI, donors, TFPs, NGOs, etc.) must combine their efforts in order to:

- Consider the clients of the system not as people looking for charity but people that can be put back to work when they have access to the basic requirements (capital and training) to climb the economic scale at their own pace, with dignity and self-respect
- Strengthen the instruments the MFIs use (proximity, accessibility, satisfaction through quality service and improving the access time to MFI services)
- Continue to support rural credit unions so as to ensure that they are adapted to their environments and to the objectives of the fight against poverty
- Target the poor and identify their financial needs to create new products and financial services that meet those needs in terms of entrepreneurship
- Transform the poor into consumers with access to services and products that meet their daily needs, through the creation of food banks
- Give priority to groups in situations of vulnerability but who are economically active

- Provide support to MFI to enable them to produce databases with a wealth of information regarding the clients and DFS operational reports that enable an assessment of the real impacts of the DFS on the living conditions of the beneficiaries

VII Conclusion

Overall, the DFS has performed unsatisfactorily in the case of Niger, even though much is still to be done. Regarding the emergence of the system, available information showed that the microfinance system's development is in full swing in Niger, as seen in the increase in the number of MFIs, the volume of credit granted and the increasing number of beneficiaries, notably women.

The decentralisation supported by the DFS through projects and credit unions also contributes to increasing rural producers' capacities and creating jobs not only through micro-projects and cooperative initiatives in the area of farming and stock breeding but also for small trade.

An econometric analysis has also enabled an assessment of the relevance and effectiveness of the DFS in reducing poverty through an empirical relationship between the status of poverty and the system's characteristic variables which include using microfinance services, satisfaction with MFI services, access time to MFI services and the possibilities of taking out a loan in the case of financial difficulties. The results of the regressions showed an increase of the probability of reducing poverty through the use of MFI services.

Despite some obstacles that exist to long-term viability, micro-credit remains a financial possibility of vital importance to the poor in Niger. Poor people need financing not only to be able to subsist but also to overcome unexpected events and to improve their well-being. Access to credit and to financial institution services is an effective instrument to enable the poor to benefit from basic daily-life needs. Financial services enable the poor to save small sums of money, to invest in their activities and to face expenses related to consumption, healthcare and education.

The analysis of available data also demonstrated that the system is developing in Niger but that several challenges remain. Restructuring the institutions in difficulty and an intervention strategy based on an in-depth analysis that identifies the poor are required to improve the system's effectiveness in reducing poverty.

References

ANIP-MF (2006), Association Nigerienne des Institutions Professionnelles de la Micro-Finance, Rapport des Activités 2006. Niamey, Niger
BCEAO (2004), Rapport Annuel 2004: Dakar, Senegal

227

Chen, Shaohua and Ravallion, Martin (2007), 'Absolute poverty measures for the developing world, 1981–2004', *Policy Research Working Paper Series 4211*, The World Bank.
Economic Commission for Africa (2005) 2005 Report. Addis Ababa, Ethiopia
Goldberger, A.S. (1964), Econometric Theory. New York: Wiley.
International Labour Organisation (2004), 2004 World Youth Employment Trends, Geneva, Switzerland.
Ministry of the Economy and Finance, INS (2006), 'Questionnaire des Indicateurs de Base du Bien-être (QUIBB2005)' *Rapport sur les indicateurs sociaux.*

Chapter 12
Financing Agriculture and the Food Crisis in Africa: What Role Can Microfinance Play?

Sandra Kendo

Abstract In the context of a growing food crisis with more than a billion people suffering from hunger, it is clear how important it is to study optimising the farming sector by increasing the ways it is financed in order to serve a larger number of the poor. The issue is to analyse how microfinance can contribute to improving the financing of farming in order to favour an improvement in the living conditions of poor populations. This financing could be improved and efficiently ensured if microfinance services were innovative and adapted to this purpose. Farm households' capacities capacities have a dual influence on the poverty-reduction process through their productivity, on one hand, and through distribution of income, on the other. More specifically, we use these facts as the basis to evaluate the impact that the financial sector can have on agricultural productivity and the impact that agricultural productivity can in turn have on poverty. It emerges that the financial sector, having reached a certain stage in its current development, is not contributing to improving productivity but is a key factor that acts positively on reducing poverty. In addition, there is a negative, non-linear relationship between agricultural productivity and poverty. Yet, in view of improving the actions of the financial sector with respect to farmers, one could develop a framework that promotes financial intermediation based on microfinance. As a result, it is necessary to valorise and popularise microfinance actions directed at farmers. The development of adequate and adapted financing through microfinance in the farming sector should be a priority for West African countries in order to enable the latter to experience the positive influence in both the process of improving productivity and in the process of reducing poverty.

S. Kendo (✉)
University of Lorraine/Yaouandé II, Cameroon, Lorraine, France
e-mail: sandra2172003@yahoo.fr

E.T. Ayuk and S.T. Kaboré (eds.), *Wealth Through Integration*, Insight and Innovation in International Development 4, DOI 10.1007/978-1-4614-4415-2_12,
© International Development Research Centre 2013

I Introduction

An awareness-raising campaign launched by the international community has highlighted the key role played by more inclusive financial services, right in line with achieving the Millennium Development Goals. Consequently, 2005 was named the international year of microcredit.[1] In 2003, Kofi Annan[2] gave a general overview of the situation of the poor, with regard to the financial sector. The heads of state and government that met at the headquarters of the United Nations for this world summit in September 2005 declared: "We recognize the need to ensure the poor special access to financial services, notably through the use of micro-finance and micro-credits".[3] Access to credit remains, therefore, an issue of concern for a good number of decision-makers with respect to the marginalised populations in general and those of the rural areas in particular, whose main income-generating activity is farming.

Myrdal highlights the fact that farming is an activity of great importance for the majority of developing country economies, in general, and for those of African in particular. It makes a large contribution to the value of the GDP in these various countries, and it represents not only a promising sector but also one that is beneficial for these economies. Since the period of independence, actors in the financial sector have focussed a lot more on agricultural production of products such as cacao, coffee and cotton, among others. Yet the agricultural sector is vast and offers a number of opportunities that receive little attention today. Exploiting the multiple opportunities offered by the agricultural sector requires certain factors such as a sufficient level of education, acceptable health, access to funding (agricultural credit, savings, etc.) and the endowment of agricultural equipment, among other things.

Furthermore, as highlighted by Morvant-Roux (2008), the majority of farmers in developing countries are excluded from the banking system due to their precarious conditions that offer little in terms of guarantees. We should note that the rate of bank usage in Africa and South Asia is less than or equal to 6% for the agricultural sector (Christiaensen and Demery 2007).[4] These farmers who practise agriculture reside primarily in rural areas and are mostly poor. However, farming contributes considerably well to reducing poverty in low-income countries, because it is strongly linked

---

[1] See the United Nations bluebook called "Building inclusive financial sectors," United Nations, New York, 2006.

[2] Kofi Annan spoke in these terms in December 2003, following the designation of 2005 as the international year of microcredit: "The stark reality is that most poor people in the world still lack access to sustainable financial services, whether it is savings, credit or insurance. The great challenge before us is to address the constraints that exclude people from full participation in the financial sector... Together, we can and must build inclusive financial sectors that help people improve their lives." DAES and FENU (2006) Building inclusive financial sectors, United Nations, New York.

[3] See the United Nations bluebook called "Building inclusive financial sectors", United Nations, New York, 2006.

[4] Christiaensen and Demery (2007) "Agriculture et réduction de la pauvreté en Afrique : une analyse terre à terre."

with other sectors and because the poor benefit more from growth in the agricultural sector than in any other sector. An analysis led by the African Development Bank in 2008 showed that extreme poverty affects more than 50% of the population in at least ten or so countries in sub-Saharan Africa.

According to a report produced by the ECOWAS and the United Nations in 2008, less than a third of the population found in Benin, Ghana and Togo are poor. On the contrary, more than a third of the population are poor in Cape Verde and Côte d'Ivoire. In Burkina Faso, Gambia, Nigeria and Senegal, we note that around 50% of the population are poor. In Guinea-Bissau and in Niger, nearly two-thirds of the population are poor, and more than two-thirds are poor in Mali and Sierra Leone. In the majority of the ECOWAS countries, poverty is more prevalent in rural areas than in urban areas. In Mali and Sierra Leone, more than three-fourths of the rural population are poor, and two-thirds of the rural population are poor in Niger, Nigeria and Senegal. An evaluation of the difference in the living conditions between urban and rural areas reveals that the poverty rate is three times higher in rural areas than in urban areas in Ghana and two times higher in Burkina Faso, Cape Verde, Guinea and Mali.

The 2008 ECOWAS-United Nations poverty profile analysis shows, for example, that the poverty rate was 39% in rural areas versus 11% in urban areas in Ghana in 2005/2006 and 81% in rural areas versus 33% in urban areas in Mali in 2003. Nevertheless, there are countries where the poverty rate is comparatively high both in rural and urban areas. In Senegal, for example, in 2001/2002, the poverty rate was 42% in Dakar, 50% in other urban areas and 65% in rural areas.

II   The Problem Statement

The agricultural policy in the 1970s was marked by strong state intervention. This situation prevailed until the beginning of the 1980s. The strategies employed to finance agriculture were many and varied. In effect, the success of good production is the optimal combination of the capital factor, which is physical here (financing, farm implements), and the labour factor (primarily manpower). As manpower is abundant, the definition of efficient mechanisms to transfer funds is required. As Lapenu (1997) emphasised, access to credit is a problem faced by poor populations in rural areas in developing countries. We should first note that 5-year plans were developed in which a central element was the implementation of large-scale development projects. Agriculture was not neglected, as during the 1960s and 1970s, it constituted a driving force of the economy.

It benefited from funding through the major development projects. These funds were distributed by public institutions in the form of short-term credit to cooperatives used to boost the agricultural sector so as to respond to the main concern of the time, which was to attain food self-sufficiency. These public institutions faced certain difficulties that led the measures that had been deployed to fail. These difficulties included low rates of repayment and fraud (poor governance). Following these problems, specific agricultural banks saw the day, again marked by a strong state presence. However, in the 1980s, the majority of the agricultural banks also failed, leading to multiple collective bankruptcies (Adams 1994). The causes were, among other things, low interest rates that were inadequate for financial services such as savings and credit.[5]

Note that these banks lent more to the local political elite who were then reticent when it came time to pay back the loans. In addition, with the lack of required collateral, the development of a "top-down" distribution scheme for credit is not attractive enough to stimulate borrowers. Finally, the use of "cold cash" does not stimulate repayment and increases credit risks (Houedanou 1999). Faced with the incapacity of the state to successfully finance the agricultural sector, combined with rising debt resulting from a raw materials crisis, it was recommended that the state disengage itself from the majority of economic activities. The IMF recommended "market fanaticism" (an expression attributed to the economist Stiglitz), with three areas of focus: an austerity policy, privatisation and liberalisation. Those in the agricultural sector were left to themselves to face very tough international competition, and they not only had to find solutions to overcome the existing credit constraints but also to find new sources of financing. This was not easy in a context of liberalisation where the interest rates on credit granted were set based on the market and proved to be inaccessible to farmers.

The state's retreat from the financial system, along with financial liberalisation, was not compensated by the development of a banking sector that offered financial services adapted to the needs of farmers. Numerous commercial banks showed very little interest in the rural sector, and the few existing agencies saw their doors close in rural areas (Zeller 2003). The commercial banks, depending on their credit-granting policy, limited access to their services. Rural areas experienced a predominant lack of use of banks. This was strengthened by an informational asymmetry that gave rise to two major problems: moral hazard and adverse selection. In effect, in developing countries, it is difficult for these commercial banks, also called modern banks, to know their borrowers well and, above all, the area in which they live (Fry 1995) and to understand the profitability of the proposed projects and the various risks that they entail.

These banks are also less flexible in their actions due to the regulations and obligations imposed on them by the central bank. Generally speaking, a certain number of factors have been listed as impeding the development of financial services in terms of accessibility of farmers (Morvant-Roux 2008). Among them are (1) the location of these activities in hard-to-access zones that are essentially characterised by low population density and a lack of infrastructure, (2) dependence on climate conditions and the temporality of cycles, (3) seasonality of income coupled with a limited amount of available monetary income, (4) volatile prices for agricultural products and (5) the low reliability of guarantees. These specific characteristics require the development of adapted financing.

---

[5] The cost of credit is not covered by the repayment rate.

In response to the above mentioned difficulties, the poor have turned to an informal financing system (tontines and loan sharks) that practises usury rates. We should note that their mode of financing does not respect the standards of a classic competitive market (Hoff and Stiglitz 1995). Decentralised financial systems, or semiformal systems, arose between the formal and informal systems. These establishments specialise in granting microcredit and are located close to their clients, who they know. In order to better understand this area of finance, it is interesting to first define the terms used by the financial system and by microfinance establishments.

The financial system can be viewed as a continuum that goes from simple loans between family and friends to banks that are strictly regulated by a central bank. On the continuum are loans from traders and retailers, possible lending and deposits offered by a variety of informal savings and loan groups, and loan sharks. Microfinance establishments are accredited institutions that provide financial services to their clients such as microcredit, micro-savings and micro-insurance. One should note that the analysis of the issue of financing agriculture is developing in the context of the liberalisation of agricultural economies. In West Africa, this analysis of the financing of agriculture in terms of the contribution made by microfinance is not the first of its kind. Already in 2002, an international seminar on the topic was organised by the Centre de Coopération Internationale en Recherche pour le Développement (CIRAD) and the Comité d'Echanges de Réflexion et d'Information sur les Systèmes d'Epargne-Crédit (CERISE). This seminar emphasised above all the lack of access to funding, which remains a major limitation to the development of agricultural households.

Yet, the said farm households have real needs such as intensification, modernisation and technical and organizational innovation (Wampfler 2002). This seminar proposed solutions in view of improving the contribution made by microfinance. These solutions focus primarily on the supply of micro-finance services, improving the coordination between the microfinance sector and the farming sector and coordinating the agricultural sector and public policies. Solutions that focus on coordination, modernisation and improving farmers' demand were developed in greater depth. A closer look at two elements—the capacity of agricultural households and the constraints linked to farming—provides a better understanding of the constraints linked to agricultural financing.

Note that increasing agricultural production in an economy can bring considerable transformations and has positive effects in terms of improving economic growth and the standard of living of populations living under limited conditions. Hayami and Ruttan (1998) analysed the chain of effects related to increasing agricultural production. They highlight the following facts: (1) Increasing agricultural production creates a surplus that complements the households' subsistence income. This surplus is considered to be a wage base for entrepreneurs and enables the hiring of more manpower. (2) This wage that comes from increasing agricultural production will increase following a juxtaposition of supply and demand. This wage base increase is accompanied by an increase in wage rates and a decrease in capital yield rates. (3) Increasing wage rates leads to an increase in population growth. The result of this population rate increase is accompanied by an increase in demand for food products. (4) The surplus in demand for food products leads to a price increase for food products, which translates into a decrease in real salary.

The decrease in real salary following an increase in agricultural production impacts the economic process and can be compensated by energizing other sectors of activity. In consequence, one would think that an increase in agricultural production must be managed in such a way as to negate the inflationist effects that suppress the initial positive effect. As a result, public policies that aim to stabilise the economic system in view of ensuring an equitable distribution should be implemented. However, increasing agricultural production is essential and necessary in countries where farming is one of the main vectors for economic growth. Promoting and improving its contribution should not only be highlighted but also popularised within these economies.

It is therefore essential to assess the needs farmers could face in a context where access to financing is very selective and offers little incentive. The ability to adapt the type of financing that fits with agriculture requires the identification of farmers' needs based on their way of life (Wampfler and Lapenu 2002). Three main needs are directly linked to farming—(1) short-term needs: Depending on what kind of farming they do, farmers have needs such as input, fungicides, market gardens and crops under 12 months, wage-earning labour, rental and sharecropping, hiring, storage and product transformation; (2) midterm needs such as endowment of equipment for intensification, commercialisation, storage (buildings), animal acquisition and land acquisition and (3) long-term needs such as creating larger plantations of perennial crops.

Buying farm equipment such as animals for traction, a tractor and a motorised pump is an important need for farm households. Other needs include family needs linked to healthcare, education of children and relatives, housing, access to drinking water, purchasing home goods and equipment. Then comes savings, because savings is a key resource for financing the establishment of a farming activity and the hope of obtaining credit afterwards. The process of accumulating income from agriculture passes first through acquiring income external to farming in view of launching this activity. Accumulating savings also makes it possible to complement the monetary income that comes from very small farms. Finally, non-financial services related to accessing public goods and developing technical support programmes. Regarding public goods, these are essentially linked to developing adequate infrastructure in view of facilitating the wide dissemination of innovative farming practices. The technical support programme developed by farmers in a spirit of development-oriented research, in partnership, enables an improvement of the endowments in human capital and the acquisition of experience in the area of farming practices.

With respect to the limited capacity[6] of agricultural households that has been observed, the consequences include the difficulty in mobilising material guarantees, a constraint to accessing the information necessary for assessing and limiting risks,

---

[6] A household's capacities refer to physical capacities such as level of education, health, standard of living and farmland. There are also material capacities that are related to finance, which are savings and credit granted.

and the acquisition of small credit amounts that do not enable households to realise a profit margin. As for farming activities, they involve endogenous and exogenous risks. Among the endogenous risks is the discrepancy between the technical progress to consider and the existing level of development of the family farm. When the production system is not very diversified, there is a very high risk of loans default by individuals. The exogenous risks include climate variations such as drought and flood, epidemics and other problems linked to inputs supply, market outlets for the products, setting sales prices and being late in payments.

Financing agriculture raises two aspects that impact microfinance both directly and indirectly. They the constraints linked to farm household capacity and the constraints linked to farming as an activity. As a result, we focussed primarily on the question of strengthening the capacity of farm households in these terms: *How can microfinance contribute favourably to improving financing conditions for farming that will enable an improvement in the living conditions of the poor? What, specifically, is the impact of credit granted on the level of agricultural productivity? What is the impact of agricultural productivity on poverty?*

III   Study Objectives

From the above, the main objective of our study is to analyse how microfinance contributes favourably to improving the financing of farming in view of improving the living conditions of the poor. Specifically, it is a question of assessing the impact of credit granted on agricultural productivity and evaluating the impact of agricultural productivity on poverty.

IV   Study Methodology

This methodological part is organised as follows: We will first present the source and type of data used, then the variables used and finally the study's models and estimations methods.

Data Used

We will carry out an applied analysis in the West Africa zone. Our sample will be primarily composed of 15 of the subregion's countries, which are the following: Benin, Burkina Faso, Cape Verde, Côte d'Ivoire, Ghana, Guinea, Guinea-Bissau, Liberia, Mali, Niger, Nigeria, Sao Tome et Principe, Senegal, Sierra Leone and Togo. Our data will be collected in the form of panel data covering a period of 5 years: 1995, 2000, 2003, 2004 and 2005. The data collected are secondary data coming primarily from the databases of the African Development Bank (ABD 2008a, b) and the World Bank's World Development Indicators published in 2008.

The Study Variables

We have the following dependent variables: productivity of farming, which is defined in our database as being agriculture's per capita added value contribution to the national GDP for each country in the subregion, and the variable-noted *added value*. *Added value²* represents the square of agricultural productivity. The poverty index will be evaluated with the help of the human poverty index and is listed as *Poverty*.

The independent variables include all the factors that make it possible to determine an agricultural household's capacity. These include among others household consumption expenditure, called *expenditure*. Financial development, which is private sector domestic credit over GDP, captures the activity of the financial sector and evaluates the availability of the credit that is granted. This variable is written as *credit*. *Credit²* represents the square of financial development. The percentage of land set aside for farming in relation to the surface area of available land is written as *land*. *Land²* represents the square of the percentage of land set aside for farming. The composite fertility index evaluates the number of births per woman in the country and is written as *fertility*. The primary schooling rate is noted as *primary*. The secondary-education schooling rate is noted as *secondary*. The percentage of women working in agriculture is noted as *woman_agri*. *Woman²* represents the square of the percentage of women working in farming. The percentage of men working in agriculture is noted *man_agri*. The percentage of the population between the ages of 15 and 64 years in relation to the total population is referred to as *popul*. The percentage of mobile agricultural material used in the country, which evaluates the number of tractors and other materials used on farmland, is noted as *machine*. The percentage of public health expenditure in relation to GDP is *Health*. The inflation rate, which measures the variation of the consumer price index, is *Inflation*.

Presentation of the Study's Model

In our sample, one notes an apparent selection bias problem in addition to a number of unobservable data. In a time-based logic, we have few statistics in the case of West African countries. Our panel model, built with the Poisson distribution, will be estimated by the maximum likelihood. The Poisson distribution defined in Wooldridge (2002) and Baltagi (2008) is as follows:

$$Pr\left(Y_{it} = \frac{y_{it}}{x_{it}}\right) = \frac{e^{-\lambda_{it}}\lambda_{it}^{y_{it}}}{y_{it}!} \tag{12.1}$$

where $y_{it} = 0, 1, 2, \ldots$; $i = 1, 2, \ldots, N$; $t = 1, \ldots, T$

With i representing the 15 countries in the West Africa zone and t representing the number of years being considered which is 5. The determination of λ_{it} is done with the help of a semi-logarithmic model that is defined as follows:

$$\lambda_{it} = \mu_i + x'_{it}\beta \tag{12.2}$$

with μ_i representing the specific unobservable individual effects. For the fixed effect model, the hypothesis is that the average is equal to the variance, that is:

$$E\left(\frac{y_{it}}{x_{it}}\right) = Var\left(\frac{y_{it}}{x_{it}}\right) = \lambda_{it} = e^{\mu_i + x'_{it}\beta} \tag{12.3}$$

And our marginal effect of the explanatory variable x_k is given by:

$$\frac{\partial E(y_{it}/x_{it})}{\partial x_k} = \lambda_{it}\beta_k \tag{12.4}$$

Our likelihood function associated with this Poisson distribution in panel data presents as follows:

$$L(\beta, \lambda_{it}) = \sum_{i=1}^{N}\sum_{t=1}^{T}\left[-\lambda_{it} + y_{it}(\mu_i + x'_{it}) - \ln y_{it}!\right] \tag{12.5}$$

This Poisson model, thus defined from Eq. 12.1, will be estimated using the dependent variables of agricultural productivity on one hand and poverty on the other. In the model's productivity model, the explanatory variables x_k are the following: financial development (**Credit**), squared financial development (**Credit^2**), use of agricultural equipment (**machine**), land allocated for farming (**land**), the consumer price variation index (**inflation**), household consumer expenditure (**expenditure**), the rate of primary schooling (**primary**), the rate of secondary schooling (**secondary**), the number of births per woman (**fertility**), the square of the number of births per woman (**fertility^2**), the percentage of women working in farming (**woman_agri**), the percentage of men working in farming (**man_agri**) and the working-age population between the ages of 15 and 64 years (**popul**).

Regarding the explanatory variables for the poverty model, we have agricultural productivity (**added value**), squared agricultural productivity (**added value^2**), financial development (**Credit**), land allotted for farming (**land**), the square of land (**land^2**), state of health (**health**), consumer price index variation (**inflation**), household consumer expenditure (**expenditure**), the rate of primary schooling (**primary**), the rate of secondary schooling (**secondary**), the number of births per woman (**fertility**), the percentage of women working in farming (**woman_agri**), square of women working in farming (**woman^2**), the percentage of men working in farming (**man_agri**) and the working-age population between the ages of 15 and 64 years (**popul**).

The indicator used in our study to carry out our test is that of the relationship of maximal likelihood that follows the law of χ^2. The hypothesis to be tested is the following:

$$\begin{cases} H_0 : \beta_j = 0 \\ H_1 : \beta_j \neq 0 \end{cases} \tag{12.6}$$

where β_j designates the jth vector component of the parameters $\beta = (\beta_1, \ldots, \beta_k)$ $\in \mathbf{R}^k$. H_0 is accepted if $\mathrm{LRT}_j \prec \chi^2_{95\%}$ and is rejected if the contrary is true. In terms of P value supplied by STATA software, the hypothesis H_0 is accepted if the P value is higher than 5%. If that is not the case, that is, if the P value is less than 5%, then the alternative hypothesis H_1 is accepted. This hypothesis H_0 corresponds to the non-significance of the explanatory variable considered in the model as specified.

V   Results

The tables containing our various results are presented in the appendix. First of all, in Table 12.1, we have presented the statistical analysis of our various variables. We observe based on this table that the number of observations is not the same for all the variables. The number of observations variable varies between 66 and 75, and our sample is small. One also notes that our sample has a high degree of dispersion around the observable average and that it is not spread symmetrically. Concerning the Poisson distribution estimations, we have obtained robust estimators using maximum likelihood. The interpretation of the signs of influences is done in the regression tables (Tables 12.2 and 12.4 in the Appendix), which give the coefficient signs, and the coefficients considered for the analysis of the coefficients are taken in the tables on marginal effects (Tables 12.3 and 12.5 in the Appendix).

Regarding our productivity model, whose variable in our estimation tables is the added value of agriculture, we have seven explanatory variables that are all significant at the 1% threshold. These variables are credit, credit squared, land, inflation rate, consumption expenditure, rate of secondary schooling, fertility rate, fertility rate squared, percentage of women in agriculture and percentage of men in farming. Among these factors, one can note that certain have a negative influence thus decreasing the added value of agriculture and others have a positive influence hence increasing the added value of agriculture. The financial development indicator, called credit in Table 12.2, has a negative influence on agricultural productivity.

We can note the existence of a non-linear inverted U relationship between financial sector development and agricultural productivity. This non-linear negative effect can be explained by the numerous financial sector reforms that were put in place following financial liberalisation. The financial sector is dominated by commercial banks that put restrictions in granting credit in sectors like agriculture.

The state's retreat from granting agricultural credit led to the emergence of huge difficulties, including the negative effects that come across in our results. The other variables that have a negative influence on agricultural productivity are the inflation rate, the proportion of men working in farming and the percentage of the population between the ages of 15 and 64 years. At the end of 2006 and 2007, a large price increase was recorded on basic products and those of first necessity. From this estimation, we note that the price increase acted negatively on farming. An increase of 1% in the inflation rate contributed to reducing the productivity value by 0.1966%.

An increase of 1% in the number of men working in farming contributed to reducing the productivity value by 0.8815%. An increase of 1% in the population group between the ages of 15 and 64 years reduced the added value of agricultural productivity by .5%. Among the variables that have a positive influence is ownership of farmland. Thus, an increase of 1% in the proportion of land allotted to farming contributed to increasing agricultural productivity by 0.3943%. Another variable is household consumption expenditure. The more the households consume, the more productive farming is; this leads one to think that consumption stimulates productivity. An increase of 1% in consumption expenditure increased the added value of agriculture by 0.5294%. As for women's fertility rate, one notes that the positive effect follows a non-linear tendency.

The optimal fertility after which one observes a change in the trend is 3.946, for a value of 4 children per woman. This result supports the fact that children constitute a considerable asset for families with small family farms. The entire family organises the activities seasonally, and the production mechanism requires know-how and labour from each of the family members. Taking into consideration that the active population in the farming sector is dis-aggregated by gender, we have a percentage of active women that has a positive influence and the percentage of active men that has a negative influence. An increase of 1% in the number of women working in farming contributes to increasing the value of productivity by .6767%. While elsewhere, one already noted that an increase of 1% in the proportion of men working in farming reduces the agricultural productivity value by .8815%.

The variables that have a significant influence on poverty at the 1% threshold are added value and added value squared, land and land squared, inflation rate, fertility rate, percentage of women working in farming and percentage of men working in farming. At the 5% threshold, we have consumption expenditure and the square of women working in agriculture. At the 10% threshold, we have the credit variable. Agricultural productivity has a positive influence on reducing poverty. One notes that there is a negative and non-linear relationship between poverty and agricultural added value. The fact that the poor have access to credit also has a positive influence on reducing poverty. An increase of 1% in the development of the financial sector promotes a reduction of the poverty index by .1508%. There is also a negative and non-linear relationship between the percentage of land allotted to agriculture and poverty.

With regard to the variation in the consumer price index, we note that there is a inverse relationship between the two variables. An increase of 1% in the consumer price index contributes to reducing the poverty rate by .1638%. Other variables having a positive influence on the poverty rate in terms of reduction include the proportion of women men in agriculture. We have also noted that the proportion of women in agriculture positively influences productivity by increasing its value. There is a linear relationship between these two variables. Regarding poverty and the proportion of women working in farming, we note that although it has a negative effect by the second variable, we observe a non-linear relationship. Regarding men in agriculture, an increase of 1% contributes to reducing poverty by .6277%.

Regarding household consumption expenditure and fertility rates, we have noted that there is a positive relationship between these two variables and the poverty rate. A variation of 1% in consumption expenditure contributes to increasing the poverty rate by .17%. A variation of 1% in the fertility rate contributes to increasing the poverty rate by 10.24%. The fertility rate is the variable with the highest negative effect on poverty. This explains the interest there is in controlling the number of births per woman, despite the fact that we have noted a non-linear positive relationship between fertility rates and agricultural productivity.

VI Economic Policy Implications and Recommendations

In numerous African countries in general, particularly in West Africa, farming makes a major contribution in terms of added value to the GDP. One notes that a good number of factors favour an improvement in the capacities of farm households. These factors are secondary schooling rate, percentage of land allotted to farming, consumption expenditure, fertility rate and the percentage of women working in farming. It is true that one of the millennium development goals is to promote schooling for all and to encourage governments to develop measures to enable the population to benefit from a minimum of primary school education. When we look at the minimum level of schooling in West Africa, we note that it is evaluated at around 6 years of study, which is equivalent to a primary school education and remains insufficient.

This is the case for a large part of the population in the West African countries, and policy-makers are encouraged not to stop at this level and to develop strategies that favour secondary education, rather than focussing essentially on primary education access for everyone. In this way, it is easier to strengthen the technical capacities of farmers, because manpower in the agricultural sector remains very ineffective and less efficient than international standards. In addition, one of the major drawbacks in the agricultural sector in Africa, today, is training that would allow farmers to better integrate innovations. This era is dominated by the wind of globalisation, which produces effects at all levels of society and influences trade on the international scene.

It is essential to develop a strategy aimed at encouraging farmers to become more specialised, which would positively contribute to improving the level of agricultural productivity. However, boosting education policies already in place could be done through setting up structures that train farmers by also preparing them to integrate new techniques and technologies that could improve yield. We have also highlighted that the percentage of farm land has a positive influence on agricultural productivity. One should note that improving the profitability of land comes through the acquisition of new equipment and the integration of new agricultural techniques. Yet, in sub-Saharan Africa in general, and in West Africa in particular, one notes a decrease in land profitability relative to that observed on the international scene in a context of globalisation and competition. We note the development of inefficient farming in the subregion.

It would therefore be interesting for decision-makers to promote new techniques for enriching the soil, while raising the awareness of the population regarding the benefits, as they seem adverse to integrating any form of agricultural innovation that they do not master. This could be done through subsidies and of new input, new techniques and available farm equipment (tractors, clearance machinery, dehuskers, etc.) made available to farmers. We also note targeted strengthening of the capacities of active women who are found in large numbers in the farming sector but do not have the resources needed to grow effectively. Furthermore, we have noted that the development of the financial sector has a negative influence on productivity.

However, this same financial sector is an important factor in the poverty-reduction process. As decision-makers already emphasised in 2003, it is important that the poor have access to credit. The poor represent a layer of the population that is marginalised by the financial sector. Yet, improving their access to this sector could positively contribute to improving their living conditions. Improving the impact of the financial sector could be done via microfinance. A case study done in Cameroon on the impact of the development of the financial sector based essentially on access to microcredit showed the opposite results (Kendo et al. 2010). In this study, the authors highlight the fact that the development of the financial sector, by disseminating and emphasising the importance and contribution of the microfinance sector, could produce a positive effect on the productivity of the poor. In addition, one finds a non-linear relationship between development of the financial sector and productivity of poor populations. Other studies also noted the benefits of microcredit on the lives of small farmers. Thus, the microcredit sector reveals its importance and that it can considerably influence small farm income. Exogenous actions to undertake in this direction concern the public authorities, while endogenous actions that concern the microfinance institutions are primarily related to the products offered.

For policy makers, a special emphasis could be placed on the major issues such as education and financing farm equipment, that is, medium- and long-term credit that microfinance institutions have done little to develop. These medium- and long-term credits could be made available to households via microfinance institutions, which have strong local relationships with these poor populations and could develop time-scaled equipment renting programmes. The local microfinance institutions have to face the problem of self-financing, which does not allow them to cover medium- and long-term financing. Additional strategic actions are required, such as implementing plans to monitor the financing of investments in view of remedying the problem of corruption and embezzlement, which are still issues in African countries.

These problems represent a major obstacle to the effective implementation of development plans in a number of African countries. Subsidies for credits that could be developed as a priority include input credit, equipment credit and social credit. Inputs credit entails enabling microfinance establishments to make available to farmers inputs equivalent to the monetary value of "cash" credits that they would have obtained. Reimbursement would depend on the proportion of the harvest and evidence of the existence of an intercommunity grouping to which the farmer belongs and that would serve as a guarantor. Belonging to this intercommunity grouping indicates that the farmer has accepted his/her responsibilities and is committed to reimburse the debt promptly.

Members of the group address the lack of punctuality in making payments by imposing on the member a reimbursement plan. As for equipment credits, heavy equipment like tractors, combines and dehuskers can be made available to an entire farming community, and the percentage of repayment would be based on the activity undertaken by the farmers belonging to the intercommunity grouping who practise essentially the same kind of farming. Social credits, such as education credit, can be attributed with the goal of improving the level of human capital for upcoming generations. The concept of educational loans is very little developed in banking and microfinance institutions and has practically never been done in Africa. The action of the public sector is not enough, despite considerable efforts to finance these sectors.

The participation of the financial sector through services such as credit and insurance is essential for broadening the effectiveness of these two sectors. In view of sensitisation on the importance of theses financing-related actions, an awareness-raising and education campaign should be undertaken among the illiterate and those with little schooling. Microfinance could be perceived as a practice to be widely distributed among farmers. Yet, this is far from the case. This practice is largely employed by rotating credit associations commonly called tontines in certain countries, who practise usury rates. Microfinance establishments continue to have poor coverage and are poorly targeted. Thus, an analysis of endogenous areas imputable to individuals remains to be done.

The endogenous needs of farmers are primarily self-training acquired through their participation in specialised technical sessions organized within the framework of innovations for agricultural practices. The labour force would have to adapt itself in a context of globalisation where a spirit of competition reigns.

VII   Conclusion

Our study shows that development of the financial sector does not contribute to improving productivity but does produce a positive effect on the process of poverty reduction. Development could be improved among farmers through microfinance. This explains the necessity of enriching and widely disseminating among farmers micro-finance activities. Thus, the development of financing that is adequate and adapted to the agricultural sector should be a priority for West African countries so as to have a positive influence both on the process of improving productivity and that of reducing poverty. This financing should take into account secondary education, the availability of farm equipment, ownership of farmland and self-sufficiency of women working in farming.

The priority of these questions has been emphasised due to the too large a bias they cause to credit applicants, who are farmers. We can note that the year 2005, decreed the "international year of microfinance", highlighted the role that microfinance can play in the process of poverty reduction by helping reach the first millennium development goals, which is reducing extreme poverty and hunger. Thus, the development of the financial sector that enhances the supply of micro-finance services that works effectively on reducing poverty must promote a promising environment where the creation of wealth is valued via the channel of productive and profitable investments.

Appendix

Table 12.1 Descriptive statistics of variables

Variables	Observations	Average	Standard error	Min	Max
Added value	73	34.89	16.332	6.827	81.825
Credit	73	15.271	17.910	1.579	142.03
Credit	73	549.564	2369.396	2.493	20172.52
Machine	65	15.008	48.925	0.088	312.5
Land	75	46.002	17.215	17.37	81.25
Inflation	65	11.518	16.648	−3.503	72.756
Expenditure	70	79.773	12.372	36.742	101.1
Primary	67	81.168	21.978	32.765	128.82
Secondary	66	28.015	14.821	6.805	67.704
Fertility	68	5.944	1.048	3.529	7.746
Fertility	68	36.409	12.004	12.451	60.000
Woman_agri	75	29.836	10.857	7.5	48.3
Man_agri	75	33.461	9.610	12.1	47.3
Popul	75	52.171	2.277	47.838	57.361
Poverty	65	44.714	11.898	15.8	64.4
Health	65	5.312	1.619	3.5	12.1

Table 12.2 Estimation of the impact on productivity

Added value	Coefficient	Semi-robust standard error	Z	$P > \lvert Z \rvert$
Credit	2.055×10^{-2}	4.762×10^{-3}	4.32	0.000***
Credit	-1.197×10^{-3}	2.097×10^{-4}	−5.71	0.000***
Machine	1.547×10^{-2}	1.970×10^{-2}	0.78	0.433
Land	1.331×10^{-2}	1.98×10^{-3}	6.71	0.000***
Inflation	-6.637×10^{-3}	7.261×10^{-4}	−9.14	0.000***
Expenditure	1.787×10^{-2}	4.396×10^{-3}	4.07	0.000***
Primary	-4.029×10^{-3}	2.458×10^{-3}	−1.64	0.101
Secondary	2.198×10^{-2}	2.701×10^{-3}	8.14	0.000***
Fertility	−0.746	0.202	−3.69	0.000***
Fertility	9.46×10^{-2}	1.012×10^{-2}	9.34	0.000***
Woman_agri	2.284×10^{-2}	4.827×10^{-3}	4.73	0.000***
Man_agri	-2.976×10^{-2}	5.575×10^{-3}	−5.34	0.000***
Popul	-1.680×10^{-2}	3.007×10^{-2}	−0.56	0.576
Cons	3.339	2.819	1.18	0.236

GEE population-averaged model **Number of observations: 50**
Variable group: year **Number of groups: 5**
Link: log **Observation by group: min = 9**
Family: Poisson **Average = 10.0**
Correlation: exchangeable **Max = 12**
Parameter scale: 1 **Wald chi2(3) = 106.7**

Table 12.3 Marginal effects on productivity

Variables	dY/dX	Z	P > |Z|
Credit	0.609	4.41	0.000***
Credit	-3.546×10^{-2}	-6.14	0.000***
Machine	0.458	0.79	0.428
Land	0.395	6.36	0.000***
Inflation	-0.197	-10.60	0.000***
Expenditure	0.529	4.21	0.000***
Primary	-0.119	-1.60	0.109
Secondary	0.651	9.04	0.000***
Fertility	-22.098	-3.69	0.000***
Fertility	2.801	9.88	0.000***
Woman_agri	0.677	4.81	0.000***
Man_agri	-0.881	-5.51	0.000***
Popul	-0.497	-0.56	0.578

Marginal effects after xtpoisson; $Y = \exp(xb)$ (predict) = 29.623
*** denotes significance at the 1% significance level; ** significance at the 5% level; and * denotes significance at the 10% level

Table 12.4 Estimations of impact on poverty

Poverty	Coefficient	Semi-robust standard error	Z	P > |Z|
Added value	1.54×10^{-2}	5.767×10^{-3}	2.67	0.008***
Added value	3.718×10^{-4}	8.29×10^{-5}	-4.48	0.000***
Credit	-3.50×10^{-3}	1.812×10^{-3}	-1.93	0.053*
Land	2.58×10^{-2}	6.802×10^{-3}	3.79	0.000***
Land	-2.051×10^{-4}	7.6×10^{-5}	-2.70	0.007***
Health	1.028×10^{-2}	2.379×10^{-2}	0.43	0.666
Inflation	-3.801×10^{-3}	4.771×10^{-4}	-7.97	0.000***
Expenditure	3.836×10^{-3}	1.860×10^{-3}	2.06	0.039**
Primary	7.345×10^{-4}	6.966×10^{-4}	2.06	0.039**
Secondary	5.518×10^{4}	1.963×10^{-3}	0.28	0.779
Fertility	0.238	3.453×10^{-2}	6.88	0.000***
Woman_agri	2.102×10^{-2}	7.734×10^{-3}	2.72	0.007***
Woman	-1.965×10^{-4}	9.71×10^{-5}	-2.02	0.043**
Man_agri	-7.306×10^{-3}	4.028×10^{-4}	-18.14	0.000**
Popul	-1.457×10^{-2}	1.284×10^{-2}	-1.13	0.257
Cons	1.87	0.713	2.62	0.009***

GEE population-averaged model   **Number of observations: 51**
Variable group: year   **Number of groups: 5**
Link: log   **Observations par group: min = 9**
Family: Poisson   **Average = 10.2**
Correlation: exchangeable   **Max = 12**
Parameter scale: 1   **Wald chi2(3) = 75,01**

Table 12.5 Marginal effects on poverty

Poverty	dY/dX	Z	$P > \lvert Z \rvert$
Added value	0.663	2.58	0.010***
Added value	-1.16×10^{-2}	-4.25	0.000***
Credit	-0.151	-1.93	0.054*
Land	1.112	3.74	0.000***
Land	-8.838×10^{-3}	-2.68	0.007***
Health	0.443	0.43	0.665
Inflation	-0.164	-8.15	0.000***
Expenditure	0.165	2.05	0.041**
Primary	3.165×10^{-2}	1.05	0.293
Secondary	2.378×10^{-2}	0.28	0.779
Fertility	10.24	7.44	0.000***
Woman_agri	0.906	7.44	0.000***
Woman	8.465×10^{-3}	-2.02	0.043**
Man_agri	-0.315	-15.82	0.000***
Popul	-0.628	-1.12	0.263

Marginal effects after xtpoisson; $Y = \exp(xb)$ (predict) $= 43.094$
***1%; **5%; *10%

References

Adams, R. (1994), 'Non-farm income and inequality in rural Pakistan: a decomposition analysis', *Journal of Development Studies*, 31(1) : 110–133.
ADB (2008a), *Indicateurs sur le genre, la pauvreté et l'environnement sur les pays africains*. Département des statistiques économiques et sociales de la BAD, 9.
ADB (2008b), *Statistiques choisies sur les pays africains*. Département des statistiques économiques et sociales de la BAD, 27.
Baltagi, B.H. (2008), *Econometric Analysis of Panel Data*. John Wiley & Sons, Ltd, Fourth edition.
Christiaensen, L. and L.Demery (2007), *Agriculture et réduction de la pauvreté en Afrique: Uneanalyse terre à terre*. The International Bank for Reconstruction and Development//The World Bank
DAES and FENU (2006), *Building inclusive financial sectors*. United Nations New York.
Fry, M.J. (1995),*Money interest and banking in economic development*. 2nd ed, The Johns Hopkins University Press, Baltimore, 346.
Hayami, Y. and V.M. Ruttan (1998), *Agriculture et Développement, une approche international*. INRA Editions.
Hoff, K, and J.E. Stiglitz (1995), 'Introduction: Imperfect information and rural credit markets-puzzles and policy perspectives', *The World Bank Economic review*, 4 (3): 235–250.
Houedanou, M. C. (1999), 'Des systèmes de financements décentralisés pour le monde rural : Défis et perspectives, Dans Financer autrement le développement du monde rural en Afrique', *Dossier de développement AGRIPROMO, Abidjan; INADES- Formation* P 100.
Kendo, T.C.S, F. Baye, .F and S. Fondo (2010), 'Développement du secteur financier et réduction de la pauvreté selon le genre : cas du milieu rural Camerounais', Banque Africaine de Développement et Commission Economique pour l'Afrique des Nations Unies (eds), *Globalisation, Institutions et Développement Economique de l'Afrique* -Actes de la Conférence Economique Africaine 2008, Economica : Paris.
Lapenu,C. (1997), *La microfinance dans les pays en développement : Théories évolutions et pratiques*, Montpellier, CIRAD.

Morvant-Roux, S. (2008), 'Quelle microfinance pour l'agriculture des pays en voie de Développement ?', *Synthèse du colloque organisé par FARM (Fondation pour l'agriculture et la ruralité dans le monde)*.

United Nations (2006), *Construire des secteurs Financiers accessibles à tous*. éd Département de l'information de l'ONU.

Wampfler, B. (2002), 'Le financement de l'agriculture familiale dans le contexte de lab liberalisation: quelle contribution de la microfinance?' *ATP-CIRAD 41/97; Séminaire International, Dakar, Sénégal*.

Wampfler B. et C. Lapenu (2002), 'La microfinance au service de l'agriculture familiale', Résumé exécutif du séminaire international, 21-24 janvier 2001 Dakar Sénégal, *Afraca/Cirad/Cta/Mae/ Enda-Graf/Fida Cerise, Français/Anglais, Ministère Français des Affaires Etrangères Série « Partenariats »*

Wooldridge, J. M. (2002), *Econometric Analysis of cross-section and Panel Data*. MIT Press, Massachussetts

Zeller, M. (2003), 'Models of rural financial institutions' in *Paving the way forward for rural finance, USAID*

Chapter 13
Common External Tariff (CET) and Targeting the Poor in Mali

Massa Coulibaly and Balla Keita

Abstract The WAEMU's common external tariff (CET) went into effect in January 2000 and is divided into four categories of products with customs duties of 0, 5, 10 and 20%, respectively. This study analyses the "benefits" of this categorisation for the poor, using targeting indicators calculated with the help of data from the Mali 2006 ELIM. For category 0, which is exempt of customs duties, the results indicate that there are proportionally fewer poor people who consume or purchase these products. However, poor consumers benefit more from category 1, made up of basic necessities subject to a 5% customs duty. The targeting is neutral for the products in category 3. The analysis of the percentage of total consumption shows that the poor consume proportionally more goods from category 1, but proportionally fewer goods from categories 0 and 3. The poor in rural areas get more advantages from the reduced duties and taxes on products in categories 0 and 1 when compared with their urban counterparts. The results also show that the poor do not benefit from tax exemptions, with a more marked disadvantage for the rural dwellers than for city dwellers. The key challenge remains to find out how to improve the effects and benefits of the CET in favour of the poor. Other than resolving the difficulties linked to applying the CET and the free movement of goods, improving the pro-poor characteristics of the community tariff structure requires improving the tariff targeting of the poor and the priority allocation of fiscal income obtained in favour of sectors that benefit primarily the poor.

M. Coulibaly (✉)
University of Bamako, Bamako, Mali
e-mail: massa@greatmali.net

B. Keita
National Institute of Statistics, Bamako, Mali

E.T. Ayuk and S.T. Kaboré (eds.), *Wealth Through Integration*, Insight and Innovation in International Development 4, DOI 10.1007/978-1-4614-4415-2_13,
© International Development Research Centre 2013

I Introduction

We have calculated a certain number of "targeting" indicators based on data concerning Mali in order to understand the weight the poor have in the "benefits" of the WAEMU's CET categorisation. These data come from the 2006 ELIM database, which contains all the products consumed by households. This consumption has three main sources: personal consumption, purchases and gifts received. In establishing the level of the targeting indicators, reference will be made either to total consumption or to purchase as being the main forms through which the "benefit" of the CET is transmitted. First, the report gives a brief overview of the WAEMU CET and the trade categorisation of household expenditure and presents the main indicators used in the estimation methodology to target the poor.

II The CET and the WAEMU

In virtue of the 1994 WAEMU treaty, the customs duties rate applied by the Union countries on merchandise imported from countries outside the Union was progressively harmonised from 1997 to the end of 1999. The CET came to effect on 1 January 2000 and included the following objectives, among others: (1) simplification of the tariff systems in force in the Union (in the face of the proliferation of duties and taxes, an excessive differentiation among tariffs and a relatively high level of overall taxation), (2) opening the Union to the world economy (considering the Union's small economic dimension, which limits the possibilities of self-focussed development), (3) protection of the community production (positive effective protection through low nominal tariffs on incoming goods) and (4) fighting diversion of trade (the existence of non-uniform tariffs among the member states creates competitive distortion with the risk that exporters from third countries bring their products into the Union through the country with the lowest external tariff to then re-export it towards the countries with higher external tariffs, which raises the problem of product origin).

Within the Union, goods are exempt from customs duties and taxes. For this to apply, they must be accompanied by a WAEMU certificate of origin, except for products of agriculture and stock breeding and for handmade products, which are exempt from this requirement. In the terms of the Additional Protocol III/2001 dated January 2003, a good from the WAEMU is either a good that is entirely obtained in the Union or manufactured from at least 60% raw materials from the WAEMU, or a good obtained from foreign raw materials that has undergone sufficient processing or transformation that translates into a change in tariff position or by an added value of at least 30%.

The CET foresees a normative structure that includes (1) a 10-digit tariff and statistics nomenclature, based on the harmonised merchandise classification system established by the World Customs Organisation (WCO); (2) product categorisation; and (3) a basic tariff structure with temporary additional measures to regulate the economy and trade.

The tariff nomenclature has four categories: (1) *category 0*: essential social goods found on a limited list, for reasons of public health (medication, re-education apparatus, notably cardiac stimulators, wheelchairs) or of educational policy (books, journals); (2) *category 1*: basic necessities (powdered milk, grains), basic raw materials (seeds, reproducers, base metals), equipment (industrial machines, computers), specific inputs and inputs that are not likely to be produced in the short or medium term (chemical products, Chaps. 39 and 40 of the plastics and rubber industries); (3) *category 2*: inputs and intermediary products that have undergone the beginning of a transformation and require finishing (crude oil, plywood, rolled paper, raw fabric, sheet metal) and (4) *category 3*: end-use products.

The WAEMU SH2007's 5,546 tariff lines break down into 72 items under category 0; 2,006 items under category 1; 1,150 items under category 2; and 2,258 items under category 3.

Customs duties are thus separated out based on these product categories, whose basic criteria remain the degree of transformation of the said products. The rates are, respectively, 0, 5, 10 and 20%. One can reasonably anticipate that the tax advantages of categories 0 and 1 target poor and vulnerable households more. In addition to the customs duty, there is a statistical charge (1%), the WAEMU community solidarity levy (1%) and the ECOWAS community levy (0.5%).

The statistical charge applies to all the products that pass through WAEMU customs from a country outside the WAEMU, including products exempt from customs duties. The community levy does not apply to oil products or to transiting merchandise, or to those that benefit from a customs warehousing system.

In addition to the basic duty made up of permanent taxes, addition measures, so-called safeguarding measures, are foreseen to protect sectors and to preserve the region for disturbances from the world market. These are, at least in principle, temporary measures and can therefore apply independent of the tariff category (including on basic necessities such as rice, sugar and vegetable oil) that is based on the degree of transformation or on social priorities. These additional measures or safeguarding measures are supposed to remedy insufficiencies in the basic tax system and truly contribute to making the CET an instrument not only for trade policy but also for the agricultural and other policies, to help reach several sector objectives.

The CET's additional tax measure included at first a decreasing protection tax, a reference value and the special import tax. The latter is the only one still in force in the Union. The basic list of products eligible for this special tax includes beef, poultry, concentrated milk, potatoes, onions, bananas, corn, rice, millet-sorghum, wheat flour, raw and refined vegetable oil, sugar, tomato concentrate and cigarettes.

III Trade Categorisation and Household Expenditure

Statistics on imports in 2006 were collected so that customs data could conform to those of the ELIM. The tariff lines were classified into the four categories mentioned in the CET. Then, household expenditure was categorised after identifying the corresponding tariff lines in the WAEMU SH2007.

2006 Import Structure

In 2006, Mali imported 903 billion CFA francs of diverse merchandise, on which was levied in overall tax around 215 billion CFA francs, representing a 24% overall tax burden, with an average customs duty of 6.4% or a little less than 58 billion CFA francs (Table 13.1). Thus, the customs duty represents 27% of the taxes and duties collected at the customs barrier, including interior taxes such as the VAT and the ISCP.

In total, therefore, there were 3,191 import tariff lines for Mali out of the 5,546 that were foreseen, or 57.5% of the actual imports in 2006. These 3,191 tariff lines divide up into 55 lines in category 0, 953 in category 1, 557 in category 2, 1,357 in category 3 and 269 discordant tariff lines in the tariff chapter.

The 269 discordant or undetermined lines (8.4% of the 3,191 actual import tariff lines) covered a volume of import of 59 billion CFA francs, or around 6.5% of the total value of 2006 imports. For the 2,922 concordant tariff lines, 46% were in

Table 13.1 Tariff structure of imports and taxes and duties in Mali in 2006 (millions of CFA francs)

	Category					
	0	1	2	3	ND	Total
Tariff lines (units)	55	953	557	1,357	269	3,191
Import	47,920	256,650	305,669	233,616	59,403	903,258
DD	2	7,885	22,659	22,582	4,501	57,630
RS	274	1,911	2,360	1,268	448	6,262
PCS	265	1,484	767	1,197	398	4,111
PC	132	874	1,165	583	204	2,958
TCI[a]	0	0	0	0[a]	0	0[a]
TPP	0	819	17,685	0	0	18,504
ISCP	0	0	15	3,526	1	3,542
VAT	103	23,459	49,791	39,829	8,420	121,602
Tax burden						
Millions of CFA francs	776	36,432	94,442	68,985	13,972	214,609
Percentage (%)	1.6	14.2	30.9	29.5	23.5	23.8
Rate, DD (%)	0.0	3.1	7.4	9.7	7.6	6.4

Source: Malian Customs Statistics and author calculations
[a]In total, there were 217,990 CFA francs of TCI

Table 13.2 Geographic structure of imports in Mali in 2006 (in %)

	Category				Total
	0	1	2	3	
WAEMU	2	16	65	19	33
Rest of ECOWAS	0.5	2	6	2	3
EU	27	29	8	17	18
Asia	18	9	8	16	11
Rest of the world	52	24	5	20	18
ND	0.5	20	8	26	17
Total import	5	29	33	33	100

Source: Author calculations

Table 13.3 Geographic structure of customs income in Mali in 2006 (in %)

	Category				Total
	0	1	2	3	
WAEMU	1	22	71	12	39
Rest of ECOWAS	0	1	6	2	4
EU	32	29	5	18	15
Asia	14	7	6	20	11
Rest of the world	51	24	4	24	15
ND	2	17	8	24	16
Total tax income	0	17	44	39	100

Source: Author calculations

category 3 and 19% in category 2. The 35% remaining were in categories 0 and 1, for which tax allowances were made for so-called social goods or basic necessities. These two categories are particularly important in the analysis of targeting for the poor. The imports from other WAEMU countries are also important in this analysis if you suppose that they are exempt of duties and taxes, and they represent a third of the volume of imports.

The WAEMU countries remain Mali's primary trade partners, and the other ECOWAS countries only represent 3% of imports. The European Union and Asia represent 29% of imports (Table 13.2).

By product category, categories 2 and 3 absorb nearly two thirds of the imports in Mali, the remaining third being covered by categories 0 and 1. Category 2 dominates imports coming from the WAEMU (65%), while categories 0 and 1 come for the most part from the EU and the rest of the world. This structure is also reflected in the tariff structure by geographic import zone. More than a third of the 215 billion in tax income come from the WAEMU and 26% from the EU and Asia. The WAEMU pays 71% of the category 2 income, and the rest of the world 51% of category 0 (Table 13.3).

When analysing the actual tax burden by category and by geographic zone, it appears that the actual burden is less than the official rate no matter the category considered. In total this burden is 6.4% of the import volume, with rates varying from 5.5% for the WAEMU to 9% for Asia or the ECOWAS not in the WAEMU. For categories 1 and 2, the burden is higher towards the WAELU than on imports from the EU or from Asia (Table 13.4).

Table 13.4 Geographic structure of customs burden in Mali in 2006 (%)

	Category				Total
	0	1	2	3	
WAEMU	0.0	3.7	7.3	1.1	5.5
Rest of ECOWAS	0.0	4.4	9.2	12.5	9.0
EU	0.0	3.3	6.8	11.5	6.2
Asia	0.0	2.2	6.9	15.1	9.0
Rest of the world	0.0	3.0	6.5	12.4	6.3
ND	0.3	2.7	8.9	7.5	6.1
Total tax income	0.0	3.1	7.4	9.2	6.4

Source: Author calculations

Table 13.5 Tariff structure of household import expenditure (millions of CFA francs)

	Category				Total
	0	1	2	3	
Tariff lines (units)	36	84	58	534	712
Import	43,401	46,504	102,865	119,899	312,669
DD	0	1,777	8,811	12,927	23,515
RS	261	416	914	712	2,303
PCS	253	245	489	699	1,687
PC	126	207	455	342	1,130
TCI[a]	0	0	0	0	0
TPP	0	182	11,684	0	11,866
ISCP	0	0	0	3,477	3,477
VAT	15	5,134	20,593	21,076	46,818
Tax burden					
Millions of CFA francs	655	7,961	42,946	39,233	90,796
%	1.5	17.1	41.7	32.7	29.0
Rate DD (%)	0.0	3.8	8.6	10.8	7.5

Source: Malian customs statistics and author calculations
[a]In total, there were 217,990 CFA francs of TCI

Household Import Expenditure in 2006

The analysis of the basic 2006 ELIM data allows one to distinguish 365 products. When looking for their equivalents in the 10-digit SH2007, we identified 767 tariff lines, of which there were 712 in actual imports in 2006. Out of these 712 tariff lines covering the four CET categories, one has to add the 62 non-tradable product codes and 21 not traded in 2006. The 2006 ELIM data then made it possible to estimate the household expenditure on imported consumer products and diverse equipment, for a total sum of 313 billion CFA francs and customs revenue of 91 billion CFA francs, which represents around 35% of the total imports for the year and 42% of the income for that same year. This ratio rises to 90% of import if we consider only those in categories 0 and 3, which cover social goods and end-use products directly aimed at consumption (Table 13.5).

Table 13.6 Potential taxation on non-traded products in Mali in 2006 (%)

CET category	Lines	DD	RS	PCS	PC	Port duty	VAT	Total burden
		Percentage						
1	8	5	1	1	0.5	7.5	0	7.5
2	2	10	1	1	0.5	12.5	0	12.5
3	33	20	1	1	0.5	22.5	18	26.3
Total	43	16.7	1	1	0.5	19.2	13.8	22.1

Source: Authors' calculation

The tax burden was, therefore, 29%, with an average customs duty of 7.5% of all imports. The applied customs duties come to 3.8% into category 1, 8.6% in category 2 and 10.8% in category 3. The actual applied duty differs from official duties, with customs exemptions being granted for certain products for a variety of reasons, including those related to investment laws, mining laws and policies to stabilise internal prices. Thus, for category 1 products, the applied customs duty was 3.8% versus the theoretical 5%, or a discount of 1.2 percentage points (equivalent to an actual reduction of 24% of the official duty) following the exemptions or the imports authorised by the WAEMU and the ECOWAS, exempt from customs duties. The reduction is even greater in category 3, representing 9.2 percentage points, or 46% reduction over the official tariff.

The 21 non-traded products cover 43 tariff lines, including 33 in category 3, 2 in category 2 and 8 in category 1. The potential taxation on these non-traded products is an official rate of 22.1% for a just as official customs duty of 16.7% and an average applied rate of 10.6% (Table 13.6).

IV   Methodology

Once the 2006 ELIM data has been matched to the 2006 import statistics, a certain number of targeting indicators then enable an assessment of whether the CET is pro-poor or not. It is considered to be pro-poor if the tariff gradient on consumer expenditure is increasing in household income (Gautier 2001). In other words, the CET would be called pro-poor if there are proportionally more poor people among those who benefit than non-poor (Cadot et al. 2004). In this case, one supposes that the CET has the effect of redistribution in terms of equity, both in categorisation and in distribution of tax burden. Equity means exactly that households with more modest income bear a proportionally less heavy tax burden than those with higher income (Mouncif and Hassane 2007). Therefore, on the contrary, one expects that households with higher levels of consumption or purchases bear a high proportion of the tax burden than those with lower income.

The redistribution effect of the CET can also be negative if, for example, the budget allocated to the importation of so-called social goods and/or essential goods is smaller for the poor than for the non-poor. In the analysis, the emphasis will be placed on this CET redistribution effect rather than on the feedback of the backwash effect of the collected tariff (including on the poor) benefiting the poor in the form, for example, of free public transport. Again because there is not enough data in the 2006 ELIM database, we will not treat the question of net tariff protection that requires that goods produced by the poor be more protected than those produced by the non-poor or that the tariff gradient on production be increasing in income. Thus, the analysis is limited here to the CET effect on consumption, where the "benefits" of the CET aim at being proportionally more favourable to poor consumers/buyers than to non-poor consumers/buyers.

To appreciate the impact of the poor on CET "benefits", we will use a certain number of "targeting" indicators usually applied in the assessment of poverty-reduction programmes. These indicators are borrowed from Lavallée et al. (2009) as well as from Yablonski and O'Donnel (2009). We chose four of them, depending on whether they refer to the number of poor, consumption or buying, tax burden on purchases and exemptions. These are, for each CET product category and for the total if possible, the targeting differential between poor and non-poor, the standardised percentage of consumption/purchases by the poor, the standard percentage of tax burden on purchases by the poor and the standardised percentage of exonerations returning to the poor.

For each category j ($j = 0, 1, 2, 3, 8, 9$), the targeting differential (dC) is defined as difference between the proportion of poor who are consumers/buyers of the product and the proportion corresponding to the non-poor:

$$dC = \frac{N_j^{\mathrm{P}}}{N^{\mathrm{P}}} - \frac{N_j^{\mathrm{NP}}}{N^{\mathrm{NP}}}$$

where N_j^{P} is the number of poor consumers/buyer of product j, N_j^{NP} the number of non-poor consumers/buyers of product j, N^{P} the total number of poor people and the N^{NP} total number of non-poor people.

This indicator, which ranges between -1 and $+1$, measures targeting performance as the difference between the ratio of poor CET "beneficiaries" and that of non-poor: $-1 \le dC \le +1$. It does not take into account the distribution of the poor and non-poor consumption/purchasing amounts, while the targeting will be all the more favourable to the poor when they receive larger proportions of the categories with less tax burden, such as categories 0 and 1.

Two indicators can be used to measure the standardised portion of poor consumption/purchases in each type of product. The first relates the proportion of poor people's consumption or purchases for each product to the proportion of poor consuming all products. The second relates the proportion of poor people's consumption or purchases in each product to the incidence of poverty or the poverty rate (P_0). They are noted as α and β and are written out as follows:

- On consumption: $\alpha_{cj} = \dfrac{C_j^{\mathrm{P}}/C_j^{\mathrm{P}} + C_j^{\mathrm{NP}}}{C^{\mathrm{P}}/C^{\mathrm{P}} + C^{\mathrm{NP}}}$ and $\beta_{cj} = \dfrac{C_j^{\mathrm{P}}/C_j^{\mathrm{P}} + C_j^{\mathrm{NP}}}{P_0}$

- On purchases: $\alpha_{aj} = \dfrac{A_j^{P}/A_j^{P} + A_j^{NP}}{A^{P}/A^{P} + A^{NP}}$ and $\beta_{aj} = \dfrac{A_j^{P}/A_j^{P} + A_j^{NP}}{P_0}$

where C designates consumption and A purchases.

Regarding the standardised proportion of tax burden or the tariff duty received for purchases by the poor, it relates the proportion of the burden borne by the poor out of the total tax burden to the proportion of purchases the poor make out of all purchases. For each product j ($j = 0, 1, 2, 3, 8$), it is defined as follows:

$$\beta_{Tj} = \frac{T_j^{P}/T_j^{P} + T_j^{NP}}{A^{P}/A^{P} + A^{NP}}$$

with T designating successively total import duty and the port duty.

Finally, the standardised proportion of exemptions reserved for the poor relates, for each product j ($j = 1, 2, 3, 8$), the proportion of exemptions granted to the poor to the incidence of poverty (P_0). It expresses the proportion of tax reductions granted to the poor divided by the proportion of poor in the total population. If the rate of reductions is not differentiated by poor and non-poor, this indicator is then identical to the standardised proportion of poor purchases. It can be defined by the formula:

$$\gamma_j = \frac{Exo_j^{P}/Exo_j^{P} + Exo_j^{NP}}{P_0} = \frac{\left(t_{0j} - t_{ej}\right)A_j^{P}/\left(t_{0j} - t_{ej}\right)\left(A_j^{P} + A_j^{NP}\right)}{P_0}$$

where t_o is the official tax rate and t_e the actual tax rate.

For a given product, if γ_j is greater than one, the exemptions go proportionally more to the poor than to the non-poor and the contrary if it is smaller than one. When $\gamma_j = 1$, targeting will be considered to be neutral.

Each of these indicators will be calculated based on the 2006 ELIM data matched with the customs data. The estimated levels of the indicators will then enable an exploration of whether the CET is pro-poor or not. Finally, once could imagine tariff options that could better target the poor, including in the area of indirect internal taxation. This is all the more relevant as the WAEMU member states move towards harmonising their indirect taxes, VAT, excises taxes, taxes on oil products, etc.

V Empirical Results

The 2006 ELIM data establish poverty at 44.5%, if one takes into account transfers between households and gifts that many households receive that result in them either getting out of poverty or at least decreasing the depth or severity of the

Table 13.7 Distribution of poverty and poor people in Mali in 2006 (%)

	Incidence of poverty	% poor people	% Pop.	Poverty versus poor
Kayes	31.6	9	13	Poverty
Urban	15.6	8	11	
Rural	37.3	9	14	
Koulikoro	43.5	16	17	Poverty
Urban	16.7	8	11	
Rural	50.4	18	19	
Sikasso	64.5	26	18	Poor
Urban	27.7	21	16	
Rural	79.1	27	19	
Ségou	43.6	17	18	Poverty
Urban	26.3	16	12	Poor
Rural	48.6	17	20	Poverty
Mopti	51.9	19	16	Poor
Urban	14.8	6	8	Poverty
Rural	58.8	21	20	Poor
Tombouctou	54.4	5	4	Poor
Urban	38.9	7	4	
Rural	60.2	5	5	
Gao	38.9	3	4	Poverty
Urban	36.1	10	6	Poor
Rural	41.6	2	3	Poverty
Kidal	19.6	0.2	0.4	Poverty
Urban	16.3	0.5	0.6	
Rural	22.0	0.1	0.4	
Bamako	15.4	4	10	Poverty
Urban	15.4	24	32	
Mali	44.5	5,482,925	12,317,562	
Urban	20.9	15	32	Poverty
Rural	55.5	85	68	Poor

Source: Authors' calculations

poverty. This incidence of poverty is established based on poverty thresholds chosen by stratum, that is, environment or region (World Bank 2007), and on the basis of total household consumer expenditure. In total, the rural area has proportionally more poor than urban areas, with 85% of the poor living in the countryside, while the rural population represents 68% of the overall population. On the other hand, 15% of the poor live in cities, while the urban population represents 32% of the country's population. So, there are more rural poor than there is poverty and the contrary in urban areas. Such structuring can be undertaken for each stratum, where it appears that cities in the regions of Ségou, Mopti and Gao are more cities of poor people than cities of poverty (Table 13.7).

The indicators for targeting the poor are calculated taking into account the above distribution of poor people, particularly by milieu, in view of the levels of household consumption and purchasing, based on the 2006 ELIM data.

Table 13.8 Distribution of consumers and buyers per product category

	NP (%)	P (%)	$dC = P\% - NP\%$	Targeting to the advantage or disadvantage of the poor
Consumer 0	66.7	66.2	−0.5	Disadvantage
Buyer 0	66.7	66.2	−0.5	Disadvantage
Consumer 1	99.9	100.0	0.1	Advantage
Buyer 1	99.3	99.0	−0.3	Disadvantage
Consumer 2	99.8	100.0	0.1	Advantage
Buyer 2	99.8	99.6	−0.2	Disadvantage
Consumer 3	100.0	100.0	0.0	Neutral
Buyer 3	100.0	100.0	0.0	Neutral
Consumer 8	98.3	98.7	0.3	Advantage
Buyer 8	92.3	86.0	−6.4	Disadvantage
Consumer 9	99.9	99.8	−0.1	Disadvantage
Buyer 9	99.7	99.7	−0.1	Disadvantage

Source: Authors' calculations

Targeting Differential

The targeting differential is established at −0.5% for CET category 0, the one that has a 0% customs duty. There are proportionally fewer poor people who consume or purchase these products than non-poor. It is the same for buyers of products in category 1, which has a customs duty of 5%. However, in this category, poor consumers benefit more, no doubt thanks to the transfers they receive from non-poor households (Table 13.8).

Targeting is neutral for category 3 products, which is a disadvantage for the poor especially when there should be proportionally more non-poor buyers of these products than poor buyers. Curiously, there are proportionally fewer poor than non-poor who buy non-traded or non-tradable products, which are supposed not to bear the actual customs duty. These results, on the whole, remain to be supported by taking into account the actual household consumption and purchasing expenditure for the poor and the non-poor.

Standard Proportion of Poor People's Consumption and Purchases

For all products, consumption by the poor represents 30% of the total value of consumption for goods and services. It reaches 40% for category 1 products and is even less for categories 0 (24%) and 3 (26%). Whatever the category, the poor consume fewer products than the non-poor proportional to their percentage of the entire population (44.5%) (Table 13.9).

By referring to the percentage of total consumption of all products taken together, one notes that the poor consume proportionally fewer goods from categories 0, 3 and 9. That deprives them of the benefits of the so-called social

Table 13.9 Distribution of consumption and percentage of consumption (millions of CFA francs and %)

	Consumption			Percentage of consumption (%)		
	Non-poor	Poor	Total	Non-poor	Poor	Total
Consumption 0	48,213	15,413	63,626	76	24	100
Consumption 1	168,982	113,684	282,666	60	40	100
Consumption 2	311,472	159,480	470,952	66	34	100
Consumption 3	785,329	269,099	1,054,428	74	26	100
Consumption 8	178,680	93,228	271,908	66	34	100
Consumption 9	542,008	228,128	770,136	70	30	100
Total	2,034,685	879,031	2,913,716	70	30	100

Source: Authors' calculations

Table 13.10 Standard percentage (%) of poor people's consumption

	α_C (%)	Targeting to the advantage or disadvantage of the poor	β_C (%)	Targeting to the advantage or disadvantage of the poor (%)
Consumption 0	80	Disadvantage	54	Disadvantage
Consumption 1	133	Advantage	90	Disadvantage
Consumption 2	112	Advantage	76	Disadvantage
Consumption 3	85	Disadvantage	57	Disadvantage
Consumption 8	114	Advantage	77	Disadvantage
Consumption 9	98	Disadvantage	67	Disadvantage
Total	100		68	

Source: Calculations by authors

and non-tradable goods, which are the categories on which there are no customs duties. For category 3, that could be interpreted as an advantage, considering the high taxation of the goods. Using the indicator (α_C), the poor consume proportionally more essential goods from category 1, which has a customs duty of 5%.

Compared to their weight in the population, the poor's percentage of consumption is 68%. According to this indicator (β_C), none of poor people's consumption reaches poverty incidence. So, the poor do not get any advantages from categories 0, 1, 8 and 9, and so therefore, the tariff advantages linked to these products go to the non-poor (Table 13.10). One could, however, imagine that for categories 2 and 3, which are taxed higher than the others, the indicator suggests more of an advantage for the poor than a disadvantage, as shown in the table.

When analysing by milieu, one notes that the poor from urban areas only consume 16% of the total consumption for that milieu, the remaining 84% being attributed to the non-poor, which shows great inequality in the consumption of goods and services. In rural areas, this percentage is 46%. In both cases, it is less than the incidence of poverty, which is 20.9% in urban areas and 55.5% in rural areas. The poor in the countryside have an even lower rate of consumption in the categories 0, and the poor in the cities, products from categories 3 and 9 (Table 13.11).

Table 13.11 Distribution of consumption and percentage of consumption by milieu (millions of CFA francs and %)

	Consumption (millions de CFA francs)			Percentage of consumption (%)		
	Non-poor	Poor	Total	Non-poor	Poor	Total
Urban areas						
Consumption 0	30,827	6,171	36,999	83	17	100
Consumption 1	73,130	15,644	88,773	82	18	100
Consumption 2	171,569	33,558	05,127	84	16	100
Consumption 3	536,954	82,839	619,793	87	13	100
Consumption 8	113,478	35,061	148,540	76	24	100
Consumption 9	365,221	64,879	430,100	85	15	100
Total	1,291,178	238,152	1,529,330	84	16	100
Rural areas						
Consumption 0	17,386	9,242	26,627	65	35	100
Consumption 1	95,853	98,040	193,893	49	51	100
Consumption 2	139,904	125,922	265,826	53	47	100
Consumption 3	248,375	186,259	434,635	57	43	100
Consumption 8	65,202	58,167	123,368	53	47	100
Consumption 9	176,787	163,249	340,037	52	48	100
Total	743,506	640,879	1,384,385	54	46	100

Source: Calculation by authors

Table 13.12 Standard percentage (%) of consumption by the poor by milieu

	α_C (%)	Targeting to the advantage or disadvantage of the poor	β_C (%)	Targeting to the advantage or disadvantage of the poor (%)
Urban areas				
Consumption 0	107	Advantage	80	Disadvantage
Consumption 1	113	Advantage	84	Disadvantage
Consumption 2	105	Advantage	78	Disadvantage
Consumption 3	86	Disadvantage	64	Disadvantage
Consumption 8	152	Advantage	113	Advantage
Consumption 9	97	Disadvantage	72	Disadvantage
Total	100		74	
Rural areas				
Consumption 0	75	Disadvantage	63	Disadvantage
Consumption 1	109	Advantage	91	Disadvantage
Consumption 2	102	Advantage	85	Disadvantage
Consumption 3	93	Disadvantage	77	Disadvantage
Consumption 8	102	Advantage	85	Disadvantage
Consumption 9	104	Advantage	87	Disadvantage
Total	100		83	

Source: Calculations by authors

On the whole, the standardised percentages of consumption are to the disadvantage of the poor for products in category 0. But by milieu, they are more favourable to the poor in urban areas in the ratio of the percentage of consumption by the poor

Table 13.13 Distribution of purchases and percentage of purchases (millions of CFA francs and %)

	Purchases (millions of CFA francs)			Percentage of purchases (%)		
	Non-poor	Poor	Total	Non-poor	Poor	Total
Mali						
Purchase 0	48,213	15,413	63,626	76	24	100
Purchase 1	106,185	45,574	151,759	70	30	100
Purchase 2	271,183	125,553	396,736	68	32	100
Purchase 3	765,861	250,538	1,016,399	75	25	100
Purchase 8	142,916	53,767	196,684	73	27	100
Purchase 9	469,357	191,966	661,322	71	29	100
Total	1,803,715	682,811	2,486,525	73	27	100
Urban areas						
Purchase 0	30,827	6,171	36,999	83	17	100
Purchase 1	62,775	11,784	74,559	84	16	100
Purchase 2	163,885	31,223	195,108	84	16	100
Purchase 3	531,842	81,041	612,883	87	13	100
Purchase 8	107,520	32,507	140,026	77	23	100
Purchase 9	320,438	54,563	375,001	85	15	100
Total	1,217,287	217,288	1,434,575	85	15	100
Rural areas						
Purchase 0	17,386	9,242	26,627	65	35	100
Purchase 1	43,410	33,790	77,200	56	44	100
Purchase 2	107,298	94,330	201,628	53	47	100
Purchase 3	234,019	169,497	403,516	58	42	100
Purchase 8	35,397	21,260	56,657	62	38	100
Purchase 9	148,918	137,403	286,321	52	48	100
Total	586,428	465,522	1,051,950	56	44	100

Source: Calculation by authors

in this category to their percentage of total consumption. This advantage disappears when the ratio is calculated with respect to the incidence of poverty in urban areas. The urban poor also have an advantage in consuming non-traded goods (Table 13.12).

If one replaces consumption by expenditures on purchases, the percentage of poor goes from 30 to 27%, under the combined effect of self-consumption and gifts received by poor households. For all the products, consumption by the poor represents 30% of the total value of consumption of goods and services. It reaches 40% for the category 1 products, which it is still less for categories 0 (24%) and 3 (26%). This percentage is only 24% for products in category 0. As for consumption, whatever the category, the poor buy proportionally fewer products compared with their percentage of the population (44.5%) than do the non-poor (Table 13.13), in the entire country and whatever the milieu, with the exception of category 8, for which poor people in urban areas purchase proportionally more than the percentage of poor people in the urban population (Table 13.13).

The analysis of the standardised percentage of purchases made by the poor remains the same for the standardised percentage of consumption, with the poor purchasing less in categories 0 and 3, deprived of the benefit of category 0, which

Table 13.14 Standardised percentage of purchases by the poor

	α_C (%)	Targeting to the advantage or disadvantage of the poor	β_C (%)	Targeting to the advantage or disadvantage of the poor (%)
Mali				
Purchase 0	88	Disadvantage	54	Disadvantage
Purchase 1	109	Advantage	67	Disadvantage
Purchase 2	115	Advantage	71	Disadvantage
Purchase 3	90	Disadvantage	55	Disadvantage
Purchase 8	100	Advantage	61	Disadvantage
Purchase 9	106	Advantage	65	Disadvantage
Total	100		62	
Urban areas				
Purchase 0	110	Advantage	80	Disadvantage
Purchase 1	104	Advantage	76	Disadvantage
Purchase 2	106	Advantage	76	Disadvantage
Purchase 3	87	Disadvantage	63	Disadvantage
Purchase 8	153	Advantage	111	Advantage
Purchase 9	96	Disadvantage	70	Disadvantage
Total	100		72	
Rural areas				
Purchase 0	78	Disadvantage	63	Disadvantage
Purchase 1	99	Disadvantage	79	Disadvantage
Purchase 2	106	Advantage	84	Disadvantage
Purchase 3	95	Disadvantage	76	Disadvantage
Purchase 8	85	Disadvantage	68	Disadvantage
Purchase 9	108	Advantage	87	Disadvantage
Total	100		80	

Source: Calculations by authors

does not have customs duties. Only the poor in urban areas purchase proportionally more in category 1, which is made up of basic necessities, at a customs duty of 5%.

The conclusions also remain the same when the ratios are established in relation to the incidence of poverty, on the whole and based on place of residence, with the percentage of purchases by the poor covering 62% of the overall incidence, for 72% in urban areas and 80% in rural areas. Only those in urban areas benefit from the advantage of non-tradable products (Table 13.14).

Standard Percentage of Import Duty and Port Duty of the Poor

The poor pay the same percentage of duties and taxes on purchases (27%) as on purchases as is. The percentage is also the same for each category of product. The analysis remains the same for the targeting indicator based on the standard percentage of purchases by the poor (Table 13.15). The poor in rural areas benefit more

Table 13.15 Standard percentage of import duty for the port (millions of CFA francs and %)

	Import duty (millions of CFA francs)			Percentage of import duty (%)				Targeting to the advantage or disadvantage of the poor
	Non-poor	Poor	Total	Non-poor	Poor	Total	β_T (%)	
Mali								
Category 0	723	231	954	76	24	100	88	Advantage
Category 1	25,166	10,801	35,967	70	30	100	109	Disadvantage
Category 2	113,083	52,356	165,439	68	32	100	115	Disadvantage
Category 3	250,436	81,926	332,362	75	25	100	90	Advantage
Category 8	31,585	11,883	43,467	73	27	100	100	Disadvantage
Total	420,993	157,196	578,190	73	27	100	99	
Urban areas								
Category 0	462	93	555	83	17	100	110	Disadvantage
Category 1	14,878	2,793	17,670	84	16	100	104	Disadvantage
Category 2	68,340	13,020	81,360	84	16	100	106	Disadvantage
Category 3	173,912	26,500	200,413	87	13	100	87	Advantage
Category 8	23,762	7,184	30,946	77	23	100	153	Disadvantage
Total	281,354	49,590	330,944	85	15	100	99	
Rural areas								
Category 0	261	139	399	65	35	100	78	Advantage
Category 1	10,288	8,008	18,296	56	44	100	99	Advantage
Category 2	44,743	39,336	84,079	53	47	100	106	Disadvantage
Category 3	76,524	55,426	131,950	58	42	100	95	Advantage
Category 8	7,823	4,699	12,521	62	38	100	85	Advantage
Total	139,639	107,607	247,246	56	44	100	98	

Source: Calculations by authors

from reduced duties and taxes on products in categories 0 and 1, unlike the poor in urban areas who do not benefit from them at all. In total, the poor benefit from low duties on category 0, whose customs duty is 0%.

The benefit for the poor of taxation on products does not change when we look at only the actual port duties, without taking into account the internal taxation levied at the customs barrier. The disadvantage for the urban poor is linked to the higher standard percentage they endure in the form of port duties on their purchases: they pay 16% of the duties paid by all urban people even though their percentage of purchases is 15%. In terms of paying port duties, the rural poor benefit from the tariff reductions on categories 0 and 1 (Table 13.16).

Standard Percentage of Exemptions for the Poor

The percentage of total exemptions that benefited the poor is 24%, although they represent 44.5% of the population, which represents a standard percentage (by incidence of poverty) of 55% and is therefore disadvantageous to the poor (Table 13.17). Here, these are official duty rates applied at the customs barrier, a

Table 13.16 Standard part of actual port duties paid by the poor (millions of CFA francs and %)

	Port duties (millions of CFA francs)			Percentage of port duties (%)				Targeting to the advantage or disadvantage
	Non-poor	Poor	Total	Non-poor	Poor	Total	β_T (%)	of the poor
Mali								
Category 0	723	231	954	76	24	100	88	Advantage
Category 1	7,114	3,053	10,168	70	30	100	109	Disadvantage
Category 2	28,203	13,057	41,261	68	32	100	115	Disadvantage
Category 3	93,435	30,566	124,001	75	25	100	90	Advantage
Category 8	27,440	10,323	37,763	73	27	100	100	*Neutral*
Total	156,916	57,231	214,147	73	27	100	97	
Urban areas								
Category 0	462	93	555	83	17	100	110	Disadvantage
Category 1	4,206	790	4,995	84	16	100	104	Disadvantage
Category 2	17,044	3,247	20,291	84	16	100	106	Disadvantage
Category 3	64,885	9,887	74,772	87	13	100	87	Advantage
Category 8	20,644	6,241	26,885	77	23	100	153	Disadvantage
Total	107,241	20,258	127,498	84	16	100	105	
Rural areas								
Category 0	261	139	399	65	35	100	78	Advantage
Category 1	2,908	2,264	172	56	44	100	99	Advantage
Category 2	11,159	9,810	20,969	53	47	100	106	Disadvantage
Category 3	28,550	20,679	49,229	58	42	100	95	Advantage
Category 8	6,796	4,082	10,878	62	38	100	85	Advantage
Total	49,675	36,974	86,648	57	43	100	96	

Source: Calculations by authors

Table 13.17 Standard percentage of exemptions for the poor (millions of CFA francs and %)

	Exemptions (millions of CFA francs)			Percentage of exemptions (%)				Targeting to the advantage or disadvantage
	Non-poor	Poor	Total	Non-poor	Poor	Total	γ (%)	of the poor
Category 1	240	76	317	76	24	100	54	Disadvantage
Category 2	674	215	889	76	24	100	54	Disadvantage
Category 3	4,436	1,418	5,854	76	24	100	54	Disadvantage
Category 8	2,643	872	3,514	75	25	100	56	Disadvantage
Total	7,992	2,582	10,574	76	24	100	55	Disadvantage

Source: Calculations by authors

rate dependent on exemptions granted as well as probably on customs fraud. In general, the majority of the exemptions are granted as a result of the investment laws or the mining laws and therefore are without direct incidence on households, including on poor households. The indirect incidence benefits non-poor households more than poor households, which explains why these exemptions do not benefit the poor, who can at best benefit from exemptions granted as part of price stabilisation

Table 13.18 Standard part of urban poor people's exemptions ($P_0 = 20.9\%$)

	Exemptions (millions of CFA francs)			Percentage exemptions (%)				Targeting to the advantage or disadvantage of the poor
	Non-Poor	Poor	Total	Non-Poor	Poor	Total	γ (%)	
Urban areas								
Category 1	154	31	185	83	17	100	80	Disadvantage
Category 2	430	86	517	83	17	100	80	Disadvantage
Category 3	2,836	568	3,404	83	17	100	80	Disadvantage
Category 8	1,875	370	2,245	84	16	100	79	Disadvantage
Total	5,296	1,055	6,351	83	17	100	79	Disadvantage
Rural areas								
Category 1	87	46	132	65	35	100	62	Disadvantage
Category 2	243	129	372	65	35	100	62	Disadvantage
Category 3	1,599	850	2,450	65	35	100	63	Disadvantage
Category 8	767	502	1,269	60	40	100	71	Disadvantage
Total	2,697	1,527	4,223	64	36	100	65	Disadvantage

Source: Calculations by the authors

policies, as was the case in 2008 in response to the food crisis the populations were facing.

The lack of benefit for the poor of tax exemptions is independent of milieu, being perhaps slightly more marked in rural areas than in urban areas because the standard percentage of urban poor is 79% (therefore closer 100%) versus 65% for people in rural areas. This difference in milieu can be observed in each of the four categories of products analysed (Table 13.18). There you have the effect of the large disparity between the rural incidence of poverty (55.5%) and the percentage of the poor in this milieu who benefit from exemptions (36%), or 19.5 percentage points of difference versus 3.9 percentage points in urban areas (20.9% incidence of poverty and 17% of the urban poor in the total exemptions impacting all urban residents).

VI Conclusions and Recommendations

This study analyses the benefits that the WAEMU's CET product category tariff structure has on the poor.

The results indicate that there are proportionally fewer poor people who consume or purchase products in category 0, which is exempt from customs duties. On the other hand, poor consumers benefit more in category 1, which is made up of basic necessities and subject to a customs duty of 5%, due undoubtedly to the transfers they receive from non-poor households. Targeting is neutral for category 3 products, which in itself is a disadvantage for the poor since there should have been proportionally more non-poor people buying these products than poor people. Curiously, there are proportionally fewer poor than non-poor who purchase the non-traded or non-tradable products, which are supposed not to bear an actual customs duty. Only city dwellers benefit from non-traded products.

In referring to their percentage of total consumption, all products considered together, one notes that the poor consume proportionally more goods in category 1, but proportionally fewer goods in categories 0 and 3. The poor in rural areas derive more advantage from the reduced taxes and duties on category 0 and 1 products compared with their urban counterparts. The results also show that the poor do not benefit from tax exemptions, with a more marked disadvantage in rural areas than in urban areas (standard percentage of 79% among urban dwellers compared with 65% for rural dwellers).

How to ensure that the poor are the primary beneficiaries of poverty-reduction policy measures, and notably the CET, remains a key issue to resolve. Besides resolving the difficulties inherent to the CET (lack of uniform application, poor handling of the rules regarding origin, various impediments to trade, etc.), the answers include (1) investing resources dedicated to fighting poverty into sectors that benefit mainly the poor people, such as primary education or basic healthcare services, and (2) identifying the poor in order to allocate the benefits of the measures as a priority to them.

Better targeting is required "to increase the impact of the CET on poverty reduction and food security". It is a question of reducing as much as possible errors in targeting (inclusion and exclusion errors). Five main measures can contribute such as (1) taking into account the WAEMU SH in the categorisation of goods and services in the budget-consumption surveys in order to facilitate the passage from survey data to customs data, (2) deepening the analysis by taking into account production so as to include actual protection defined as the difference between nominal protection on production and that of incoming goods used in this production, (3) extending the study to all WAEMU countries in order to determine the CET effects on the poor and to assess potential pro-poor solutions, (4) identifying a possible pro-poor categorising approach and (5) undertaking measures of sensitivity of poverty to reassigned categories of certain goods for social reasons and to fight poverty and refine the methodology of targeting the poor in the WAEMU CET categorisation.

References

Cadot O., De Melo J. and Olarreaga M. (2004), 'Lobbying, Counterlobbying, and the Structure of Tariff Protection in Rich and Poor Countries', *World Bank Economic Review*, 18(3):345–366

Atelier fiscalité de développement au sein de l'UEMOA, Bamako, 6 – 8 December

Gautier, Jean-François (2001), 'Taxation optimale et réformes fiscales dans les PED – Une revue de littérature tropicalisée', DIAL DT/2001/02

Lavallée, Emanuelle,Anne Olivier, Laure Pasquier-Doumer, Anne-Sophie Robillard (2009), 'Le ciblage des politiques de lutte contre la pauvreté – Quel bilan des expériences dans les pays en développement', *DIAL Document de travail*, mars

Touil Mouncif, El Amrani Hassane (2007), 'Systèmes fiscaux comparés' FES WAEMU (2005), 'Note sur la libéralisation des échanges commerciaux au sein de l'UEMOA et la levée des entraves non tarifaires aux échanges', Réunion des ministres chargés des douanes, de la gendarmerie et de la police, Ouagadougou, 8 – 10 December 2004

World Bank (2007), *Tendances et déterminants de la pauvreté au Mali (2001 – 2006)*

Yablonski, Jennifer and Michael O'Donnell (2009), 'Lasting benefits–The role of cash Transfers in tackling child mortality' Save the Children UK.

Chapter 14
How Does Communication Enrich Integration Policies

Ahmed Barry, Augustin Niango, and Kathryn Touré

Abstract When public institutions focus excessively on their survival or on their reproduction, they run the risk of progressively distancing themselves from reality and of not serving the citizens and their communities. The West African Economic and Monetary Union (WAEMU) and the International Development Research Centre (IDRC) took the initiative to encourage discussions focused on the necessary complementarity among three key players in regional integration who until now have ignored each other or, at least, have not understood each other: researchers, decision makers and journalists. This chapter is a retrospective critique of the experience of an encounter among stakeholders coming from different social areas with different approaches and interests and who nevertheless need to cooperate in their everyday professional lives. This chapter draws lessons from this three-way discussion and explores how these players—those who design and implement public policies, researchers and journalists—can invent and lead discussion forums in order to influence policies that are closer to citizens' reality and expectations and that accompany integration.

We express our gratitude to all those who reread and improved this chapter and particularly to Catherine Daffé, Aghi Bahi and Jerome Gerard. However, the authors are solely responsible for the facts they report and their opinions.

A. Barry (✉)
L'Evénement Newspaper, Ouagadougou, Burkina Faso
e-mail: bangreib@yahoo.fr

A. Niango
West Africa Economic and Monetary Union, Ouagadougou, Burkina Faso

K. Touré
West and Central Africa Regional Office, International Development
Research Centre, Dakar, Senegal

E.T. Ayuk and S.T. Kaboré (eds.), *Wealth Through Integration*, Insight and Innovation in International Development 4, DOI 10.1007/978-1-4614-4415-2_14,
© International Development Research Centre 2013

I Introduction

West Africa is experiencing good economic growth that is not benefiting everyone and, above all, not benefiting the poor. The West African Economic and Monetary Union (WAEMU), as part of its fifteenth anniversary celebrations in December 2009, organised a regional conference with the International Development Research Centre (IDRC), the Canadian International Development Agency (CIDA) and the University of Ouagadougou's Institut Supérieur des Sciences de la Population (ISSP) in Burkina Faso. The topic of the conference was "Regional Integration and Poverty-Reduction Strategies".

Various players involved with regional integration, along with researchers, journalists and representatives of civil society, attended this conference. It was organised in order for the WAEMU to examine and discuss the development, implementation and follow-up of its regional poverty-reduction policies through the comparative perspectives of researchers, journalists and civil society.

In this chapter, we will review this actual experience so as to examine what happens in the field when these players meet. This analysis is intended to enable institutions to be more open to the points of view and the concerns of citizens.

Using the example of regional integration within the WAEMU, we will highlight the idea that institutions have a vital need to change their working methods and to focus more on the impact of their actions. One means to meet this objective could involve creating a synergy with researchers and journalists. This requires abandoning old "protectionist" reflexes. This chapter sets the context and provides readers of this book with the context in which these scientific presentations and discussions took place.

II Preparing for Synergies among Actors

The conference did not only aim to bring people together into the same room to discuss development policies. The preparation of this conference last one year and was made up of several steps, the first being reconciling the visions of the major organisers. During one of the first meetings, the latter discussed their interests and expectations, along with the advantages and risks linked to such an encounter that puts a major regional integration institution under the spotlight of constructive criticism.

The "decision makers" and the "researchers" had to begin to understand each other and to speak the same language. To give a single example of the efforts of reconciling vision and language, the WAEMU representatives wanted the conference to look at the effectiveness of its "instruments" in order to draw some lessons. When social science researchers hear the word "instruments", they think of the instruments used to collect data, such as questionnaires and interview guidelines. For the WAEMU, the "instruments" are mechanisms used to implement its policies, such as the Banque

Régionale de Solidarité (BRS) and the Regional Agricultural Development Fund (RADF). Without this preparatory meeting, which made it possible to reconcile visions and means and to create a better mutual understanding and feeling of trust among the organisers, there would have been little likelihood of the conference reaching the substantial level of interactions and discussions that were hoped for.

It was decided that each type of actor be sufficiently prepared before the conference. As a result, the members of the Scientific Committee selected researchers based on the quality of the papers they submitted. The researchers, once selected, then benefited from advice from the committee members in order to improve their presentations. This precaution proved insufficient, however. In order to avoid the use of academic language by researchers, it would have been necessary to organise a workshop to prepare them for sharing the results of their research using language that was more adapted and accessible to the diversity of conference participants. Below, we will discuss the moments of misunderstanding that arose during several presentations. As one researcher said, "in order to have an impact on those outside our own research communities, we have to learn to know others' points of view and ways of communicating" (Porter and Prysor-Jones 1997).

An "events" media that is not particularly professional or analytical limits the role journalists play in the discussions on societal development (Nyamnjoh 2005). As a result, in order to improve the quality of the discussions and ensure more in-depth participation in the conference, the journalists prepared themselves ahead of time with the help of MediaDevAfrica, a media support structure based in Dakar, which IDRC chose to be a key actor with this goal in mind. Journalists were chosen by way of a call for participation, which proved to be a good practice. One journalist was chosen for each of the eight countries in the Union. Unfortunately, no women applied. This demonstrates the necessity of encouraging the latter to become more interested in economic issues.

During a discussion workshop held before the conference, the journalists shared their relative discomfort with the technocratic language used by decision makers and the technical jargon used by researchers. It was therefore necessary to "arm" the journalists by giving them access to documents and analyses regarding regional integration and poverty-reduction strategies. It was also necessary to organise discussions with three researchers who have different visions about economic and social development. A spirit of attentive listening and mutual learning among peers reigned at the workshop—somewhat like the training workshops described by Marquez (2005: 327), which are not looking to "infuse participants with theoretical dogmas or academic prejudices, but rather to strengthen their skills . . . so they can benefit from the experience that he has himself acquired through practicing the profession".

The workshop discussion led to further examination of Union policies, their implementation, their strengths and their weaknesses. A representative of the WAEMU Commission participated in them, in order to help his "decision-making" colleagues to better understand the goals of the conference so they would be able to prepare for it.

III   Stereotypology of Decision Makers, Researchers and Journalists

Understanding where others are coming from can improve the quality of discussions. As a result, the conference began by an overview of the (stereo) typologies of decision makers—always in a hurry—and researchers—lost in their Ivory Tower (see Fig. 14.1). Although the typologies are caricatured, they amuse the researchers and decision makers who recognise themselves in them.

Even a researcher that becomes a policy maker tends to adopt the characteristics of a decision maker, who needs to be pragmatic and find immediate solutions. A decision maker wants answers that are certain, while researchers are careful and nuanced in their recommendations. Decision makers are impatient, while researchers seem to take their time. Decision makers accuse researchers of being incomprehensible when they speak. Researchers accuse decision makers of being too selective in the implementation of their recommendations. While decision makers sometimes hold their positions for too short a time, due to the high rotation rates within the public authorities in West Africa, researchers are often victims of financial necessities, which require them to neglect their research in order to take on consulting contracts that improve their wage earning. By putting all of this prior information on the table, it enables frank discussions, taking into account the needs and constraints that each have.

Journalists are not perceived as communication professionals but as disruptive elements or as people looking to confront policy makers. They can be perceived as activists rather than specialists in social intermediation. When journalists are seeking out information, some decision makers and researchers fear them and avoid them. Journalists are accused of not understanding the facts or of deforming them. Furthermore, journalists are not associated with projects but are called on at the last minute to "cover" an event for which they have not received any information. Journalists are not spared from looking for the easy road, and certain institutions accept to pay for articles in the press, thus contributing to the continued disdain for the profession.

Decision Makers		Researchers
Pragmatic	⇔	Academics (Ivory Tower)
Need solutions now	⇔	Need time
Short-and medium-term planning	⇔	Long-term results
What answers that are certain	⇔	Careful and nuanced
Benefits of research little known	⇔	Policy processes little known
Selective	⇔	Not very concrete and not very comprehensible
Very mobile among ministries	⇔	Absorbed by consultation
Impatient to know the answers	⇔	Little consideration for policy feasibility

Fig. 14.1 Stereotypologies of decision makers and researchers (Source: Adapted from Ndiaye 2009)

After discussing these issues, the players can go beyond these stereotypes and open up to each other, rather than staying confined within the limits of a corporation, feeding their own fears and prejudices. The meeting of interests, opinions and perspectives can then be explored. A shared discussion can be much richer and contribute to improving the relevance and effectiveness of policies.

IV Communication: At the Heart of Synergies Among Key Actors

One of a researcher's obligations is to share and publish the fruit of his/her work in a highly-respected journal. The foundation of the scientific approach has, as a result, an obligation to "divulge" and to submit to "discussions" with peers. Isaac Newton (1676) expressed this eloquently in these terms: "If I have seen further, it is by standing on the shoulders of giants." Joseph Ki-Zerbo says it differently: "An old man seated sees farther than a young man standing."

Yet, the evolution of modern society, in which citizen participation is taking on a larger and larger role in implementing public policies, imposes another concept of communication. It is not only about circulating research results among insiders to have it validated but taking into account the requirement of "citizen information". This new right in "modern democracies" implies that "citizens have the right to be informed, to express their opinions, to know what the government is doing and why it is doing it" (Stiglitz 2005: 44). This requirement should govern public interventions. Research activities are subject to this obligation, which explains the ever more important role communication and journalists play for researchers and for decision makers. In all cases, it is a question of avoiding the apprehension that one "is using special arguments to demonstrate that the decisions made to serve special interest in reality serve the general interest" (Stiglitz 2005).

How can one build a society and integration without communication? Even if politicians communicate and researchers communicate, communication specialists and especially journalists also have a role to play. When the latter listen to politicians or researchers, they listen with the ears of their readers or audience and ask questions related to the concerns of the latter. Through the journalist's active listening, he/she nearly brings the audience in the meeting room with him/her. Through his/her questioning, the representatives of an institution can better understand the concerns of the citizens they are supposed to serve.

A certain lazy routine has settled in, reducing a journalist's assignment to the "transmission" of messages, while denying them the right to interpretation. Journalists are not simply a channel for transmitting the messages of decision makers or researchers. Far from it, they bring their own point of view and their interrogations. In Ouagadougou, "what was new at this conference was certainly the participation of journalists from the sub-region's countries as interested actors in the discussions...." Yet there were many who "had trouble getting used to this practically indiscrete presence" (Ndao 2009).

Communication is essential for relevance

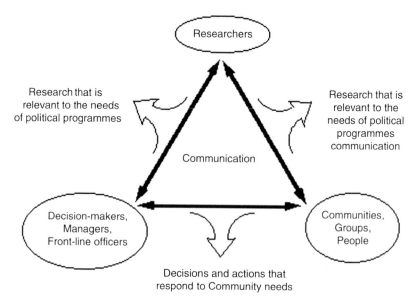

Fig. 14.2 Representation of the three-way dialogue between researchers, decision makers and citizens (Source: Porter and Prysor-Jones 1997)

A Three-Way Dialogue

The three-way dialogue (see Fig. 14.2) between researchers, decision makers and citizens puts communication at the centre of these interactions that are capable of responding to research and action needs that address community needs. But this representation can be a little difficult to implement.

Rotating or Horizontal Dialogue

While preparing for the regional integration conference, an economist in conversation with journalists explained the dangers of representing this communication as "polarised".[1] So, the IDRC consultants who opened the conference made an effort to represent a dialogue that aims to create a relationship that is stripped of any idea of superiority (see Fig. 14.3). The use of the circle perhaps best illustrates a

---

[1] Thanks to Gaye Daffé from Cheikh Anta Diop University in Dakar, Senegal, for these thoughts, based on years of observing and experience.

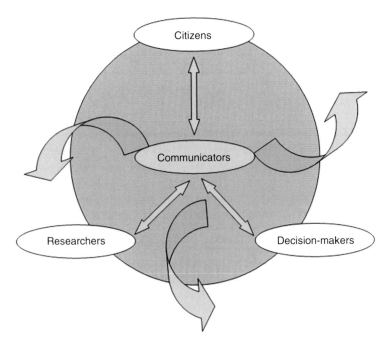

Fig. 14.3 Representation of a dialogue stripped of all ideas of superiority, in which communicators occupy a space at the crossroad (Source: Adapted from Ndiaye and Houenou 2009)

non-polarised dialogue in which the participants can be open-minded, flexible to move easily in the other's direction and also going from one perspective to another in order to find the most appropriate path, instead of remaining camped in a corner or stuck in a position. The dialogue is more horizontal and rotating. Each observes and listens or takes turns speaking, and the journalists communicate outside the meeting about the discussions. All this is done in order to build a multidimensional comprehension of social and economic dynamics and to build integrations strategies to enrich everyone. It is neither the researcher nor the decision maker who dominates. And for there to be a dialogue, one needs to work with the communicators, allowing them to occupy a space at the crossroad.[2]

According to the journalists (Ndao 2009), despite all the preparatory efforts and their level of professionalism, "the central position" of the media in the researcher-decision-maker dialogue did not always manifest itself in reality. In effect, the two

---

[2] Thanks to Jerome Gerard for this concept of a "crossroads area". He noted that the "central space" is slightly in contradiction with what this paragraph seems to affirm, the need for horizontality between equal players. The centre is often perceived as the dominating element around which the rest is organised. Perhaps here, we should propose the idea of a "crossroads area" that promotes circulation/confrontation of information and ideas from everyone involved.

actors—researchers and decision makers—are often inaccessible or reticent to give the information the journalists asked for.

But this constraint did not keep the journalists from leading panel discussions and sharing, following discussions about scientific articles. The exercise, carried out in the presence of civil society organisations, makes it possible to "raise the real problems citizens in the Union face at a national level and from a subregional perspective". As a result, essential questions were discussed such as isolation, lack of quality economic infrastructure, the technocratic nature of the Regional Poverty-Reduction Strategy Document (DSRRP) and "the mercantilism of researchers who have been called by the market to become consultants". This "round-table format is very relevant as a space to draw the attention of researchers and decision makers, as well as an approach to training, in that the participating journalists have an obligation to do their research in order to play an active role" (Ndao 2009).

The trust between the different actors is built as they get to know each other and over time. During the 3 days of the conference, the tone of "free speech encouraged frank discussions among researchers, journalists and WAEMU decision makers. The journalists benefited from having a space to better understand regional policies but also to draw the attention Union decision makers about the issues raised by researchers with respect to the conference's topics…" The conference enabled journalists "to build strategic alliances with researchers who are accused of being inaccessible. The conference gave journalists more advanced analytical points of reference about economic integration issues as witnessed in the quality of certain articles" (Ndao 2009).

Before the conference, the journalists initiated discussions or at least raised the national issues in terms of the conference's themes, for example, through the reports on 87-million person market (*Fraternité Matin*, Côte d'Ivoire) and the 15 years of WAEMU (Guinea-Bissau; *Les Echos*, Mali). After the conference, they wrote press articles on the obstacles of tariff and non-tariff barriers on free movement (Le Quotidien, Senegal), the impact of common external tariffs or community taxes on the national strategies to fight against poverty (Senegal; Les Echos, Mali). They also wrote about channelling cash transfers to productive activities (*Savoir News,* Togo), "the high cost of a trip from Dakar to Bamako" (Senegal) and the competitiveness of industries as a way of fighting poverty in the WAEMU area (Niger). The interview on the central bank reserves in OuestAf News was circulated by a world bank blogger and caused reactions around the world. A simple "event" coverage of the conference would not have given the journalists such an opportunity to deepen their ideas and writings further in the public space.

Main Characteristics of the Discussions Between Decision Makers, Researchers and Journalists

Researchers and Decision Makers: Roles, Missions and Responsibilities Poorly Understood on Both Sides

What is a researcher's role? What is his/her social responsibility?[3] What can be expected of him/her in terms of their missions? What are the limits of a decision maker's responsibilities? What is the scope of his/her missions? These are all questions whose answers determine the quality of the researcher-decision-maker dialogue.

During the conference, particularly animated discussions illustrated a reciprocal lack of understanding between researchers and decision makers, and excessive expectations on both sides. Thus, it is expected that the WAEMU takes on the responsibility of persistent poverty in the weakest member states such as Guinea-Bissau and that regional integration tools provide answers regarding poverty (see, e.g. Diery Seck's contributions on WEAMU results and Massa Coulibaly's work on the common external tariff and targeting the poor).

In reality, the question is much more complex, the Union being the result of a constant compromise (Fondation Jean Monnet 2009) through which the states accept to give up a part of their sovereignty to a regional body. As shown in Massa Coulibaly's contribution, although certain community measures could have an impact on the situation of the poorest members of the population, the question of the states' responsibilities remains in full. In effect, when you look closely at the Union's decision-making mechanisms, it becomes quickly clear that a community decision is, above all, a decision made by its member states, who are stakeholders. From this point of view, the question of the Union's responsibility is necessarily nuanced.

This necessary prudence is valuable in another way. In effect, during the conference, it was highlighted that decision makers tend to expect that researchers provide immediate solutions to the issues raised in their analyses. It is as if ultimately it were a discussion among the deaf where it is difficult, or even impossible, to discern any relevant recommendation.

Analytical Grids and Concepts for Which Agreement Does Not Come Easily

How can one have a discussion when both parties use different analytical grids and concepts? These questions are linked to those of the wide dissemination of research results and emphasise the necessity for both researchers and decision makers to

---

[3] "When you talk about responsibility, in effect, you talk about *answering to* in space and in time, providing a three-dimensional response": responsibility (i) to the environment, (ii) to others/to society and (iii) to oneself (Vermersch 2009).

communicate in a way that is understood by the others. The reaction of one participant, who was a member of civil society, to a researcher mentioning the "Dutch disease" shows to what extent this lack of a shared vocabulary can impede the quality of discussions. A simple comment on the major risk run by any state whose economy is based exclusively on the exploitation of natural resources would have been much better understood by everyone.

Furthermore, the discussions between researchers and the WAEMU Commission representatives about the various views on the *convergence* of macroeconomic policies show to what extent the question of a common language is important. It is clear that what characterises a researcher are the tools he or she uses to have the scientific nature of his or her results recognised by peers. The necessity of using them should not be brought into question. It remains, however, that to contribute to discussions with decision makers, it is essential that researchers make their observations and scientific analyses accessible. We are not talking about simplifying them but about using language that is appropriate to one's audience.

During the conference, two notions were used abundantly: *sigma convergence* and *beta convergence*. What do these terms mean to decision makers in their daily work? Nothing, at least for decision makers who are not economists. Is it not simpler to talk about nominal convergence and real convergence and to give the meaning of each of these concepts? Nominal convergence is simply measured by the fact that the countries of the Union respect or do not respect the eight convergence criteria set by the Union (i.e. non-accumulation of payment arrears, higher wage bill than tax income, interior investments that are higher than tax income). Real convergence is less strictly defined. It refers to a measurement in which standards of living, levels of productiveness and, more generally speaking, the economic structures of the Union's member countries become more similar. Said in this way, it is certain that decision makers understand what beta and sigma convergence mean.

Another example of using tools meant to prove the scientific nature of these researchers' papers is the major role modelling plays in communicating their research. What is at play here is not the relevance of the models but their accessibility to decision makers. In what way is it useful for a decision maker to go into the detail of the models used as a basis for the researcher? The question was raised many times by participating members of the civil society.

When Professor Wetta of the University of Ouagadougou explained that greater investment in education could greatly improve the distribution of the per capita gross domestic product, it appears to us that he is saying something essential. Particularly when he affirms that the divide between the "rich" and the "poor" could be reduced by half in 10 years instead of 50 with greater investments in education. Yet, such obvious statements are nearly missed, first because they are buried deep in a paper whose very title gives the impression that the scientists are only talking among themselves: "Real convergence in the WAEMU area: a Bayesian analysis". Indeed, the economists at the conference seemed to be more interested in debating the "Bayesian approach" used by the professor rather than the basis of the research results and their implications on regional policies. With habits like these, how can we go from science to a dialogue that is capable of informing and guiding policies?

On the other side, one could note during the conference and excessive simplification that appeared in the documents written by the decision makers and their excessively descriptive nature with little analysis. The WAEMU's presentation of the Regional Poverty-Reduction Strategy Document (DSRRP), developed as a framework to bring consistency to relevant regional programmes that are complementary to national poverty-reduction strategies, was particularly criticised from this point of view. Speakers criticised it for being too descriptive and for lacking a strategic approach. The question did indeed come up again: What resource prospects do the Union use as a basis for quantifying this DSRRP? For many participants, the lack of an answer to this question reduces the strategy's chances of success.

Certain researchers also questioned the fact that the DSRRP was developed based on the Washington consensus[4], which demonstrated its limitations during the 2008 crisis. When then did the Union decision makers continue to refer to it at a time when we need alternative paradigms? In other words, the relevance of the model at the basis of the strategy appeared questionable and reflects the incapacity decision makers have to renew their theoretical references, as prisoners of a short-term results culture, little inclined to ask for insight from research.

This lack of theoretical renewal seems to be major flaw that impacts the very coherence of all of the community programmes. There seems to be a lack of a unifying theme in the development of regional policies, which gives the impression of being redundant and sometimes of overlapping, as with the DSRRP and the Union's agricultural policy, for example.

Furthermore, several participants emphasised the impression of community policy measures piling up. For example, the Union's Agricultural Policy (PAU) consists of actions that are so diversified and varied in three major areas that its implementation is complicated.

Finally, other participants wondered about the involvement of the major beneficiaries in the development not only of the DSRRP and the PAU but also for the transport policy, raising the question of the legitimacy and the effectiveness of these policies at the time of their implementation.

Decision Makers Seen as Little Concerned by the Impact of Their Decisions and Programmes

For the researchers, the decision makers seemed to be little concerned by the weak impact of their decisions on the daily lives of citizens, content to adopt laws and develop policies whose implementation remains limited. Here is one illustration: the reactions that followed the WAEMU Commissioner's presentation of the

---

[4] The Washington Consensus refers to a corpus of standard measures (reform packages) applied to economies in difficulty to handle their debt; it was theorised in 1989 by the economist John Williamson.

Regional Agricultural Development Fund (RADF) and the criticisms raised about it in the researcher's contributions.

The academic Kimseyinga Savadogo (whose paper is not included in this book) noted in his analysis of the Union's Agricultural Policy (PAU) that in 7 years, its implementation has been essentially limited to setting up regulatory and institutional measures. He also emphasised that the follow-up and evaluation of the policy seem to be insufficient to such an extent that its impact on poverty, the structure of external trade, and food security and crises continues to lack credibility.

For Savadogo, the success of the PAU confronts at least three challenges: (1) the introduction of foreign direct investment (FDI) in the economic area, (2) the choice between protecting and not protecting the agricultural sector and (3) the harmonisation with the Common Agricultural Policy (PAC) of the Economic Community of West African States (ECOWAS).

In addition to the criticism that the WAEMU does little to question the relevance of its choices, several questions arose concerning the long delays involved in implementing Union programmes.

One will also note criticisms made regarding the slow implementation of the Regional Agricultural Development Fund (RADF), the limited impact of the Banque Régionale de Solidarité (BRS), the small contribution the states make to support the BRS in its mission to finance the fight against poverty, the small contribution made by microfinance institutions to the fight against poverty, the poor use of migrant cash transfers and the regional financial market to fight poverty on a regional scale, etc.

A relevant observation made by researchers also concerns the paradox that exists in the fact that the Union authorities count on European Union (EU) resources to finance the regional PAU in a context marked by the prospect of competition between European exports and WAEMU products that will result from the upcoming signature of the Economic Partnership Agreement (EPA). These contradictions obviously limit community decisions' chances of success.

Finally, the conference participants emphasised the decision makers' slow reaction to new, urgent challenges as illustrated in the case of the PAU. It was adopted in 2001 but has still not been implemented, and it already appears out of date due to new challenges such as the reform of the ECOWAS common external tariff (CET), the persistence of the food crisis and the emergence of biofuel and other alternative energies aimed to protect the environment and reduce carbon dioxide (CO_2) emissions.

Researchers' Conclusions and Recommendations Are Often Hasty and Not Very Practical

It is useful to highlight the way in which decision makers consider the conclusions and recommendations made by the researchers. On one hand, the conclusions and recommendations are considered to be somewhat hasty, with little consideration for the constraints faced by decision makers. To this effect, it is useful to review the recommendations found in articles by young researchers.

This is the case with the necessity for a social pact, which was recommended in several papers, whose authors seem to forget the paradigm behind the creation of the WAEMU. In effect, the WAEMU was founded with the goal of responding to needs in terms of coordinating macroeconomic policies in order to preserve monetary stability and not to respond to social concerns that seem to be more the responsibility of national policies than regional policies. This is also the case with the recommendation or creating structural funds aimed at development. The decision makers ask where the resources will come from.

One of the main criticisms made of these recommendations is that they do not take into consideration their own feasibility. How can a social pact be financed? How can the Union's responsibilities be broadened in a context where state sovereignty is jealously guarded? In considering these actual concerns, the researchers could have nuanced their recommendations or, at least, added prerequisite conditions.

In Samuel Kaboré's paper on the integration of financial services in strategies to fight poverty, the author notes that people's lack of access to financial services is for the most part dependent on the lack of credit, which limits the creation of income-generating activities. To this effect, he recommends the promotion or real access to financial services for the poor. For decision makers, the question remains how to promote this access to financial services for the poorest people taking into account the decision makers' constraints, which are well known. There is no answer to this in the paper, which explains the dissatisfaction expressed by decision makers during the conference.

It was mostly the journalists who remarked the lack of knowledge about the real economies in the region and insisted on the need to domesticate the approaches. During the debates on financing poverty-reduction strategies and their limited, not particularly operative, nature, the following was emphasised: (1) regional integration appears to be insufficiently or poorly theorised with objectives that lack precision, (2) research on integration and on development is often led with instruments that are not domestic enough and (3) the DSRRP is clearly inspired by the outside, notably the famous Washington consensus that was theorised and financed by the World Bank.

How, and under what conditions, is it possible to move beyond these contradictions? Few things were said (or proposed) on this subject at the conference.

In the End, What Can Be Said About the Dialogue Between Decision Makers and Researchers?

It is true that this conference, despite the misunderstandings that arose here and there, was very useful in everyone's opinion. There are several reasons for this. The exercise was an opportunity to put the WAEMU civil servants in front of researchers and journalists, who did not always deal with them tenderly by, in many areas, pointing out the weaknesses of community choices. The three-way discussion was the opportunity to publicly raise questions that are usually handled by insiders. The meeting brought to light leads for improving professional practices among civil servants and made people aware of the fact that in the Union's methods, there are areas of thought that need more exploration. Finally, sharing experience was an opportunity for reciprocal demystification and opened the way to strengthening the collaboration between the world of research, journalists and the regional institution WAEMU.

For the WAEMU, this conference occurred at an important time in its history, when it was raising a lot of questions about its relationship to its environment and about how its actions are understood by the general public.

In effect, for the WAEMU, it is no longer possible to work on a purely technocratic basis. Various initiatives have, for that matter, been taken in this direction: creating bodies that involve the social partners, opening up to the civil society, for the most part, dictated by the following reasons:

- The requirement that the states and the regional groupings take into account the social dimension of the ongoing globalisation process. The WAEMU should not be, as a result, at the margins of such a general movement.
- The experiences of dialogue between public organisations and civil society throughout the world are considered to be additional factors of effectiveness in reaching the goals set by these organisations. On the contrary, the lack of dialogue leads to the rejection of decisions they have made.
- Social actors need to be aware of the necessity of being associated in the decisions made or at least to be heard.
- The social crises that have arisen in certain WAEMU countries shed light on the necessity and the urgency of opening the Union to its environment and, in this way, of having instruments to prevent conflicts.

Certainly, such a dialogue could, for certain questions, weigh down the decision-making process and slow the pace of adopting certain community measures. Its generalisation could be a risk to the pace of reforms in the Union. However, the advantages of the dialogue outweigh the risks.

In effect, if discussions with researchers and the media are well led and used by the region's decision makers, they would offer the Union a good relay for community measures to reach the Union's populations. They constitute an opportunity to involve citizens in the Union's decisions that concern them first. This perspective is, without a doubt, what could guarantee greater social legitimacy for the measures the Union takes and makes them more effective.

V   Research and Policies That Are Anchored in Reality and Well Understood by the Citizens

What purpose does research serve? Improving the living conditions of populations, responding to a problem, finding a solution to a concern. In Africa, it is usual to say that researchers research, but they never find the answers, when in fact, research activities are very extraverted. The best African research is aimed at the major journals in developed countries so as to meet the requirements of an academic career.

The Need to Make the Research Process More Domestic

African research needs to be endogenous, certainly by using tools invented by others because there is no reason to reinvent the wheel but by making its tools reflect local conditions, so they are more efficient when used with realities that are totally different from those that presided over their invention. It is necessary to follow in the footsteps of Western automobile manufacturers. The cars produced for Europe and the United States are not the same as those made for Africa. You need to strengthen the joints and the shock absorbers for African roads.

Better Public Communication About Research

Citizens' right to information is placing a new obligation on researchers and policy makers; that of improving "the information and the rules that preside over its dissemination", according to Stiglitz (2005: 42), who was recognised for his work on transparency in the public sphere. Because "information is an integral part of the process of government" and can reduce the cases of citizen abuse, that is, when the government in place applies policies "that could serve their own interests more than those of the citizens".

What does this requirement mean for research? It is more a question of remedying what Stiglitz refers to as information asymmetries not only between policy makers and citizens but also between researchers and citizens. Research is an activity of creation, invention and discovery. As an individual or a group of individuals produces research, it must benefit the researcher in terms of his/her professional standing. But that should not deprive citizens of knowledge that could have important implications for societal development. Knowing how to bring value to one's work and one's research results supposes knowing how to communicate and provide information about one's work. But that cannot be an isolated act.

As recalled by the research of the Burkina economist Samuel Kaboré presented above, in order to have efficient results in the fight against poverty, one needs to target rural areas (see also Gemandze 2006), "the pocket of poverty, par excellence", with a credit system that is aimed in priority to "subsistence producers". Yet the current practice of credit in rural areas favours cash crop producers. If this information were broadly disseminated, would it not have a certain impact on poverty-reduction policies? If they were informed, would members of civil society not have the means to influence poverty-reduction policies with decisive arguments? On this specific issue of fighting poverty, one can measure all the relevance of Stiglitz's words (2005): "the lack of information, like all artificial forms of rarity, generates income".

It is not enough, however, to establish collaboration with journalists in order to resolve the issue of disseminating and informing people about research results. This objective implies taking several factors into account.

African research on the whole is still largely ruled by the rules of organised knowledge dissemination established during the seventeenth century (CNRS 2007: 2), while the vectors for disseminating information are evolving rapidly, notably with the rise of Internet. This requires researchers to adapt their need to communicate and to inform, all the while remaining in control of "the opportunity and the relevance of ... communicating their results" (CNRS 2007: 2). In this way, at the same time as a researcher publishes scientific communications with complex titles that are aimed at peers and insiders, shouldn't he or she also work on producing summarised policy notes available on the Internet and understandable by all?

Knowledge production is an important act in a society's evolution. It is therefore important to surround it by certain safeguards, notably in terms of financing. Using public financing guarantees that as many people as possible have access to knowledge, which is considered to be a "universal good". It would therefore be a good time to envision greater support for research within the WAEMU but also to the publishing structures, along with possibly greater visibility and accessibility of the research results in the Union through the Internet. In effect, quality scientific work is only of interest if it can be found.

It is the interest or goal of the collaboration of specially prepared members of the media with researchers "capable of describing their research well and filing their data" (CNRS 2007: 12). In this context, organising collaboration between researchers, decision makers and journalists takes on its full meaning. In this perspective, the publication would be "appropriate, balanced and justified, going beyond just the motivations of career advancement or the presence of international competition" (CNRS 2007: 3).

It is primarily a question of meeting the demand created by the citizen's right to information that is imposed on researchers and on science. "Experiments should be conducted before 'real' witnesses who attest to the observed facts; and thanks to the records of experiments that have been duly recorded, readers become 'virtual' witnesses, capable or reproducing the experiment in order to verify it. The academic community therefore functions like its own 'republic of the sciences', independent of the Church, public opinion and the monarch, even though it is under his patronage" (CNRS 2007: 6). Collaborating with journalists presents, at this level, some interest because the publication of information does not necessarily make it accessible or enable citizens to form an opinion because they do not always have the means to identify data that has meaning. Greater interaction between researchers and journalists could contribute to enabling the Union's citizens to benefit more from research results.

Closer Cooperation Between Researchers and Journalists

It is important to point out a few prerequisites to smooth cooperation between researchers and journalists. They each need to have a good understanding of the other's role. The Ouagadougou conference could prove to be the beginning of this necessary cooperation.

Journalists are not researchers. There are, obviously, scientific journalists, but that does not make them specialists in everything. It is therefore necessary to begin by training journalists in research procedures. They need to understand what is at stake in research in order to better translate it into communication and information actions. It requires that a relationship of trust be developed.

Researchers are not journalists. Some know how to or have a talent for communicating, but that does not make them communication professionals. But researchers could and should be trained in techniques for communicating and disseminating messages. They should learn how journalists think in order to communicate their results better. At the WAEMU conference, many researchers presented research that only they could understand.

There are examples of when good communication of research results could lead to political adhesion and trigger actions. This is the case of research on cassava in Burkina Faso. A feasibility and profitability study of cassava farming in Burkina Faso in 2002 done by national experts was presented in an appropriate way led to its appropriation by the Ministry of Agriculture (Ndiaye 2009). This led the Burkina government to develop a national policy for the cassava sector and submitted a request for funding from the United Nations.

In order to have promising results when it comes to communication, it is necessary to develop a long-term process of cooperation. Timely actions are necessarily limited in impact and do not last. In a partnership, it is possible to think about the approach, to choose the best supports, to adapt the messages and to use appropriate language. Galileo and Descartes understood these demands in the seventeenth century, which led them to prefer vernacular languages to Latin, in order to ensure a broader dissemination of their writings.

VI   Conclusion

Decision makers do not actively seek out research. Researchers are criticised for not taking into account the concerns of decision makers and for their lack of effort in disseminating their research. Both avoid journalists. The conference we used as an example here was the first of its kind in the 15 years the West African Economic and Monetary Union (WAEMU) has existed. It is not very surprising that the speeches and contributions carried the mark of each of the social actors.

The analysis of the dynamics of communication during the conference suggests several things. First, if regional institutions open up to knowledge and various points of view, this could contribute to regional policies that take more into account the aspirations of the people. Also, cooperation between researchers, decision makers and journalists with the goal of policy dialogue can be favoured by prior preparation and by practice, taking into account the internal approaches specific to each group and a determination of going beyond one's self interests and taking into account the interests of others. This kind of cooperation could encourage decision makers to seek out more research and researchers to communicate better. At the same time, it could promote more in-depth relations with journalists and communication professional to ensure a link to and interaction with society.

Stiglitz demonstrated the beneficial effects of sharing information within an area. The question remains on how to find the most appropriate means to do so in West Africa in the context of regional integration. The organisation of the 2009 conference constitutes an experiment that, through these crossed discussions, made it possible to draw some important conclusions and as such deserves to be replicated and improved. Policy decisions should be informed by research and understood by citizens, notably with the help of dedicated media. The conference therefore served as a place where the people involved in the integration process could meet. According to certain people, the "circulation of information stimulates the public to demand more effective institutions, which has a positive influence on governance and the economic and social situation" (World Bank press release[5] 2002).

At the same time, the determination to put communication at the centre of discussions about integration policies in West Africa is not enough to achieve policies that are anchored in reality and well understood by citizens. Questions that are equally important include the quality of research, making the research process to reflect local conditions, leadership being interested in openness, the quality of institutional governances and the relations between member countries. Communicate does not mean to understand, but communication could contribute nevertheless to understanding the expectations of the people and the means to fulfil them. There is still work to be done among researchers, decision makers and journalists in order to strengthen a mutually beneficial approach to cooperation that helps citizens (MediaDev 2009) and appropriate and intelligible policies.

References

CNRS [Centre national de la recherche scientifique]. (2007), *Réflexion éthique sur la diffusion des résultats de la recherche*. Avis du Comité éthique du CNRS, Paris, France. www.cnrs.fr/fr/organisme/ethique/comets/docs/reflexionethique070521.pdf

Fondation Jean Monnet pour l'Europe. (2009),*Construction européenne : crises et relances*.

Marquez, G.G. (2005). Le plus beau métier du monde. In Banque Mondiale, *Le droit d'informer : le rôle des médias dans le développement économique* (pp. 321–327). Brussels, Belgium: De Boeck Université.

Ndao, M. (2009), *Médias pour un dialogue politique sur l'intégration régionale*. MediaDev activity report submitted to IDRC. Dakar, Senegal, 14 pages.

Ndiaye, A. (2009),*Chercheurs et décideurs d'Afrique : quelles synergies pour le développement ?* Dakar, Senegal : CODESRIA and IDRC. www.idrc.ca/fr/ev-140737-201-1-DO_TOPIC.html

Ndiaye, A., and P. Houenou (2009), *Dialogue décideurs-chercheurs en Afrique de l'Ouest: quelle synergie pour le développent ?* Présentation pour le colloque UEMOA - CRDI sur « Intégration

---

[5] Press release: "Better Institutions Key to Poverty Reduction" http://go.worldbank.org/2RSCB5Z840.

régionale et stratégies de réduction de la pauvreté », Ouagadougou, Burkina Faso, 3–10 December. www.idrc.ca/braco/ev-149118-201-1-DO_TOPIC.html

Nyamnjoh, F. (2005). *Africa's Media: Democracy and the Politics of Belonging.* London, United Kingdom: Zed; Pretoria, South Africa: UNISA.

Porter, R.W. and S. Prysor-Jones (1997), *Influencer les politiques et les programmes : un guide pour les chercheurs.* Academy for Educational Development, Washington, DC, USA. http://sara.aed.org/publications/cross_cutting/policy_programs/html/fr_intro.htm

Stiglitz, J. (2005), 'Gouvernement et transparence', In Banque Mondiale, *Le droit d'informer : le rôle des médias dans le développement économique* (pp. 41–62). Brussels, Belgium: De Boeck Université.

Vermersch, D. (2009),*De la responsabilité éthique du chercheur.* Support écrit de l'exposé à l'UMR SAS Agrocampus Ouest, 14 décembre, http://espace-ethique.agrocampus- ouest.fr/infoglueDeliverLive/digitalAssets/10032_091214RespCherchSAS.

World Bank (2002). *Rapport sur le développement dans le monde: des institutions pour les marchés. / Development Report: Building Institutions for Markets.*

Chapter 15
Conclusions and Prospects: Creating Wealth through Integration

Elias T. Ayuk and Samuel T. Kaboré

Abstract This chapter summarizes the main findings and conclusions of the seven integration issues addressed in the book. The appraisal of integration efforts within the WAEMU shows both successes and failures. The chapter identifies seven strategic prospects for successful regional integration and for maximising its impact in the UEMOA community. These answer the question of how to create wealth through integration.

This book covers seven key issues related to integration, creating wealth and reducing poverty in the WAEMU space, along with their economic policy implications. These are (1) the evolving trend of some economic and social performance indicators, (2) real convergence, (3) structural convergence, (4) credit constraints, (5) free movement of goods, (6) common external tariff and (7) issue of future prospects, research and actions. This conclusion will review the key messages found in the above chapters and discuss the implications and prospects for regional economic policy drawing on the conclusions that emerged from the discussions among researchers, decision-makers and journalists that occurred during the conference.

Between 1990 and 2007, the human development index (HDI) within the WAEMU indicates a steady decline of the average ranking of countries in the zone, making the Union one of the most disadvantaged community spaces in the world. During the same period, the per capita GDP increased, but there

E.T. Ayuk (✉)
United Nations University, Institute for Natural Resources in Africa,
Accra, Ghana
e-mail: ayuk@inra.unu.edu

S.T. Kaboré
UFR/SEG (Research and Training Centre in Economics and Management), University
of Ouagadougou II, Ouagadougou, Burkina Faso

E.T. Ayuk and S.T. Kaboré (eds.), *Wealth Through Integration*, Insight and Innovation
in International Development 4, DOI 10.1007/978-1-4614-4415-2_15,
© International Development Research Centre 2013

was significant and increasing income disparity among the member countries, with an increase of 56% in the income gap between the three poorest countries (Guinea-Bissau, Niger and Togo) and the three richest countries (Côte d'Ivoire, Senegal and Benin), going from US$594 in 1990 to US$926 in 2007.

Financially speaking, the Union maintained its tradition of low inflation, with an annual rate under 3%, in conformity with its first level convergence criteria and except for Guinea-Bissau, which was victim of a civil war and suffered during the initial period following the CFA devaluation. The money supply (M2) to GDP ratio and the private sector financing to GDP ratio between 1990 and 2007 showed notable progress, with the exception of the Ivory Coast due to a socio-economic crisis, of Niger of Guinea-Bissau, which had a low level of access to credit.

The statistical review found in Chap. 2 that covers a few socio-economic and financial indicators brings to light four major facts: (1) the level of well-being and human development remains low and precarious, despite progress in GDP and control over inflation; (2) the income disparity is significant and increasing between member countries, which weakens convergence; (3) the countries' economic and financial performance is very sensitive to sociopolitical crises, making the Union's economic growth strongly dependent on the existence of peace and good governance and (4) the weak countries need attention and specific, targeted actions to catch up on a structural level in order to accelerate convergence. The persistence of the sociopolitical crisis in the Côte d'Ivoire and in Guinea-Bissau, as the existence of pockets of rebellion in Niger, Mali and Senegal, threaten socio-economic performance and convergence. The Union should make more efforts to resolve these issues. Similarly, the Union continues to face the challenge of improving the transmission of the effects of growth to the most disadvantaged.

One of the main measures of WAEMU's success resides in the convergence of its member states' economies towards sustained growth marked by the weakest countries catching up with the more advanced countries. The empirical tests of real convergence (sigma-convergence) and structural convergence (beta-convergence) show diverging results.

The results of tests for real convergence show both its absence and its presence, depending on the periods and the variables that were considered. The review of the literature found in Chap. 2 shows that most of the research concludes in a lack of sigma-convergence, which in the case of the WAEMU, indicates that the richest countries remain so over time and the poorest remain the poorest, a result that concords with the per capita GDP statistics and that shows an increasing disparity among the countries. Chapter 3 concludes in the existence of real convergence. Chapter 3, which looks at per capita GDP, shows the existence of real convergence for the period from 1975 to 1991, but real divergence for the periods 1970–1974 and 1992–2005. The real convergence observed for the 1975–1991 period is not absolute but conditional to structural convergence. It emerges that the policies implemented by the WAEMU were not enough to support real and structural convergence in the member countries. Chapter 5 shows that the convergence, stability and growth pact (CSGP) has a positive impact on real convergence. Chapter 6 concludes in the presence of sigma-convergence for the periods 1980–1994 and 2000–2008, but an absence of this convergence for the period 1994–2000.

The results of structural convergence tests also show both an absence and a presence of it depending on the periods and the variables that were considered. Chapter 2 indicates that the rare tests of absolute convergence (beta-convergence) for WAEMU country economies also show contradictory results regarding the existence or non-existence of absolute convergence. Chapter 3 concludes in the existence of beta-convergence within the WAEMU. Chapter 4 uses gross capital formation and total factor productivity to demonstrate the existence of structural convergence for the period 1971–1991, but structural divergence for the periods 1970–1974 and 1992–2005. Chapter 4 shows that the economic growth of WAEMU countries is not based on foundations such as investment and demography but rather on residual elements related to work organisation and production techniques that could be influenced by the institutional and macroeconomic frameworks. It follows that convergence of WAEMU countries would not be stable because all it takes is that one economy acts differently than the others to a shock for convergence to be disturbed. The results found in Chap. 6 show that there is weak absolute convergence within the Union. Assessing real and absolute convergence remains dependent on data limitations and quality, whose resolution by the researchers led to a diversity of methods and results that make comparability difficult.

Credit and financing constraints have negative effects on convergence, as well as on the development of investment and income-generating activities, growth in agricultural productivity and poverty reduction. The analyses found in Chaps. 7, 9, 10, 11 and 12 demonstrate the following major facts: (1) there are credit constraints that keep countries—notably those with low levels of credit such as Niger, Burkina Faso and Guinea-Bissau—from fully benefiting from transfers of technologies and push them away from the growth frontier by considerably showing down their speed of convergence, which implies the need for financial policy measures that target rapid improvement of access to credit for all member countries and particularly for those with low levels of credit; (2) cash transfers by migrants represent an estimated average of US$79.8 million a year for all the WAEMU countries and could be a major source for funding for domestic investment and for promoting economic growth if joint, practical, realistic and effective measures are taken to channel and stimulate investment efforts by migrants; (3) the agricultural sector is the sector with the highest concentration of poverty in the Union, yet financing efforts, notably agricultural credit, reach very few of the sector's poor; (4) despite the multiple limitations and relatively high interest and usury rates found in the decentralised financial system (DFS), it still provides hope to a number of poor to have access to financing; (5) the development of adequate and adapted financing through microfinance in the agricultural sector should be a priority for West African countries due to its positive influence both on improving productivity and reducing poverty.

The free movement of people and goods is a requirement for the Union's development, but it encounters objective tariff and non-tariff obstacles that the WAEMU Commission is unable to remove due, among other reasons, to a lack of a legal and judicial framework within the community (Chap. 8).

The effects of the WAEMU's CET on households, particularly those with a modest standard of living, were assessed for Mali (Chap. 13). The results show that

CET's category 0, which represents social goods, benefits proportionally more non-poor than poor. The same applies for poor buyers of basic necessities found in the CET's category 1. This shows the need for an in-depth and extensive assessment of the CET but also for the integration of the "poverty" dimension into the development and implementation of the Union's trade policies.

The review of integration efforts made within the WAEMU shows successes and failures. The question of how to create wealth raises the problem of prospects for the success of regional integration and how to maximise its impacts within the WAEMU community. The discussion of prospects is based on two sources: (1) the results and policy implications found in the various chapters and (2) additional proposals and observations that arose in discussions between researchers, media professionals and regional integration policymakers during the conference organised from 8 to 10 December 2009 in Ouagadougou, during which the studies in chapters found in this book were presented and discussed.

In total, the strategic prospects for improving regional integration and its effects in the WAEMU can be found at seven levels: (1) improving the strategic planning mechanisms to better ensure the links between actions and expected results; (2) boosting the Commission's regional policy competence; (3) setting up a stricter policy to strengthen the Union's weaker countries; (4) creating a social pact; (5) increasing mobility of goods, people and capital; (6) developing adequate and adapted financing that is accessible, notably to the agricultural sector and to the poor and (7) strengthening the dialogue between researchers, decision-makers and journalists regarding development policies.

Improving Strategic Planning Mechanisms

The following shortcomings were noted in the assessment of economic convergence and the fight against poverty: (1) the slow pace of economic convergence reached by the Union's countries, (2) the weak link established between the level of economic convergence reached and the decrease in poverty, (3) the insufficient real impact of progress made in terms of economic convergence on the well-being of the populations, (4) the insufficient levels of intra-community trade within the Union and (5) the lack of support to the Union's most economically fragile countries such as Guinea-Bissau and Niger as part of the solidarity pact imposed by regional integration. The policy recommendations that emerged during the discussions include (1) the need to identify a permanent strategic planning mechanism that is inspired by introverted rather than extroverted sources, (2) the need to undertake strong actions to boost intra-community trade (see below), (3) the need to renew the paradigms underlying regional integration actions and the choice of convergence criteria for the WAEMU, (4) the need to revisit the convergence criteria and notably those related to improving living conditions and (5) the need to include social convergence criteria into the WAEMU's integration approach by setting up a regional integration social pact (cf. details below).

Extending Economic and Social Policy Competence

Achievement has been made and strengthened in the monetary area, but the economic and social potential has not been particularly exploited. Chapter 4 demonstrates that growth in WAEMU countries is not especially linked to economic fundamentals such as investment and demographic growth but rather by total factor productivity generally assimilated with work organisation and production techniques that could be influenced by the institutional and macroeconomic frameworks.

Boosting the Union's Weaker Countries

Such measures should facilitate the process of weaker countries catching up with stronger countries and help decrease the possible perverse effects of disparities or divergence impacting the poorer economies. In effect, in a context in which certain countries have comparatively marked advantages, combined effects can affect the integration process, increasing the economic weight of the more developed countries, such as the coastal states. Chapter 2 demonstrated a significant and rising disparity in income between member countries, which weakens convergence.

Developing a Social Pact to Improve the Living Conditions of Residents

Similar pacts in the economic area have showed encouraging results. Chapter 5, which assesses the effect of the convergence, stability and growth pact (CSGP), shows that the latter tripled the speed of levelling of real per capital GDP for WAEMU member states during the period 1997–2008.

Removing Non-tariff Barriers and Developing Infrastructures

Chapter 3 demonstrates that trade supports income convergence in the WAEMU space and recommends policy measures that aim to promote intra-regional trade. However, Chap. 8 shows that states do not hesitate to marginalise the right to free movement of goods, particularly when it leads to a loss of tax income. The absence of a legal and judicial framework within the Union is a key cause. The WAEMU Commission should therefore ensure that community law is put fully into effect (primacy, direct and immediate applicability) throughout the entire WAEMU space. Strengthening the common market in general and the free movement of goods in particular are a sine qua non condition for economic development within the WAEMU space.

Discussions regarding the insufficient transport policies within the Union made it possible to be more specific about what limits free movement: (1) the multitude of road checks, (2) the collection of illicit payments, (3) the complexity of transit procedures and documents, (4) the long waits at the borders and time lost during road checks, (5) the excessive weight of heavy trucks (premature degradation of infrastructures, high-maintenance costs), (6) the insufficient consideration for lack of safety on the roads, (7) the responsibility of high-level authorities in the impunity observed regarding the delays experienced on the roads, (8) the lack of communication notably in national languages regarding the abnormal practices observed by the observatory of abnormal road practices and (9) the lack of involvement on the part of the Commission against abnormal practices. The measures related to control posts combined with setting up of the observatory of abnormal practices (OPA) and weighing vehicles have proven to be insufficient.

Developing Adequate and Adapted Financing

Chapter 7 shows that credit constraints keep the countries from fully benefiting from technology transfers and push them away from the growth frontier by considerably slowing down the speed at which they converge. Financial policy measures should aim to rapidly improve access to credit for all the member countries and especially for Niger, Burkina Faso and Guinea-Bissau, which have the lowest levels of credit access in the Union.

A review of the links between regional financing instruments and the fight against poverty revealed the following shortcomings: (1) the slow pace in implementing the Regional Agricultural Development Fund (RADF); (2) the limited results and impact of the Banque Régionale de Solidarité (BRS); (3) the low contribution by the states to supporting the BRS in its mission to finance the fight against poverty; (4) the low contribution of microfinance institutions in the fight against poverty, notably due to the little access that the poor have to sources of financing; (5) the issues linked to the sustainability, relevance and role of microfinance institutions in financing activities that enable the beneficiaries to exit poverty and (6) the lack of use of migrant cash transfers and the regional financial market to finance the fight against poverty at a regional scale.

The main recommendations made to the community institutions to address the lack of financing are (1) accelerate the actual implementation of the RADF, which is urgent; (2) improve the mechanisms used to finance agriculture and the informal sector; (3) learn from the imperfect experiences of the BRS and microfinance initiatives by setting up appropriate mechanisms for funding the informal sector and rural activities; (4) clarify the debate on the use of foreign exchange reserves to boost the capacity to finance the regional financial market; (5) look more deeply into the possible use of migrant cash transfers to finance the fight against poverty;

(6) strengthen the states' capacities to pilot better national instruments that fund the fight against poverty; (7) identify financing mechanisms based on resources that come primarily from the region's own wealth and (8) ensure the establishment of structural funds aimed at funding development actions in the most disadvantaged countries.

Strengthening the Dialogue Between Researchers, Policymakers and Journalists

The usefulness of dialogue between researchers, decision-makers and journalists to contribute to developing, implementing and evaluating regional integration policies has been reaffirmed. Strengthening this dialogue requires (1) a better knowledge and understanding of the factors that promote or impede this dialogue and of the advantages of the dialogue between researchers, policymakers and journalists in the mobilisation around regional integration strategies; (2) for the WAEMU to emphasise strengthening the research capacities of institutes and universities at a regional level to support discussions about regional integration strategies; (3) for intellectuals to contribute to discussions related to renewing the key paradigms that underlie regional integration strategies; (4) identifying sources of financing to increase the support of regional research in view of improving research and scientific production capacities on economies, policies and local and regional dynamics and (5) revalorising the role played by researchers and increasing their independence.

To meet these challenges related to strengthening research, the following practical measures were proposed: (1) define and support a community research agenda and programme in view of contributing to strategic discussions about regional integration and fighting poverty; (2) set up a regional research plan dedicated to the evolution of WAEMU policies that are based on regional expertise; (3) increase university research through WAEMU centres of excellence and support higher education and (4) redefine a more dynamic Union communication strategy, taking into account the three-way discussion between policymakers, researchers and journalists, in order to improve the understanding WAEMU citizens have of the regional integration and poverty reduction strategies and programmes.

In conclusion, economists since Ricardo have shown that economic integration can increase well-being (Baldwin 1997), particularly for economies that are of the same size (Palley 2002, 2003). The economic integration theory developed by Balassa (1961) identifies the advantages for the countries that integrate. As Palley (2003) indicates, the reasons for integration are obvious. The big question is how to ensure that regional integration is designed and led in such a way as to generate the expected benefits for the population. The expected gains of integration require certain conditions that have been identified in this book.

References

Balassa, Bela (1961), *The Theory of Economic Integration*, Richard D. Irwin, INC, Homewood, Illinois.

Baldwin, R.E. (1997), 'Review of the theoretical developments on regional integration' Dans OyejideA., Elbadawi I. and Collier P. (eds) *Regional Integration and Trade Liberalization in sub-Saharan Africa*. Volume 1: Framework, Issues and Methodological Perspectives. Londres: Macmillan Press Ltd: 24–88.

Palley, T.I. (2002), 'A New Development Paradigm: Domestic Demand-Led Growth, *Foreign Policy in Focus*, September 2002, at: www.fpif.org.

Palley, T.I. (2003), 'Export-Led Growth: Is There Any Evidence of Crowding-out?' in Arestis et al. (eds), Globalization, Regionalism and Economic Activity. Cheltenham, UK. Edward Elgar, 2003.

Index

A

Absolute convergence, 8–10, 35, 45, 48, 50, 53, 61, 63, 64, 73, 74, 81, 95–96, 112, 114, 116, 119–120, 123, 127, 128, 288, 289

Accumulation effect, 5–7

Agricultural credit, 189–208, 289

Agricultural productivity, 13, 122, 233–239, 289

Allocation effect, 5

B

Bayesian estimation, 9, 116–119

Beta-convergence, 6, 9, 71, 97, 102–106, 276, 288

C

Cash transfers, 171–186, 274, 278, 289, 292–293

CET. *See* Common external tariff (CET)

Citizens, 10–11, 38, 268, 271, 272, 274, 277, 280–283, 293

Common external tariff (CET), 3, 13, 24–26, 149, 152–153, 247–265, 275, 278, 287, 289

Common market, 2–3, 5, 10, 11, 24, 25, 148–150, 161–163, 165, 166, 291–292

Communication, 14, 25, 126, 159, 160, 204, 267–284, 293

Community law, 11, 147–166

Community taxation, 162

Comparative advantage, 4, 5, 37, 85

Conditional convergence, 9, 45, 50, 51, 53, 61–65, 73, 75, 80–81, 86, 92, 93, 95–100, 104, 105, 107, 112, 116, 117, 120–123, 127, 288

Convergence clubs, 9, 45, 48, 49, 60, 61, 65, 95–98, 102, 107, 138, 140–141

Convergence criteria, 2, 6, 8, 23, 24, 26, 28, 30, 31, 33, 34, 37, 50, 71, 77, 87, 93, 97, 99, 100, 105, 107, 108, 114, 124, 126, 276, 287, 290

Convergence, track record, 8, 9

Creating trade flows, 3

Credit constraints, limitations, 136

Critical level of private credit, 10, 141

Customs union, 2, 4, 153–154

D

Decentralised financial system (DFS), 12, 13, 193, 211–225, 231, 289

Decision-makers, 14, 107, 115, 161, 177, 228, 238, 239, 268–280, 282–284, 287, 290, 293

Deposits, 3, 12, 140, 179, 181–186, 215–217, 231

DFS. *See* Decentralised financial system (DFS)

Dialogue, 31, 272–276, 279–280, 283, 290, 293

E

Economic and monetary union, 2–3, 22, 27, 114, 115, 149

Economic and social review, 8, 30, 32–33

E.T. Ayuk and S.T. Kaboré (eds.), *Wealth Through Integration*, Insight and Innovation in International Development 4, DOI 10.1007/978-1-4614-4415-2, © International Development Research Centre 2013

Economic convergence, 6–11, 22, 34, 50, 55, 61, 70–71, 86, 92, 95–97, 106, 115, 122, 131–144, 290
Economic cycles, 3, 5
Economic growth, 1, 3, 10, 11, 22, 26–27, 34, 44, 47, 49, 63, 69, 70, 84–86, 93–95, 100, 105–107, 115, 125, 132–134, 138, 140, 142, 172, 175, 177–181, 183–185, 232, 268, 288, 289
Economic integration, 4–6, 31, 70–71, 73, 87, 95, 115, 123, 124, 127, 133, 134, 142, 148, 150, 159, 293
Economic union, 27, 40, 148
Economic union wealth benchmarks, 23
Effectiveness of targeting indicators, 191, 194, 197, 204
Effects of variety, 5, 6
Efficiency of credit targeted to the poor, 12, 190, 191, 194
Eligibility of the poor, 12, 194–196, 198–200, 203, 204

F
Fixed effects, 9, 53, 65, 96, 99, 104, 235
Food crisis, 13, 227–244, 264, 278
Free movement of goods, 147–166, 287, 289, 291–292
Free trade, 2, 4, 125

G
GDP growth, 20, 44, 48, 50–51, 58, 60, 63, 100, 101, 131, 137, 140, 177–179, 186
General method of moments (GMM), 9, 50, 52, 53, 60, 61, 75, 99, 100, 102, 104, 105, 132, 134, 139, 143
GMM. *See* General method of moments (GMM)
Growth frontier, 132, 137–142, 289, 292

H
HDI. *See* Human development index (HDI)
Human development index (HDI), 8, 30, 38, 113, 287

I
Impact of credit, 13, 134, 190, 199, 233

J
Journalists, 249, 268–274, 279–284, 287, 290, 293

M
Migrant cash transfers, 171–186, 278, 292
Monetary overview, 7

N
Nominal convergence, 6, 23, 34, 37, 49, 70, 71, 77, 87, 92–94, 97, 100, 105, 107, 114, 276
Non-tariff obstacles, 11, 155, 289

P
Panel, 9, 43–67, 95–96, 99, 107, 115–117, 132, 134, 137–139, 233–235, 274
Perspectives, 7, 14, 38, 48, 54–55, 95, 126, 147–166, 191, 194–195, 203, 214, 268, 271, 273, 274, 280, 282, 287–293
Perverse convergence, 49, 101
Policy makers, 29, 178, 180, 270, 281
Poverty reduction, 1, 2, 4, 6, 7, 13, 14, 106, 107, 122, 149, 190, 192, 203, 204, 211–225, 241, 265, 268, 269, 274, 277, 279, 281, 289, 293
Productive investment, 11–12, 20, 172, 177–185, 241
Prospects, 7, 14, 21, 26, 44, 50, 277, 278, 287, 290

R
Real convergence, 6, 7, 9, 34–36, 49, 54, 59, 69–87, 93–95, 97, 99, 101, 102, 104–107, 111–129, 276, 288
Real efficiency, 12, 201
Regional integration, 2–7, 14, 38, 44, 50, 85, 105, 107, 114, 268, 269, 272, 275, 279, 284, 290, 293
Regional trade zones, 4
Regulatory framework, 11, 165
Researchers, 1, 2, 14, 268–284, 287, 289, 290, 293
Ricardo model, 4
Ricardo–Viner model, 4

S
Savings, 6, 8, 12, 34, 35, 46–48, 72, 133, 183, 185, 192, 212, 213, 215–216, 223, 228, 230–232
Sigma-convergence, 6, 8–10, 97–98, 101–102, 107, 111, 115, 116, 123–124, 127, 276, 288
Smoothing cubic spline regression, 71, 73, 74, 79, 87

Social pact, 9, 20, 36–40, 279, 290, 291
Speed of convergence, 9, 10, 47, 98, 104,
  105, 107, 114, 116, 119–121, 127,
  141, 142, 289
Structural convergence, 6, 9, 69–87, 287, 288
Synergies, 3, 37, 39–40, 268–269, 271–280

T
Targeted credit efficiency index, 12,
  189–208

Targeting the poor, 13, 189–208, 212, 218,
  224, 240, 247–265, 275
Tariff obstacles, 5, 11
Technological frontier, 132, 136, 141
Trade diversion, 4, 5
Trade expansion, 4

W
WAEMU institutional measures, 23–30
Worldwide growth frontier, 132, 139–142